Penguin Education

Public Finance

Edited by R. W. Houghton

Penguin Modern Economics Readings

General Editor
B. J. McCormick

Advisory Board
K. J. W. Alexander
R. W. Clower
G. Fisher
P. Robson
J. Spraos
H. Townsend

D1329508

Public Finance

Selected Readings

Edited by R. W. Houghton

Penguin Books

Penguin Books Ltd, Harmondsworth,
Middlesex, England
Penguin Books Inc., 7110 Ambassador Road,
Baltimore, Md 21207, U.S.A.
Penguin Books Australia Ltd, Ringwood,
Victoria, Australia

First published 1970
This selection copyright © R. W. Houghton, 1970
Introduction and notes copyright © R. W. Houghton, 1970

Made and printed in Great Britain by
Cox & Wyman Ltd, London, Reading and Fakenham
Set in Monotype Times

Contents

Contents

Contents

Introduction

Everyone is interested in the getting and spending activities of governments, if only because he pays taxes or benefits from government expenditure. For many it is but a short step from taking an interest in to becoming an authority on public expenditure and taxation. Anyone, particularly if he has managed the affairs of a household or firm with a modicum of success, may succumb to the temptation to become a member of the club of self-appointed public finance experts. The evidence for this is to be found in parliamentary debates and in the speeches of such well-established figures as company chairmen, trade union leaders and bankers, as well as in the correspondence columns of the newspapers. The atmosphere of a democratic society encourages all to make their contribution to a continuing debate. Even if enlightened self-interest indicates silence – as it seldom does in these matters – what is conceived as social obligation may compel speech. The continuous discussion of public finance problems at the common-sense level allows no lack of solutions: most of them depending on the naïve premise that the government is simply a large firm or household whose chief problem is that of matching expenditure to income. Folk wisdom of this kind, like folk history, is absorbed by members of the society which creates it, and is often a positive handicap to the scientific student of public finance who is required both to rebut it and to prevent its insidious invasion of his work. If there were no other justification for what he does, the prevalence of misconceptions and their apparent immortality would be sufficient.[1] Not that popular discussion is to be deprecated: on the contrary it is a medium for increasing general understanding of public finance activities and for revealing the effectiveness of existing institutional arrangement for purposes of public policy. If policy makers and administrators as well as those at whom their efforts are directed become better informed, both the quality and efficiency of arrangements may be expected to improve.

The complaint then is not that there is discussion – of course

1. For a lively account of some prevalent misconceptions see Peston (1965).

not – but that too much of what is alleged to be knowledge or fact consists of untested or unsubstantiated hypotheses. It does not follow that because each adult has one vote that all are equally competent to comment on decisions made in the government sector of the economy. The absurdity of the contrary view is clear. No answer to a technical question is acceptable from a man who does not know the relevant theory and has no factual information. The attitude that the government sector does not deal with technical problems – and if it does, it ought not – can be dismissed. Clearly in a community of people equally well informed in all matters, the views of the man-coming-out-of-the-bank or the woman-going-into-Woolworth's on the origin of the universe as well as on devaluation, might well be of interest. Purely economic considerations suggest that specialization will persist: that however much improvement is achieved in the general appreciation of the nature, scope and consequences of public sector activities, details of policy to secure (perhaps) generally agreed objectives will have to be left to 'experts'. This in no way impairs the argument for continued study and discussion to provide more information so that both the formulation of policy and the development of institutions can be improved. As the store of knowledge expands and access to it improves there is less room for folk wisdom and less scope for the pseudo-expert.

Some indication of the contributions of economists to public finance studies is given by the articles reprinted in this volume. The subject has always been in the main stream of political economy, itself brought into being by the coalescence of the ideas of political philosophers on the one hand and thoughtful practical men on the other. The great classic codification of political economy, Adam Smith's *The Wealth of Nations* (1776), provides, in the last of its five books, an early treatise on public finance; the subject figures largely in nineteenth-century Anglo-Saxon writings from Ricardo to J. S. Mill to Edgeworth; and two twentieth-century treatises have become classics: A. C. Pigou's *A Study in Public Finance* (1947) and Henry Simons' *Personal Income Taxation* (1938). To a highly distinguished Continental literature, the German, Italian and Swedish contributions are outstanding.

The articles collected here are recent contributions to two traditional branches of public finance: the allocation of resources between public and private sectors and the distribution of incomes; the third branch, which covers macro-economic questions relating to stability and growth, is to be dealt with separately in another volume. Selection is always brutal; in this instance it was painfully apparent that no single guiding principle had clear claim to pre-eminence. In fact a seemingly endless string of possible objectives confronts the editor of a volume such as this. It is desirable to provide complete coverage of the chosen topics; to show how thinking on the various issues has developed over time; to indicate current trends; to provide background material for the discussion of topical issues and proposals for reform; to throw light on unsettled and on neglected questions; to include the results of empirical work, and so on.

To try to do everything means taking the risk that nothing is fully achieved; yet all the foregoing are desirable objectives from the point of view of the student of public finance. My compromise was not to try and achieve all of them in each section but, over the book as a whole, to attempt to give a picture of public finance studies at the present stage of their evolution. It is hoped that the book provides, in an interesting and useful form, some of the essential outside reading required in an undergraduate course in public finance. It has been assumed that such a course would be concerned more with principles than with description and that a good grounding in economic theory would already have been given to those taking it. A difficulty had to be faced with survey articles – on the one hand, the reason is obvious, these are the most useful articles; on the other, they are not the most appropriate because they belong to the same family – the distilled group – as the textbooks which readings are intended to complement. To provide a series of surveys on the main topics seemed a very heavy approach to the subject. Original, seminal articles have the great virtue that their exciting flavour of discovery is retained; the disadvantage of using them, together with subsequent comments, is that the rounded picture of the present state of play may not be given. The trade-off between flavour and convenience is a highly subjective matter; my tastes have led me to use a few surveys. I have reluctantly not included some highly original work which has been well assimilated in the literature: Dupuit's immortal *De l'Utilité des Travaux Publiques* (1844) does not appear, nor

Wicksell's magnificent 'Ein neues Prinzip der gerechten Besteuerung' (in *Finanztheoretische Untersuchungen und das Steurwesen Schwedens*, 1896).

It is an uncomfortable fact of life that in most economies, existing public finance arrangements are the result of an evolutionary process of adaptation to changing circumstances (including increased knowledge). In this process, piecemeal addition has played an important part, for the relative size of the public sector tends to grow, and revenue requirements correspondingly increase as the economy matures.[2] It would be surprising if in these circumstances a country would choose to establish *de novo* the set of public finance arrangements it has. The speed at which improvements occur is not high; possible changes for the better are neither obvious nor easy to carry out. Once discovered, desirable changes, even if not frustrated by those with a vested interest in the *status quo*, require the creation of efficient administrative arrangements – and over what is administratively feasible there are great possibilities for honest disagreement.[3] All this comes out clearly in the *Report of the Canadian Royal Commissioners (1966)*; an extract from which appears as Reading 7.

A Prefatory Note on Government Expenditure and Revenue

Government expenditure may be either *exhaustive*, that is, it uses up some of the nation's available resources, or it may take the form of unrequited payments to individuals, sometimes called *transfer* payments. This distinction may be illustrated by comparing the salary paid to a civil servant and the pension benefit paid to a retired person. Both are clearly sources of income to the recipient. The first, however, is a requited payment: a man's labour services are secured for the government or public sector of the economy and are not available to the private sector. In the case of the pension no *quid pro quo* exists and no resources are absorbed by the public sector when it is paid. Both the civil servant and the pen-

2. This is sometimes known as *Wagner's Law*; see Peacock and Wiseman (1961), pp. 16–21, 23–6.

3. The introduction of the P.A.Y.E. system in the U.K. in September 1943 is a classic example of 'needs must when the Devil drives'. As late as the spring of 1942 a White Paper (*The Taxation of Weekly Wage Earners*, Cmnd 6348) had presented powerful arguments against such a scheme. For details see the interesting discussion in Sayers (1956), pp. 99–111.

sioner exert pressures in markets when they dispose of their receipts: the important difference is that while in securing the services of the civil servant the government has competed in the labour market there is no corresponding effect anywhere in the case of the pension payment. The example indicates the two branches of government activity dealt with in this volume: one involves the allocation of productive resources between the private sector and the public sector, the other is concerned with the re-allocation or redistribution of incomes or spending power between individuals in the private sector of the economy.

Governments may obtain resources either by commandeering them, with or without compensation, or by purchasing them in the market. The first method is not much used in most societies in normal times;[4] in a monetary economy the government finances its payments, both exhaustive and unrequited, from one or more of the following: income from the ownership of state property and profits from the operation of state enterprises, tax revenues, taxes, loans, newly created money. It may be observed in passing that when there are unemployed resources in the economy, the last is uniquely efficient for, unlike all the other devices, the method does not itself have demand-reducing effects. In western societies, state property and enterprise are not major sources of funds; normally taxes and loans are the main revenue raising instruments. The question of when it is appropriate to borrow and when to tax is a most interesting one; moreover, the loan method gives rise to a further alternative; borrow at home or borrow abroad? Among taxes the choice is vast but any tax raises considerations of equity – or fairness – between taxpayers, and efficiency – its effects upon the use of resources; these may conflict, a fair tax being judged inefficient and an efficient tax unfair. Such considerations also arise in the choice between taxes and loans, and between either of these, and adjustments in the prices at which government-owned goods and services are offered. Indeed to differentiate the latter from taxes is difficult. As is shown later, such conflict is not inevitable: taxes may be used to promote efficiency without unfairness. However, further sources of possible conflict are present if government objectives also include a parti-

4. The interesting problems which are raised by its use are discussed by Pigou (1947), pp. 3–18.

cular rate of economic growth, full employment, stable prices and balance-of-payments equilibrium.

Enough has been said to show that despite its traditional name most of the problems in public finance studied by economists are not financial in any fundamental sense. The point was succinctly made by Pigou (1947, p. 4):

Though ... money is practically always the medium of public finance, it is not the thing in which it really deals. The money is merely a ticket embodying command over services and goods. It is these, not the money that represents them, which constitute the real object of all transactions. This is, of course, a truism. But it is a truism the detailed implications of which are complex ... apart from creations of new money, every completed act of public finance is alike in form. £100 million are obtained by the government from the public and are paid over to certain other persons. This money is purchasing power. When it is taken away, those persons from whom it is taken are constrained to give up other things (including perhaps some leisure) which they would have had if it had not been taken away. The Government then pays out the £100 million. It is evident that there are a great number of different ways in which the providers of taxes or fees or loans can modify their purchases and activities in order to furnish the £100 million: and a great number of different ways in which the £100 million can be paid out and in which the output of different sorts of goods and services can accordingly be affected. Thus important divergences of substance underlie the similarities in money form.

References

DUPUIT, J. (1844), *De l'Utilité des Travaux Publiques*. Translated into English by R. H. Barback, *International Economic Papers*, vol. 2 (1952), pp. 83–110. Reprinted in D. Munby (ed.), *Transport*, Penguin Books, 1968, pp. 19–57.

PEACOCK, A. T., and WISEMAN, J. (1961), *The Growth of Public Expenditure in the United Kingdom*, Oxford University Press.

PESTON, M. (1965), 'On the nature and the extent of the public sector', *Three Banks Review*, September.

PIGOU, A. C. (1947), *A Study in Public Finance*, Macmillan, 3rd edn.

SAYERS, R. S. (1956), *Financial Policy 1939–45*, H.M.S.O.

SIMONS, H. (1938), *Personal Income Taxation*, University of Chicago Press.

SMITH, A. (1776), *The Wealth of Nations*. (Everyman edn, 1956.)

WICKSELL, K. (1896), 'Ein neues Prinzip der gerechten Besteuerung', in *Finanztheoretische Untersuchungen und das Steurwesen Schwedens*. Translated into English by J. M. Buchanan, in R. A. Musgrave and A. T. Peacock (eds.), *Classics in the Theory of Public Finance*, Macmillan, 1952, pp. 72–118.

Part One Equity and the Choice of Tax Base

A first approach to public finance studies is to assume that
government expenditure is given, so that the important question is
the equitable distribution of taxes among citizens. A further
simplification is made if government expenditure, like tribute paid
to a foreign power, is assumed to confer no benefits on taxpayers.
In this way are avoided problems of measuring the benefits of
expenditure which, whether the ability to pay taxes is defined by
income, consumption or wealth, must affect taxable capacity. This
simplified approach provides the easiest interpretation of the early
ability-to-pay school who were enthusiastic utilitarians. Regarding
tax payments as utility sacrifices, they produced *inter alia* a simple
and strong injunction to tax collectors: minimize sacrifice. If it is
assumed that individuals have identical income utility curves and
that these slope downwards, the least aggregate sacrifice doctrine
requires only the rich to be taxed; and by the same arguments it
shows that so long as incomes are unequal, utility can be increased
by equalization; if society's aim is to maximize utility, equalization
of incomes must follow. Some of those who accepted the utilitarian
basis for these conclusions, such as Pigou, proposed qualifications to
them on efficiency grounds. However, in recent times the
underpinnings have fallen into disrepute. That interpersonal utility
comparisons are possible is often denied; that income utility curves
are identical certainly lacks proof; and doubt has been cast on the
continuous downward slope hypothesis. The last is perhaps the most
interesting argument. If income utility curves sloped upward, total
utility would be increased by increasing the degree of inequality;
but few would then favour utility maximization or least aggregate
sacrifice taxation.

Henry Simons (Reading 1) elegantly discloses the fragility of the
support afforded to the case for progressive taxation by the utility
sacrifice doctrines and proceeds to a magnificently phrased defence of
progression on equity grounds. He follows this with a beautifully

constructed argument for a comprehensive definition of income for tax purposes (Reading 2).

To the *Report of the Royal Commission on the Taxation of Profits and Incomes (1955)* there was attached a well-argued Memorandum of Dissent (Reading 3). This first shows how income was defined for tax purposes in the United Kingdom, criticizes the narrowness of the definition in the spirit of Henry Simons and goes on to make suggestions for extending the tax base by, among other measures, introducing a tax on capital gains. One of the Commissioners, Kaldor, in a subsequent book, argued for the use of expenditure rather than income as the index of taxable capacity; he showed that tricky definitional problems, inherent in the use of income, are avoided when expenditure is the tax base. His chapter explaining how the tax might be used in practice is reprinted as Reading 4. Vickrey (Reading 5), reviewing Kaldor's proposals and discussing these alternative tax bases, suggests that Kaldor's comparisons are too kind to the expenditure tax, in that the income tax with which comparison is made is highly imperfect and capable of much improvement. The studies are completed by Due's study (Reading 6) of the controversial net worth or wealth tax. The Canadian Royal Commission Report (Reading 7) contains detailed proposals for reform of the Canadian income tax system. Although the context is a special one, the issues are discussed in such a way that they are of general interest. One interesting difference between the United Kingdom and Canadian Commissioners may be noted: the latter, because they also propose a radical change in the income tax structure with a top marginal rate of 50 per cent felt able to propose that capital gains should be treated on a par with other kinds of income, rather than be subject to a special flat tax rate.

The Canadian Report in six volumes, which took over four years to compile, has been most favourably received by public finance experts. The conformity of its proposals with Henry Simons' ideas, published nearly thirty years earlier, is remarkable, suggesting that there is a basic truth in that last paragraph of Keynes' (1947) which emphasizes the influence of 'academic scribblers' and goes on to proclaim: 'soon or late it is ideas not vested interests which are potent for good or evil'.

Reference
Keynes, J. M. (1947), *The General Theory of Employment, Interest and Money*, Macmillan p. 384.

1 H. C. Simons

The Case for Progressive Taxation

Excerpt from H. C. Simons, *Personal Income Taxation*,
University of Chicago Press, 1938, pp. 1–29.

Economics, as a separate discipline among the so-called social sciences, takes its rise and derives its essential meaning from specific problems of public policy. It deals, ultimately, with two kinds of practical questions, (1) What are likely to be the results of specified measures? (2) By what kinds of measures may specified results be attained? In its special branches, such as public finance, the main problems are obviously problems of 'control' – problems of legislative policy, for the most part. Thus, the specialist in government finance becomes of necessity a sort of propagandist – a protagonist of 'sound fiscal practices' and a hostile critic of measures which fall outside the pale. It is incumbent upon him, therefore, to set up fundamental objectives and criteria of fiscal policy. He must build upon a set of values – and these will usually be things which he brings with him to the special field, not end results of his specialized researches.

It has become conventional among students of fiscal policy, however, to dissemble any underlying social philosophy and to maintain a pretense of rigorous, objective analysis untinctured by mere ethical considerations. The emptiness of this pretense among economists is notorious; yet people who cannot solve a simultaneous equation still regard 'unscientific' as the ultimate in critical invective and themselves live in constant terror of that characterization. Having been told that sentiments are contraband in the realm of science, they religiously eschew a few proscribed phrases, clutter up title-pages and introductory chapters with pious references to the science of public finance, and then write monumental discourses upon their own prejudices and preconceptions.

One means of avoiding this unfortunate procedure is to introduce at the outset a confession of faith or recital of preconceptions. For present purposes, brief discussion of the question of justice in taxation may adequately serve this end. We intend, in what follows, no real contribution to that subject,[1] or even a study of its extensive and exceedingly dull literature. It may be possible, however, to define some objectives of policy which will seem acceptable to many readers; at the least, subsequent chapters should be less unintelligible to one who understands the writer's tastes.

How tax burdens should be apportioned among individuals has no doubt been the subject of discussion and controversy since the beginning of political organization. So long as poverty and insecurity compel the sovereign to employ every available fiscal device in order to maintain sovereignty, questions of justice are naturally subordinate. Once stable government and a measure of economic freedom appear, however, considerations of equity are forced to the front. More revenue devices are available than are required. To what extent shall each kind of levy be employed? Questions of relative collection costs, of stability and flexibility of yield, are relevant of course. But, at the center, is the question of how the burden *should* be allocated, of what is the most equitable system.

1. A significant position regarding taxation and tax reform is properly a derivative, or subordinate part, of a broader position on general questions of economic policy. Taxation is only a small element in the structure of rules and conventions which constitute the framework of our existing economic system; and problems of taxation can be clearly apprehended only as phases of the broad problem of modifying this framework (the rules of the game) in such manner as to make the system more efficient and more secure. Those who reject revolutionary upheavals as a means to progress must analyse the shortcomings, the weaknesses, and the unlovely features of the system as it stands. They must determine which of its faults most urgently need correction and which are most easily amenable to correction. Finally, they must ascertain what kinds of measures are appropriate in each case. Thus, one's position regarding taxation can hardly be stronger than one's position on economic policy generally. Sound proposals for tax reform imply sound conception of the role of taxation changes in some larger scheme; they imply sound insights as to what tax reform may properly undertake to accomplish, and sound insights as to the urgent problems which may best be dealt with along other lines. At all events, the writer's argument regarding income taxation in these essays may properly be interpreted, and perhaps better understood, as part of a scheme of policy outlined in a short tract (Simons, 1934).

A familiar answer to this question is found in the doctrine of taxation according to benefit. Each person may be called upon, as in his dealings with private enterprise, to pay according as he receives. It is fair to say, however, that this principle, with reference to the allocation of the whole tax burden, is now of interest only for the history of doctrine. It finds a diffident proponent here and there; but, on the whole, it has been repudiated as completely by students as by legislatures.

Taxation according to benefit, as a slogan, has an interesting history, which illustrates what a variety of uses and masters a good phrase may serve. In eighteenth-century France, when public expenditures were made largely with regard for the benefit of the tax-exempt nobility and clergy, it epitomizes a protest against obvious injustice. It was then a forward-looking doctrine, defining a proximate goal of liberal reform. Later on it serves those opposing the movement toward taxation of individuals differentially according to their circumstances; thus it becomes a significant element in a reactionary social philosophy, constructed from the gratuitous implications of *laissez-faire* economics. And it still survives in the vigilant wisdom of the courts, protecting property against democracy.

The slogan, of course, has little more than emotive content. At best, it represents an ill-defined protest against obvious injustice (in the movement for 'universality'); at worst, an empty evasive sort of conservatism (in the opposition to progression); but it defines no real basis for apportionment. In some cases, to be sure, its implications are fairly clear. Where the government distributes goods and services which may be bought and sold in the open market, pricing according to cost is feasible. Where expenditure is made for purposes of general welfare (national defense, internal security), the benefit principle leads nowhere at all; and, where the government undertakes deliberately to subsidize certain classes (the economically unfit) or certain kinds of consumption (education, recreation), taxation according to benefit is sheer contradiction.

On the other hand, one cannot deny the importance of benefit considerations for modern fiscal problems. Sound fiscal measures for the future must be designed, at many points, with regard (a) for the fact that particular classes will derive special benefits from certain kinds of government expenditure and (b) for what tax arrangements have been in the past. There is a decisive case for retention of a substantial element of *ad rem* taxation – for resort in part to levies which classify persons with respect to characteristics other than net income or net worth or 'ability to pay'.

The end of conciseness in argument will be served, if we leave the foregoing assertions for the present, without attempting to support them, and proceed to the problem of personal taxation. For purposes of this chapter, the general problem must be broken into three parts: (1) the problem of personal taxation; (2) the problem of *ad rem* taxation; and (3) the problem of the combination of these two types of levies in a complete system. To define the scope of discussion under (1), we may start by asserting that *ad rem* taxation should form an important, if minor, part of the system, and by assuming solution of the question as to what part of total revenues should be provided by levies in this latter form. Thus, we may proceed to the traditional question of justice in taxation.

The greater part of what has been written about justice in taxation has been couched in terms of sacrifice. This concept, along with 'ability' and 'faculty', is a more or less legitimate progeny of 'utility'; and it has contributed about as much confusion, with respect to the ethics of public policy, as has 'utility' with reference to the explanation of human behaviour. Yet the doctrines built from and around these concepts deserve attention, if only because they are so firmly intrenched in the literature and even in lay discussion.

There is first the doctrine of equal sacrifice – that tax burdens should so be distributed that the same total sacrifice is imposed upon every individual. This we may associate with Mill, who asserts the position and then points out rather casually, as though it were axiomatic, that equal sacrifice among individuals means minimum sacrifice for the *community* as a whole (Mill, 1909, ch. 2, sec. 2). This latter position has been subjected to devastating criticism at the hands of Mill's most sympathetic followers. Edgeworth (see Edgeworth, 1925, vol. 2, pp. 100–25 ff.), notably, turns the whole argument around, starting with the proposition that taxes should impose minimum total sacrifice; and he then demonstrates conclusively – so far as is possible with such dialectical tools – that equal individual sacrifice by no means minimizes the total burden. Minimum sacrifice, as he demonstrates, calls for not equal but equimarginal sacrifice among individuals – i.e. for equality not in the total burden on each person but in the burden of the last small increment of tax. Intermediate between these positions, incidentally, is that of, notably, Cohen-Stuart, who contends that there should be equality of proportional sacrifice (proportional to the total utility of income!). (See Seligman, 1908, pp. 278 ff.)

Definite interpretation of these doctrines is exceedingly difficult. They all relate to taxation on the basis of income; and they surely involve the conception of a functional relation between the amount of income and its marginal utility. Moreover, the area under the income-utility curve, or the integral of the function, is conceived to measure total utility. Sacrifice is defined as the loss of total utility.

Let us, then, postulate a generalized utility curve for 'money income', i.e. a functional relation between amount of income and its marginal utility, applicable to all persons and to all income classes. If this curve be rather flat – if the arc elasticity be less than unity for all pairs of significant points – then equal sacrifice would mean regressive taxation, and proportional sacrifice would call perhaps for a mild sort of progression. If the curve were a rectangular hyperbola, proportional levies would produce equality of sacrifice (see Pigou, 1928, p. 109). All this, however, is not very illuminating. One derives practical implications from the criterion of equality, or proportionality, of sacrifice precisely in proportion to one's knowledge of something which no one ever has known, or ever will know, anything about. Perhaps this goes far toward explaining the popularity of these doctrines among academic writers.

It is a peculiar relative merit of the Edgeworth doctrine that it depends for some definite interpretation merely on the assumption that the utility curve has everywhere, within significant limits, a negative slope; and common sense, if it accompanies us at all in flight to such dialectical altitudes, will surely support this assumption. Thus, minimum sacrifice would appear to dictate a tax rate of 100 per cent, with an initial bracket of income exempt from tax, and with the level of exemptions adjusted according to revenue requirements.

This definiteness, however, is only apparent. To admit, as one must, the reality of differences in standards of living, is to concede that the simple income-utility function is only a locus of points on much steeper, 'short-run' curves at the various income levels. The simple function tells us nothing about the proximate consequences for marginal utility to a normal Jones, if his income is changed from b to a. It only tells us what the marginal utility of the smaller (or larger) income will be to Jones *after* he has completely revised his standard of living, after he has become a thoroughly 'a-dollar' man, and only after he has quite forgotten his better (or worse) days. While these considerations do not dispose of the doctrine, or deny a certain relevance to the simple income-utility function, they do place the minimum-sacrifice legislator under the unfortunate disability of not knowing where to start.

Minimum-sacrifice doctrine, while proposing the outright slicing-off of income peaks, has yet the political wisdom to postpone that arrangement for an infinite period of time. It leads, under any reasonable assumptions as to the short-run functions, to progressive taxation; yet, while its sister-doctrines tell – quite equivocally – just how taxes should be apportioned, it says not only that taxes should be progressive now but also that they should be increasingly progressive for all time to come.

A system which produces least aggregate sacrifice this year will fail to achieve that result in the next fiscal year. The marginal utilities of the large taxpayers will at first be indignantly high; but time will drag these utilities down toward the long-run utility curve as a limit. As taxpayers become adjusted to their new circumstances, their utility curves, like their indignations, will recede; and every such change will require an increase in the degree of progression. Thus, if the minimum-sacrifice principle were continuously applied, income differences would be in process of continuous moderation, with concomitant changes in standards of living and in the utility functions. Ultimately, it would give merely a confiscation of all income above a certain level – but only ultimately.

But there are further complicating considerations. The long-run income-utility function is itself a function of the prevailing distribution of income; and the short-run function for a member of any income class is one thing when other incomes remain unchanged and something quite different when all incomes within this and neighboring classes are changed concomitantly and systematically at the same time. The fact that consumption, especially in the upper-income classes, is so largely competitive and invidious constitutes by itself a powerful argument for steep progression. For the minimum-sacrifice program, it implies that the rates of tax should be much more progressive at the outset, and should be more rapidly increased afterward, than would otherwise be appropriate.

This consideration, as Pigou suggests, gives strong support to that persistent, but seemingly indefensible, notion that even equal sacrifice requires distinctly progressive levies. The loss of utility from curtailment of large incomes would be less great if that curtailment were general; or, in Pigou's words, 'the satisfaction which a man derives from the possession of a given income depends, not only on the absolute amount of the income, but also on the relation subsisting between it and the incomes of other people' (see Pigou, 1928, p. 111). At all events, the logic of least aggregate sacrifice leads far beyond the simple utility functions of Bernouilli and Cramer.

Minimum-sacrifice theory has done wonders toward sustaining the vitality of hedonism, at least in liberal economics. If we believe that science and logic point no highroad to justice and beauty, we still resent it; and, if we discourse on questions of policy, we dissimulate the conviction. We crave some ultimate sanction for our tastes and sentiments; at all events, we crave their company even within the 'science' of finance. So, we invent and seize upon all manner of disguises – and even build up a professional code which frowns upon our not acccepting some things merely for what they seem to be. Edgeworth and his followers have made good costumes; they have written our sentiments in a sort of logic; they have served a worthy cause and served it well. But from it all hedonism derives a blessing which is unearned and undeserved and, indeed, unfortunate for economics as a discipline.

What really commends the Edgeworth doctrine to liberal students, of course, is its conclusion – its pseudo-scientific statement of the case against inequality. Consequently, it is important to see that the doctrine derives not only all its practical implications but all its noble ethical quality from an assumption usually introduced or recognized without much ceremony. This is the assumption that all individuals are, or must be treated as, equally efficient as pleasure machines. Pigou disposes of the matter in two sentences:

Of course, in so far as tastes and temperaments differ, allowance ought, in strictness to be made for this fact. ... But, since it is impossible in practice to take account of variations between different people's capacity for enjoyment, this consideration must be ignored, and the assumption made, for want of a better that temperamentally all tax-payers are alike (Pigou, 1928, p. 76).

To a person who found Professor Pigou's conclusions uncongenial, this method of reaching them simply by confession of ignorance might seem absurdly easy. Such a person might maintain, not unfairly, that this confession, far from reconciling hedonism and equalitariansm, really implies that they belong to different universes of discourse.

The conclusions, to be sure, may be salvaged to some extent by proper amendment of the premises. Instead of merely professing ignorance, one might maintain (a) that there is no presumption favoring the existence of significant positive correlation between individuals' incomes and their respective efficiencies as pleasure machines; (b) that such differences as exist merely because the income distribution has been what it has been may be ignored for long-run policy; (c) that the assumption of equality in original, innate capacities for pleasure is a sufficiently precise approximation to the facts; or (d) that no other assumption is either politically practicable or morally tolerable. The last argument would evidence frankness and candor; but it invites suspicion of logical legerdemain. Certainly it would reduce the whole hedonistic calculus to a merely superfluous embellishment of the argument. The other premises, to many persons, will therefore seem more inviting. For votaries of hedonistic welfare economics, however, they all have the disadvantage of revealing the crucial importance of this step in the argument.

Indeed, one may well insist that hedonistic ethics is not less absurd than hedonistic 'explanation' of human behavior, or less naïve than the productivity ethics which we associate with J. B. Clark. This latter brand of apology, though somewhat out of fashion now, deserves a moment's attention, even at risk of laboring the obvious.

Let us imagine a competitive economy, without inheritance, where all persons have substantially equal talents for straight thinking, imagination, salesmanship, and chicanery, but are enormously unequal in physical strength. Here, of course, the millionaires will be the persons with strong backs; and the apology of productivity ethics will be that they are entitled to share in the social income according to their respective differential contributions (productivity). A dose of Calvinist theology would make this doctrine more palatable to the masses; but persons of a critical temper might be led to restate the implications and to revise the conclusions simply by reversing them. If a person has been greatly favored by the Creator in the dispensation of rare physical blessings, it is hard to regard that initial good fortune as a basis for preferential claims against his fellows with respect to scarce goods whose distribution is amenable to some deliberate, human control. Indeed, one is almost obliged to admit the reasonableness of the opposite system of ethical book-keeping, whereby rare physical blessings would be debited to the recipient's account with the universe. Let us now build up the analogy with respect to hedonistic welfare economics.

Let us imagine a world where people, while substantially equal in other respects, display enormously different efficiencies as pleasure machines. Let us imagine also that these efficiencies vary inversely as the cube of the cephalic index. In such a world the criterion of least aggregate sacrifice would require that taxation leave the longheads with very large incomes; and a consistent policy would require that all impecunious longheads be generously subsidized. Now, to support such a scheme, one finds an appropriate theology not only convenient but utterly indispensable. The criterion implies that the primary objective of policy on earth should be that of generating *through* the human population the maximum output of pleasure for the contemplation of some external Spectator; and the appropriate supporting religion would assert that this Spectator dispensed blessings and punishments to humanity according to the adequacy of the pleasure output.

A critical, disinterested Spectator, contemplating such a world, would probably conclude, however, that the ethical claims of the longheads were, if anything, weaker and more specious than those of the strongbacks in the other world. If a person obtains, by virtue of luck or divine favoritism in the dispensing of genes, a remarkably efficient mechanism for converting income into pleasure, would not a meticulously equitable system equalize as between him and his fellows not marginal or incremental utility but simply total utility? It might seem somewhat ungenerous and vindictive for his fellows to insist upon such an arrangement; and the corollary implications respecting the treatment of the round-heads would sorely try economists' souls. But a deity could hardly be called unjust if he built a world on this general pattern. At all events, if the longheads succeed in getting and keeping as large incomes as the roundheads, they would do well to rest content. Certainly they should try to discourage speculative inquiries into questions of justice.

If there is any cogency in these remarks, one may conclude that the case for equality (for less inequality) is enormously stronger than any utility foundation on which it can be rested; indeed that hedonistic ethics, no less than productivity ethics, shrivels almost to absurdity when confronted with the creed of 'the greatest good *of the greatest number*'. To grant this is to demand that hedonism, repudiated as a basis of explanation of human behavior, be denied domicile in the 'economics of welfare'.

Such a demand will fall, in many quarters, upon deaf ears. Many professors of economic dialectic still find comfort and intellectual satisfaction (and 'filler' for courses and textbooks) in the 'explanations' of hedonism; and a larger group will continue to practice a kind of utility therapy and to write their prescriptions for the economist's millennnium in the hedonistic code. But serious students of fiscal policy and fiscal therapy cannot afford to achieve callousness to that always disturbing, and usually fruitful, question: What of it? Unless they can find some intelligible reasons for trying to maximize total social utility or to minimize aggregate sacrifice, they will do well not to spend their lives trying to define the conditions under which these ambiguous ends would be realized.

More sensible and more important than the contributions of utility theorists is the so-called sociopolitical theory of Adolph Wagner. Wagner contends, in effect, that taxation must be conceived as an instrumentality for altering or correcting the distribution of wealth and income and, what is more important, that only in this light do maxims of taxation according to ability or faculty or sacrifice have any real meaning. He would say that, if one regards the prevailing distribution of wealth and income as the only righteous, just, or expedient distribution, then it is idle to talk about ability to pay, to defend progression, or even to support the exemption of small incomes. His views (if we pursue them no farther) seem eminently sensible and represent sound criticism of other writers. (See Wagner, 1890, pp. 381–5 *passim*.)

Wagner's candor and clarity on these points have exposed his position to many adverse comments; and some writers have found his doctrine a too severe test of their tolerance. Seligman, to take an extreme case, deals with Wagner most severely and, in so doing, has considerably influenced American opinion. The cogency of Seligman's criticism, and his facility with emotive language, may fairly be judged from two statements which seem especially revealing:

It [Wagner's doctrine] would land us not only in socialism, but practically in communism.[2]

Legal justice means legal equality, and a legal equality which would attempt to force an equality of fortune in the face of inevitable inequalities of native ability would be a travesty of justice (Seligman, 1908, p. 132).[3]

The first statement requires no comment; and the second, if one looks behind the obvious ambiguity, reveals an unquestioning acceptance of the productivity ethics which we have referred to above.

The passages are quoted from Seligman's *Progressive Taxation in Theory and Practice*. Here the author, after roundly condemning the notion that improvement of the income distribution is a proper objective of tax policy, goes on to argue, in the very next paragraph, that public expenditures may properly be directed to attainment of that end. This conviction that expenditure is a

2. Seligman (2nd edn, 1908, p. 131) was taken to task severely by H. C. Adams (1898, p. 342) for his discussion of Wagner.

3. Actually this quotation follows the first edition (*Publications of the American Economic Association*, vol. 9, nos. 1 and 2, p. 69). In the second edition, the phrase 'equality of fortune' becomes 'inequality of fortune'; but the change is undoubtedly a typographical error.

proper instrumentality for controlling the income distribution but that taxation must not so be conceived is surely an amazing achievement of academic reflection. Nor is it less amazing that Seligman should argue strongly, later on, for progression, on the grounds that it is required by his totally ambiguous 'principle' of taxation according to faculty. (Seligman, 1908, ch. 4.)

Such curious methods of defending progression are commonplace. The practice typically is that of admitting progression through the back door, under the cloak of Adam Smith's first maxim. Tons of paper have been employed in teaching the world that taxes should be levied according to ability – perhaps for the reason that this word utterly defies definition in terms of any base upon which taxes are or ever might be levied. Whereas the question is as to how taxes should be allocated with respect to income, consumption, or net worth, the answer is that they should be proportional to ability or faculty, which cannot be conceived quantitatively or defined in terms of any procedure of measurement. Such an answer indicates that the writer prefers the kind of taxation which he prefers; that he is unwilling to reveal his tastes or examine them critically; and that he finds useful in his profession a basic 'principle' from which, as from a conjurer's hat, anything may be drawn at will.

To avoid dissimulation and circumlocution, one may begin by saying what one thinks about inequality. Indeed, one may assert a substantially equalitarian position; or, at least, that there is a presumption in favor of equality and that the burden of proof rests with him who would depart from it. With such a start, one may hold that every increase in the degree of progression is, *with reference merely to distributional effects*, a desirable change, and without limit short of substantial equality among those taxed. The same position may be acceptable even to persons not sympathetic toward a thoroughgoing equalitarianism, for the existing distribution may bear no trace of the *kind* of inequality which they approve. And all the practical implications may commend themselves to cautious critics committed only to the view that inequality is sadly excessive here and now.

At any rate, it may be best to start by denying any justification for prevailing inequality in terms of personal desert. This position has the great virtue of being definite; and it seems more nearly defensible than any other simple position relevant to the immediate problem. If one refuses to accept this dogma, one's error cannot be demonstrated by resort to scientific or dialectical analysis. We may plead, remonstrate, preach, and exhort; but we cannot prove. But one dogmatic assertion is permissible, namely, that by no other means can the problem be dragged out into the open. Taxation must affect the distribution of income, whether we will it so or not; and it is only sensible to face the question as to what kinds of effects are desirable. To do this is to reduce the discussion frankly to the level of ethics or aesthetics. Such procedure, however, is certainly preferable to the traditional one of 'describing' the attributes of the good life in terms which simply are not descriptive.

The case for drastic progression in taxation must be rested on the case against inequality – on the ethical or aesthetic judgement that the prevailing distribution of wealth and income reveals a degree (and/or kind) of inequality which is distinctly evil or unlovely.

Such a view obviously takes account merely of the distributional effects of progression. Indeed, that is as far as traditional discussions of justice in taxation may properly go. Yet this is obviously but one side of the problem. The degree of progression in a tax system may also affect production and the size of the national income available for distribution. In fact, it is reasonable to expect that every gain, through taxation, in better distribution will be accompanied by some loss in production. The real problem of policy, thus, is that of weighing the one set of effects against the other.

Two simple points should be noted at the outset. First, the effect of a higher degree of progression in taxation upon the distribution of income is certain; the effect upon production, problematical. One is a matter of arithmetic; the other, largely, of social psychology. Second, if reduction in the degree of inequality is a good, then the optimum degree of progression must involve a distinctly adverse effect upon the size of the national income. Prevailing opinion to the contrary notwithstanding, it is only an inadequate degree of progression which has no effect upon production and economic progress.

But what are these sources of loss, these costs of improved distribution? There are possible effects (a) upon the supplies of highly productive, or at least handsomely rewarded, personal services, (b) upon the use of available physical resources, (c) upon the efficiency of enterpriser activity, and (d) upon the accumulation and growth of resources through saving. Of these effects, all but the last may be regarded as negligible, under any degree of progression which is at all likely to obtain; at least, this position is not indefensible, and surely it is a lesser distortion of the truth than the essentially opposite position so commonly implicit in popular discussion and in the writings of conservative economists.

The attractiveness of jobs as jobs surely varies, on the whole, directly and markedly with the remunerations which they carry. What competing firms must pay to get experts away from one another is vastly different from what society would be obliged to pay in order to keep the experts from being ditch-diggers. Physical resources will always be more profitable to employ than to leave idle, so long as progression falls short of 100 per cent or does not rise precipitously to that level. Our captains of industry (enterprisers) are mainly engaged not in making a living but in playing a great game; and it *need* make little difference whether the evidence of having played well be diamonds on one's wife or a prominent place in the list of contributors under the income tax. Besides – and this may be emphasized – the mere privilege of excercising power is no mean prize for the successful enterpriser.[4]

4. This is not the place for more cautious and judicious discussion of the economic effects of income taxes. What would otherwise be careless and offensive dogmatism is perhaps justified where the main purpose is that of revealing the writer's biases and, in particular, of presenting the tentative conclusion that, within significant limits, only the possible effects on capital accumulation are of first-rate importance. More thorough treatment would consider especially the possible effects upon investment in more venturesome undertakings, i.e. on the gambling aspects of enterprise. It seems, however, that too much importance is likely to be attached to such effects. In the first place, some deterrent against the more uncertain and risky commitments might well be economically salutary. In spite of our obvious indebtedness to those who have been wisely venturesome in the past, one feels that modern social and economic arrangements are conducive to an excessive wagering of resources at long odds, to overrapid development of new areas, and to undue haste in the exploitation of new technical discoveries which, with only a little more delay and patience, might be adopted and applied (or discarded) with great reduction of the relevant uncertainties. The mere existence of commercial gambling is significant evidence on this score; and a careful accounting of our total outlays in prospecting for gold

These remarks define, of course, an extreme and not wholly tenable position. But the adverse effects of increasing progression may be estimated only in terms of predictions of human behavior; and one may well doubt that most of them would be important, at least under any degree of progression which is politically possible or administratively practicable for the significant future. With respect to capital accumulation, however, the consequences are certain to be significantly adverse. How increased progression would affect the *incentive* to accumulation or saving, it would be rash to predict. Here the ultimate question is essentially that of the probable effect of small changes in the rate of interest upon the rate of saving. That the incentive, within wide limits of tax practice, would be unaffected, is as reasonable as any other position, many economists to the contrary notwithstanding (see Schmoller, 1863, *passim*).[5]

Nevertheless, it is hardly questionable that increasing progression is inimical to saving and accumulation. Under an individualistic system, great inequality is necessary to rapidly increasing indirectness in the productive process – necessary to the increasing use of resources in the production of more (and different) resources. The cost of our present stock of productive instruments was, in a significant sense, decades and centuries of terrible poverty for the masses. Conversely, the cost of justice will be a

and oil would probably be very illuminating. Second, if the effect of progressive, personal taxes on speculative investments is undesirable, it is attributable in no small measure to gross defects of existing taxes which are easily amenable to correction. Our tax laws are crude, niggardly, and patently unfair in their treatment of losses. With these defects removed, the possibility of deducting losses would largely counterbalance the prospective tax on speculative gains, except for persons and enterprises whose small resources prohibit diversification of investments. At the worst, some measure of inhibition against long-odds ventures is a perhaps inevitable, but relatively unimportant, cost of more equitable tax arrangements.

5. As Schmoller argued so clearly, the rate of saving would appear to depend on many other factors more intimately than upon the rate of interest. Certainly it will depend upon the prospects with reference to the security of the institution of property and of the whole economic and political system. Moreover, mitigation of the grosser inequalities in the distribution of income, wealth, and power would surely fortify the existing system against attack and contribute to the prospects of its stability and security. Thus, highly progressive taxation might serve, historically, to sustain and strengthen the incentive to accumulation.

slowing-up in our material advance (though this effect may be modified if and as governments assume the role of savers).

Increasing progression means augmenting incomes where saving is impossible and diminishing incomes too large to be used entirely for consumption. Thus, it means diversion of resources from capital-creation to consumption uses. The classes subject to the highest rates will not greatly curtail consumption; and persons at the bottom of the income scale, paying smaller taxes, will use their additional income largely to improve their standard of life. Some curtailment of consumption at the upper end of the scale may be expected, as may some increase of saving at the lower end. That the net effect will be increased consumption, however, hardly admits of doubt.

Here perhaps is a real cost, a limitation, a poser for one who would lead us away from extreme inequality via taxation. Increased saving is a true blessing, other things being equal;[6] its curtailment,

6. Of course, saving may be a real affliction during a depression. When unfavorable cost-price relations discourage investment, an increase of saving will aggravate hoarding and thereby aggravate maladjustments between the flexible and sticky prices. In such periods, incidentally, the income tax has great advantages over other taxes, by virtue of its effect on saving, and because it does not contribute to the cost-price maladjustments. No other important type of levy can be imposed with less adverse effects per dollar of revenue.

Many devotees of 'oversaving' theories would argue, of course, that the adverse effects of progression upon saving are desirable or even necessary for purposes of fuller or more stable employment. We repudiate this argument entirely; and we wish scrupulously to avoid the temptation, which must face every ardent advocate of progression, to support his case by recourse to sophistries of the kind recently propagated by Mr Keynes in England and, more journalistically, by David Cushman Coyle in this country. One may concede that their arguments contain an obscure element of practical insight and are more nearly respectable intellectually than earlier doctrines of over-saving. Our economy is more dangerously exposed to catastrophic deflation than to excesses in the opposite direction; and, historically, we have had perhaps less increase in the quantity and/or velocity of money than would have been ideal. Urgent as is the need for a sound program of monetary reconstruction, however, it seems improper to regard progressive taxation as a part of such a program. To concede that increase in money turnover is often, if not typically, desirable is not to argue for every kind of measure which would operate in this direction. Those who advocate progressive taxes because they curtail hoarding by curtailing saving, seem to take no account (1) of the need for minimizing monetary uncertainty through the establish-

undeniably a loss. Nevertheless, the position that progression should be applied only moderately, because of its effect upon accumulation, is by no means inviting when one considers precisely what it means.

There is, first of all, a question as to whether society should make large sacrifices to further accumulation. To stress obligations to our children's children is often a means of diverting attention from patent obligations to our contemporaries. For the future there is a responsibility of maintaining a respectable proportion between population and resources – which surely admits of more than one method. Of course progress should be encouraged; but its costs should give us pause, in a society mature enough to exercise some deliberate control. Both progress and justice are costly luxuries – costly, above all, in terms of each other. Let us raise the question, in passing, as to whether we have been quite safely removed from the predicament of that hypothetical society which employed every increase in its income for the purposes of further increase, and so on until the end of time.

There is also a difficult question, from the point of view of the

---

ment of definite rules of policy, (2) of the need for rigid economy in the kinds of devices for implementing those rules, or (3) of the need for sharp focusing of responsibility for observance of the rules. Moreover, such taxes, as a device for controlling the velocity of money, have the disadvantage of working only in one direction; at any rate, no one appears to advocate their reduction or abolition in boom times as a means for checking a movement of dishoarding!

The advocates of these intriguing heresies appear to argue that we cannot afford prosperity because additional income promotes hoarding; but the paradox, however salable and entertaining, is intellectual rubbish. One means for reducing hoarding, to be sure, is to keep people very poor. The excuse for killing of the goose, however, is very lame. There is no need for restricting saving in order to restrict hoarding; appropriate monetary rules, implemented by mandatory changes in the quantity of money, can assure adequate (or excessive) spending by making the alternative cost of hoarding as high as may be necessary, and without any deliberate diversion of funds from would-be savers to the more profligate or necessitous. Thus, to paraphrase a previous statement, the case for progression is enormously stronger than any monetary considerations on which it might be rested; and those who seek to support it in this way only raise doubts about an otherwise strong position.

For statement of the writer's views on monetary questions see Simons (1936, pp. 1–30).

economics of welfare, as to the relative importance of productional and distributional considerations. There is real point, if not truth, in the suggestion that, within wide limits, the quality of human experience would be about the same at one income level as at another if the *relative* position of persons and classes remained unchanged. Poverty, want, and privation are in large measure merely relative. Thus, something can be said for mitigation of inequality, even at the cost of reduction in the modal real income.

It is important to recognize that each generation inherits a system of property rights, as well as a stock of means of production – that it receives its resources with mortgages attached. If we deliberately limit the degree of progression, out of regard for effects on accumulation, we are in effect removing taxes from those who consume too much and transferring them to classes which admittedly consume too little; and against the additional capital resources thus painfully acquired are mortgages, property rights, in the hands of those freed from tax. While the saving will really have been done by those at the bottom of the income scale, those free from tax and their assigns will enjoy the reward. This method of fostering increase in productive capacity thus increases the concentration of property and aggravates inequality.

If the productivity of capital were highly elastic – if the long-period demand for investment funds were not extremely elastic – the phenomenon of diminishing returns might be relied upon to mitigate the distributional effects. The masses would surely participate to some extent in the blessings of greater productive capacity. In fact, however, the scheme looks a bit like taxing small incomes to reduce consumption in the hope that those relieved of tax will save more after consuming all they can, and then allowing 1 per cent to those who have really done the saving and 4 per cent to those who have served merely by paying smaller taxes. We are thus placed under the strange necessity of lamenting the flatness of the productivity curve – of lamenting the otherwise glorious prospect of using additional capital goods very productively. The anomaly arises, of course, merely from the institution of property, which largely sets the distributional problem of taxation.

A possible solution of this difficulty is budgetary provision for capital accumulation on the part of governments. In this way, fiscal policy might promote or sustain accumulation without incurring the doubly unfavorable terms involved in restricting progression to that end. Whether and how far this is really feasible are questions of political morality and administrative efficiency. The same questions arise when one asks how large government expenditures should be and, indeed, are at the heart of the problem of social control through fiscal devices. If governments can administer and effectively direct the production and distribution of certain classes of goods and services, expenditures and taxation may properly be high. If governments could handle effectively the business of investment, more drastic measures for modifying the degree of inequality would be desirable and expedient.

Opportunities for extending the scope of socialized consumption are clearly numerous. Many goods and services, of great importance for general welfare, might be distributed freely or with substantial relaxing of prevailing price controls. The prospect for public administration of saving is much less promising. For the immediate future, however, the retirement of public debts will provide an adequate offset to the adverse effects of progression on saving;[7] and, after debts were entirely retired, governments might still contribute somewhat to the volume of savings available for private investment by adhering to a pay-as-you-go policy. Moreover, they might proceed gradually with investment in private industry.[8] The techniques of a conservative investment business

7. No case can be made for lowering the higher surtaxes, in order to foster saving, when this proposal contemplates reduction in the rate at which the government debt is being retired, for the taxation and expenditure together will in this case increase rather than diminish the amount of funds available for private investment. At least it is highly probable (almost certain) that a larger proportion of the funds will be saved if transferred to bondholders in exchange for their bonds than if left in the hands of the taxpayers.

8. Here, again, there are some immediately attractive opportunities, especially in the case of the public utilities. Regulation is a peculiarly unsatisfactory and anomalous expedient, justifiable only on the dubious grounds that governments are more nearly competent to regulate than to own and operate. Under a sound, long-term program, the government, while undertaking to preserve competitive controls for industry as a whole, should plan gradually to acquire and operate those industries where competition simply cannot serve as an implement of control. At least, there would seem to be no proper place for regulation of private industry (as to prices and investment) under anything like our existing economic system or under anything like democratic government.

are fairly well established; and governmental bodies might, on a moderate scale, function quite as well as the investment departments of the better banks and insurance companies. Considerable investment might be made without involving the government in the management of private business – just as governments may distribute all sorts of consumption services while leaving many steps in their production in the hands of private enterprise. Indeed, governments might well remain, special cases apart, in a quite passive, creditor role, merely dispensing investment funds according to interest return and security.

To the inevitable protest that this means socialism, one may reply that the program is properly part of a promising scheme for saving the free-enterprise system and the institution of political freedom.[9] The growth of government investment in private industry might be thoroughly gradual; steps could be taken forward or backward according to the dictates of expediency; and perhaps the maintenance of accumulation would not justify or require continued saving through the government. The contention here is not that there should be correction of the effects of extreme progression upon saving but that government saving, rather than modification of the progression, is the appropriate method for effecting that correction, if such correction is to be made.

Any such scheme implies increasing reliance upon political

9. These paragraphs were written years ago, at a time when the writer was less sensitive to the difficulty or impossibility of maintaining representative government in the face of increasing centralization and collectivism. Complete revision has not seemed necessary, however, for, although the shades of emphasis are sometimes unfortunate, the central position seems sound. The direct provision by governments of capital funds for private industry is something which can be viewed only with grave misgivings. However, if we were faced with a dangerous tendency toward capital consumption and disaccumulation, such a policy would seem preferable to that of making taxes less progressive (or more regressive) than otherwise would have been expedient. Actually, it is altogether academic to consider how the government might find adequate outlets for its own saving, with our present debt, and with great industries which can never be effectively competitive still under private ownership. To suggest that the government might protect our capital resources by assuming the role of saver is not to suggest that it become even a passive investor in competitive, private industries during the next century!

controls. The vital issues in economic policy, however, have to do with the form of political control rather than with its extent, for increase is inescapable. Moreover, the control of the distribution of income through taxation represents a form of control which democratic governments can be expected to exercise somewhat correctly, i.e. without undermining the foundation of their own existence. No fundamental disturbance of the whole system is involved. Business would still be conducted for profit; the prosperous would still exercise power; the game should remain substantially as interesting and attractive as ever; and the control of relative prices might still be left to the forces of competition.

References

ADAMS, H. C. (1898), *Science of Finance*.

EDGEWORTH, F. Y. (1925), *Papers Relating to Political Economy*, vol. 2, Heffer.

MILL, J. S. (1909), *Principles*, Book 5, W. J. Ashley edn.

PIGOU, A. C. (1928), *A Study in Public Finance*, Macmillan, 3rd edn.

SCHMOLLER, G. (1863), 'Die Lehre vom Einkommen in ihrem Zusammenhang mit den Grundprinzipien der Steuerlehre', *Zeitschrift für gesamte Staatswissenchaft*, vol. 19.

SELIGMAN, E. R. A. (1908), *Progressive Taxation in Theory and Practice*, Princeton University Press, 2nd edn.

SIMONS, H. C. (1934), 'A positive program for *laissez faire*: some proposals for a liberal economic policy', *Public Policy Pamphlets*, no. 15, University of Chicago Press.

SIMONS, H. C. (1936), 'Rules versus authorities in monetary policy', *Journal of Political Economy*, vol. 44, no. 1.

WAGNER, A. (1890), *Lehrbuch der Politischen Oekonomie*, vol. 6, Teil II, 2nd edn.

2 H. C. Simons

The Comprehensive Definition of Income

Excerpt from H. C. Simons, *Personal Income Taxation*,
University of Chicago Press, 1938, pp. 49–58.

Although personal income is not amenable to precise definition, it has, by comparison with the concept of social income, a much smaller degree of ambiguity. Its measurement implies estimating merely the *relative* results of individual economic activity during a period of time. Moreover, there arises no question of distinction between production and predation. Social income implies valuation of a total product of goods and services; while personal income is a purely acquisitive concept having to do with the possession and exercise of rights.

Personal income connotes, broadly, the exercise of control over the use of society's scarce resources. It has to do not with sensations, services, or goods but rather with rights which command prices (or to which prices may be imputed). Its calculation implies estimate (a) of the amount by which the value of a person's store of property rights would have increased, as between the beginning and end of the period, if he had consumed (destroyed) nothing, or (b) of the value of rights which he might have exercised in consumption without altering the value of his store of rights. In other words, it implies estimate of consumption and accumulation. Consumption as a quantity denotes the value of rights exercised in a certain way (in destruction of economic goods); accumulation denotes the change in ownership of valuable rights as between the beginning and end of a period.

The relation of the income concept to the specified time interval is fundamental – and neglect of this crucial relation has been responsible for much confusion in the relevant literature. The measurement of income implies allocation of consumption and accumulation to specified periods. In a sense, it implies the possibility of measuring the results of individual participation in economic relations *for an assigned interval* and without regard for anything which happened before the beginning of that (before the end of the previous) interval or for what may happen in subsequent periods. All data for the measurement would be found, ideally, within the period analyzed.

Personal income may be defined as the algebraic sum of (a) the market value of rights exercised in consumption and (b) the change in the value of the store of property rights between the beginning and end of the period in question. In other words, it is merely the result obtained by adding consumption during the period to 'wealth' at the end of the period and then subtracting 'wealth' at the beginning. The *sine qua non* of income is *gain*, as our courts have recognized in their more lucid moments – and gain *to* someone during a specified time interval. Moreover, this gain may be measured and defined most easily by positing a dual objective or purpose, consumption and accumulation, each of which may be estimated in a common unit by appeal to market prices.

This position, if tenable, must suggest the folly of describing income as a flow and, more emphatically, of regarding it as a quantity of goods, services, receipts, fruits, etc. As Schäffle has said so pointedly, 'Das Einkommen hat nur buchhalterische Existenz.' (Quoted by Schmoller, 1863, p. 54, from Schäffle, 1861.) It is indeed merely an arithmetic answer and exists only as the end result of appropriate calculations. To conceive of income in terms of things is to invite all the confusion of the elementary student in accounting who insists upon identifying 'surplus' and 'cash'.[1] If one views society as a kind of giant partnership, one may conceive of a person's income as the sum of his withdrawals (consumption) and the change in the value of his equity or interest in the enterprise. The essential connotation of income, to repeat, is *gain* – gain *to* someone during a specified period and

1. This point, with all its triteness, can hardly be overemphasized, for it implies a decisive criticism of most of the extant definitions of income. Professor Hewett, e.g., asserts and implies consistently that income is merely a collection of goods and services which may, so to speak, be thrown off into a separate pile and then measured in terms of money. He and others too, no doubt, know better; but, when one undertakes the task of definition, one may expect to be held accountable for what one literally says.

measured according to objective market standards. Let us now note some of the more obvious limitations and ambiguities of this conception of income.

In the first place, it raises the unanswerable question as to where or how a line may be drawn between what is and what is not economic activity. If a man raises vegetables in his garden, it seems clearly appropriate to include the value of the product in measuring his income. If he raises flowers and shrubs, the case is less clear. If he shaves himself, it is difficult to argue that the value of the shaves must also be accounted for. Most economists recognize housewives' services as an important item of income. So they are, perhaps; but what becomes of this view as one proceeds to extreme cases? Do families have larger incomes because parents give competent instruction to children instead of paying for institutional training? Does a doctor or an apothecary have relatively large income in years when his family requires and receives an extraordinary amount of his own professional services? Kleinwächter suggests[2] that the poorest families might be shown to have substantial incomes if one went far in accounting for instruction, nursing, cooking, maid service, and other things which the upper classes obtain by purchase.

A little reflection along these lines suggests that leisure is itself a major item of consumption; that income per hour of leisure, beyond a certain minimum, might well be imputed to persons according to what they might earn per hour if otherwise engaged. Of course, it is one thing to note that such procedure is appropriate in principle and quite another to propose that it be applied. Such considerations do suggest, however, that the neglect of 'earned income in kind' may be substantially offset, for comparative purposes (for measurement of relative incomes), if leisure income is also neglected. For income taxation it is important that these elements of income vary with considerable regularity, from one income class to the next, along the income scale.

A similar difficulty arises with reference to receipts in the form of compensation in kind. Let us consider here another of Kleinwächter's conundrums. We are asked to measure the relative incomes of an ordinary officer serving with his troops and a

2. Simons (1938, introduction). We have drawn heavily, in this and other passages, on Kleinwächter's conundrums.

Flügeladjutant to the sovereign. Both receive the same nominal pay; but the latter receives quarters in the palace, food at the royal table, servants, and horses for sport. He accompanies the prince to theater and opera, and, in general, lives royally at no expense to himself and is able to save generously from his salary. But suppose, as one possible complication, that the *Flügeladjutant* detests opera and hunting.

The problem is clearly hopeless. To neglect all compensation in kind is obviously inappropriate. On the other hand, to include the perquisites as a major addition to the salary implies that all income should be measured with regard for the relative pleasurableness of different activities – which would be the negation of measurement. There is hardly more reason for imputing additonal income to the *Flügeladjutant* on account of his luxurious wardrobe than for bringing into account the prestige and social distinction of a (German) university professor. Fortunately, however, such difficulties in satisfactory measurement of relative incomes do not bulk large in modern times; and, again, these elements of unmeasurable psychic income may be presumed to vary in a somewhat continuous manner along the income scale.

If difficulties arise in determining what positive items shall be included in calculations of income (in measuring consumption), they are hardly less serious than those involved in determining and defining appropriate deductions. At the outset there appears the necessity of distinguishing between consumption and expense; and here one finds inescapable the unwelcome criterion of intention. A thoroughly precise and objective distinction is inconceivable. Given items will represent business expense in one instance and merely consumption in another, and often the motives will be quite mixed. A commercial artist buys paints and brushes to use in making his living. Another person may buy the same articles as playthings for his children, or to cultivate a hobby of his own. Even the professional artist may use some of his materials for things he intends or hopes to sell, and some on work done purely for his own pleasure. In another instance, moreover, the same items may represent investment in training for earning activity later on.

The latter instance suggests that there is something quite arbitrary even about the distinction between consumption and accumulation. On the face of it, this is not important for the definition of income; but it must be remembered that accumulation or investment provides a basis for expense deductions in the future, while consumption does not. The distinction in question can be made somewhat definite if one adopts the drastic expedient of treating all outlays for augmenting personal earning capacity as consumption. This expedient has little more than empty, formal, legalistic justification. On the other hand, one does well to accept, here as elsewhere, a loss of relevance or adequacy as the necessary cost of an essential definiteness. It would require some temerity to propose recognition of depreciation or depletion in the measurement of personal-service incomes – if only because the determination of the base, upon which to apply depreciation rates, presents a simply fantastic problem. It is better simply to recognize the limitations of measurable personal income for purposes of certain comparisons (e.g., by granting special credits to personal-service incomes under income taxes).

Our definition of income may also be criticized on the ground that it ignores the patent instability of the monetary *numéraire* (see Viner, 1923, esp. pp. 494–504), and it may also be maintained that there is no rigorous, objective method either of measuring or of allowing for this instability. No serious difficulty is involved here for the measurement of consumption – which presumably must be measured in terms of prices at the time goods and services are actually acquired or consumed.[3] In periods of changing price levels, comparisons of incomes would be partially vitiated as between persons who distributed consumption outlays differently over the year. Such difficulties are negligible, however, as against those involved in the measurement of accumulation. This element of annual income would be grossly misrepresented if the price level changed markedly during the year. These limitations of the income concept are real and inescapable; but it must suffice here merely to point them out.

Another difficulty with the income concept has to do with the

3. In a sense relevant to income measurement, two persons' consumption of, say, strawberries might be very unequal for a period, though the physical quantities involved were identical, provided one consumed them largely in season and the other largely out of season.

whole problem of valuation. The precise, objective measurement of income implies the existence of perfect markets from which one, after ascertaining quantities, may obtain the prices necessary for routine valuation of all possible inventories of commodities, services, and property rights. In actuality there are few approximately perfect markets and few collections of goods or properties which can be valued accurately by recourse to market prices. Thus, every calculation of income depends upon 'constructive valuation,' i.e. upon highly conjectural estimates made, at best, by persons of wide information and sound judgement; and the results of such calculations have objective validity only in so far as the meager objective market data provide limits beyond which errors of estimate are palpable. One touches here upon familiar problems of accounting and, with reference to actual estimates of income, especially upon problems centering around the 'realization criterion'.

Our definition of income perhaps does violence to traditional usage in specifying impliedly a calculation which would include gratuitous receipts. To exclude gifts, inheritances, and bequests, however, would be to introduce additional arbitrary distinctions;[4] it would be necessary to distinguish among an individual's receipts according to the intentions of second parties. Gratuities denote transfers not in the form of exchange – receipts not in the form of 'consideration' for something 'paid' by the recipient. Here, again, no objective test would be available; and, if the distinctions may be avoided, the income concept will thus be left

4. The greater part of the enormous German literature on *Einkommenbegriff* may be regarded as the product of effort to manipulate verbal symbols into some arrangement which would capture the essential connotations of *Einkommen* (as something distinct from *Ertrag*, *Einnahme*, *Einkünfte*, etc.), provide a not too arbitrarily delimited conception, and yet decisively exclude gifts and bequests. It is as though an army of scholars had joined together in the search for a definition which, perfected and established in usage, would provide a sort of 'linguistic-constitutional' prohibition of an (to them) objectionable tax practice. For summary of this literature see Bauckner (1921).

Of course, we must avoid the implication that our definition establishes any decisive presumption regarding policy in income taxation. The case for or against taxation of gratuitous receipts as income ought not to be hidden in a definition.

more precise and more definite.[5]

It has been argued that the inclusion of gratuities introduces an objectionable sort of double-counting. The practice of giving seems a perhaps too simple means for increasing average personal income in the community. But philosophers have long discoursed upon the blessings of social consciousness and upon the possibilities of improving society by transforming narrow, acquisitive desires into desire for the welfare of our fellows. If it is not more pleasant to give than to receive, one may still hesitate to assert that giving is not a form of consumption for the giver. The proposition that everyone tries to allocate his consumption expenditure among different goods in such manner as to equalize the utility of dollars-worths may not be highly illuminating; but there is no apparent reason for treating gifts as an exception. And certainly it is difficult to see why gifts should not be regarded as income to the recipient.

The very notion of double-counting implies, indeed, the familiar, and disastrous, misconception that personal income is merely a share in some undistributed, separately measurable whole.[6] Certainly it is a curious presumption that a good method for measuring the relative incomes of individuals must yield quantities which, summated, will in turn afford a satisfactory measure of that ambiguous something which we call social income. This double-counting criticism, in the case of some writers (notably Irving Fisher), carries with it the implied contention that all possible referents of the word 'income', in different usages, must be definable or expressible in terms of one another. We have pointed out several different usages of the term in order to show that they represent distinct, and relatively unrelated, conceptions – conceptions which only poverty of language and vocabulary justifies calling by the same name.

5. The force of the foregoing argument is perhaps diminished when one remembers that the distinction creeps in unavoidably on the other side of the transaction – i.e. in the distinction between consumption and expense in the case of the donor. But there remains a presumption against introducing the distinction twice over if once will do.

6. Some writers explicitly avoid the implication that social income should be definable in terms of individual incomes or vice versa: Held (1872), ch. 4, esp. pp. 92 ff.; F. J. Neumann (1899), pp. 220–21; Schmoller (1863), p. 78; Ammon (1932), pp. 21–6; Meyer (1887), ch. 7.

References

AMMON, A. (1932), 'Die Begriffe Volkseinkommen und Volksvermögen und ihre Bedeutung für die Volkswirtschaftslehre', *Schr. d. Verein für Sozialpolitik*, vol. 173.

BAUCKNER, A. (1921), *Der privatwirtschaftliche Einkommenbegriff*, München.

HELD, A. (1872) *Die Einkommensteuer*, Bonn.

MEYER, R. (1887) *Das Wesen des Einkommens*, Berlin.

NEUMANN, F. J. (1899), *Grundlagen der Volkswirtschaft*, Tübingen.

SCHÄFFLE, A. E. F. (1861), 'Mensch und Gut in der Volkswirtschaft', *Deutsche Vierteljahrschrift*.

SCHMOLLER, G. (1863), 'Die Lehre vom Einkommen in ihrem Zusammenhang mit den Grundprinzipien der Steuerlehre', *Zeitschrift für gesamte Staatswissenchaft*, vol. 19.

SIMONS, H. C. (1938), *Personal Income Taxation*, University of Chicago Press.

VINER, J. (1923), 'Taxation and changes in price levels', *Journal of Political Economy*, vol. 31.

3 Royal Commission on the Taxation of Profits and Incomes

The United Kingdom Income Tax System *and* The Case for Taxing Capital Gains[1]

Excerpts from the *Report of the Royal Commission on the Taxation of Profits and Incomes*, Cmnd 9474, H.M.S.O., 1955. Memorandum of Dissent signed by G. Woodcock, H. L. Bullock and N. Kaldor, pp. 354–82.

The United Kingdom Income Tax System

[. . .]

2. The purpose of progressive income taxation is to allocate the burden of tax fairly between different members of the community. As the Majority point out in the Report (para. 33), a graduated tax differentiated according to personal circumstances is necessarily a tax on persons according to their respective total incomes, and not a tax on a 'body of income . . . as such', considered impersonally under some system of classification. It follows that equity between persons cannot be secured – however nicely the effective rate of tax is graduated according to an individual's total taxable income and however meticulously it is differentiated to allow for personal circumstances – unless the tax base itself (that is to say, the definition of income for tax purposes) provides a measure which is uniform, comprehensive and capable of consistent application to all individuals. Impartial assessment of the relative taxable capacity of individuals is impossible if the definition of taxable income is unduly restricted, ambiguous or biased in favour of particular groups of taxpayers.

3. A system of personal income taxation which operates without any clear definition of what constitutes 'income' is exposed to a double danger. On the one hand the simple view that income is an

1. This was written before the introduction of a capital gains tax in the United Kingdom and was clearly a strong influence on the introduction of the present (1968) capital gains taxes. [Ed.]

unambiguous word, not subject to various interpretations, may ensure general complacency, and the particular notion of 'taxable income' hallowed by legal tradition tends to become identified with taxable capacity as such. On the other hand, in the absence of any clear underlying principle, revisions and interpretations of the law proceed, in the light of particular considerations, to introduce successive concessions which have the effect of constantly shifting the tax burden in a manner which is no less far-reaching for being unobtrusive. Lacking a firm basic conception, neither the public nor the legislature nor the Courts are conscious of the extent to which the tax system, behind a façade of formal equality, metes out unequal treatment to the different classes of the taxpaying community.

4. It has therefore seemed to us most important to state at the outset what, in our view, is the 'true conception of income' (cf. para. 28 of the Report) required to secure an allocation of taxation that is in accordance with taxable capacity, or 'ability to pay'.

The definition of income

5. In our view the taxable capacity of an individual consists in his power to satisfy his own material needs, i.e., to attain a particular living standard. We know of no alternative definition that is capable of satisfying society's prevailing sense of fairness and equity. Thus the ruling test to be applied in deciding whether any particular receipt should or should not be reckoned as taxable income is whether it contributes or not, or how far it contributes, to an individual's 'spending power' during a period. When set beside this standard, most of the principles that have been applied, at one time or another, to determine whether particular types of receipt constitute income (whether the receipts are regularly recurrent or casual, or whether they proceed from a separate and identifiable source, or whether they are payments for services rendered, or whether they constitute profit 'on sound accountancy principles', or whether, in the words of the Majority (para. 31), they fall 'within the limited class of receipts that are identified as income by their own nature') appear to us to be irrelevant. In fact no concept of income can be really equitable that stops short of the comprehensive definition which embraces all receipts

which increase an individual's command over the use of society's scarce resources – in other words, his 'net accretion of economic power between two points of time'.

6. Definitions of income giving expression to this basic principle have been offered by various writers on public finance, all of which, subject to minor differences, agree in regarding 'income' as the sum of two separate elements, namely personal consumption and net capital accumulation. In the words of one writer income can be looked upon either as '(a) the amount by which the value of a person's store of property rights would have increased, as between the beginning and the end of the period, if he had consumed (destroyed) nothing; or (b) the value of rights which he might have exercised in consumption without altering the value of his store of rights'. Hence income is the 'algebraic sum of (1) the market value of rights exercised in consumption, and (2) the change in the value of the store of property rights between the beginning and the end of the period in question' (see Simons, 1938 [p. 39 above – Ed.]).

7. The above definition focuses attention on two fundamental aspects of the concept of income which reflects the increment of 'spending power' or 'economic power' in a period. One is that income is a measure of the increase in the individual's command over resources in a period, irrespective of how much or how little of that command he actually exercises in consumption. The private choice of an individual as to how much he spends and how much he saves is irrelevant to this notion: income is the sum of consumption and net saving. The second is that 'net saving' (and hence income) includes the whole of the change in the value of a man's store of property rights between two points of time, irrespective of whether the change has been brought about by the current addition to property which is saving in the narrower sense, or whether it has been caused by accretions to the value of property. From the point of view of an individual's command over resources, it is the change in the real value of his property which alone matters, and not the process by which that change was brought about.

8. In applying the basic conception of income as the power to satisfy material needs to any workable tax system, a number of guiding principles need to be introduced.

i. The first of these is, in the words of the Majority (para. 29), that 'no income [should be] recognized as arising unless an actual receipt has taken place, although a receipt may take the form of a benefit having money's worth received in kind as well as of money or of a payment made to a third party in discharge of another's legal debt'. The obvious corollary to this principle is that no deduction should be recognized from any gross receipt in arriving at the net receipt unless an actual outlay has taken place, whether in money or money's worth.[2] Hence improvement or deterioration in the market value of a man's property should not be recognized until it is reflected (as in the long run it must be) in his actual receipts, or in the outlays that he can properly charge against those receipts. (We shall refer to this point more fully in our treatment of the problem of capital gains.)

ii. The second guiding principle is that receipts which cannot reasonably be brought within the scope of taxation because their control and enforcement is beyond the power of any efficient tax administration are better ignored altogether (even though they are beneficial receipts) since their inclusion creates unfairness to the disadvantage of the honest taxpayer. (Gambling winnings may be regarded as an example of this.) The obvious corollary to this principle is that outlays or expenses chargeable against gross receipts which cannot be efficiently and uniformly administered (because it is beyond the powers of an efficient tax administration to control or check whether (a) they have actually been incurred or not; or (b) whether they have actually been laid out for the purposes stated; or (c) whether they are properly deductible as necessary expenses incurred in connexion with, and for the purpose of obtaining, the receipts) should similarly be ignored, since their inclusion may create more unfairness between taxpayers than it remedies. (We shall refer to this point more fully in connexion with the difference in the definition of income charged under Schedules D and E.)

iii. Thirdly, under a progressive system of taxation, recognition needs to be given to the fact that unique or non-recurrent receipts

2. Our tax system generally obeys this principle subject to two important exceptions. The first consists (as is stated by the Majority) in the taxation of the owner-occupier of a house or land in respect of the annual value represented by his occupation. The second consists in the concession which allows a reduction in the market value of unsold stock-in-trade below its actual cost of acquisition to qualify as a deduction against the year's receipts from trading activities.

obtained in any particular period do not confer the same spending power on the recipient within that period as recurrent receipts of like amount.

The present legal definition of taxable income

9. Our tax system has not been developed in obedience to such general principles; and to the extent that they do receive recognition in the tax code, it is more the result of *ad hoc* considerations or of administrative necessities than of any systematic application of a basic conception. The current legal definition of what constitutes taxable income has been arrived at by a process of piecemeal statutory revision and judicial interpretation of the provisions of Five Schedules, introduced by the Income Tax Act of 1803, under which the various kinds of taxable receipts and benefits are enumerated and which collectively define the limits of taxable income. As the Majority state, 'While the fundamental structure remains signally unaltered, additions and alterations have, of course, been made from time to time either by changing or enlarging the list of sources or by *ad hoc* provisions to the effect that a particular kind of receipt is to rank as taxable income' (para. 31). But the original Act of 1803 already included a 'sweeping up clause', in Case VI of Schedule D, under which 'any annual profit or gain' is taxable which is not enumerated under any of the other Cases or Schedules. Since the law employs the terms 'income', 'profit' or 'gain' interchangeably, the very insertion of such a clause is incongruous within a system which identifies income only by a process of categorization and which in consequence nowhere defines what it is that is to be swept up.

10. The circularity inherent in this legal conception is well illusstrated by the juxtaposition of two well-known judicial interpretations of the statute. 'Income tax', according to Lord Macnaghten's famous dictum,[3] 'is a tax on income'. But 'as regards the word income' said Lord Wrenbury,[4] 'it means such income as is within the Act taxable under the Act'. The law faces the same dilemma as the medieval Schoolmen who were forced to deny to exotic birds and beasts, captured by travellers in strange lands, the status of birds and beasts, since they relied for their definition

3. Attorney-General *v.* London County Council (1900), 4 T.C. at p. 293.
4. Whitney *v.* C.I.R. (1925), 10 T.C. at p. 113.

on an exhaustive list of birds and beasts reported by tradition to have entered the Ark with Noah.

11. The inclusion or exclusion of particular types of receipts assumed an entirely different significance as income tax was gradually transformed from a small flat-rate impost to a steeply graduated tax calculated with reference to an individual's total income from all sources. Yet the trend towards the comprehensive tax base implied in the very notion of progressive taxation has been checked at various points, mainly on the basis of two distinct considerations. First, as the Majority point out (para. 32) there has been a tendency to avoid the special problem of the heavy incidence of a steeply graduated tax on receipts which by their very nature are realized irregularly, instead of being spread evenly over the years in which they may be regarded as accruing, by the simple expedient of excluding such receipts altogether from the tax charge. Secondly, the ancient constricted conception of income as something which recurrently emerges and is separated off from its perpetual source, like the harvest from the soil, has lingered in the tax code from times when, by and large, income was the harvest from the soil. It has only been abandoned gradually, through the piecemeal adoption of basically inconsistent provisions, and without the consequences of its abandonment ever having been systematically taken into account. Thus the old view of the rigid separation between the income flow and its permanent source has been blurred by the allowances introduced for capital wastage and even losses, as permissible deductions in the calculation of income. The old boundary-line afforded by the regularity or recurrence criterion has been discarded in judicial decisions which have established that casual or isolated gains are taxable provided that they are not of the character of 'capital profits'.

Casual and capital profits

12. Indeed this question of the status of 'casual' and of 'capital' profits has been a matter of uneasiness in this country for at least forty years; and the accession of case law, far from gradually evolving any clear principle, has left matters in greater uncertainty than they were before.[5] The exploitation of exceptional oppor-

5. cf. also Appendix I of the Board's Memorandum on Capital Gains printed on p. 454 this report [not included here].

tunities to make and enjoy profits which emerged from no regular profession or trade, during and after the First World War, brought into public question the justice of exempting from taxation fruits of luck and speculation which, in the economic benefits their possession conferred, seemed indistinguishable from taxed earnings more hardly won. The 1920 Royal Commission on the Income Tax recommended (Cmnd 615, para. 91 [not included here]) that 'a transaction in which the subject matter was acquired with a view to profit-seeking, should be brought within the scope of the Income Tax, and should not be treated as an accretion of capital simply because the transaction lies outside the range of the taxpayer's ordinary business, or because the opportunities of making such profits are not likely, in the nature of things, to occur regularly or at short intervals'. On the other hand they stated 'profits that arise from ordinary changes of investments should normally remain outside the scope of the tax, but they should nevertheless be charged if and when they constitute a regular source of profit'. In the view of the 1920 Commission therefore (1) the basic test of whether a particular gain is taxable should lie not in the regularity of recurrence of its character, but in the question whether the subject matter of the transaction was acquired with a view to profit-seeking or not; (2) when the subject matter of the transaction is an 'investment', the motive of profit-seeking should not be presumed, unless such transactions occur with sufficient frequency to constitute a regular source of profits. (The second of these propositions is not stated in this form in the Report of the 1920 Royal Commission. But in our view it is the only interpretation of their position which makes the two recommendations, quoted above, consistent with one another.)

13. No subsequent action was taken by Parliament on these recommendations; and we agree with the Majority (para. 113) that the line of approach adopted by the 1920 Commission is unsatisfactory. We consider a test based on motive to be not merely defective in its vagueness and the uncertainty of proof, but irrelevant. The sole relevant test, in our view, as to whether a gain is to be taxable or not is whether it secures a net material benefit to the recipient. From the point of view of taxable capacity it is irrelevant whether an increase in spending power occurs as a result of an unexpected windfall, or whether it was expected,

planned or achieved in the course of a business organized for the purpose.

14. As the Majority explain (para. 86), a series of Court decisions since 1920 have radically changed the state of the law. We believe however that these developments have only served to increase the ambiguity and uncertainty in the status of non-taxable 'capital profits' without effecting any notable advance towards equity. The position now appears to be that a purely isolated profit is taxable, if the underlying transaction carries with it 'the badges of trade'. But the question whether it carries such a badge or not, appears to be decided not on motive, nor on whether a business had to be organized for the purpose, but simply on whether the transaction involved speculation of a rare kind (such as the purchase and sale of toilet paper by a money lender;[6] of whisky in bond by a woodcutter;[7] or of farms by a motor engineer[8]) rather than speculation of the more usual kind involving operations on the Stock Exchange or the produce exchanges. In the case of the purchase and sale of investments, 'an accretion to capital', as Lord Buckmaster put it, 'does not become income merely because the original capital was invested in the hope and expectation that it would rise in value.'[9]

15. The Majority defend what appears to be the present position of the law by a more subtle piece of reasoning. According to this view (para. 31) 'referability to a defined source is essential to permit of a receipt being categorized as income'. Though 'all profits that arise from the utilization of property are made in a sense out of capital (para. 109) only those profits are income 'which arise out of something more substantial than the mere occasion of the profit itself. Income, it has been said, is the fruit that ripens on and can be plucked off the tree. If there is to be income therefore there must not only be fruit but also a tree. This substance is to be found where the person concerned has been conducting a venture or concern in the nature of trade out of which the profit arises. That is equivalent to saying that he was a dealer, even if he made only one deal. But the profit that is taxed in such a case is the income

6. Rutledge v. C.I.R. (1929), 14 T.C. 490.
7. C.I.R. v. Fraser (1942), 24 T.C. 498.
8. Reynolds' Executors v. Bennett (1943), 25 T.C. 401.
9. Leeming v. Jones (1930), 15 T.C. 333, at p. 357.

arising from the venture: it is meaningless to say that what is taxed is the profit from the sale itself' (para. 84).

16. We are unable to follow these arguments. It seems to us that the motor engineer who buys and sells a farm or the woodcutter who buys and sells bonded whisky is in no different position from the Stock Exchange operator who buys and sells particular shares. If the one is deemed to have committed his capital to a venture, so has the other; if the one is to be decorated for the occasion with the 'badges of trade', so should the other. The ordinary man (whether he accepts it as adequate or not) might be able to follow a line of reasoning according to which the profits of a regular business are to be distinguished from isolated or casual profits which a man might obtain outside his regular activities once or twice in a lifetime. But we submit that he would be quite unable to appreciate the equity of regarding certain profits as taxable even though they be isolated or casual, and other profits as exempt, even though they may be recurrent or regular – simply because in the one case the transaction is deemed to have an atmosphere of a 'venture in the nature of trade' about it, and in the other case this atmosphere (owing to the very ease with which the transactions can be conducted) is absent.

17. Nor are we satisfied that even if this distinction were a tenable one, the question of the taxability of the so-called capital profits could be dismissed on the ground that they are a fruit without a tree. 'Referability to a defined source', even under present law, is not invariably required to 'permit of a receipt being categorized as income'; there is also that 'limited class of receipts that are identified as income by their own nature' (para. 31). In our view it would still be necessary to show cause why these profits should not be admitted to the membership of that limited class.

18. Though the Majority do not propose to widen in any way the present legal conception of taxable income, they are conscious of the ambiguity created by the vagueness of the present boundary-line that separates taxable from non-taxable profits. They therefore put forward, without wishing to lay down any fixed rule, a set of guiding considerations for determining whether any particular profit is to be regarded as taxable or not (para. 116). We do not share the expectation that these 'relevant considerations'

would serve to reduce the present legal uncertainty surrounding the notion of income, nor do we find that they clarify the meaning of the 'true conception of income' for tax purposes. If the six considerations were to be regarded as six necessary constituents of the definition of taxable profits, they would serve to make the concept of taxable profits considerably narrower than it is under present law. This clearly was not the Majority's intention. Nor did they look upon them as six independent conditions, any one of which should be sufficient in itself to establish taxability – especially since some of the criteria are matters of degree rather than of kind (as, e.g., length of the period of ownership or the frequency of transactions). In fact, in all doubtful cases some of the tests suggested are bound to give results contradictory to the others; and there is no indication how such contradictions are to be resolved. Thus the profits of a man who speculated in a commodity on a produce exchange – by buying and selling tea, for example – would pass the first test (since the subject matter of the realization is normally the subject of trading rather than investment) but completely fail in the fourth (since 'nothing at all is done' to bring the commodity into a more marketable condition). In our view the enumeration of these 'relevant considerations' serves not only to emphasize the uncertainty of the present legal border-line that separates taxable from tax-exempt profits, but to reveal how wide that border-line or border-area is, relatively to the area which it encloses.

Treatment of expenses

19. Enough has been said to show that the present legal distinction between taxable and non-taxable receipts cannot be justified on any reasonable criterion of equity. The other main respect in which the present legal definition of taxable income causes inequality of treatment between classes of taxpayers concerns not receipts, but outlays. As the Majority point out (para. 38) one particular source of these differences consists in the allowances given for the wastage of capital. The original theory which ignored the wastage of capital altogether 'has been profoundly modified in the course of time, but not to the same extent or in the same way in respect of all the different sources of income' (para. 38). While incomes derived from trades, vocations or professions 'now receive a

full allowance out of taxable income to make good money expended in acquiring assets that are used up in the production of the income' (para. 39), no allowances are given with respect to the capital expenditure incurred in vocational and educational training or for the expenditure which a man incurs 'in developing and improving his expert knowledge' (para. 41).

20. We cannot follow the Majority in the argument which they put forward in justification of this difference in treatment (in para. 42) according to which the wastage involved in the case of an individual's capital equipment 'is the obsolescence of the human machine itself, not the obsolescence of its skill or experience'. We agree however with their view (in para. 43) that it would be impracticable to extend the scheme of capital allowances to expenditure incurred on investment in the human person; and we believe therefore that short of withdrawing capital allowances altogether – a course that, on grounds of expediency, we should not favour – the difference in treatment cannot in this respect be avoided and ought therefore to be recognized and compensated for.

21. Another and, in our view, even more important cause of such inequality arises out of the difference in the legal definition of deductible expenses in respect of income from a trade, profession or vocation assessed under Schedule D, and in respect of income from an office, employment or pension, assessed under Schedule E. In the latter case only such expenses are deductible as are 'wholly, exclusively and necessarily' incurred 'in the performance of' the duties of the office or employment. In the former case all expenses are deductible which are 'wholly and exclusively laid out or expended for the purposes of the trade'. As we shall argue in more detail in chapter 4 [not included here] this difference in wording implies that in the case of incomes assessed under Schedule D the calculation of the individual's actual liability proceeds on the basis of provisions for deductions which are without parallel in the case of incomes assessed under Schedule E; and which bring it about that the true taxable capacity represented by a unit of taxable income is normally considerably greater in incomes assessed under Schedule D than in incomes assessed under Schedule E. Here again we are of the opinion that the difference in treatment ought to be openly recognized and com-

pensated for in so far as, for administrative reasons or on grounds of expediency, it cannot be eliminated.

Tax avoidance and escape

22. The full tally of inequities arising from the defects in the calculation of the tax base – whether on the side of receipts or on the side of the allowances for expenses – can be reckoned only after those taxpayers who are in a position to do so have adjusted their activities and transactions so as to benefit from gaps and ambiguities in the definition of taxable income.[10] The incentive to make such adjustments (which may not be a matter of tax evasion, and frequently may not even be classed as tax avoidance within the accepted meaning of that term) is in direct proportion to the effective marginal rate of tax and is inevitably powerful at the present level of taxation. Thus the exclusion of capital profits from the tax base leads to the conversion of taxable income into tax-free capital gains. Since this manoeuvre can in fact be accomplished within wide limits and through various channels the taxpayer finds that his taxable income, and therefore the size of his tax bill, is left in large measure to his own discretion, provided he is a man of property.[11] Generous provision for business expenses invites

10. The ambiguity of the law in this context is just as important as the gaps in the law. So long as the taxability of certain classes of profits is subject to so much uncertainty, it is hardly to be expected that the taxpayer will regard such profits as part of his income for tax purposes when he comes to make out his tax return. The question of the assessment of such profits is therefore largely dependent on information reaching the Revenue authorities independently of the taxpayer – which must necessarily be a rather chancy affair. We feel that quite apart from any change in the present legal conception of taxable income, the hands of the Revenue would be greatly strengthened if there were a statutory obligation on taxpayers to return all profits made in the year; non-taxable or capital profits being shown separately.

11. Several pieces of legislation on the Statute Book have been devised to stop particular methods of converting taxable income into tax-free capital gains, but alternative facilities remain readily available, and as we shall argue (para. 47 [not included here]) the problem cannot be effectively dealt with by means of special anti-avoidance provisions. Thus the Finance Act of 1937, Part II, Section 12, is designed to prevent tax escape through the sale of securities 'cum dividend' and their repurchase 'ex-dividend' in so far as sale and repurchase is accomplished in the same agreement or any collateral agreement. The Finance Acts of 1922 (Section 21) and 1937

the dressing up of personal expenses as business expenses and the dressing up of income payments as expense allowances.

23. Moreover, the social cost of defects in the tax base is to be reckoned not only in terms of inequity between different taxpayers, but in distortions of normal economic behaviour. Such distortions take two main forms. Firstly, the desire and pursuit of short-term speculative gains, artificially stimulated by the tax-free character of such gains, tends to distort the allocation of the community's savings between different forms of investment. Secondly, the liberal provision for expenses of kinds that are not directly and inevitably associated with the making of the profits against which they may be offset, involves encouraging, by means of a considerable subsidy from the Exchequer, expenditure (e.g. on advertising and entertaining) of doubtful value which might not have been incurred at all in the absence of taxation.

The erosion of the tax base

24. When the base on which a tax is levied lacks precise definition the system is particularly exposed to the danger that successive concessions, designed to take care of special situations, will cause a progressive erosion of the tax base until its efficacy as an instrument of taxation is seriously weakened. For once a new principle is admitted into a tax system on the basis of which additional concessions are given, the pressure for further concessions based on arguments of close analogy becomes well-nigh irresistible. Every time some particular interest can make out a case of inequitable treatment under the existing provisions of the law and a fresh concession is granted, it invariably follows that some other interest finds itself disadvantageously treated as a result and can make out an even stronger case for a further concession that can be shown to follow logically from the original concession made.

25. It could not be maintained that as a result of this whittling down process the allocation of the tax burden became any more

(Section 14 (2) (b)) attempted to check avoidance of surtax, by shareholders in closely held corporations, through failure to distribute profits and subsequent realization of accumulated earnings through the sale of shares. The Finance Acts of 1936 (Section 18) and 1938 (Section 28) prevent tax avoidance through transfer of securities to controlled foreign holding companies for the purpose of converting earnings into capital gains under the guise of repayments of capital, etc.

equitable than it was before unless it could be shown that each new principle introduced was consistent with, and logically followed from, a comprehensive basic conception of taxable income. In the absence of any such conception the allocation of the tax burden is likely to become less rather than more equitable. In some cases a new 'principle' may be officially recognized, and a range of concessions deduced from it, without it being realized that the principle conceded is but one aspect of a larger principle: with the result that it narrows the concept of taxable income for certain groups of taxpayers while leaving a wider concept applicable to others. In other cases a new 'principle' may be induced from a particular concession granted in special circumstances for a specific purpose, and originally conceived as of strictly limited application: with the result that in time the grounds for an exceptional concession are elevated into a general principle. The net result of the whole process is that the Government has to impose higher rates of taxation to obtain a given amount of revenue without any compensating gain in the general equity of the tax system.

26. There is less danger of this happening when a new tax instrument of wide application is introduced for an avowedly economic purpose, as for example in the case of initial or investment allowances or of non-distribution relief in connexion with profits tax. Such concessions can be withdrawn at any time (as indeed the initial allowances were withdrawn in 1951 for a period). Their presence in the tax code is apparent and unlikely to escape notice and their retention needs continued justification on grounds of public expediency. But with concessions granted in response to pressure from particular interests, and whose justification is regarded, or comes to be regarded, as lying in equity rather than economic expediency, the situation is different. Once they are introduced it is difficult to withdraw them and they become the focal point of agitation for further concessions.

27. The last twenty years have witnessed the introduction of a whole crop of new concessions of this kind. One of these was the introduction of relief from foreign taxation which grew out of a concession originally granted (mainly for economic reasons) to Dominion taxation; that led to an extension covering other countries on the basis of reciprocity, and then to a full extension

to all countries, and this in turn to demands for an extension of the range of foreign taxes that qualify for the relief; and finally, when the anomalous consequences of these concessions had been demonstrated, to arguments for the complete exemption of overseas profits from home taxation. Another example is provided by the great extension of the scope of capital allowances in the 1944, 1945 and 1949 Acts and the consequent demand for still further concessions, described in paragraph 193 of the first Tucker Report (Cmnd 8189). Indeed the Tucker Report acknowledges the validity of the general principle that the 'Income Tax system should give relief in respect of the wastage of all assets that are used up or consumed in the course of carrying on a business'. The incorporation of such a general principle in the tax code would logically carry with it (in our view) the tax recognition of the assets built up (and not only of the assets consumed) in the course of carrying on a business – in the form of goodwill for example. Another example is the extended recognition of losses for tax purposes, and the offsetting of losses against income from other sources (described by the Majority in paragraph 483 of the Report [not included here]).

28. The present Royal Commission has been faced with a series of demands for further concessions and exemptions of this character. We shall confine our treatment of these issues to the cases in which we dissent from the conclusions of the Majority, though we are not always in agreement with the reasoning of the Majority in the other cases.

Income or expenditure as the basis of taxation

29. As was explained in paragraphs 6 and 7 above, income taxation sets out to tax each individual according to the increase, in a period, in his command over society's scarce resources – irrespective of how much of that command he actually exercises in consumption and how much he leaves unspent, in the form of saving or capital appreciation. To the extent that this spending power is actually exercised in consumption its measurement raises no difficulty in principle, since it can be assumed that equal expenditures in terms of money in a given period represent claims of equal real value on the resources of society. But with regard to that part of a man's spending power which is not currently spent

but saved up for the future (irrespective of whether this is the result of a deliberate act of saving or of capital appreciation or capital gains) there is an additional problem that equal amounts of such unspent income in terms of money value need not represent equal additions to the command over real resources in the hands of different individuals. In times of rising prices, the real increase in 'spending power' represented by a given addition to the value of a man's store of rights will vary, not only with the size of that addition, but with the ratio of that addition to the value of his store of rights at the beginning of the period. Analogous problems arise from the fact that the real value of a man's store of rights at any particular point of time may be looked upon either as the amount of goods and services it represents in terms of purchasing power at that moment or as the flow of such goods and services (i.e. the flow of real income) it commands over time. When interest rates are changing, measurement of the 'command over resources' in the one sense will not yield consistent results with measurement in the other sense; and it depends on a man's future disposition of his resources (and not on his resources as such) whether the proper measure of his spending power is in terms of the stock of goods his resources command at any one time or the flow of goods they command over time.

30. In the light of these considerations it is a matter for examination whether any definition of the term 'income' capable of translation into a measurable tax base could approximate an individual's spending power as closely as his actual spending does; and whether a tax assessed on personal expenditure might not secure a more equitable distribution of the burden of taxation than a tax assessed on income, whatever the definition of income chosen as the basis of taxation. Such an examination could take into account the spending power realized through dis-saving (living on capital) which must be ignored under a system which sets out to tax Income rather than Consumption – even though dis-saving may in fact be an important source of spending power, and despite the fact that large property owners are likely to dis-save extensively when marginal rates of taxation have reached a level which makes it rational for them to do so.

31. Since, however, the consideration of a personal expenditure tax (which would bring spending out of capital within the tax

net) has been explicitly ruled out from the Commission's terms of reference we shall not consider this aspect of the problem but shall limit ourselves to the question of how the present system of charging a tax on income could be reformed so as to mitigate the existing inequities.

Scope of the present memorandum

32. The major inequities, in our view, arise from the present tax immunity of capital gains, and from the differences in the treatment of the trader assessed under Schedule D, and the treatment of the wage and salary earner assessed under Schedule E. Accordingly our main recommendations are concerned with these matters. The taxation of capital gains raises related issues concerning the reform of company taxation and we shall discuss these two problems in direct sequence. The differences in tax treatment between profits and other kinds of income arise partly out of general differences in the definition of taxable income which call for general remedies; partly out of specific provisions such as those concerning losses, capital allowances, stock valuation or double taxation relief which need to be considered in detail. Finally there are a number of particular issues concerning the taxation of individual income – expense allowances and benefits in kind, superannuation, covenants, etc. – on which we wish to comment as we are not in entire agreement with the Majority's views.

33. Before turning to particular issues we feel impelled, in the light of the discussion of Tax Avoidance in the Report [chapter 32, not included here], to record unequivocally our view that the existence of widespread tax avoidance is evidence that the system, not the taxpayer, stands in need of radical reform. We agree with the basic view expressed in that Chapter that it would be wrong to assert that a man owes a duty to the community not to alter the disposition of his affairs so as to reduce his liability to taxation. It is up to the community, acting through Parliament, so to frame the tax laws that they do not leave wide loopholes or open broad avenues for tax avoidance.

The Taxation of Capital Gains

34. The tax exemption of the so-called capital profits of various kinds represents the most serious omission in our present system of income taxation.

35. The basic reason for the inclusion of capital gains in taxation is that capital gains increase a person's taxable capacity by increasing his power to spend or save; and since capital gains are not distributed among the different members of the taxpaying community in fair proportion to their taxable incomes but are concentrated in the hands of property owners (and particularly the owners of equity shares) their exclusion from the scope of taxation constitutes a serious discrimination in tax treatment in favour of a particular class of taxpayer. The manner in which capital gains (of certain kinds at any rate) augment the taxable capacity of the recipient, has been convincingly shown, in our view, in the memorandum by the Board that is reproduced as an Annexe to the present Memorandum[12] and we do not therefore consider it necessary to argue this at length.

Arguments against taxing capital gains

36. The main arguments habitually used to justify the exclusion of capital gains from taxation are:

(a) that the rise in capital values in the course of, or in consequence of, inflation represents illusory, and not real gains;

(b) equally the capital gains arising as a result of a fall in interest rates may be illusory, since they do not increase the investor's future income;

(c) capital gains are not only irregular, but may also be unsought or unexpected, and do not therefore represent the same kind of taxable capacity as regular and expected income;

(d) only a tax on realized capital gains is administratively feasible, and this is inequitable because (i) it imputes the gains on any realized asset to the particular year in which the realization takes place, whereas the appreciation may have accrued over a series of years; (ii) the realized capital gains of any particular year may be offset by the depreciation in the value of unrealized assets in that year; (iii) if in a particular year the realized losses exceed realized gains, it would not be practicable to allow such

12. As recorded in para. 11–12 of the Introduction to the Report, the Commission decided, on grounds of economy, not to publish the voluminous written evidence received both from the Board and from outside bodies and individuals. In agreement with our colleagues, however, we are making an exception in the case of the Board's memorandum on capital gains, in view of the importance of the subject.

losses to be set off against other income, and yet it would be unjust merely to allow such losses to be carried forward as an offset against future gains.

The Majority base their commendations mainly on arguments connected with (b), (c) and (d) above. We shall deal with all four types of argument in turn.

Capital gains in an inflation

37. We do not deny that the rise in capital values that occurs in the course of an inflation does not increase the taxable capacity of the recipients in the same way as a rise in capital values during a period of steady prices. But we cannot regard this as a justification for excluding capital gains from taxation within the general framework of a tax system which sets out to tax income and not consumption, and which therefore taxes that part of income which is saved as well as that part which is spent – although, as we shall argue below, it does constitute a case for certain well-defined exceptions. If the proceeds of the gain are spent the recipient derives the same benefit as he does in spending taxed income. If the gains are saved, the argument about their illusory character applies equally to all saving, and not merely to capital appreciation. If a man regularly saves up a part of his earnings by adding to his savings deposits or paying premiums on a life assurance, it may equally happen that as a result of inflation the real value of his accumulated savings is constantly shrinking. He is in no different position from another man who attains the same increase in the money value of his capital as a result of capital appreciation. The fact that in times of inflation money appreciation will not mean a corresponding real appreciation may be regarded as an argument against the taxation of savings as such. It is not an argument for the differential treatment of capital appreciation as against other forms of saving.

38. It must also be remembered that taxable capacity is essentially a relative concept, and those property owners who make capital gains during an inflation are undoubtedly in a better position than those who own fixed interest securities, and who therefore lose part of their real capital as a result of the rise in prices. Equity cannot be secured by ignoring relative changes in the taxable capacities of different property owners; and, if it were held to be

desirable (and possible) to exempt that part of capital appreciation which was commensurate with the general price rise, it would follow that any lesser degree of capital appreciation should be regarded as a loss. It is not our view that the tax code should be so devised as to insure taxpayers against the risk of inflation. Indeed we should consider any such intention singularly inappropriate, for taxation must be regarded as one of the principal weapons in the armoury of the central government for combatting inflation. In the event of a drastic depreciation it might become necessary to revise the basis of all monetary obligations and commitments, including tax payments – as was done in Belgium after the First World War, and in Belgium and France after the Second World War. But we do not regard such a situation as within the foreseeable circumstances which tax regulations, or tax reforms, should take into account.

Capital gains and interest rates

39. An appreciation of capital values which results from a fall in the 'pure' rate of interest is not in the same category as a rise in values which merely reflects higher prices, since in this case the capital gain is real enough in the sense that it increases the gainer's command over goods and services. As the Majority emphasize, however, if the proceeds of the gain are reinvested 'a reinvestment of sale proceeds has to be made upon the terms that the investor must accept a lower yield upon his money and he needs therefore all or most of his gain to maintain the same nominal income' (para. 93 [not included here]). This is true, but ignores the fact that the holders of long-term bonds still gain on such occasions relatively to other savers who save out of current incomes, or whose past savings were not invested in long-term bonds. When rates of interest fall, some savers (e.g. those whose savings are invested in savings deposits) must accept a reduction of income, whilst other savers manage to offset the effect of the fall in interest by the capital gains on their existing holdings. We do not see that equity is better served by ignoring the relative improvement in the position of the second group of taxpayers altogether rather than by recognizing it; even though we would agree that a capital gain resulting from a reduction in the yield of long-term bonds does not add to taxable capacity as much as an equivalent

gain on equity shares resulting from higher dividend payments.

40. Further, it should be noted that whereas general movements in the price-level tend to be irreversible, there is no reason to suppose that the long-term trend of interest rates is either falling or rising. Past experience suggests on the contrary that periods of falling interest rates alternate with periods of rising interest rates, with little net change on balance. The man or the beneficiary of a settled estate who is unduly heavily taxed as a result of a fall in interest rates is correspondingly lightly taxed as a result of a rise in interest rates.

Capital gains and taxable capacity

41. We wish to emphasize, however, that – ignoring the exceptional periods following in the wake of great wars or great economic depressions – capital gains are not, to any important extent, the consequence of either rising prices or falling interest rates. The great bulk of capital gains in normal periods is the result of rising real incomes (higher profits and larger dividend payments) to which therefore none of the above considerations apply. In a modern industrial community such as ours a high proportion (four-fifths or more if American experience can be taken as a guide) of all capital gains are derived from transactions in securities, and mainly in ordinary shares of business corporations. There is a steady long-run trend of rising share values which simply reflects the growth of the real earning power and the growing dividend payments of companies.

42. We take the view therefore that the great bulk of capital gains is of a kind to which the description 'neither anticipated at the time of acquisition nor sought for by the recipient' (para. 94 [not included here]) does not apply. It may be true that at any one time the majority of ordinary shares are held by their owners in the hope of long-term appreciation rather than of any definite expectation of an early sale at a quick profit, but this does not mean that the expectation of such long-run appreciation is not an important part of the benefit which the owners expect to derive from the acquisition or the holding of ordinary shares. The value which successful businesses acquire in the form of 'goodwill' – the excess of their market capitalization over their share capital and reserves – is not an isolated windfall like a lucky draw in a sweep-

stake. It is part of the normal reward of successful enterprise: indeed, under present day conditions it is by far the most important part of that reward, the expectation of which is a crucial factor in the supply of risk capital and business ability to new ventures. We do not wish to deny that the prospect of high rewards to successful enterprise plays an important role in the economic progress of society. But this does not alter the fact that it is grossly unfair to allow the rewards to the successful property owner or business man to remain so largely exempt from taxation when successful authors, actors, inventors, lawyers, surgeons or civil servants are all fully taxed on their earnings.

43. Our first concern has been to show that, in the circumstances of present day Britain, it is not a sensible view to look upon capital profits generally as isolated and non-recurrent windfalls; but we also unreservedly reject the view that by virtue of being a windfall, incidental and unforeseen, a gain ought to be exempt from tax. Windfall gains confer material benefit just as expected gains do. The Majority argue that to tax a pure windfall 'would inflict very small proportionate sacrifice on the taxpayer' but it would still leave open the question whether 'a gain in respect of a single piece of property, isolated and non-recurrent, bore any recognizable sign of being income' (para. 94 [not included here]). If this is taken to mean that the recipient will not adjust his scale of living, as a result of the receipt of such a non-recurrent gain in the same way as in the case of an increase in his regular receipts, the point is obvious; but it is hardly relevant to a tax system which sets out to tax savings as well as spendings.[13]

44. In paragraph 98 [not included here] on the other hand the Majority argue that even if a man does spend his capital gains it would be unfair to tax him on that account so long as spending out of capital in general is left untaxed. 'Two persons, one with a capital of £100,000 on which no gains are being made, the other with a capital of £30,000 on which he is making gains, may each of them be selling assets in order to finance their

13. As we shall argue below, there is a case (under a progressive tax) for taxing non-recurrent receipts in a different way from recurrent receipts, since, as was stated in paragraph 8, they do not confer the same taxable capacity in a particular period. This, however, is a problem common to all forms of non-recurrent or irregular receipts and not just to gains of a windfall character.

expenditure; but why should the second be taxed on his excess expenditure while the first is untaxed?' Here the Majority seem to be disputing the justice of electing Income as the base for personal taxation. The objective of income taxation is to tax a man, not in accordance with his spendings as such, nor in accordance with his disposable wealth as such, but in accordance with his 'increment in economic power' over a given period. Under an income tax capital gains represent taxable capacity precisely because they provide a distinct addition to the amount of goods and services which an individual is in a position to command, quite irrespective of whether he chooses to spend them or save them.

Capital gains and tax avoidance

45. The full significance of the omission of capital profits from taxation only becomes clear, however, when it is appreciated that the extent to which rewards take the form of tax-free capital gains rather than taxed dividend income is not something that is fixed by Nature, but is very much subject to manipulation by the taxpayer. A community with a highly developed capital market like Britain offers wide opportunities for an individual so to arrange his affairs that the accrual of benefits from his ownership of capital takes the form of capital appreciation instead of taxable income. It is well known (indeed it is constantly broadcast by the financial press) that it 'pays' a surtax-payer to select securities which have a low dividend yield but a high degree of expected capital appreciation, owing to rising dividend payments over time; to purchase bonds that stand at a discount, or bonds that can be bought in an 'unassented' form (like German and Japanese issues at the present time) so that the value of the interest that is periodically paid on them appears as an appreciation of capital, and not as taxable income; or to convert income into capital appreciation in innumerable other ways. [. . .]

In our view so long as capital gains remain exempt from taxation it is impossible to deal with the problem of the conversion of income into capital gains in all its possible forms by specific pieces of legislation.

48. All these opportunities, moreover, are far more readily available to the large property owner than to the small saver;

and it is well known from American experience that capital gains are a major source of large incomes but unimportant as a source of smaller incomes. The Report, while it pays a great deal of attention to the alleged inequities that the taxation of capital gains would involve as between one property owner and another (discussed in paragraph 61 below), makes no mention of the far more serious inequities that arise as a result of the exclusion of capital gains from taxation as between those who can (and do) manipulate their affairs so as to augment their tax-free gains at the cost of their taxable income and those who are not in a position to minimize their tax liability in this manner. In fact the Majority find no occasion to refer to problems of tax avoidance in connexion with capital gains at all.

Capital gains and undistributed profits

49. With regard to the capital profits associated with ordinary shares, the Majority admit that as companies are growing through the steady retention of part of their current profits and the consequent growth of their earnings and dividends, 'a process is detected which has the effect of adding to the capital of the shareholder through savings made out of the company's income without his share of the savings ever having been subjected to surtax as income in his hands' (para. 96 [not included here]). They argue, however, that since undistributed profits bear the whole of the profits tax as well as income tax at the standard rate, even though this charge 'has no ascertainable relation to the benefit that some shareholders may obtain from the fact that their share of retained profits is, in effect, saved for them in the corporate pool', 'it is impossible to ignore the countervailing circumstance that profits made in corporate form do in fact bear a supplementary charge which is not imposed on other forms of profit or income'.[14]

50. This argument implies that undistributed profits are the source and the measure of the appreciation of ordinary shares so

14. The U.K. situation is now changed. Company profits are taxed to Corporation tax and only distributed profits bear income tax and surtax. The system gives an incentive to portfolio investment by companies on behalf of shareholders, for the amount available in the hands of the company is greater than if it is distributed to shareholders and taxed to income tax and surtax. [Ed.]

that the case for taxing the appreciation of these shares arises from the difference between the tax actually paid by the companies on undistributed profits and the tax that would have been payable if the aliquot share of undistributed profits had been imputed to the individual shareholders. This approach completely overlooks the fact that in the case of successful companies the growth in market capitalization resulting from the growth in earnings and dividends may greatly exceed the growth in the companies' reserves through the continued ploughing back of profits. To show how important that fact can be it is sufficient to refer to a few leading equities. In the case of Woolworth for example the market capitalization of the ordinary capital amounted (in February 1955) to some £280 million whereas the share capital and accumulated reserves together amounted to £39 million. In the case of Marks and Spencer the market capitalization amounted to £128 million whereas capital and reserves amounted to £20 million. In both these cases therefore 83 to 86 per cent of the accrued appreciation in the value of the shareholders' capital has never borne any form of tax, however indirect; nor can that appreciation be described as bearing the character of isolated, unexpected or non-recurrent gains, considering that it has accrued over a long series of years – in fits and starts no doubt, with fluctuations in the sentiment of the capital market, but unmistakably as a by-product of the growth in the companies' profits and dividends.

51. The cases where the market capitalization of companies' 'goodwill' exceeds by as much as 7 to 1 its share capital and the accumulated reserves are no doubt exceptional. Indeed, under present circumstances and for reasons not unconnected with the present tax régime, which will be discussed more fully below in the Chapter on Corporate Taxation (paragraphs 98–100 [not included here]), the disparity is frequently the other way round. What is important in the present context is that such disparity is common and may be very marked; and that it is the growth of the companies' reserves only which is taxed under the present system.

52. We agree with the Majority that the tax which the companies pay on their undistributed profits bears no ascertainable relation to the benefits which the shareholders obtain in the form of capital appreciation. This is so not only because the growth in market

valuation is likely to differ from, and may exceed greatly, the increase in taxed reserves. It is also because a shareholder is not indissolubly wedded to any particular holding of shares but can buy and sell shares at more or less frequent intervals so that the capital gains or losses that he may realize on any particular holding of shares need bear no relation whatever to his aliquot share of the undistributed profits during his period of ownership. It is true, however, that the taxation of undistributed profits, to the extent that it reduces the amounts which companies put to reserve, may reduce the rate of growth of businesses and in this manner exert an adverse effect on the long-run appreciation of share values. We believe therefore that if capital appreciation were brought into charge in the form of a capital gains tax there would be a case for reducing the present burden of taxation on undistributed profits.

Realized and accrued gains

53. We should now like to turn to the objections against the taxation of capital profits that are particularly directed against a scheme of taxation of realized capital gains. As is explained in the Report (para. 29), it is a basic principle both of the tax system and of business accounting not to take account of profits until they are realized. This means that ordinary trading profits are reckoned as the year's receipts (whether in actual money or in money's worth), less the expenses that are attributable to those receipts, the latter being evaluated by reckoning the difference between the opening and the closing stock at actual cost. Unrealized gains which take the form of an appreciation in the market value of unsold goods relatively to their costs of acquisition are not taken into account; though accountancy principles approve, and the tax system by special concession allows, the anticipation of unrealized losses in permitting stocks to be valued at market prices, when market prices are below cost.

54. We agree with the view expressed in paragraph 12 of the Board's memorandum that both administrative and other considerations make it inevitable that a tax on capital profits should follow analogous principles. From an administrative point of view it would be extremely difficult, if not impossible, to make a periodic valuation of all capital assets with sufficient accuracy

to permit a tax to be levied on the change in the market value of all assets between two points of time. [. . .]

59. Under a system of taxation which taxes only realized capital gains the very fact that the timing of the realization of gains is under the taxpayer's own control would serve to even out the fluctuations in his annual liability. If the gains on realized assets are reckoned as the gains of a single year, so are the losses; if losses can be offset against the gains, and unabsorbed losses carried forward against future gains, the taxpayer is given, in fact, full facilities for moderating the effects of fluctuations in his taxable gains over time.

60. On the other hand there are circumstances in which a tax on realized gains inevitably involves a bunching of gains in time, and hence, under a progressive tax, would involve the tax-payer in heavier liability owing to the incidence of timing. This would obviously occur where the capital profits are derived from a single indivisible asset – as for example when a man who has gradually built up a business sells it as a going concern or it changes hands at his decease. But it may occur more generally in cases where the capital assets are not easily marketable and can only be realized infrequently or when a wholesale realization of accrued but unrealized gains is deemed to have occurred through death. This familiar problem in equity under progressive taxation[15] arises in connexion with capital gains whenever a property owner is not in a position to spread out or regulate the realization of his net capital profits. It should be emphasized that the problem dis-appears under a flat-rate tax, and that it constitutes the main argument, in equity, for a flat rate rather than a progressive rate of tax on capital gains.

61. Independently of the above considerations we recognize the force of the argument which leads to the conclusion that it would be inexpedient to tax capital gains at the full progressive rate of income tax and surtax combined. The arguments in favour of confining the charge to income tax – which would mean in effect

15. Theoretically the problem could be met by an arrangement permitting the averaging of income over a series of years (in a manner similar in principle to the cumulative averaging of weekly income under the present P.A.Y.E. system); but we understand that for administrative reasons this solution is regarded as impracticable.

a flat rate of tax once total income (including capital gains) is above the point at which the taxpayer becomes liable to the standard rate – are more powerful in our view when considered from the point of view of expediency than when considered from the strict point of view of equity. The great bulk of capital gains accrue to the higher income groups; the fundamental reason for this is that the accrual of capital gains is closely linked with the investment of capital in risky ventures, and it is the large property owner, and not the small saver, who is able to commit his resources to ventures involving risk. If capital gains were subjected to both income tax and surtax the effect would be that a great part of these gains would be taxed at an extremely high rate (mounting at present to 19s. 0d. in the £) which would be bound to have a destructive effect on the willingness to assume risks. Added to this is the consideration that since a great deal of capital investment is made in the expectation of distant and not immediate appreciation even those investors not currently liable to the higher surtax rates would be in considerable uncertainty as to the rate at which their ultimate gains would be taxed when realized. Finally the full charging of capital gains to both income tax and surtax would have a negative effect on the incentive to save and encourage capitalists to dissipate their capital. Though we do not share the view of the Majority that capital gains are generally saved and do not contribute to the spending of the property-owning classes,[16] it is true of course

16. The Majority are much concerned to show (para. 106 [not included here]) that 'on the whole, capital gains will be saved' so that a tax on capital gains would not in itself 'contribute to the control of inflation'. We do not know on what evidence this particular conclusion is based. It is certainly not in accord with the official view – as is shown for example by the Economic Survey for 1953 where the Government explicitly refer to the effect of the fall in Stock Exchange prices in the previous year in reducing consumers' expenditure (Cmnd 8800, para. 38). The view is plainly contrary also to the undoubted effect of the rise in Stock Exchange values on the level of consumption of luxury goods in the course of 1954. Nor is it correct to suppose (as the Majority suggest in para. 105 [not included here]) that any restraining effect of a capital gains tax would depend on the actual realization of the gains on which the taxes are paid. If a property owner knew that half his gains would be payable in tax on realization he would behave in much the same way as if he were making only half the gains; and as the Majority observe, the characteristic form of such spending follows upon the rise in capital values as such and is not dependent on the actual realization of the gains. A capital gains tax will reduce 'boom spending' precisely because it

that the present opportunity to save tax free in the form of capital appreciation must provide an incentive to the large property owner not to dissipate his capital, despite the strong temptations which the high taxation of income combined with the tax exemption on spendings out of capital provides in this direction. We think therefore that the taxation of capital gains beyond a certain rate would have highly undesirable effects on risk-bearing, saving and capital formation.

62. We cannot agree on the other hand that these considerations of economic expediency justify the continued tax exemption of an important source of income and the consequent grave injustice in the distribution of the tax burden between different groups and different social classes. We certainly do not share the view of the Majority (expressed in para. 99 [not included here]) that he gains should either be taxed at the full progressive rate or else not at all. There is no principle of equity which leads us to suppose that if something cannot or should not be taxed at 95 per cent it should be taxed at zero per cent. We therefore recommend that subject to the qualifications and on the definitions suggested below capital gains should be subjected to income taxation but not to surtax.

Short-term and long-term gains

63. Subject to the above recommendation that capital gains should not be liable to surtax we recommend that no distinction should be made between short- and long-term gains. Any such

reduces the extent to which an '[individual's] position on capital account is strengthened' by the boom. Quite apart from this the Majority's view that people will live on capital whether they make capital gains or not and *therefore* the mere fact of capital gains does not add to the volume of spending (para. 104) is self-contradictory. If people live on capital, but do not make capital gains, their spending must come to an end when their capital is exhausted. But if their spending is offset by capital gains, it can continue indefinitely.

It is true on the other hand that a capital gains tax so severe in its incidence as to cause the property owner to wish to dissipate his capital would, for a short period, increase spending. But while such a tendency might become serious in case of a capital gains tax which taxed away nine-tenths or more of the gains, we do not believe that there is any such danger if the tax is limited to one-half or less of the gains earned.

distinction is bound to be arbitrary and an invitation to tax avoidance. The distinction in the U.S. tax system makes it worth while for the taxpayer to realize short-term losses in less than six months and short-term gains in more than six months and has in many cases the effect that the taxpayer's liability is less than it would have been if short-term gains had been taxed at the long-term rate. We do not share the view that long-term gains have any inherent claim to more favourable treatment than short-term gains. We agree with the view expressed in the memorandum of the Board (para. 17) that 'looking at the matter purely as one of taxable capacity there may seem little justification for distinguishing between two gains of equal amount simply because in one case the asset was held for a longer period than in the other'.

64. As already indicated we strongly support the suggestion that contrary to the existing American practice change of owner-ship of property by gift or bequest should count as realization in the same way as the transfer of ownership by way of sale (the property being valued for the purpose by the same rules as apply to stamp duties). Without this provision, not only would a large part of capital gains escape the tax net altogether, but the taxpayer would have every incentive so to manipulate the realization of his losses and his gains as to make his net unrealized gains as large as possible.[17]

17. According to the provisions of the American law a change in the ownership of property by way of gift or bequest does not count as realization. In the case of gifts *inter vivos* there is a partial remedy in that the property so transferred is valued for the purpose of any future realization at the donor's cost and not at its value at the time of its transfer to the recipient. In the case of transfer by inheritance, however, not only is no gain recognized in the hands of the deceased but the property is valued at probate value in the hands of the beneficiary. Hence all accrued capital gains are automatically wiped out for tax purposes whenever property passes by death.

We have little doubt that these provisions (together with the distinction between short- and long-term gains) have been responsible for the fact that net reported capital losses have continued to be so large in relation to net reported capital gains and largely explain why the yield of the American tax continues to be so small in relation to the probable rate of accrual of capital gains.

Treatment of losses

65. We agree with the suggestions made by the Board as to the treatment of losses. Realized losses ought to reckon as an offset to realized gains; net unabsorbed losses ought to be permitted to be carried forward indefinitely as an offset against the taxpayer's future gains. As the Board's memorandum explains (para. 13), it is always open to a taxpayer to turn a paper loss – at least in easily marketable securities – into a realized loss, and to cover himself (if he has no real desire to liquidate his investment) by repurchasing the security afterwards. So long as losses only count as an offset against current or future realized gains, the taxpayer's incentive to do so will be confined by the extent of the realization of his gains, and will tend to have the effect of confining the concept of net taxable gains in any particular year to the excess of net realized gains over net accrued losses. If, however, losses could be offset against past gains, the taxpayer would find it worth while to 'realize' paper losses as they accrued, so that the tax would become one where the recognition of accrued losses was not limited to the amount of currently realized gains. In those circumstances the taxpayer could so manipulate his realizations (by formally selling securities whenever their price happened to be low enough to show a loss) that in an extreme case he would avoid paying tax altogether during his lifetime even though he might enjoy a steady appreciation on the total of his assets and / or a growing total of net gains on 'genuine' realizations. It is true that all such manipulations will involve a correspondingly higher liability on his estate at death but under a flat-rate tax (unless he has a definite expectation of a rise in the rates of taxation) he can only gain by them, since he saves the interest on the tax during the period of postponement. Analogous considerations apply to the question of allowing capital losses as an offset against other income. In that case the taxpayer would not only be able to avoid paying tax during his lifetime on his capital gains but to 'borrow' money from the Revenue during his lifetime to be repaid only when his accounts are closed on his death. These particular considerations might not be so important if capital gains were taxed at a full progressive rate since in that case the taxpayer would have a clear incentive to even out in time the rate of realization of his gains. But under a flat-rate tax the need to regard the taxpayer's

account with the Revenue in respect of liability for net realized capital gains as a separate running account is the more obvious.

66. The need for such restrictions on the manner and extent to which capital losses are taken into account seems to have weighed heavily with the Majority of the Commission in their rejection of the taxation of capital gains. In paragraph 99 [not included here] which sums up their general view of the problem, the Majority state that: ... 'indeed no form of the tax that was based on realized gains and realized losses – and there is no alternative – would escape the serious objection to its foundation in equity that it would tax to the same extent a man who had realized a gain on one of his assets, though showing a net loss on others that he retained, as the man who had realized a similar gain without any current depreciation of his other assets to set against it'. Here their concern seems to be misplaced, and the reasoning behind it somewhat circular, since the main reason, or one of the main reasons, for restricting the way in which losses are taken into account (which in paragraph 91 [not included here] the Majority appear to recognize) is precisely the ease with which a man can realize a paper loss, and the likelihood that he will do so whenever by so doing he effects a reduction in his tax bill. The situation described would therefore only be likely to occur, in any particular year, in the relatively rare circumstance of the depreciated asset being of a kind that is not readily saleable. Even so this 'serious objection to its foundation in equity' is only an objection if equity is so narrowly conceived as to require full equality of treatment between different taxpayers for each particular year. Under a flat-rate tax a taxpayer's cumulative liability would be unaffected by any delay he experienced in realizing his loss.

67. There may be cases, however, in which a taxpayer realizes a true loss but has no opportunity during his lifetime to offset that loss against gains, since he makes no subsequent gain. This case may be what the Majority have in mind when they state that the result of the proposed treatment 'would not be to hold the balance evenly as between capital gains and capital losses, for, whereas a [realized] gain would be chargeable even if there were no realized loss, a loss would not be allowable except so far as there was a realized gain'. We do not believe that such cases are likely to be numerous. But they undoubtedly could occur; and whenever they

do, the taxpayer's estate will show net unabsorbed losses at his death. Any possible inequity resulting from this would be mitigated if the tax claim arising out of net unabsorbed capital losses shown by an estate at probate valuation were allowed to be credited against estate duty liabilities. Provided the tax on capital gains is a flat-rate tax (so that the Exchequer is not committed to bearing the major share of unabsorbed losses, in a manner which might indeed tempt the aged into a last speculative fling) we are prepared to recommend that this should be allowed.

Other considerations

68. We agree with the Majority that in times of inflation a tax on capital gains would inflict hardship on the owner-occupier who for personal or business reasons has to sell his house and find a new home somewhere else, and who may need all the money received from the sale of his old house for the purchase of another house of the same quality and condition. If the scope of the capital gains tax were extended to the case of the owner-occupier this might have the further undesirable effect of hindering mobility since people might be deterred from accepting new jobs if it meant that they had to sell their existing home. We therefore recommend that the gains arising out of the sale of owner-occupied houses, to the extent of one residence for each taxpayer, should be exempted from the capital gains tax.

69. We believe, on the basis of the consideration of the various alternatives suggested in the Board's memorandum (para. 20) that for the purpose of the capital gains tax assets purchased prior to the appointed day should, in the case of securities quoted on the Stock Exchange, be deemed to have been purchased at the middle price ruling at the appointed day. In the case of other assets, the actual cost of acquisition should reckon as the purchase price, but the taxable gain should be reduced to that fraction of the total gain which the period between the appointed day and the date of realization bears to the total period of ownership.

70. We do not wish to enter into a detailed consideration of the administrative problems created by a capital gains tax except to record our view that we do not believe that these problems would prove so formidable as is sometimes suggested. The experience of several European countries – such as the Scan-

dinavian countries – as well as of the United States show that a tax on capital gains is by no means beyond the powers of an efficient tax administration. We believe that the institution of an automatic reporting system in connexion with property transfers (such as is already in force in some countries, e.g. in Sweden) would greatly ease the administrative task of checking the transactions recorded on the taxpayer's return. We are in accord with the view that for an initial period the tax should be limited to gains arising from the sale of businesses, securities of all kinds and real property and that there should be an exemption limit (of say, £50 or less on any particular sale, when the annual gain is £400 or less) to reduce the administrative task involved.

Other forms of capital receipts

71. The argument for the taxation of capital gains on the above lines applies equally to various other forms of receipts which are now exempt from taxation as being receipts of a capital nature. Such receipts are premiums on leases, moneys received for the surrender of leases, receipts on account of the sale of terminable rights of enjoyment or possession such as the sale of mineral rights, etc. We agree with the Majority that such receipts represent 'a commutation of the future income which the vendor would have received had he retained it' and are 'capable of being described as anticipations of future income in the hand of the recipient and, as such, as partaking of the nature of income' (para. 32). We do not agree with the Majority, however, that 'common fairness argues against [their] inclusion in the range of taxable income' merely on account of the fact that the receipt 'is in substance the equivalent of the discounted income of several years'. This argument could equally be applied to the sale of patent rights, for example, which under present law are fully subject to tax. But, whether or not it would be fair to tax them at the full progressive rate of income tax and surtax combined, we certainly cannot admit the validity of the reasoning which argues that if they would be too severely hit under the full progressive rate they should for that reason be exempted from tax altogether. We therefore recommend that the net receipts (i.e. after deduction of any sum that may have been paid for the acquisition of these rights) on account of the sale of terminable rights which are now exempted from taxation

should be subjected to income tax in an analogous manner to capital gains. [. . .]

77. In our view any reasonable estimate of the long-term rate of capital appreciation in this country should chiefly be based on estimates concerning the long-term trend in trading profits, dividends and the value of ordinary shares. At the present time the total value of privately owned capital may be put at some £40,000 million of which some £12,000 million are in the form of ordinary shares whilst another £8000 million are in the form of real property. Capital appreciation, in the long run, mainly reflects the appreciation on these two kinds of assets. The price level of gilt-edged and other fixed interest securities – if past experience is any guide – is not likely to give rise to any long-term appreciation or depreciation, since periods of rising and falling interest rates are likely to alternate with each other without any significant trend in either direction. Whilst the long-term rate of appreciation in real property is less predictable, the long-term rise in ordinary shares will be closely related to the rate of increase in dividends which in turn can be assumed to increase at much the same rate as company profits.[18]

78. In the 44 years 1870–1914 gross profits assessed to Schedule D increased at an average compound rate of over 3 per cent a year. In the 33 years 1914–47 the rate of growth was $4\frac{1}{2}$ per cent a year. In the six years 1947–53 company profits grew at a compound rate of 8 per cent a year. The first of these periods included a long period of falling prices between 1870 and 1900, and a subsequent period of rising prices up to 1914; but this only brought the wholesale price level to around 80 per cent of its 1870 value. The second period included the two inflationary periods following the First

18. As we explain in paragraphs 98 et seq [not included here] this has not been the case since 1938 owing to dividend limitation and related factors. There is no reason to suppose, however, that, unless it be the result of deliberate Government policy, there will be any further decrease in the proportion of profits distributed as dividends. The experience of the last four years has shown, on the contrary, that despite the discriminatory tax on dividend distributions, dividends have increased at a faster rate than profits, and this is likely to continue for some years. According to figures recently published by the Stock Exchange ordinary dividends, since 1950, increased at a rate of 12 per cent a year. The rise in company profits in 1950–53 was only 6 per cent a year.

and Second World Wars as well as the prolonged slump of the 1930s. The third period was one of full employment and rising prices. It appears to us that any estimate of the long-term growth of profits in this country would have to take into account the fact that Governments since the war have assumed responsibility for maintaining high and stable levels of employment. To the extent that future Governments will suceed in carrying out this policy the rate of growth in industrial production will be higher than in the past and the long-term trend of prices is more likely to be rising than falling.

79. We believe that the rate of growth of industrial production in this country cannot be put at less than 3 per cent a year. On this basis the long-term rate of growth of profits is unlikely to be below 3–5 per cent a year. The lower of these estimates assumes that the inflationary trend in prices experienced since the war will be completely eliminated in the future. The upper estimate also assumes that Governments will succeed in controlling inflationary trends more successfully in the future than in the past; but it takes into account the possibility of the continuance of a moderate degree of price inflation. Assuming that dividends keep pace with the rise in earnings, this implies an annual increase in dividend payments of the order of £25 million–£40 million, and an average increase in the value of ordinary shares of £500 million–£800 million a year.[19]

80. The percentage rise in the value of real property cannot be estimated with any such confidence but is not likely to be as great.

19. We have chosen the figure £25 million–£40 million – in preference to the figure of £20 million–£30 million which represents 3–5 per cent of *current* dividend payments – simply because we do not believe that the relationship of dividends to earnings will remain at its present ratio. Since the ending of dividend limitation in 1950 ordinary dividend payments have increased by some £210 million, £100 million of which occurred in 1954. In the four years ending 31st March 1954 the increase in the value of securities quoted on the Stock Exchange was £5000 million of which about £3000 million represented the rise in the value of ordinary shares. The rise in the market value of *all* ordinary shares in personal ownership over the period may be put at £4000 million or £1000 million a year. (According to figures recently published by the Stock Exchange the ordinary shares of United Kingdom registered and managed companies, quoted on the London Stock Exchange, excluding investment trusts, rose by £1500 million in the second half of 1954.)

Assuming an increase of the value of real property of the order of 1–2 per cent a year and taking into account capital gains on the sale of unincorporated businesses, capital appreciation in forms other than ordinary shares cannot be put at less than £100 million–£200 million. Hence the long-term rate of capital appreciation in this country in all forms should be put at a minimum of £600 million–£1000 million a year.

81. An alternative approach which yields much the same results takes the rate of accumulation of company reserves as its starting point. While the market values of shares at any particular time can move independently of the underlying assets of companies, past experience suggests that over longer periods the rise in share values keeps pace with the growth of assets: indeed to the extent that the market puts a value on companies' 'goodwill' the rise in market values should outstrip the rate of increase in reserves.[20] The current rate of increase of undistributed profits of companies (after deduction of depreciation measured in terms of current replacement cost) is of the order of £800 million a year. Hence additional dividend payments of £40 million a year represent no more than a return of 5 per cent on the additional capital annually reinvested by shareholders through the ploughing back of profits; and that in turn involves the appreciation in the value of shares by £800 million a year.[21]

82. Assuming that the rate of capital appreciation will be of the order indicated, there will be a long gestation period before the appreciation is fully reflected in realized capital gains. But, for reasons explained in paragraphs 55–6 above [not included here], the ultimate rate of realized capital gains should correspond with a time lag of a number of years, with the rate of accrual of gains.

83. We understand from the Board that after making allow-

20. If this has not been the case since the war, the reason is again to be found in the great reduction in the proportion of earnings distributed as dividends. Earnings of companies have risen fully as much as reserves.

21. The Board's estimate implies in effect that the sums annually reinvested by companies on behalf of their shareholders is 'money down the drain', from which the owners derive no appreciable benefit, present or future. Otherwise it would be impossible to regard as 'quite unrealistic' an average appreciation of more than £200 million to £250 million, when ploughed back company profits alone represent £800 million.

ance for the effect of stamp duties in reducing the extent of the gains, and allowing for gains accruing to exempt bodies and to non-resident holders, and assuming an average marginal rate of 7s. 6d. to 8s. 0d. in the £, the ultimate annual yield of the tax on our calculation of the rate of appreciation of capital would be between £200 million–£350 million (including £20 million–£30 million payable by companies at the 33⅓ per cent rate suggested in paragraph 109 [not included here]). This does not allow for the consequential loss in the yield of estate duties. The Board estimate this consequential loss at 35–40 per cent of the yield of the capital gains tax, or £65 million–£130 million a year. In our view the consequential loss from estate duties could not exceed 25–30 per cent of the total revenue from estate duties after a lapse of thirty years from the initial introduction of the tax;[22] hence the Board's estimate would be consistent only if the annual yield of estate duties were also assumed to be twice as large as at present. This in turn implies that there would be no spending out of capital gains, that estate duties would be paid out of saved-up income rather than out of capital and that there would be no avoidance of duties through *inter vivos* settlements.

84. In putting forward this estimate we do not wish to deny that international political uncertainties, world economic crises or domestic elections may interrupt or reverse for prolonged periods the trend in the rate of accrual of the investors' capital appreciation. The capital gains tax is certainly not a tax that could be relied on as a steady source of revenue. Nevertheless we believe it right to estimate the yield of such a tax on the assumption that Governments, of whatever political party, will be bent on, and will succeed

22. Assuming that estates become liable for death duties on the average once every thirty years, the average capital appreciation on all estates, on the above assumptions as to the annual rate of capital appreciation, will be 60–100 per cent in thirty years' time. Assuming further that the gains will be concentrated on the top 50 per cent of estates, the average appreciation on those estates will be 120–200 per cent. The reduction in the dutiable value of those estates due to the capital gains tax assuming a marginal tax of 9s 0d in the £, will therefore be between 220–100/220 × 0·45 and 300–100/300 × 0·45, or between 25 and 30 per cent. Assuming the present yield of £140 million from estate duties on the top 50 per cent of estates, the loss of estate duty will be £35 million–£42 million.

in maintaining the state of economic prosperity of the nation. It is precisely this newly-assumed responsibility for maintaining the economy on an even keel which makes the case for the imposition of such a tax so much stronger than it was in the past. The risks which were formerly associated with the holding of ordinary shares – the risks that profits are wiped out, or that companies go bankrupt, during the periodic economic crises of capitalism or during prolonged periods of economic stagnation – have been largely removed as a result of the new methods of economic control, and the new responsibilities assumed by the State. If the owners of risk capital profit from these policies, as in the long run they are bound to do, fairness demands that part of the benefit of these gains should be shared by the taxpaying community in general.

Reference
SIMONS, H. C. (1938), *Personal Income Taxation*, University of Chicago Press.

4 N. Kaldor

Is a Personal Expenditure Tax Practicable?

N. Kaldor, 'Is a personal expenditure tax practicable?', *An Expenditure Tax*, Allen & Unwin, 1958, pp. 191–223.

Some of the early advocates of the expenditure tax mentioned in the Introduction [not included here] thought of the tax either as a general tax on commodities and services of all kinds, or as an income tax from which special exemption is made for 'savings' in so far as the latter are embodied in particular forms. Neither of these two methods could however effectively translate into practice the real purpose of the tax. A uniform tax on all commodities and services would at best imply a *proportionate* tax on personal expenditure; and a proportionate tax on expenditure (as distinct from a progressive tax) would mean from a social point of view a more regressive form of taxation than a proportionate tax on income. The alternative of approaching a tax on expenditure from the income tax end, through the exemption of particular forms of savings, is subject to the fatal objection, already perceived by Mill, that it would exempt savings without bringing dis-savings into charge, and thus make a purely fortuitous concession to people who 'save with one hand and get into debt with the other'.

It was thus generally recognized by the later writers on public finance that the principle could only be given effect by the method of direct assessment of personal expenditure; and this was thought to be wholly impracticable owing to the difficulty of compelling taxpayers to keep accurate records of their personal expenditure and of checking the returns (cf. Pigou, 1928, pp. 123–4).

It was left to Irving Fisher to show that comprehensive records of personal expenditure are in fact unnecessary for the administration of the tax since expenditure could in principle be computed as the difference between certain money incomings and outgoings. Fisher's idea was that since what a man spends is nothing else but the difference between what he had available for spending and what he is left with, personal expenditure can be computed for tax purposes by taking his income (as at present), *adding* monies received from the sale of capital assets, depletion of bank balances, etc. and *deducting* sums spent on the purchase of capital assets and on 'non-personal' or 'non-chargeable' expenditure.

This method of assessment can perhaps best be understood by seeing what a tax return would look like. The return would be drawn up on the following broad lines:

£   s.   d.

1. Bank balances and cash at beginning of year
2. Receipts (in money or money's worth) such as wages and salaries, business drawings, interest and dividends, and all other kinds of income to which the present Income Tax applies; in addition, bequests, gifts, winnings, etc.
3. Money borrowed, or money received in re-payment of loans
4. Proceeds of sales of investments (including houses)

                           Total receipts

Less:

5. Money lent or money paid in repayment of previous borrowing
6. Purchase of investments (including houses)
7. Bank balance and cash at end of year

                       Gross expenditure

Less:

8. Exempted expenditure
9. Allowance for spreading of expenditure on durable goods

Add:

10. Proportion of expenditure on durable goods incurred in previous years and chargeable in the current year

                    Chargeable expenditure

Items 1 to 4 represent the total amount of money at the taxpayer's disposal from all possible sources; items 5 to 7 represent the total amount of money which is applied in ways other than personal spending. The difference beween the two represents the 'gross personal expenditure' from which, after a number of deductions and adjustments, net chargeable expenditure is arrived at.

Looking at the matter in another way a man obtains spending cash (a) from regular income sources – such as a wage or salary, interest and dividends, etc.; (b) from gifts and bequests or winnings; (c) by depleting his cash balances or bank accounts; (d) by selling capital assets (stocks and shares, real property, etc.) *in excess* of his purchases; (e) by borrowing. Some of these items can be negative or positive. At present only (a) figures on the income tax return. Under an expenditure tax on the lines suggested by Fisher the liability would still be assessed in a similar manner – starting from 'income' so to speak – but there would be a series of additions and deductions the net result of which should make spendings, and not earnings, the basis of the charge.

The primary question to decide with a tax of this kind is whether the legal basis of the charge should remain Income, subject to specific additions and deductions the intent of which is to exempt savings (as specified) and bring dis-savings (as specified) into the charge; or whether the legal basis of the charge should be Personal Expenditure, in which case, whilst an indirect method of computation would normally be used for the assessment, the basic intention of the law, governing both the statutory rules of accountability and exemptions, and guiding the Courts in cases of dispute, would be to base the charge on a reasonable everyday conception of 'personal expenditure'. Though the first, and less revolutionary, alternative may seem simpler at first sight, I have little doubt that only the second would satisfy the requirements of equity and efficient administration. Reasons for this will become evident in detail in the course of this chapter. They may be summed up by saying that if one started with the first conception one would soon find that considerations of equity and administrative needs forced so many additions and qualifications to the original rules of computation as to make the tax too difficult to administer without a positive underlying conception of what the law intended to be the basis of taxation. If one started with the second conception the taxpayer would be required in effect to declare his personal expenditure for the year (in much the same way as a trader is now required to return his profits for the year) and whilst he would only be asked to give details concerning his receipts of various kinds and his exempted outlays of various kinds there would be a clear obligation on him to bring the results of his computation into broad conformity with his actual expenditure – i.e. to see to it that his return was sufficiently comprehensive to ensure broad consistency between his computed and his actual spending. This does not mean that taxpayers would need to keep comprehensive records of personal expenditure (any more than a trader is obliged to keep books under present law); it does mean however that the Revenue would have powers to ask questions concerning a taxpayer's mode of living – the house or houses he maintains, servants kept, cars owned, etc. or what he spent in the year on particular items or for particular purposes – and such evidence would be admissible in the Courts in cases of a disputed assessment.

Assuming a tax conceived on these lines the main questions for discussion are (i) how 'chargeable expenditure' should be defined, having regard both to equity considerations and administrative needs; (ii) the specific administrative problem of preventing, or minimizing, the possibility of evasion. Under the first head the chief problems are the treatment of what may be termed 'consumers' capital expenditure', and the parallel question of the notional benefits derived from the possession of durable goods; the treatment of gifts, bequests and gambling winnings; the method of allowing for differences in the personal circumstances of the taxpayer; and finally, the categories of expenditure which ought to be exempted from charge. Under the second head, the main questions are whether the administration of the tax should follow the American practice of 'self-assessment' or the British system which attempts to limit as much as possible the extent to which assessment is dependent on information directly supplied by the taxpayer; assuming the British practice were followed, how it could be applied in the case of an expenditure tax; and finally, the problems connected with the initial introduction of the tax. We shall deal with these in turn.

Questions of Chargeable Expenditure

Consumers' 'capital' expenditure

For any comprehensive system of personal taxation costly durable goods bought and owned by consumers constitute a special problem because of the element of investment in their purchase, or of capital wealth – conferring a flow of benefits or notional income – in their possession. The greater the disparity between the cost of their purchase and the value of annual consumption which they afford the stronger is the element of investment in their purchase. The more durable the commodity, that is the less it is subject to physical depreciation in use, the more closely it resembles other forms of capital wealth. Looked at from the point of view of a comprehensive tax on income, possession of such goods provides the owner with an income in kind, and/or a source of possible capital gains. For purposes of an expenditure tax it has to be decided whether to regard the purchase price of any or all such goods as taxable expenditure or to exempt it from tax as capital investment. If, under a progressive tax, purchases are treated as taxable expenditure something must clearly be done to remove or reduce the inequity which would be involved if the *whole outlay* were reckoned as taxable expenditure *in the year of purchase*. If, on the other hand, purchases are exempted as investment something must certainly be done to remove or reduce the inequity between owners and non-owners which would arise if the flow of benefit conferred by ownership were ignored for tax purposes. The substance of this point becomes obvious when the contrast is made between two men one of whom is able to buy a piece of expensive equipment outright, while the other, to obtain similar benefits, must rent or hire the equipment or repeatedly pay someone else to provide comparable services.

Two classes of consumers' capital expenditure need to be distinguished. Firstly, there are durable, or highly durable, pieces of equipment bought for direct use – of which the dwelling house bought for owner-occupation is the most important example. Secondly there are valuables which a man may buy predominantly for purposes of investment – that is as a means of storing wealth, and for the sake of capital appreciation – but in respect of which the owner draws not a money income, as from stocks and shares or real estate, but some form of direct enjoyment which might be described as a 'psychic income'. Pictures by rare masters, antiques, jewellery, etc. fall in this class.

In the case of a dwelling house bought for owner-occupation the obvious course under an expenditure tax would be to exempt the expenditure on purchase and to impose an annual charge on the value of benefits derived from possession. This procedure raises no difficulties, particularly in this country where there has always been a 'Schedule A' charge on the notional income from owner-occupied houses. Should ownership of yachts, motor cars and certain household chattels be dealt with similarly? Such possessions undoubtedly confer a notional income, or flow of benefits, of an analogous kind. The freedom from tax of such notional income under our existing conception of taxable income is indeed one of the factors which tilts the scales in favour of the man of property as against the wage or salary earner. In practice, however, proposals to extend the category of 'capital' goods on whose owners an annual charge is imposed would, very reasonably, meet with stiff administrative opposition. The greater the physical depreciation in use of the article the more complicated would be the administration of the annual charge and the less justifiable the administrative cost and bother. Moreover it would in practice be difficult to draw a firm line delimiting 'capital' expenditure of this class. There is no need to dwell on all the peculiar features and circumstances which make it practicable to put land and buildings under a different tax régime from other things.

Hence, except in the case of houses,[1] the procedure of exempt-

1. In the case of houses, the existence of a Schedule A charge on owner-occupiers makes the principle of the spendings tax much easier to apply in Britain than e.g. in America where there is no such charge. It is important however that the Schedule A charge should reflect the full rental value of houses if serious inequities between owner-occupiers and rent-paying tenants are to be avoided. At present all Schedule A charges are based on pre-war valuations (although the property may not be rent-controlled at all, and may have recently been purchased) – and under the Local Government Act, 1948, the new rating values for dwelling houses are also to be expressed in terms of pre-war prices which makes it probable that valuation in terms of pre-war prices will be perpetuated for Schedule A charges also.

ing expenditure on this class of consumers' capital purchases, but imposing an annual charge on the value of benefits from ownership, must generally be rejected. Instead we should look to reasonably generous spreading provisions to take care of the disparity, in an annual period, between expenditure and consumption in connexion with such goods. There could be no objection if money spent in a year on the purchase of motor-cars, furniture and other durable goods (also heavy irregularly incurred consumers' expenses such as payments for repair and re-decoration of houses) were spread over, say, five years for tax purposes *at the taxpayer's option*. It might at first sight appear that the introduction, and limitation, of such spreading provisions would raise formidable administrative problems. This is not so. There would be no need for the Tax Inspector to inquire too closely whether some particular item of expenditure qualified for the spreading provisions or not, since any tax relief obtained on this account in the current year would automatically swell the taxpayer's chargeable expenditure in the following and subsequent years. Spreading would be against the taxpayer's interest except in so far as it genuinely assisted to even his rate of expenditure over time. In other words there could be no objection on grounds of equity to the taxpayer claiming a 'spread' for as much of his current spending as would smooth out irregularities in his expenditure-flow; and he would find, under a progressive tax, that he would soon incur heavy tax penalties if he went beyond this.

So long as expenditure on the purchase of a particular type of object is not exempted there is no need, of course, to reckon the money received from the sale of such objects as part of the year's cash receipts since (i) if the cash received from the sale is not spent but saved it would not be chargeable in any case; (ii) if it is spent it represents a kind of 'swopping' of personal possessions and does not give rise to a net outlay on personal goods; it is only the *net outlay* which should form the basis of the charge. Thus if a man gives his old car in part exchange for a new one, his chargeable outlay should be the price of the new car *less* the price received for the old car; this is the amount which automatically enters into the computation by the Fisher method, provided only that the price received for the old car is *not* entered on the receipts side.

Valuables which compose the second class of consumers'

capital goods have a unique advantage, considered as investments, for the taxpayer under the present tax system. Typically they suffer little or no physical depreciation, are a source of possible tax free capital gains, while in addition their possession yields a continuous benefit of one sort or another (whether in the form of personal or domestic decoration, the contemplation of beauty, the prestige which possession confers on their owner, or some mixture of these and other benefits)[2] which is not subject to tax at all. The existing level of demand for these valuables, reflected in their prices, must obviously be influenced by their special advantages as investments to the taxpayer.[3]

The very suggestion that purchases of things like Rembrandt pictures or rare stamps should be taxed while the purchase of bonds and shares is exempt would be likely to arouse fierce opposition from art dealers and stamp dealers, who would argue with conviction that the one represents the investment of savings in much the same way as the other; and further that if such expenditure were not exempt nobody would buy works of art, with dire consequences both to themselves and to the Progress of the Arts.[4] The same holds, of course, for jewellers and antiquarians.

Whereas the analogy between purchases of consumers' valuables and other types of investment has considerable force, high-flown argument relating to the Progress of the Arts is a red-herring; and since argument of this kind could be used to oppose any change whatsoever in the present complete tax privilege afforded to such valuables it needs to be disposed of straight away. A society bent on fostering the arts undoubtedly can and will

2. Occasionally the element of 'psychic income' from the possession of such objects may seem to be quite insignificant: the joy derived from contemplating a rare stamp (whose value resides essentially in its scarcity rather than in any intrinsic beauty) hardly seems different from the joy derived from contemplating a share certificate or a row of tenement houses which a man owns down a neighbouring street!

3. The inclusion of purchases of these valuables in taxable expenditure would, therefore, undoubtedly depress their market prices; even the alternative treatment of exempting expenditure on purchase but imposing an annual charge on the benefits arising from possession would have some depressing effect.

4. This problem, curiously enough, is never mentioned in Fisher's numerous writings, nor, as far as I am aware, anywhere else in the literature of the spendings tax.

find some more vital expression of its urge than the preservation of anomalies and creation of loopholes in its tax system to tempt rich men into connoisseurship, or at least into private acquisition of valuable works. As a means of encouraging the arts tax privileges are feeble, clumsy, unfair and unnecessarily costly to society. There is no neat correlation between the aesthetic worth (let alone stimulus to aesthetic creation) and the investment appeal of valuables – the latter depending considerably on scarcity, snobbish and fashion factors: in a way, moreover, which inevitably discriminates in favour of the dead as against the living and in favour of the established as against the rising artist. The existence of tax loopholes and incentives to invest in consumers' valuables may even serve to induce false complacency about the progress of the arts, and obscure the real condition of the arts in society, by appeasing the more businesslike and vocal sections of the art world. Meanwhile wealthy individuals are artificially encouraged to buy valuables – from stamps and diamonds to old masters – and enjoy them in private, rather than to invest their savings in productive channels. It is, of course, savings productively employed, not just savings as such, which benefit the community.[5]

The strong theoretical case for looking upon purchases of such valuables as investments has nothing to do with encouraging the arts. It is based on the very close analogy with other forms of investment – the absence or virtual absence of physical depreciation, the chance of capital gains, etc. It would, in my view, be preferable to treat such purchases as investments and exempt them from tax, but to impose an annual charge on the flow of benefits which ownership confers, provided that the administrative difficulties involved can be overcome. The category or list of exempt valuables would have to be defined by a minimum price limit. The annual charge would be some fixed percentage of

5. Though the unproductive hoardings of savings in the form of gold, precious stones and ancient works of art is not as serious a problem in an industrial community like Britain as it is in India, it is a problem nevertheless. It was one of the great achievements of Keynes to have demonstrated the manner in which, and the precise reasons for which, the desire to own wealth in the form of non-reproducible assets interferes with real capital accumulation (cf. Keynes (1963), in particular the profound though extremely difficult chapter 17 of the *General Theory*).

the purchase price (of the order of, say, 5 per cent); and would relate only to goods bought after the introduction of the expenditure tax.[6] The proceeds of sales of exempt items would, automatically, have to be entered on the receipts side of a tax return along with other sales of investments, and would be chargeable unless reinvested. The administrative requirement for this procedure is that all purchases and sales of exempt items, as defined, should be accurately notified by the taxpayers. I believe that this condition could be achieved by the institution of a self-checking system of certificates of purchase and sale, exchanged by taxpayers and forwarded with the tax return to the tax authority. Collusion to evade tax could hardly arise since the interests of buyers and sellers would be diametrically opposed. Such a system is described in greater detail in the section on administrative problems at the end of this chapter.

If this procedure were rejected on administrative grounds it would be necessary to introduce generous spreading provisions for the second class of consumer's capital expenditure, as well as for most of the items in the first category.

Treatment of gifts and bequests

The basic conception of the spendings tax as a tax on per caput consumption would justify the exemption of all genuinely one-sided transfers whether in the form of casual gifts, bequests or regular allowances to other persons, and treat these as taxable (or rather accountable for tax purposes) in the hands of the beneficiaries. In practice, however, unrestricted freedom in this respect might make the tax well-nigh impossible to administer. Since, for reasons explained below, the tax would not only be a progressive tax, but one with a relatively high exemption limit, it would clearly be strongly in the interest of taxpayers liable to the tax to 'hire' persons of low spending power to do some of their spending for them – to pay some of their bills, for example – under the guise of making a 'gift' to them. There would be nothing to prevent the making of an apparent gift to a person outside

6. To value the existing stock of similar items in private possession for purposes of an annual charge would, of course, be an administrative impossibility; and in any case the retrospective nature of the taxation involved in such an extension is ethically unattractive and logically unnecessary for a tax based on current expenditure.

the scope of the tax altogether of, say, £100, of which the recipient in reality only retained a fraction, returning the major part of it to the donor.[7] And while the clear-cut illegality of the procedure might prevent people from indulging in such practices too freely there are numerous other ways in which a beneficiary could help a donor without such a clear-cut evasion of the law. (The making of gifts is very often, though not always, of benefit to the giver as well as the receiver.)

The British income tax system is almost unique in giving the taxpayer full freedom to 'alienate' his income either to persons or to trusts, provided it is done under a deed of covenant for a minimum of seven years.[8] While the obligation to sign a seven-year covenant undoubtedly imposes some check, there is little doubt that the system provides a rich source of surtax avoidance.[9] The incentive to tax avoidance would be much stronger under a spendings tax system; and it would be idle to expect that the same kind of limitation – i.e. the obligation to sign a seven-year covenant – would provide an adequate safeguard against abuse. Nor does it seem that a seven-year obligation is necessarily a reasonable restriction to impose in cases where taxpayers have genuine obligations for the maintenance of aged

7. Besides spending masquerading as a gift there is also the possibility of spending masquerading as investment – e.g., when a taxpayer controls an investment trust or a holding company, and makes it do some of his spending for him, whether in the form of the company buying pictures or jewellery and loaning them to the taxpayer, or in the crude form of paying his grocery bills. The remedy for this is to treat all such outlays by the company as a form of dividend distribution to the taxpayer – in much the same way as the 1948 legislation treats as the income of the Directors, or other highly paid employees, any expenses that the company incurs on their behalf.

8. With the exceptions of charities and of agents or employees of the taxpayer – in these particular cases the alienation is only recognized for income tax purposes, but not for surtax purposes.

9. The justification for recognizing a transfer of income for tax purposes is much less, of course, under an income tax system than under a spendings tax system. Under an income tax system there is no way of determining whether a particular gift was made out of 'capital' or out of 'income'; the system of covenants implies that it is always possible to make a capital gift into an income gift and thus get off income tax (or rather surtax) on something which may not have been paid out of income at all. Under a spendings tax system the question whether the gift is made out of income or out of capital is not relevant.

relatives, retired servants and others. The solution here (as in so many other matters concerning taxation) is to find a reasonable compromise between the requirements of equity and the dictates of administrative efficiency. Clearly one-sided transfers ought to be allowed as a deduction from personal expenditure (i) when there is a genuine 'adverse interest' involved – as e.g., in the case of payments of alimony to ex-wives, imposed by a Court order, or maintenance payments to children separated from the taxpayer; (ii) for the support of aged or incapacitated relatives, retired servants or retired employees if they have no independent means of support (or insufficient means), subject to an over-riding maximum in the case of any one person. Similarly contributions to charities might be allowed, provided the American system were followed and the maximum exemption restricted to a small percentage of chargeable expenditure, though whether they ought to be excluded at all from the notion of 'personal expenditure' (in cases other than capital gifts) is a more debatable matter. But in all other cases – e.g., payments made to grown-up children, or other relations who are neither old nor incapacitated, or to friends, not to speak of payments made to 'discretionary trusts' containing strings of potential beneficiaries, all of which are 'allowed' for income tax purposes under the present law – payments should clearly be disallowed as a deduction if the tax is to be administered efficiently.[10] (On the question of capital bequests to charities, cf. p. 97.) It may well be that considerations of equity would justify exemption in a wider category of cases. But, as the recent Report of the Royal Commission on Taxation observed (Second Report, Cmnd 9105, para. 152), 'in tax matters there is no equity in that which is not reasonably capable of being put into practical operation'.[11]

10. Fisher himself recommends in connexion with his spendings tax proposal that 'the exemption of gifts should be duly limited' (not specifying in what way). 'The limitations on charitable gifts could be made substantially as now, by making the limit a fixed percentage of spendings-plus-savings, or a new system could be devised such as a fixed percentage of savings (spendings?) alone' (Fisher, 1942, p. 202).

11. Restrictions on gifts would have to be accompanied by analogous restrictions on personal loans made by one taxpayer to another for other than business purposes – otherwise there would be nothing to prevent disallowed gifts from masquerading as 'loans' – though it would be open to a taxpayer to help another taxpayer to accommodation by a bank through a banker's guarantee (which would not automatically reduce his tax liability).

What about 'capital gifts'? Under present law, a person has an unlimited right to transfer his property to others – a freedom that accords ill with the extreme penalties (in the form of Death Duties) imposed on property that is not settled *inter vivos* but is left to be passed on through inheritance. A rational system would make no distinction between property transferred through inheritance and property transferred through *inter vivos* settlements; it would tax both equally at rates varying, not with the size of the gift nor the cumulative total of gifts received, but with the total value of the property owned by the beneficiary at the time of the transfer.[12] Given such a system of gift taxes there would be no difficulty in treating *inter vivos* settlements in the same way as the purchase of investments in the hand of the donor, and thus exempting them from the tax. But in the absence of such a reform it is doubtful whether capital bequests should be permitted to be treated as a form of savings by the donor in all cases: specific exceptions could be made to cover such cases as settlements made by parents on their children on attaining majority or in contemplation of marriage, or the transfer of property to a charitable trust. But there is no case for permitting the tax-free transfer of property in all those cases (and they are the great majority) where the motive for the transfer is mainly the avoidance of potential Death Duties.

To those accustomed to the existing British system of taxation which accords almost unlimited liberty to the taxpayer to assign his income or his property to others the above suggestions may smack of totalitarianism. Let them reflect on the fact that they would imply no more than the adoption of much the same principles as have long been accepted in the United States of America.

Whether gifts and bequests are allowed or not as a deduction in the hands of the donor they would clearly have to be treated as receipts to be brought into account in the hands of the recipient (though for administrative reasons, it would be sensible to exempt a certain minimum of such receipts, say £100 annually). The charge of 'double taxation' which this apparent asymmetry of treatment might raise is really irrelevant. The purpose of a personal expenditure tax is to levy a tax on *persons*, not on items of 'income'

12. This would mean of course that the incidence of Death Duties would be presumed to fall on the beneficiaries (on whom it does, of course, fall) and not on the estate of the deceased as such.

or 'money' as such; the issue to decide is what is the most equitable measure for the taxation of persons (having regard to the inequities that might be caused by widespread tax avoidance itself, as well as other considerations), not how to ensure that a particular streamlet of money is not taxed 'twice' in passing from hand to hand. There is necessarily 'double taxation' in all cases where the payments from A to B are given in consideration of some service rendered by B to A or benefit received by A from B, and the line between genuinely one-sided transfers, and payments rendered in exchange for compensatory benefits is often hard to draw.[13]

The treatment of betting and gambling gains or losses involves analogous considerations. Outlay on betting and gambling is really a form of consumption and quite apart from the administrative reasons, there is no reason in equity for excluding this from chargeable expenditure. Betting gains on the other hand, particularly if they are of sizeable amounts, are on all fours with other kinds of receipts. If a sweepstake winner or a large winner in the football pools were allowed to exclude his winnings from among the accountable receipts he would indeed be put in a position to avoid paying tax altogether possibly for a whole series of years (since his apparent annual savings might exceed his reported receipts). The sensible procedure again would be to ignore small gains and call for receipts to be returned if they exceed, say, £100.[14]

13. cf. Simons (1938, ch. 6), where the same asymmetrical treatment is urged in relation to income tax. 'Considerations of equity surely afford little ground for excluding (or including) particular receipts according to the intentions of second parties. Gifts are very much like earnings, and earnings are often quite like gifts. The whole return from property is, in a sense, a gift from the community. Where money is earned by common labour, the distinction may be fairly clear; but many remunerative employments only require people's doing what they would quite enjoy doing without compensation. If it is impractical to graduate taxes according to the pleasure return from one's earning activity, surely it is hard to defend exclusion of certain receipts merely because one has done nothing or given nothing in return. Thus, as regards donees, current income tax practices as to gifts find no sanction in considerations of fairness; and they do involve a distinction between gifts and compensation which introduces serious administrative difficulties and which, moreover, invites the dressing-up of real exchanges in the guise of one-sided transfers' (pp. 134–5).

14. In the U.S. income tax code all betting and gambling gains are to be returned as income, while losses are not deductible.

Differences in needs

The next problem to consider is how far allowance should be made for such differences in personal expenditure as are due to clearly recognizable differences in personal 'needs'.

At first sight it may be questioned whether the very notion of differences in 'needs' is consistent with the basic principles of tax. Any system of personal taxation must proceed from the assumption that all men are fundamentally alike; and it must perforce ignore individual differences in psychological urges which cause some men to spend a lot of money on drink, for example, and others to be abstemious; or differences of social convention or education which influence aspirations and the pattern of living. But this does not mean ignoring such differences in spending as arise, not from differences in psychological urges, in personal habits and proclivities, but from differences in objective circumstances that are, in a broad sense, outside the control of the individual. A progressive tax aims at adjusting the burden of taxation in accordance with ability to pay; and ability to pay is nothing else but the ability to satisfy personal needs – the ability, in other words, to attain a certain standard of living. Though this notion of a 'standard of living' is not one that can be defined with any great precision, it is sufficiently clear in its broad outline to enable one to say that according as a person finds himself in one set of circumstances or another he may require a greater or a lesser expenditure to attain some given 'standard of living'. In this sense, the true purpose of an equitable tax system is to vary progressively the burden of the tax in accordance with the standard of living attained, rather than the expenditure as such – which means that as far as practical and administrative considerations permit the tax system should make allowance for all those differences in individual circumstances or 'needs' which cause the attainment of a certain standard of living to involve differing amounts of personal expenditure.

These considerations apply, of course, in the case of a progressive income tax as well and they form the logical justification for all the numerous personal allowances and reliefs granted in connexion with that tax. But the case for recognizing differences in individual needs is undoubtedly stronger with an expenditure tax. If A and B have identical financial resources, i.e. own identical amounts of property and have the same income, but A spends more than B *simply* because he has a larger number of dependants to look after, or because he suffers from a severe disability necessitating special assistance, he is not, on that account, called upon to pay *more* tax than B under an income tax régime (ignoring any special reliefs or allowances which may cause him to pay less). But under an expenditure tax system – unless that system were so framed as to make allowance for these things – A's tax liability would actually be higher: so that he would be worse off than B, both on account of having to spend more money to reach the same standard of living and also because his greater expenditure would involve him in heavier tax liabilities.

Indeed, to some people this consideration might well suggest that income is a fairer measure of taxable capacity than expenditure, since under an income tax system the man with greater needs could at least spend more – out of capital or at the cost of potential savings – without attracting more tax. If all sections of the tax-paying community were equally endowed with spendable wealth (in the shape of realizable assets) in relation to their taxable incomes, and were thus equally free to vary their total spendings *relatively* to their taxable incomes, there would undoubtedly be some force in this argument. But for the great majority of taxpayers, who have no financial resources other than their income, and whose spending is thus rigidly confined to their incomes net of taxes, no such freedom exists, though they are just as likely to suffer from exceptional or fluctuating needs as the capitalists.[15] And as we have shown in earlier chapters, for those who have this freedom the actual differences in the rate of spending relatively to *taxable* incomes are as likely – in fact a great deal more likely – to reflect differences in 'standards of living' than in 'needs'. For both these reasons it is far more equitable to allow for differences in needs within the framework of the tax system than to rely on the 'free' spendings out of capital to provide relief.

Such differences of needs arise from two broad causes: (i) differences in the number of persons a taxpayer has to support;

15. This does not mean that their spendings are necessarily *equal* to their net incomes; but a great deal of the personal saving of the wage and salary earner is of a contractual character and does not reflect differences in individual needs.

(ii) the unequal incidence of the hazards of life arising out of illness, accidents, damage to personal property, etc.[16] We shall deal with each of these in turn.

Treatment of the family. As far as difference in the number of persons in the family unit is concerned, full allowance can be made for this by making the tax vary with expenditure *per head* rather than expenditure per *family unit.* This means adopting the 'quotient system', which is already applied in France for income tax purposes, according to which the income (or expenditure) of all members of the family is first aggregated and then divided into a number of parts, depending on the number of persons in each family, and tax is charged separately on each part. Children count as one-half unit each (though the fraction could be varied with the age). This means that two adults comprising a family would pay twice the tax of a single person with half that expenditure, a married couple with two children would pay three times the tax payable by a single person with one-third of the joint family expenditure and so on.[17] Nor is there any *prima facie* reason for restricting the conception of the 'family' to husband and wife and their infant children. Other relatives could be brought in (without necessarily being counted as a full 'unit' each) provided only that they effectively shared a common household, and that their individual 'gross expenditures' (as above defined) were effectively aggregated with the rest. Once it is clearly accepted that the burden of an expenditure tax should vary with the standard of living, and that the standard of living is more a matter of expenditure *per head* than of expenditure *per household*, it is obvious that equity is better served by adoption of the French

16. It is important to emphasize that it is only the *unequal incidence* of such 'necessitous expenditure', rather than the expenditure as such, which has any claim for special treatment. Pursued to the last resort, the category of 'necessitous expenditures' could be made very wide indeed (including things like burst pipes or broken-down door handles) but most of these are the normal attendants of a certain scale of living and can be presumed to stand in a reasonable relationship to total expenditure.

17. In the United States an analogous system is applied to husband and wife only and the quotient system on the above lines was recommended by the U.S. Treasury in connexion with their wartime proposal for a spendings tax.

system (or something like it) than by any other. (It is arguable of course that the standard of living is neither simply a matter of expenditure per head, nor of expenditure per household, but a mixture of both: the larger the size of the household the smaller being the per caput expenditure required to secure a given standard of living. But the principle underlying the 'quotient system' is flexible enough to take care of such refinements, if desired: it would be perfectly possible for example to vary the actual 'quotient' in inverse relationship to the size of the household.)[18]

The introduction of the 'quotient system' would also remove any justification for the claim, sometimes advanced even in relation to the income tax, that educational expenses should be exempted. Under that system each child is credited, in effect, with its *pro rata* share of the family income (or expenditure), and thus receives the same kind of progressive tax concession (though half in amount) as a single person. I do not think that the costs of education could justify a more favourable treatment than this, though there may be a case, under a progressive tax, for permitting the taxpayer to spread his educational expenses. This could most conveniently be done by treating the benefits received from educational insurance policies as exempt (i.e. as items which do not need to be accounted for), provided the initial contribution to such policies were included in chargeable expenditure.

Necessitous expenditure. There remains the question of what kinds of expenditures ought to be specially exempted on the grounds that they arise out of misfortunes or unavoidable obligations of

18. The Royal Commission on Taxation has considered the adoption of the French quotient system and rejected it on the ground that it would give an excessive concession to the family in the upper income ranges. (See *Second Report*, Cmnd 9105, paras. 121 and 176.) For the reasons explained above, the case for this system is much stronger in connexion with an expenditure tax than with an income tax. In the upper income ranges (and it is only at these ranges that the quotient system would make a substantial difference) *total* expenditure is likely to vary a great deal with differences in family size, so that, with any system of personal allowances that is short of the quotient system, larger families might find themselves burdened with a heavier tax liability than smaller families with the same income and financial resources – a situation that certainly could not arise under an income tax.

some kind and are not part of a person's 'voluntary' expenditure on which his standard of living depends. It is arguable that a great deal of an average person's expenditure consists of items which in some sense he is 'forced to' incur as a result of some unfavourable occurrence or other.[19] But the only ones that need to be taken into consideration are those that are clearly unequal in their incidence as between taxpayers (the others can be presumed to be taken into account in fixing the scale of taxation). Irving Fisher suggested (Fisher, 1942, p. 8) that medical expenses of all kinds, and the expenses connected with births and deaths, subject to specific legal limitations, and fines, forfeitures and penalties, or payments for damages imposed by the Courts ought to be exempted on these grounds.

There clearly ought to be some recognition of the additional living expenses connected with grave physical disability and this could be made by a lump sum allowance on the lines recommended in the Second Report of the Royal Commission on Taxation (Cmnd 9105, paras. 210–5). But it is doubtful whether there is a justification for exempting in general the 'costs of nursing, surgical and dental care' as Fisher suggests. In Britain under the National Health Insurance, these expenses are already covered, at any rate up to a certain point; and it is open to anyone to supplement the compulsory national assurance with private assurance giving additional benefits. There is a case for exempting all insurance contributions, compulsory or voluntary, against sickness or accidents; and for exempting all benefits received in cash or in kind, under the insurance schemes, from inclusion among the receipts which the taxpayer must account for. But the needs of equity are adequately met if the insurance benefits are exempted (as well as the contributions in this case) without exempting medical etc. expenses as such.

Analogous considerations hold as regards expenses incurred as a result of accidental damage, fire, burglary or theft, etc.

19. Some people would argue that all expenditure incurred as a result of having to 'keep up a social position' or to maintain one's 'social responsibilities' is of an unavoidable or 'necessitous' character. But the assumption of social responsibilities is essentially a voluntary act; nor could the fact that a person has acquired, or was born into, a certain 'social position' be treated as an unfavourable event, like being struck down in a street accident.

These all (or nearly all) represent insurable risks; and the best way to allow for their unequal incidence is to exempt payments received under such insurance policies from inclusion among the receipts of the year; which means, in effect, that any outlay which is covered by insurance does not attract tax. There is no ground, however, in this case for exempting the insurance contributions as well as the benefits, any more than a private individual's household or motor car insurance should be a deductible expense for income tax. (The cost of insuring motor cars, or household goods, is more properly regarded as part of the cost of the services provided by these goods.)

It follows from this that specific exemption of particular categories of expenditure ought to be limited to those cases which cannot ordinarily be covered by insurance. This is true of the expenses incurred as a result of lasting physical disability which justifies a special disability allowance; of penalties, etc. imposed by the Courts and of birth and funeral expenses.[20] The problem of medical expenditure is adequately met by exempting contributions to all health and personal accident insurance schemes. (Contributions to life assurance are of course also exempt as a form of saving.) With regard to all other types of 'necessitous expenditure the problem is adequately met, I think, by excluding the payments received from fire, burglary or accident insurance schemes from among the receipts which have to be accounted for.[21]

This concludes our survey in broad outline of the specific problems of definition thrown up by an expenditure tax. There are, no doubt, a host of minor questions (as e.g. how to treat unabsorbed expenditure, or debts outstanding at death; how to deal with double taxation relief) which have not been examined; nor have we dealt with the problems which arise equally under an

20. Funeral expenses can of course be covered by insurance, but funeral insurance is in all respects analogous to life assurance and should be treated as such. (That means that the contributions, being a form of savings, are treated in the same manner as the purchase of investments, while the proceeds of the insurance are 'brought in' on the receipts side – i.e. they are treated in the same way as the sale of investments.) Hence the actual funeral expenses need specific exemption.

21. The question whether taxes should be a deductible expense is dealt with in the next chapter (cf. ch. 8, pp. 232–8, not included here).

income tax but which might become more difficult to deal with under an expenditure tax (as e.g. the question of payments which take the form of benefits in kind, or the temptation to dress up personal expenses as business expenses).[22] Equally we have not gone into all those aspects in which an expenditure tax would be simpler to administer than an income tax, but which would only become relevant if one contemplated the abandonment of the income tax system altogether. All the problems connected with the determination of taxable profits (which take up so much of the time and brain power of accountants and lawyers under an income tax) would disappear if not the profit earned, but only the money withdrawn from the business by the proprietors, were made the basis of the charge. Problems of depreciation, stock valuation, obsolescence, allowance for bad debts, research and all other problems connected with the concept of 'profit' would no longer arise. These questions however are not really relevant from the point of view of the particular reforms advocated in this book which are confined to a limited application of the spendings tax principle.[23]

22. There can be little doubt that even with the restrictive legislation introduced in 1948, there is a great deal of income tax and surtax avoidance in connexion with business expenses, particularly entertainment and travelling expenses (as e.g., the use of the business car for private purposes). Ultimately, the solution to these problems may only be found in a much more restrictive conception of business expenses which would exclude things like entertainment and advertising altogether as deductible expenses. The extent to which the disallowance of such items would cause inequities between different taxpayers can easily be exaggerated, particularly if the broadening of the tax base were associated with correspondingly lower rates of tax.

23. Even the adoption of these proposals would however have decided advantages as against the present system in several respects. First the problem of the difference in treatment between partnerships and companies would disappear, since partnerships would no longer pay surtax on their undistributed profits. Second, the elaborate provisions designed to prevent undue withholding of distributions by closely controlled corporations (as a means of avoiding surtax) would no longer be needed – though as mentioned before, there would be need for additional provisions to prevent corporations from undertaking expenditure for the personal benefit of proprietors. Nor would there be the same need for elaborate provisions against surtax avoidance through the creation of trusts and settlements.

Problems of Administration

American and British methods

With any progressive system of personal taxation the obligation imposed on the taxpayer to make a periodic return of his income (or capital as the case may be) forms an essential element in the administration of the tax. Indeed under the American system of 'self-assessment' the taxpayer is obliged not only to compute his taxable income, but the tax charge as well, and to remit the tax together with his return by the due date. Under that system the Revenue authorities are largely dependent for the accuracy of assessments on information furnished by the taxpayer;[24] and to ensure compliance they mainly rely on a close scrutiny of a random sample of cases together with heavy penalties and the odium of public exposure in cases of detection of fraud.

The British system is built on different lines. The responsibility for assessment rests entirely with the Revenue authorities and the tax system is so framed as to minimize the extent to which the Revenue is dependent on the information directly furnished by the taxpayer. This is largely achieved by the adoption of the 'standard rate' (and the relatively wide range of marginal income to which the standard rate effectively applies) and the widespread application of the system of deduction at source which in recent years has been extended to all salaries and wages as well as rents, dividends and interest. This means that as far as income tax is concerned the Revenue is not dependent on a full return from the taxpayer disclosing his total income from all sources; and whenever the tax is deducted at source, the function of the return is mainly to credit the taxpayer with the various allowances and reliefs to which he is entitled – to prevent automatic overassessment rather than underassessment – and, in fact, with large numbers of smaller taxpayers taxed under P.A.Y.E. a return is not normally asked for. In the case of trading profits and the earnings of self-employed persons generally, however, the Revenue is necessarily dependent on information directly furnished by the taxpayer, and here the checking of evasion depends on a close scrutiny in individual cases in much the same way as under the

24. Except that for salaries and wages the same kind of automatic reporting system is in operation as in this country.

American method. (It is well known that most cases of fraudulent or negligent evasion are to be found in this field, particularly among smaller traders.)

With surtax the position is different. Here the assessment depends, in a way which it does not with income tax, on *comprehensive* information concerning the income of a particular taxpayer, from all sources; a global return disclosing total income is therefore an indispensable feature of the machinery of assessment. It is true that as far as salaries are concerned the information furnished by the taxpayer can be checked by the independent information available to the Department in the tax offices, while in the case of trading profits and professional earnings, the income tax assessments also serve the purpose of surtax assessments. As regards dividends and interest, etc., however, where income tax has been deducted at source there is no information available in the tax offices to show how much each taxpayer has received, other than that furnished by the taxpayer on his return: in this field therefore under-reporting can only be checked by the same methods of sample inquiry or scrutiny on which the American authorities rely.[25] It would be perfectly possible however to extend the same comprehensive reporting system as exists in the case of the wages and salaries of employees to the interest and dividends paid by companies to their creditors and shareholders.[26] If this were done (or regarded

25. The Revenue authorities have powers, under existing law, to obtain certified copies of registered securities from corporate bodies and to compel nominees or trustees to disclose the beneficial owners of the securities registered in their names. In this way they could track down the total income received from U.K. companies by any one taxpayer by looking through all company registers and obtaining the names of all the beneficial owners of the securities registered in the names of trustees or nominees. But such powers can only be used discriminatingly, with inquiries on a sample basis; they are not comparable to the automatic reporting system that exists in the case of salaries and wages.

26. The problem here is complicated by two factors: (1) that the true recipient of the income is frequently a different person from the one in whose name or names the stock or shares are registered, as the latter can be a trustee or nominee; (2) that whilst the affairs of the employees of a particular employer are normally dealt with in one tax office, the affairs of the shareholders of a particular company may be distributed among all the numerous tax offices of the country. Both these problems could be solved

107

as worth doing) the Revenue authorities would be no more dependent on the information directly supplied by the taxpayer in the case of surtax than they are in the case of income tax.

In the case of an expenditure tax assessment would necessarily depend on *full* information concerning the totality of affairs of a particular taxpayer, in much the same way as in the case of surtax. But in addition to all the information that is now required for surtax, there would be a series of additional items: (1) the purchase and sale of capital assets during the year (this would equally be required for a capital gains tax); (2) money borrowed or lent, or loans repaid or borrowings returned in the course of the year; (3) the state of bank balances at the beginning and the end of the year;[27] (4) bequests, gifts, capital payments received from life insurance, gambling and betting winnings, which are not now reported since they are not taxable.

This is certainly a formidable list and one's first reaction to it is bound to be that the tax could only be made administratively manageable through a system of self-reporting on the American pattern. This means that only a small sample of cases could be scrutinized in detail and one would have to rely on the heavy punishment inflicted, and on exposure with a great deal of publicity, as the main weapon for the discouragement of false or incomplete reporting in the great majority of cases where the returns could not be checked or followed up in detail.

This system seems to work tolerably well in America (there is naturally not sufficient evidence for saying just how well), and the U.S. Treasury must clearly have thought that it could be made to work sufficiently well in the case of a spendings tax to recom-

---

however by the device of furnishing each taxpayer with a particular code number and making it obligatory to include the code number of the *beneficial owner* among the particulars of registration. If copies of all dividend counterfoils issued containing this code number were regularly furnished by the companies to the Revenue, they could be distributed among the tax offices as a routine operation; at the same time the anonymity afforded by the system of nominee shareholders (which the Cohen Committee thought worth preserving) would be safeguarded.

27. A return of cash would only be required for the beginning of the first year in which the taxpayer makes a return, and then only for the excess over a certain maximum amount.

mend to Congress its adoption as an emergency tax for wartime. I have little doubt, however, that it is far less suitable for adoption in Britain. The British tradition of tax administration is to rely as far as possible on the prevention of fraud, rather than its discouragement through criminal punishment and exposure in cases of detection. Most cases of known evasion are settled out of Court without any publicity whatever. It has been said that the policy of the Board of Inland Revenue has always been to encourage the sinful and the careless to come forward and confess their sins,[28] and in pursuance of this, they are ready to accept pecuniary settlements, instead of instituting criminal proceedings, if the taxpayer makes a full confession and gives full facilities for an investigation of his affairs.[29] Nor are the Courts any too co-operative with the Revenue in convicting a man in cases in which fraudulent intent (the making of false statements 'knowingly and wilfully' in the words of the law) cannot be proven beyond any shadow of doubt. In the nature of things this is very difficult to establish in a great number of cases and there have in fact been a number of unsuccessful prosecutions among those brought before the Courts. The Revenue authorities on their side are anxious to preserve their traditionally good relations with the taxpayers – which is possible so long as they are not *too* dependent, or at any rate not exclusively dependent, on the statements furnished by the taxpayer for their sources of information.

The American system has tended to rely on penalties. The British system, despite the strain caused by heavy taxation, still relies in the main on the willing co-operation of taxpayers to fill in the gaps in the Revenue's own sources of information. The transplantation of the American system would thus not fall on fertile soil in Britain.

28. cf. memorandum by the Inland Revenue Staff Federation submitted to the Royal Commission on Taxation.

29. cf. the statement by the Chancellor of the Exchequer (Sir John Anderson) in the House of Commons, 5 October 1944, and the evidence of the Chairman of the Board of Inland Revenue (Sir Eric Bamford) before the Committee of Public Accounts, 12 December 1950. Among the 22,753 cases of under-reporting investigated between 1948 and 1953 (which yielded over £10 million in fines alone) there were only fifteen prosecutions of which thirteen were successful (cf. 95th and 96th reports of the Commissioners of Inland Revenue, Cmnd 8726 and 9030).

Application of British methods to an expenditure tax

On the other hand it would be a mistake to assume too readily that the institution of a regular reporting system that would put the Revenue in a position to check the accuracy of the items in the taxpayer's return more or less on a routine basis would prove such a formidable administrative task. We have mentioned how the gap in the case of the existing surtax could be filled by the institution of an automatic reporting system for dividend and interest payments. Similarly an automatic system of cross checking (or rather cross-reporting) could be instituted for all capital transactions mentioned under (1) and (2) above, which could also be extended to the items mentioned under (4). This, together with the obligation to furnish documentary evidence for certain items of the return (including (3)), would enable the Revenue authorities to keep a check on the whole range of items on which the computation of liability depends. (With the exception of the initial cash balance, discussed below.)

As regards capital transactions, a system of cross-reporting could be devised in the form of tax-slips, detachable into two halves, both sides of which are filled in by the party to any loan or investment transaction (let us call him X) who receives cash (i.e. the seller in the case of stocks and shares and real property; the borrower in the case of loans and the lender in the case of loan repayments). They are in effect a form of receipt which is handed over to the payer (let us call him Y) who retains one portion of it (let us call it slip A) and has the obligation to hand on the other portion (slip B) to the Revenue. (In the case of investments this would be most conveniently done when the transfer is handed in to the Stamp Office for stamping.) It would not be difficult to devise a form for slip B (by the institution of a system of code numbers) that would make it relatively easy for the Revenue authorities to route each slip automatically to X's files in the relevant tax office. Slip A on the other hand would provide the documentary proof for Y when he comes to make his return and claim exemption on these payments. (To make matters doubly sure evidence or surrender of slip A could be indicated by an appropriate official stamp on slip B.) Slip A would prevent any over-reporting on behalf of Y, whereas the collection of B slips, accumulating on X's files, would prevent effective under-reporting on behalf of X. Since the risk is only of under-reporting by X and of over-reporting by Y, there is no point in asking X to submit any evidence as regards his receipts; and equally there is no need to keep any check on Y as to whether *all* his payments have been reported. The same idea could be applied also to cases of bequests and gifts, winnings in pools, lotteries and races, etc. In fact in the case of all cash payments above a certain minimum sum, which are *not* payments for goods and services rendered for the non-exempt categories of purchases, the completion of a receipt by the payee and its surrender by the payor could be made a statutory requirement.

Some system of this sort (confined to property transactions) would be equally necessary for the efficient administration of a capital gains tax, and Sweden does in fact operate a similar system in connexion with her taxation of capital gains.

With regard to bank balances a similar check could be provided through the banks supplying a certificate to their customers showing the net balance standing in their accounts at the first day of each income tax year. (The banks have already been asked on previous occasions to furnish a list of names of all depositors to the Revenue authorities to whom more than £15 interest was paid and such a list would also serve as a check on whether all deposits had been returned.)

It is not suggested of course that each return would be automatically checked in detail with regard to all items, any more than is the case at present with income tax. But the information would all be at the Revenue's disposal to carry out such checks as frequently and as widely as efficient administration requires; there would be no need to have recourse to a close investigation of a taxpayer's personal affairs every time it was desired to scrutinize a particular return.

Nor would the system be completely foolproof – any more than is the case with the present income tax. For just as at present there is no certain way of getting reliable information on profits assessed under Schedule D independently of the taxpayer's own return, so there would be no independent check on the corresponding item 'business drawings' under the expenditure tax.

Finally, there is no way of checking the declaration of the personal holding of bank notes, which would only be required, however, the first year in which the taxpayer makes a return. (It would be expedient to ignore normal cash holdings altogether and to require a declaration only of the holding of bank notes and coins in excess of a certain sum, say £50.) With regard to this item the Inspector would be wholly dependent on the taxpayer's honesty. But the significance of this cannot be very great, since it is only in regard to bank notes possessed prior to the initial introduction of the tax that tax evasion is possible. After the initial year concealed cash hoards would be reflected in lower deposits and would thus subject the individual to tax. If the cash originated in an understatement of income, or some other kind of receipt, it would be the understatement of these other items, not the hoarding of cash, which was the cause of underassessment: in fact if a person concealed some of his profits, and kept the proceeds in ready cash which he failed to disclose in turn (so as to avoid giving cause for suspicion) the two understatements, under a spendings tax, would offset one another, leaving his tax liability much as it would have been if he had declared all items honestly. It is only in so far as the concealed income is effectively spent that tax is really evaded.

And here perhaps lies the final safeguard against large scale evasion under an expenditure tax. There may be many ways of concealing profits made by casual traders or by people with complex business or financial dealings. But there are not many ways of spending money (at least not many that people regard as worth while) which do not leave some visible mark behind them – which are not 'open for all to see'. Tax laws or other restrictive regulations would not work as well as they do if the average person did not instinctively tend to overrate the chances of being 'found out' if his contravention of the law leaves any external traces behind. For all we know there may be thousands of tax-dodgers who make thousands of pounds a year, all on cash transactions, and who keep the thousands well hidden in stockings. But they couldn't *spend* thousands of pounds a year without letting quite a number of people into the secret: the risk of being found out is undoubtedly much greater with grossly understated spendings than with grossly understated earnings.[30]

30. Even now the Revenue sometimes relies on a man's style of living as a means of detecting tax evasion when this is obviously inconsistent with the information given in his returns. The usual defence in such cases is that the

And even if it were true that the possibilities of straight-forward evasion would be greater than under the present income tax, this would need to be set against the very much narrower opportunities for legal tax escape or tax avoidance. A man who keeps a country house and a town house, several cars and a yacht, and several servants and entertains frequently on a lavish scale, might yet manage to understate his true expenditure by a few hundred or even a few thousand pounds. But he could not possibly return a figure of, say, £3000 when in fact he spent £30,000. Yet under the present tax system there is no effective limit to the extent to which he can economize on having a taxable income by converting income into capital gains, or economize on surtax by transferring property into trusts or settlements, etc.

Problems of transition

The above does, however, bring to light an important problem connected with the initial introduction of the tax – namely the anticipatory buying of durable goods and the anticipatory hoarding of cash to which the very expectation of the tax is likely to give rise. Of these the second is far more important, since the range of goods suitable for anticipatory buying is rather limited and the buying wave would soon be checked through the temporary exhaustion of current obtainable supplies. (e.g., an anticipatory buying wave for motor-cars under present conditions would be almost wholly ineffective, since there is anyhow a long waiting list for most cars.) Nor would potential heavy-spendings taxpayers be tempted to hoard 'free' purchasing power in the form of jewellery and valuables: there would be no point if these were exempt items;[31] and if they were not exempted, since the

---

money comes out of capital gains or gambling profits. Under an expenditure tax he would have no such defence; and, what is more important, he would be conscious of the need to bring the two into some sort of harmony, whereas today the average person does not feel that 'the appearances are against him' merely because his scale of living is out of line with his reported income.

31. No point, that is, in buying for purposes of re-selling later, since the proceeds of sale would become accountable receipts for tax purposes. Intending buyers might well, however, hasten to bring forward their purchases in order to escape the annual charge imposed on possession of such goods bought after the introduction of the tax.

values of these things would be likely to fall (for reasons explained) as a result of the introduction of the tax, they would not be very suitable as vehicles for tax avoidance. But there might well be a run on the banks by people who wished to hoard cash in anticipation. To forestall this the Government might find it necessary to announce, in any public statement in which reference was made to the tax, that, if introduced, it would have retrospective effect from the date of the first announcement – though such retrospective provisions might themselves raise difficult problems if the period between the first announcement and its effective Parliamentary adoption were at all prolonged.[32] And if this were not sufficient, the Government could threaten to take the more drastic step of calling in all bank notes and reissuing them in a new form at a date subsequent to the introduction of the tax, so that all cash hoards would be automatically disclosed.

Another transitional problem would arise in connexion with the limited number of taxpayers who would be affected by the proposed Expenditure tax in the period of their retirement, having saved for this period before the tax was introduced. Unless special provision were made some unfairness would be involved in so far as savings, heavily taxed as income when they were put by, were further taxed when they were spent. This problem could be met by applying a higher exemption limit, for a period of years after the introduction of the tax, to taxpayers above retirement age.

Summary

The general conclusion of this survey must therefore be that a personal expenditure tax would undoubtedly be a more complicated tax to administer than the present type of income tax;[33]

32. This is less likely to be a serious problem in Britain – where it is customary for the Chancellor to announce his proposals on Budget Day 'out of the blue' and to take effect immediately – than in America where the Administration's tax proposals are usually debated in Congress for months on end without any guarantee of their ultimate adoption.

33. The qualification 'present type' is important, for the relative simplicity of our existing income tax administration is not an inherent feature of the taxation of income as such but merely of the defective and inadequate notion of income which underlies the tax system. If income tax were based on the comprehensive definition of income advocated by Henry Simons and others, according to which each individual would be taxed on the sum of

it would make greater demands on the taxpayer in the preparation of the return, as well as on the Revenue officials in checking it; that in consequence, it may never assume the role of the present income tax as a tax embracing two-thirds, if not three-quarters, of the whole working population of the country. But subject to these limitations we have found nothing in the basic conception which would present insuperable problems from an administrative point of view, or which would necessitate a departure from the high standards of tax administration customary in Britain.[34]

It should be clear from the foregoing, however, that it would be impossible to think of *replacing* the present system with an expenditure tax system at one stroke, so to speak. There is well over a hundred years' accumulated experience in administering the income tax. There is no such experience concerning the expenditure tax; and until some practical experience is gained in its administration it is not really possible to foretell with any confidence how difficult its administration would prove in practice.

Assuming that the superiority of the expenditure tax over the income tax, from the point of view of equity, incentives and economic efficiency, is as great as was claimed in the previous chapters, the only practical line of advance is to make a cautious beginning by introducing an expenditure tax side by side with

his consumption and net capital accumulation over a period ('the algebraic sum of (1) the market value of rights exercised in consumption; and (2) the change in the value of the store of property rights between the beginning and end of the period in question'), the evaluation of a person's income would require much the same information as is needed to evaluate expenditure, even if all assets were valued at cost (i.e. only realized capital gains were reckoned as income).

34. A former U.S. Treasury tax expert, Kenneth E. Poole, writing in the *American Economic Review* for March 1943 (after the proposal was rejected by Congress) on the administrative problems connected with a war-time spendings tax, summed up the position as follows: 'From the standpoint of administration the conclusion seems reasonable that the spendings tax does not present insuperable difficulties. The most serious problem would be that of providing an adequate check over returns in view of the scarcity of manpower and the vast number of taxpayers. Finally most of the administrative details which give the spendings tax the appearance of cumbersomeness have been equally bothersome under the income tax; and the issue resolves itself into the question whether such a complicated tax ought to be introduced as a temporary measure' (p. 73).

the existing income tax, so framed as to apply to a limited number of taxpayers only in the top brackets. If the experiment proved successful after a number of years of operation it would be possible to extend gradually the scope of the new tax and to reduce the scope of the old. The proposals put forward in the following chapter serve to this end.

References
FISHER, I. (1942), *Constructive Income Taxation*, Harper.
KEYNES, J. M. (1963), *General Theory of Employment, Interest and Money*, Macmillan.
PIGOU, A. C. (1928), *A Study in Public Finance*, Macmillan, 3rd edn.
SIMONS, H. C. (1938), *Personal Income Taxation*, University of Chicago Press.

5 W. Vickrey

Expenditure, Capital Gains and Progressive Taxation

Excerpt from W. Vickrey, 'Expenditure, capital gains and progressive taxation', *Manchester School of Economic and Social Studies*, vol. 25, 1957, pp. 1–13.

Although the idea of a progressively graduated tax based on aggregate personal expenditure is by no means new, the lack of practical experience with any such tax is a perennial excuse for speculation about what such a tax would involve in practice, and the appearance of Nicholas Kaldor's recent book (Kaldor, 1955, p. 249) advocating such a tax as a substitute for the surtax on personal incomes, following close on a series of far-ranging Royal Commission reports (1953; 1954; 1955) is a further occasion for a re-examination of this tax in the light of present-day income tax practices.

Income and Expenditure Taxes Compared in Ideal Terms

In this area, more than in most, there is a sharp distinction to be drawn between considerations that would apply to the comparison of theoretically perfect taxes of the various types and those that would apply to the taxes as actually administered. Kaldor's treatment suffers considerably from a tendency to compare an idealized expenditure tax with the income tax as it exists, which is inappropriate unless indeed the tacit assumption is made that by turning over a new leaf a degree of perfection can be attained that has become difficult or impossible in the older form of taxation by reason of the accumulation of special vested interests and commitments to untenable positions. Kaldor's lack of success in getting the majority of the recent Royal Commission to accept a proposal for fuller taxation of capital gains (see Cmnd 9474, paras. 80–117, pp. 25–40; paras. 34–84, pp. 365–82) might indeed thus partly justify his approach. On the other side, even less tolerable is the reverse error of ignoring the difficulties of the present system, merely because they are somehow being lived with, while making the most of all of the difficulties, real or imagined, associated with the new.

Even-handed comparison of two taxes in terms of imperfect practice is difficult, however, not only because imperfection is always more complex than perfection, but because the nature of the imperfections to be encountered in practice are difficult to predict, particularly with respect to the new law. As a first approximation, therefore, it is helpful to compare a reasonably perfected income tax with an equally idealized expenditure tax; when this has been done it will be easier to assess what changing to a new basis of taxation may have to offer as compared to reform of the existing tax.

If we begin accordingly by considering on the one hand a comprehensive income tax that insures that all forms of income, whether as dividends, interest, or capital gains sooner or later pay income tax on the same footing, and in which irregularities in the receipt or realization of income are adequately dealt with by some system of averaging, and on the other a correspondingly perfected spendings tax, we find that at least some of the differences between the two forms of taxation disappear.

Eliminating bias against risk

For example, it is quite true that income tax laws as actually applied in nearly all countries have a considerable bias against risky investment. (See, for example, Kaldor, 1955, chapter 3, pp. 102–29.) This arises in some cases because with annual assessment and inadequate averaging under progressive rates the realization of a large profit will push income up into the higher surtax brackets, whereas a corresponding loss, even if fully deductible, will cause tax abatement at a lower marginal rate. In other cases, particularly the development of new products or processes by firms established for this purpose, profits, if the venture is successful, often present themselves most naturally in the form of dividends at a relatively high level, taxable at the full rates as income, whereas if the venture is a failure, so that much or all of the investment is lost, this will ordinarily rate as a capital loss, deductible, if at all, only subject to various restrictions and resulting in a relatively low level of tax abatement. A somewhat similar phenomenon arises even more specifically if the investment is in bonds subject to risk of default of principal, in which case again the higher rate of interest obtained in consideration of the risk is fully taxed, but the loss in the event of default gets inadequate tax consideration.

But neither of these effects is inherent in the concept of an income tax. With full consideration of all gains and losses in the tax base, averaging of income over a sufficiently long period would greatly reduce the difference between the rate at which a gain would increase tax and the rate at which a loss would diminish it, since the marginal rate would depend not on the income for a single year but on the income of an extended period taken as a whole, in relation to which the gain or loss would be much smaller and thus cause much less variation in the point on the scale of progression at which the taxpayer would find himself. Moreover, to the extent that this bias against risky investment persists even with adequate averaging, it may be considered to reflect a consistent social policy. For if the progression of the tax schedule is deemed a reflection of the extent to which public policy looks with disfavour on inequality in the distribution of income, then it will be equally in accord with public policy to discourage individuals to place such large parts of their capital in such hazardous ventures as would carry an unduly heavy risk of greatly enriching or impoverishing them. Such a degree of bias against risky investment is inherent in any progressive tax system, including an expenditure tax, since the eventual spending of the proceeds of a successful venture would be subject to higher rates of tax than would the expenditure forgone in case of loss.

Consistent treatment under almost any concept of income would seem to require the avoidance of situations where the revenue plays 'heads I win, tails you lose' with the taxpayer, and the allowance of full deduction of losses in all cases where the profits, if realized, even if in a somewhat different nominal form, would have been taxed. But it is extremely difficult to do this consistently unless substantially all gains and losses are brought into consideration in the determination of net income (with the possible exception of certain losses not of an investment nature, such as gambling losses, or casualties related to consumption such as a mishap to a personal automobile). Losses from ventures whose successful outcome will normally result in taxable profits appear in a wide variety of ways, so that it is difficult to deny deductibility to any wide category of loss from investment without introducing an anti-risk bias. And it is hardly to be expected that deductibility should be allowed for any given type of loss without correspondingly taxing the gains in what appear to be analogous cases. Thus a full taxation of capital gains would seem to be a prerequisite for avoiding this anti-risk bias in the income tax.

Curiously enough, it is as a means of mitigating this bias that partial or complete exemption of capital gains is often advocated. But it is doubtful whether any kind of capital gains exemption can do anything but substitute one kind of bias for another, namely bias in favour of investments that are likely to reap their return in capital gain form over those more likely to reap returns in forms taxable in full; this distinction does not necessarily involve any significant element of risk, witness the case of the gilt-edged short-term bond selling at a discount because its coupon rate has been fixed below the market rate, possibly with tax advantages in mind. In so far as the elimination of bias against risk is concerned, averaging plus inclusion of capital gains and losses in the income tax base can be considered an alternative to shifting to an expenditure tax. Kaldor would appear to be in error in his repeated assertion that a tax on accrued income would discriminate against risk more severely than the existing income tax (Kaldor, 1955, pp. 117, 121).

Offsetting pressures for retention of corporate earnings

Another point where existing income taxes offend is in their impact on corporate finance and more particularly on the disposition of corporate profits. Especially where corporations are owned predominantly by shareholders in the upper surtax brackets, the tax results in considerable pressure for companies to avoid the distribution of taxable dividends, and instead to retain large fractions of their net earnings, either for expansion of the company's own business, retirement of debt, or investment in securities of third parties. There is considerable difference of opinion as to whether this is on balance desirable, and the balance of considerations may shift from one side to the other over time; but whatever position is taken in general, the specific form in which the tax pressure is exerted seems to bear no relation to any public purpose. From one point of view such retention is undesirable in that it subjects the investment process to biases in the direction of pandering to the already suspect desire of corporation executives to add to their economic imperium in possible disregard of productivity considerations; in that it reduces the supply of investment funds available to rapidly growing smaller corporations through the flotation of new securities (as a supplement to what they could secure through the retention of their own earnings where this is justified by prospective returns); and in that it tends to encourage the growth of established companies with consequent tendencies for monopoly and the dominance of the economy by the very large companies. In the United States, concerns of this nature have been reflected in such phenomena as the short-lived surtax on undistributed profits of 1936-9, the notorious section 102 surtax on corporations having improper accumulations of surplus, and the special penalty taxes on person holding companies that accumulate undistributed profits.

In Britain, the quite properly greater concern for anti-inflationary considerations and the greater tolerance towards monopoly have resulted in what is to the American observer the amazing spectacle of a profits tax which discriminates against distributed profits, adding its pressures to those of the surtax. Yet it is highly doubtful whether such a provision has had any important direct anti-inflationary effects (particularly as the individuals whose dividends were thereby kept low probably had low propensities to consume and were in many cases in a position to finance consumption expenditures in other ways), even though such measures may have filled a need in making restrictive policies in other directions more palatable politically. Granting everything that may be said in favour of internal financing as being economical in avoiding the expenses connected with the flotation of securities, and as directing funds more or less automatically in the directions that have been proved most profitable in the past, nevertheless it seems hardly appropriate to further reinforce these factors, which are quite adequately under consideration by company directors, by artificial and irrelevantly modulated tax pressures. Moreover the consequence for the present seems to be that such a provision, once enacted, is difficult to eliminate without causing a windfall to shareholders in the form of increased share prices, which in turn could only be tolerated on equity grounds if there were adequate provision for the taxing of the resulting capital gains.

It is entirely possible to design an income tax structure that is reasonably free from such irrelevant and unintended influences on company policy. Indeed, under an income tax with full inclusion of gains and losses and cumulative averaging in which the interest factor is taken into account (cf. Vickrey, 1947, chapter V, esp. pp. 172 ff.), the deferment of the realization of the income by the shareholder that results from the retention of earnings by the company would not affect the ultimate burden of the shareholder, and such a tax would therefore be reasonably neutral on this point. Even if a less pretentious form of averaging is used that does not take into account the interest factor, it would be possible to keep the tax system as a whole reasonably neutral by applying to the accumulated undistributed earnings of companies an annual tax at say 1 per cent or 2 per cent, this being deemed to be equal to an interest charge of say 5 per cent on the surtax which is being postponed by reason of the non-distribution of the earnings. (cf. Vickrey, 1945, pp. 122–7.) Problems of discrimination against risk and pressures on dividend policy are thus both capable of being taken care of within the framework of the income tax concept, and it is accordingly only to a limited extent that an expenditure tax can be considered necessary to achieve these ends.

Comparative effects on saving: the net rate of return

A third major claim for the expenditure tax is that it will encourage saving. How weighty this consideration is will depend on the context of general economic conditions, anticipations regarding the future of the tax, the motives that influence the saving of individuals, and possible criteria as to the socially desirable amount of saving. If the tax is thought of as a permanent and long established tax, then as Kaldor and others before him have shown (Kaldor, 1955, pp. 79–101), the effect of changing to an expenditure tax is to permit the individual to adjust the time pattern of his consumption, through corresponding adjustments in his savings programme, so that it will bear a correct relation to the relative social costs of providing goods and services at different times as this relative cost is reflected in the market rate of interest, whereas the income tax distorts this relationship, making present rather than future consumption unduly attractive to the individual in spite of its higher drain on the resources of the community. This is the traditional analytic argument for preferring the expenditure tax to the income tax, and there is certainly no denying its validity, nor any possibility of amending the income tax so as to avoid this defect without in effect converting it into an expenditure tax. Opinions will differ, however, as to how important the changes that would occur on this basis would be. It is at least arguable that the increase in the savings of an individual in a 16 shilling in the pound tax bracket that results from increasing the net rate of return on his savings, after tax, from say 1 per cent to 5 per cent by shifting from an income tax to an expenditures tax, and similarly for other taxpayers, is not of paramount importance to the economy as a whole.

Savings in an emergency

There is a case of a different order to be made, not discussed by Kaldor, for a temporary expenditures tax to be applied at a time of great general shortage of consumer goods, as during a war or other emergency period (cf. Vickrey, 1943, pp. 165–70). In this case the tax is specifically not expected to continue after the emergency is over, or at least only at much lower rates, so that deferment of expenditure not only defers the tax, but reduces the applicable rate, and the incentive for individuals to save, at least temporarily, is greatly enhanced. In such contexts the argument for the expenditure tax is much stronger than it is for a permanent tax; indeed it can be considered as a form of graduated generalized rationing. One could even argue that the possibility of such emergency use would be a reason for using the tax in normal times in order to have the administrative machinery ready for the emergency.

Effects on the concentration of economic power

A much more controversial issue that arises in considering an expenditure tax as a permanent tax is the effect of such a change on the concentration of the ownership of wealth and of economic power. Kaldor claims that 'by making the expenditure tax sufficiently progressive it would always be possible to prevent the rich from saving too much' (Kaldor, 1955, p. 97), but this is patently erroneous, since spendings tax rates, however progressive, could have no effect on a man who persisted in living on a frugal scale in spite of his great wealth, even leaving out of account the easing of this frugality by the non-taxable perquisites that almost invariably accompany the possession of great wealth. Possibly there may be some who would view such accumulations of wealth in private hands with equanimity and even approval so long as the spendings tax rates were such as to induce their possessors to treat them as funds held in trust rather than for personal gratification through consumption of the income. It can be hazarded, however, that the weight of opinion would regard with some misgiving even that accumulation that might be made by a man such as Henry Ford within his own lifetime, let alone an accumulation continued unchecked over several generations. If a spendings tax is to be substituted for an income tax, some complementary form of progressive taxation seems called for to check the more extreme accumulations.

Corresponding adjustment of death duties

The usual recourse at this point is to invoke heavy death duties as the remedy. Even without balking at the very substantial possibilities that would still remain for the accumulation of wealth within a single lifetime, one can point to the very serious difficulties, often overlooked, that stand in the way of setting up an effective, sharply progressive succession tax that is reasonably free from untoward consequences. Present-day death duties are subject to major avoidance through gifts *inter vivos*, through skipping generations by the setting up of trusts or otherwise, and in many other ways; if these avenues of avoidance were effectively blocked, another very troublesome one of international transfers and migrations would arise that could be blocked only at the expense of seriously interfering with legitimate and desirable international movements of capital; the present international convention to the effect that only the jurisdiction of situs may tax real property would have to give way. Kaldor suggests that an appropriate succession duty should vary the rate of tax according to the net wealth of the recipient (Kaldor, 1955, p. 101); possibly also the difference in age between transferor and transferee would need to be taken into consideration (Vickrey, 1947, pp. 216 ff.) so as to avoid the incentives that would otherwise develop if the rates were at all steep to skip over as many generations as the rules against perpetuities will allow, with consequent undesirable tying up of property in various kinds of trusts to the detriment of the supply of venture capital and of flexibility in the use of property.

Thus at least one of the liabilities of the expenditure tax is that its substitution for an income tax renders more crucial the solution of the far from easy problem of developing an adequate succession duty. To make a fair comparison between the two taxes thus requires considering not merely the change to the expenditure tax itself, but also the appropriate changes in succession taxation that would be called for. This necessarily greatly complicates the comparison. However, a not too difficult comparison becomes available if in lieu of imposing a specific succession tax we merely on the one hand apply the expenditure tax to all gifts and bequests, considering them to be a form of personal consumption of the donor, while under the income tax on the other hand we consider gifts and bequests to be taxable income to the recipient. Such an arrangement would not be satisfactory in practice, because of the avoidance possibilities mentioned above, so that caution must be used in interpreting the comparison. Assume a stable price level, and suppose further that in both the income tax and the expenditure tax, to avoid the effects of fluctuations from year to year in the tax base, which with the inclusion of gifts and bequests would be particularly severe, the tax is assessed on a cumulative basis, comparable to the method used for P.A.Y.E., the final tax liability being assessed on the basis of an aggregate of the income or expenditure over the entire period, prior tax payments being considered a deposit against the ultimate liability, compound interest being credited at an appropriate rate of this deposit. The aggregate amount brought to account for tax purposes for any individual will be the same in both cases, the difference between the impact of the two taxes being entirely due on the one hand to the relative weights given the quantities reported for the various years in aggregating them, and on the other hand to the timing of the interim payments on account.

Weighting effects

As to weighting, in the case of an income tax it would be appropriate to make each year's income count the same as any other, to avoid any arbitrary effects on the tax burden due to shifts in the time of realization of income; for the spendings tax it would be more appropriate to use a present value of the expenditures of various dates at compound interest so as properly to express the slighter burden imposed on society by the later consumptions. The weighting is then such as still to preserve the difference between the two taxes in the net rate of return offered in terms of future consumption or ability to make bequests in return for present abstinence: under the expenditure tax this remains equal to the market rate of interest, in the income tax it is reduced by the marginal rate of tax, and thus the increased incentive to save produced by the spendings tax can be represented by this change in interest rate.

Timing effects

As to the difference in the timing of payments for the two taxes, this depends on the way in which income is realized for tax purposes. At one extreme, if income is realized for tax purposes only as needed to provide funds to finance personal expenditure, then the timing of the payments of the two taxes becomes quite similar. This is indeed the ultimate extreme of the policy of allowing accelerated depreciation, or granting initial capital allowances, in that in effect all investments are written off to zero as soon as made, with the implication that all subsequent amounts realized from such assets, of whatever character, would then be treated as income and not return of capital. The writing down process would presumably be limited in the case where the taxpayer had indebtedness, so as not to produce a negative nominal net worth. The effect of shifting from such a tax to an expenditure tax would then be limited to the incentive effect produced by the fact that future expenditure would be taxed relatively more lightly than present expenditure, and there would not be any element of leaving the more frugal taxpayer with greater resources at his command under the expenditures tax than under such an income tax.

Another way of looking at the matter is to consider that allowing the taxpayer to postpone the realization of income is in effect to allow him to postpone the payment of the corresponding tax, which can be considered equivalent to a loan of the corresponding funds from the government to the taxpayer. If, as under an income tax, this postponement will often depend on purely nominal differences in financial arrangements that are more or less under the control of the taxpayer, it becomes necessary, in the interests of equity between taxpayers differing in the flexibility of their finances and of avoiding the distortion of normal financial arrangements in response to tax pressures, to charge an appropriate rate of interest for these deferments or loans. This is not in present practice done, at least not in any systematic way, but it can readily be done in conjunction with cumulative averaging. On the other hand if the deferment of tax is co-ordinated with a deferment of consumption, as under an expenditures tax, then one can without inequity omit the charging of interest on the tax deferred, thus producing the appropriate incentive for saving. One can readily afford to provide such incentives for saving when the saving is net aggregate saving, but can generally ill afford to provide even more moderate incentives for particular forms of saving when these may be offset by dissaving in other forms so that the incentives would operate more to divert savings from its natural channels than to increase the total flow of savings.

Thus even within the income concept it would be possible to provide a procedure whereby tax on reinvested income would be deferred, thus avoiding the tendency of heavy income taxation to impinge on the funds that might be used by frugal and skilful entrepreneurs to expand the scale of their operations. What is inherently and necessarily different in the expenditure tax approach is merely that there is appropriate differentiation between the present values of the tax attracted by increments of present consumption as compared with increments of future consumption.

References
KALDOR, N. (1955), *An Expenditure Tax*, Allen & Unwin.
ROYAL COMMISSION ON THE TAXATION OF PROFITS AND INCOME, *First report*: 13 February 1953, Cmnd 8761; *Second report*: 9 April 1954, Cmnd 9105; *Final report*: 20 May 1955, Cmnd 9474. H.M.S.O.

VICKREY, W. (1947), *Agenda for Progressive Taxation*, Ronald Press.

VICKREY, W. (1945), 'A reasonable undistributed profits tax', *Taxes*, February.

VICKREY, W. (1943), 'The spendings tax in peace and war', *Columbia Law Review*, vol. 43.

6 J. F. Due

The Taxation of Wealth

J. F. Due, 'Net worth taxation', *Public Finance*, vol. 14, 1960, pp. 310–21.

By the term 'net worth' or 'net wealth' taxation is meant an annual tax on the net wealth of individuals. Similar taxes could be applied to corporations (and are to a limited extent in India and elsewhere), but such levies are excluded from the present discussion. Likewise the paper will not deal with nonrecurrent capital levies, or with *in rem* property taxes imposed against the gross value of various forms of property, primarily real, in the United States, Canada, and elsewhere, except incidentally for purpose of comparison. The purpose of the paper is to consider the nature and unique features of such a tax and to evaluate its role in the tax structure, with particular emphasis on equity and economic effects. Only incidental reference will be made to actual use of this form of tax, an aspect which can be discussed far more adequately by persons from the countries involved (Fisher, 1958, pp. 84–93; Eigner, 1959, pp. 151–62).

The Nature of a Net Worth Tax

A net worth tax is a personal or direct tax, imposed upon individuals or families on the basis of their total personal wealth, on a net basis, that is, net of all liabilities outstanding. The base of the tax would thus include real property (land and buildings), tangible personal property (automobiles, jewelry, furniture, etc.), and intangibles, including stocks, bonds, notes, mortgages, cash, bank deposits, and the like. It would be possible, of course, to exclude certain items by specific exemption, but to do so would destroy the generality of the tax; the present paper is concerned with the form under which all types of property are taxable. The tax would of necessity be limited to individuals with the value of corporation property reached by assessment of the outstanding stocks and bonds to their holders. To include both tangible property of corporations and the securities of the corporation would constitute discriminatory double taxation. This feature of United States property taxation in the last century proved to be unworkable, and ultimately was for the most part discontinued, by practice or law.

Two major issues of a net worth tax system are those of exemptions and rate structure. In the interests of avoiding burden on the owners of small amounts of property, a certain monetary exemption could be provided, perhaps varied according to the number of dependents. However, some high-income families own little property and would receive unwarranted bonus from such an exemption. More logically, the exemption, if given, should be related both to total property held and income; persons with incomes, as defined for income tax purposes, below a certain figure would be exempt from tax on wealth up to a certain amount. Whether such an exemption should be provided depends upon the rate of tax, the intent of the use of the levy, as noted in the next section, and the general social philosophy of the government.

Much the same considerations affect the choice between progressive and proportional tax rates. If a primary purpose of the tax is to lessen the concentration of wealth, obviously progression is desirable. But if the purpose is that of a supplement to the income tax to adjust the overall burden to some extent in terms of wealth, proportional rates will be adequate, and will minimize adverse economic effects and troublesome questions relating to the definition of the taxable unit and the spreading out of property ownership over various members of the family.

The Role of the Tax

At this point the issue of the appropriate role of a net worth tax in the tax structure must be raised. There are several major possibilities. First, the tax could be imposed with the prime purpose of breaking up or checking the growth of large concentrations of wealth. Rarely has this been emphasized. Secondly, the tax, confined, through high exemptions, to the top level income groups, could be designed to serve as a means of supplementing the progression of the personal income tax in these income brackets without the potentially disastrous effects of income tax rates above certain levels. This is the position taken by Vickrey:

Thus practical considerations may impose limits on the degree of progression obtainable with income, spendings, and succession taxes alone. If still steeper progression is desired, a tax on net worth may provide a possible method of topping off the tax structure. Such a net worth tax would be an acceptable substitute for the continuation of graduation in the upper ranges of income, spendings, or successions taxes (Vickrey, 1947, pp. 362–63).

In like vein, the Shoup Mission report on Japanese taxation states:

The most satisfactory solution to the problem posed here (the impossibility, under the circumstances, of pushing income tax rates beyond 50 per cent) involves the imposition of an annual, low rate tax on the net worth of well-to-do individuals. ... A progressive tax on net worth ... could be given a high exemption so that it would take effect only where the income tax rate schedule levels off. ... Such a net worth tax would not be subject to most of the difficulties that militate against the retention of the high rates of income tax (U.S. Tax Mission to Japan, 1949, pp. 81–2).

Kaldor regards a net worth tax as a somewhat inferior substitute for an expenditure tax, designed to reach the spending power represented by capital wealth. 'The fact that capital and income constitute two distinct though mutually incomparable sources of spending power would certainly suggest that a separate tax on each provides jointly a better yardstick of taxable capacity than either form of taxation taken by itself ...' (Kaldor, 1955, p. 33). The wealth tax, like the spendings tax, would avoid the pressure of very high rates of the personal income tax necessary if the latter is used alone.

Finally, the tax could be conceived of as one of widespread application, as the American property tax, applying perhaps without exemptions to all families owning any property at all. The rationale of such a tax would essentially be that expressed in the quotation from Kaldor in the previous paragraph, except that Kaldor is thinking in terms of a tax limited to the higher income groups. The basic argument for such a tax, as noted below, is that of the desirability of considering wealth as well as income as a measure of tax capacity.

Shifting of a Net Worth Tax

Evaluation of any tax requires assumptions with regard to shifting, and in light of the difficulties in the ascertainment of shifting, they are usually little more than assumptions! On the whole it would appear difficult for persons to pass off the burden of the tax on to others. For most persons the liability for payment of tax would be completely unrelated to any market transactions, and thus direct and immediate shifting through price increases would be impossible. This is true of the portion of the tax on cash and bank deposits, securities, existing mortgages, homes, and all tangible personal property. In turn, the larger corporation could not conceivably shift forward the tax on the holdings of stockholders. In three instances, however, some direct shifting might occur. The market for new real estate mortgages is highly imperfect, and lenders might be able to pass the tax on in the form of higher interest rates. On rental housing, shifting would be possible under conditions of scarce supply, and perhaps over a longer period through the effects on the construction of new rental housing. Small business firms might seek to shift, but competition, particularly with larger corporations, would make price increases difficult. If a tax is truly general, there are serious obstacles in the way of shifting, except under certain peculiar conditions.

Thus any shifting of consequence could occur only through the effects of the tax upon supply of factors, and particularly of money capital. To the extent to which the tax reduced total savings, as discussed in the section on economic effects, there would be some tendency for the interest rate to rise, if permitted by monetary authorities. But, as subsequently explained, the tax will encourage persons to shift away from highly liquid cash holdings, a feature which tends to lower the interest rate. The net effect is difficult to predict, but is likely not to be of great consequence – given present day monetary policies.

The Basic Difference between Net Worth and Income Taxes

It is sometimes argued that a tax on net worth is essentially the same as an income tax on property income. It is quite true, of course, that – assuming a typical interest rate of 5 per cent – a tax of 20 per cent on income is the same in amount as a 1 per cent tax on the capital sum involved. Even in this instance there could be psychological differences in reaction to the tax and thus in its economic effects; taxpayers probably have a tendency to exaggerate the significance of the rate, as such, and thus may be influenced more by the 20 per cent income tax rate. And reactions designed to reduce tax liability may be very different with the two levies.

Quite apart from these reactions, the case of the holder of securities yielding a rate equivalent to the typical current capitalization factor is quite different from the entire spectrum of owners. First, the wealth tax includes in its base substantial property which does not yield a current income taxable under the usual income tax. True, some of these yields could be made taxable, but are not, and some, on cash holdings, for example, could not be made taxable on any basis. Accordingly, the tax rate necessary to raise a given sum is less than that which provides equivalence in burden between the income tax and the wealth tax on average-rate-of-interest investments.

Secondly, the relative burdens on the owners of securities of various returns will differ substantially. For the relatively low return holdings, including savings deposits in banks and other financial institutions, government and other high grade bonds, and similar investments, the tax will be greater with the net worth tax than with the equivalent-revenue income tax on property income. Above the breaking point, that is, on the higher yield securities, the wealth tax burden will be lower. Thus the net effect of substitution of the wealth tax for a portion of the income tax would be to increase the burden on non-cash-income holdings and high grade securities and reduce it on the high-return securities. Greatest increase in burden occurs for the holders of those types of investment which yield no money income subject to the usual income tax – cash, non-interest bearing bank deposits, homes (the imputed income of which is frequently not subject to tax, although it is in some countries), and consumer durable goods, such as automobiles.

Thirdly, and of particular significance from the standpoint of economic effects, the tax on wealth applies to the entire lump sum of wealth owned, whereas in a sense the income tax applies only at the margin – that is, to additional wealth. If a person has $10,000, he will be subject to income tax on it only if he earns additional income from it. But he will be subject to wealth tax on the entire sum regardless of what he does with it – so long as he continues to hold it in some form of wealth.

Also, the wealth tax does not reach increases in the value of wealth, as such, although, of course, the wealth tax liability will be higher in subsequent years if the property has increased in value. An income tax which applies to capital gains will reach the increase directly. Capital gains, however, usually receive favorable treatment relative to other income.

These comparisons have been made between a net worth tax and an income tax on property income, either a separate levy, or a portion of the regular income tax placing a higher rate on property income than labor income. If, however, a net worth tax is introduced to replace a portion of the income tax applying to all incomes, the net effect is to increase the relative burden on property holders and to reduce the amount of labor incomes.

The Equity Case for Net Wealth Taxation

In terms of usually accepted standards of equity in taxation, the case for net wealth taxation rests in part upon the basic doctrine that tax capacity is measured not only by income, but also by wealth. Without question, a person's economic well being – his capacity to obtain the fruits of production – depends primarily upon the income he receives during the period. But it also is influenced by what may be called his reserve spending power, the ability to spend from amounts inherited or previously accumulated. Two persons with families of equal size, each with $10,000 annual income, are not equally well off, in the sense of tax capacity, if one has $25,000 accumulated wealth and the other has $1000. The former will feel under less obligation to save, and thus can afford to spend more of his income; he can spend beyond his income if he wishes, by falling back on the wealth. The mere possession of wealth, in itself, is a source of prestige and feeling of security. A basic limitation of income taxation, if used as the sole source of revenue, is its tendency to discriminate against the persons who have not yet accumulated compared to those who have.

In part the same results could be attained by the placing of a heavier income tax burden on property income than on labor income. But the line between the two types of income is by no means sharp and becomes highly arbitrary, in practice, and the income tax approach is completely ineffective if the wealth is kept in non-monetary-income-yielding investments.

Secondly, the use of a net wealth tax provides greater equity among the holders of various types of securities, a result which cannot be attained merely by a higher income tax rate on property income. The income tax, which typically applies only to money income and does not reach the liquidity and security gains of low-interest bonds, the convenience gains of bank accounts, or the imputed income of homes and other consumer durables, discriminates against the holders of high-money-yield securities. Granted, tax cannot be paid from these various nonmonetary gains, and excessive reliance on a wealth tax would be even more discriminatory than excessive reliance on income taxation. But the income tax overlooks the relatively better wealth position of holders of low- and no-yield investments. Reform of the income tax could catch some of the imputed gains, but only with arbitrary elements in assessment, more arbitrary, probably, on the whole, than those involved in wealth tax assessment. And it could not possibly catch the liquidity gains of cash and near-cash investments.

Thirdly, the tax may allow attainment of greater overall progression in the tax structure than is possible with income taxation alone without serious adverse economic effects, as discussed in the following section.

Finally, a wealth tax, while not taxing increases in capital values, as such, does reach the higher values as they accrue. By contrast, the income tax, in practice, never reaches them until they are realized – and thus gives an incentive to avoid realization (the locked-in effect). Even when realized, the gains are taxed very inadequately, under the income tax laws of many countries.

As Kaldor has stressed, in large measure inadequacies of the income tax in reaching persons with disproportionate amounts of accumulated wealth could be overcome by a spendings tax rather than a wealth tax. But in this instance no tax is collected so long as the wealth is merely held, even though it is conveying important advantages to the holders during this period.

It should be obvious that while a strong case for a net wealth tax can be made on the basis of equity, such a tax must not become the primary revenue source. Of the two determinants of tax capacity, income and wealth, the former is the more significant, under usual circumstances. Excessive reliance on wealth taxation would create serious difficulties for persons with large wealth holdings and little current income, and free from appropriate tax burden persons with large incomes but little or no accumulations of wealth. The income and wealth taxes complement each other; in no sense are they 100 per cent substitutes, and the income basis (perhaps in combination with the spending basis) must remain the primary source of revenue.

The Economic Effects of the Wealth Tax

In terms of relative effects upon investment and economic development, several advantages are claimed for the net wealth tax as a substitute for a portion of the income tax on property income. Since the tax does not rest directly upon the gain from investment or expansion, but upon the total sum accumulated by the person, regardless of the gain made from it, the argument is advanced that the adverse effects will be less, per dollar of revenue. The advantage will be attained even if the income tax were proportional; it will be greater if the income tax is progressive (assuming the same revenue in each case). There is a significant psychological difference between a tax which impinges directly on income earned this year and one which applies to the accumulated earnings at a low rate over a period of years. The former can be avoided by not earning the income, the latter only by disposing of the wealth.

So far as corporation policy is concerned, since the wealth tax does not impinge directly on the corporation, as such, but only upon the security holders, the chances of direct influence on business decision making are less than that of a personal-corporate income tax system. The fact that a portion of the tax comes from non-income-yielding investments increases still more the likelihood that the wealth tax will have less deterring effect, per dollar of revenue.

Secondly, and closely related, is the argument that the tax will discourage risky ventures less than an income tax, particularly a progressive tax, since relatively more of the revenue will come from highly safe low yield securities, land held for speculation, consumer durables, and the like. Also the tax will have less influence than the income tax in deterring the purchase of stock in venturesome companies. This argument must be interpreted with some care, however. Domar and Musgrave have demonstrated that the usual views about the effects of income taxes on risk-taking are by no means entirely valid. With the allowance of loss offsets, total risk-taking in the economy will actually be increased by an income tax. Musgrave has also shown that a tax on capital will have less restrictive effect on risk-taking than an income tax (with loss offset) only under certain specific conditions, not as a generally valid rule (Musgrave, 1959, pp. 325-7).

Nevertheless, there is good reason to believe that typically the wealth tax is likely to have less effect, particularly when the income tax alternate is highly progressive. On the one hand, loss offsets are by no means perfect; under usual income tax laws, there are in practice serious limitations to the actual ability to offset losses, particularly by new and expanding firms. Secondly, the Musgrave analysis rests on the assumption that persons give equal weight to the probability of gains and losses, whereas it can be argued that there is a bias in the direction of optimism. If this is true, the loss offset is reduced in significance.

A third type of effect is the tendency of a wealth tax to push investments out of cash and low income securities into higher yield investments. The holding of cash is made more expensive, and some persons may be forced to shift in order to avoid having to pay the tax out of capital. Thus liquidity preference is reduced, and the interest rate will tend to fall, monetary authorities permitting. This effect is not inherently advantageous, except in period in which monetary authorities are having difficulty overcoming strong liquidity preference and lowering interest rates below certain levels. The relative shift toward equity capital, as compared to the situation with an income tax alternative, may be regarded as advantageous in terms of economic development. It must be recognized that the shift will bring adjustments in relative yield rates, with lessened differential returns on the various forms of investment, which will nullify in part the initial shift. But some net change is almost inevitable.

The relative effects of a net wealth tax and an income tax on property income on the savings-consumption ratio are difficult to assess. The wealth tax is likely to be paid to a somewhat greater extent directly from liquid savings, because some of the liability for tax will rest upon persons who have inadequate current income to meet payments from this source. From an incentive standpoint, the wealth tax cannot be avoided simply by holding the savings in cash form, as can the income tax. On the other hand, to the extent to which income is saved to provide funds for business expansion, the more favorable treatment given to equity investments by the wealth tax may tend to bring greater savings with this levy. Likewise, from a purely psychological point of view, the fact that the wealth tax is spread over the entire accumulation, whereas the income tax concentrates on the earnings from additional saving, may result in the former having less deterring effect. And, in general, the income tax is more likely to be highly progressive than the wealth tax. But, on the whole, the net effect is unpredictable.

A final effect of the wealth tax is the possible shifting of consumption expenditures from durable to nondurable forms. The purchase of consumer durables gives rise to tax liability, whereas other forms of consumption do not. The amounts placed in homes, particularly, may be reduced, an effect which, if widespread, would usually be regarded as objectionable, in light of the relative inadequacy of much housing in terms of standards regarded as socially desirable. The present property tax in the United States, which concentrates very heavily upon housing facilities, and has relatively high rates, is often criticized on this basis. A general net wealth tax, applying to all forms of personal wealth, would have less allocative effect of this type.

This whole discussion of economic effects has been based upon a comparison between a net worth tax and an income tax on property income yielding equivalent revenue. If the comparison were made between the net worth tax and an equivalent-revenue income tax on all income, the net effects would obviously be different. The greater relative burden on property income to which the wealth tax would give rise would offset to some extent the relative advantages which this tax has over an income tax on property income. The reduced tax on labor income, however, would lessen the effects of the tax structure on the work-leisure ratio and other aspects of labor supply. This issue has been discussed many times and need not be reviewed here. One point, however, warrants stress. The net worth tax applies only to investment in nonhuman capital. Thus incentive would be given to persons to invest more of their capital in education, which would not give rise to wealth tax liability, and less in other forms. The net effect would be one usually regarded as desirable.

In summary: the case for the net worth tax in terms of economic effects rests primarily upon the arguments, which appear to have some validity, that there would be less direct adverse effect upon business investment and expansion than an equivalent tax on property income, since the tax applies to the whole capital accumulation, not merely to the earnings from expansion, and would likely lead to some shift in investment in the direction of more risky ventures, which would be taxed less heavily than under the income tax. These merits can easily be exaggerated, but they are certainly of some significance, and reinforce the equity case for the net worth tax.

Other Considerations

A net wealth tax would be of substantial merit in facilitating enforcement of the income tax, and of any possible future expenditure tax. Reliable statements of net worth would greatly facilitate compilation of data of national wealth,[1] now seriously deficient relative to national income statistics. The tax would likewise facilitate the checking of concentration of economic power, if high progressive rates were employed, more effectively than any other levy – if this goal is accepted as one of paramount importance.

The Primary Problems of the Tax

Any form of annual wealth tax requires an annual valuation of

1. This significant point was suggested to me by my colleague, Professor Marvin Frankel.

property. This is a task inherently more difficult than the ascertainment of income, since a constructive figure is normally required. With many types of property, the task is not insuperable. Cash and bank deposits have stated monetary values, and most bonds and stock have readily ascertainable market value figures. Typical homes create only minor problems. The greater difficulties would arise with large closely held family businesses, with no public sale of shares. It must be recognized, of course, that once accurate figures were established initially, modifications for most of these figures from year to year would be slight.

Apart from the task of assessment is the problem of underreporting, that is, of failure of taxpayers to list all assets. With a nationally administered tax, this problem would not be as serious as it might appear, since cross checking between income and wealth tax returns would reveal many omissions. Taxpayers would realize that other properties would show up at time of death. Money and personal valuables such as jewelry would be perhaps the most troublesome items to find. The problem of finding all property virtually precludes use of the tax below the national level.

A third problem is that of the assessment date. Any wealth tax must solve this issue, which does not arise with income, sales, and most other levies. For many types of property the choice of date would not be significant, but, with others, such as bank balances, it would be, and some annual average figure might be necessary.

These administrative problems, together with the substantial audit program which would be required, have without question limited the introduction of net worth taxes. While they are significant, they are not insurmountable, and they should not be allowed to obscure the important advantages of the tax on the bases of equity and economic effects. A net worth tax used in conjunction with income taxation and perhaps some expenditure-based levies gives a much better balanced tax system, in terms of usual standards of taxation, than one concentrating on income or spending alone, and the potential dangers to economic development are less. The tax is far superior to the usual property tax, which concentrates on certain forms of property only and ignores liabilities outstanding against the property.

References

EIGNER, R. M. (1959), 'Indian income, wealth and expenditure taxes', *National Tax Journal*, vol. 12.

FISHER, J. A. (1958), 'Taxation of personal incomes and net worth in Norway', *National Tax Journal*, vol. 11. Translated from 'Statistisk sentralbyrå', *Samfunnsøkonomiske studier nr. 2: skatt på personleg inntekt og midel*, Oslo, 1954.

KALDOR, N. (1955), *An Expenditure Tax*, Allen & Unwin.

MUSGRAVE, R. A. (1959), *The Theory of Public Finance*, McGraw-Hill.

U.S. TAX MISSION TO JAPAN (1949), *Report on Japanese Taxation*, vol. 1, Scap.

VICKREY, W. (1947), *Agenda for Progressive Taxation*, Ronald Press.

7 Royal Commission on Taxation (Canada)

A Proposal for Taxation Reform

Excerpts from the *Report of the Royal Commission on Taxation (Canada)*, vol. 1, pp. 3–30; vol. 3, pp. 50–51; 1966.

Objectives

A tax system can be judged from different points of view. Is the system fair? Does it contribute as much as possible to the growth and stability of the economy? Are the rights and liberties of the individual protected? Does it help to strengthen the federation? These questions reflect not only the many facets of taxation but also what we believe to be the principal objectives that Canadians wish to realize through their tax system. They want equity, more goods and services, full employment without inflation, a free society and a strong, independent federation.

Evaluating an existing tax system or designing a new tax system is complicated because we seek to realize all of these objectives simultaneously and they are frequently in conflict. In trying to achieve one objective more fully, another is less adequately realized. For example, adopting a particular tax provision might increase the rate of economic growth. However, the same provision might also reduce the fairness of the system by providing some group of individuals with a tax advantage relative to others in the same circumstances. Similarly, making a tax system more equitable may necessitate increased complexity in the tax law. This greater complexity may mean that fewer individuals know and understand the law so that individual rights and liberties are jeopardized.

Sometimes these kinds of conflict can be avoided. Frequently, other methods can be found to achieve an objective that do not have the unwanted negative effects on other objectives. The negative effects of an otherwise desirable tax provision on an objective can often be compensated for by introducing or changing other tax provisions. Obviously every effort must be made to avoid spurious conflicts.

But some conflicts among objectives are unavoidable and compromises are inescapable. The 'best' compromise depends upon two things: estimates of the extent to which one objective will be sacrificed if another is to be realized more completely; and the relative importance attached to the competing objectives.

When faced with these hard choices we have consistently given the greatest weight to the equity objective. Taxation is one method of transferring command over goods and services from individuals and families to the state. If equity were not of vital concern taxes would be unnecessary. The state could simply commandeer what it needed. The burden of a reduced private command over goods and services would then be borne by those individuals and families who happened to be within easy reach of the state.

The first and most essential purpose of taxation is to share the burden of the state fairly among all individuals and families. Unless the allocation of the burden is generally accepted as fair, the social and political fabric of a country is weakened and can be destroyed. History has many examples of the severe consequences of unfair taxation. Should the burden be thought to be shared inequitably, taxpayers will seek means to evade their taxes. When honesty is dismissed as stupidity, self-assessment by taxpayers would be impossible and the cost of enforcement high. We are convinced that scrupulous fairness in taxation must override all other objectives where there is a conflict among objectives.

Equity Principles

Equity has two dimensions. Horizontal equity requires that individuals and families in similar circumstances bear the same taxes. Vertical equity requires that those in different circumstances bear appropriately different taxes. Two questions, therefore, have to be answered. What personal circumstances should be recognized in allocating tax burdens among individuals and families? By how much should tax burdens differ between those in one circumstance relative to those in another? These are both

143

questions of belief rather than of fact. We can do no more than recommend what we believe to be fair.

We believe that horizontal equity is achieved when individuals and families with the same gains in discretionary economic power pay the same amount of tax. By economic power we mean the power to command goods and services for personal use. By discretionary economic power we mean the residual power to command goods and services for personal use after providing the 'necessities' of life and after meeting family obligations and responsibilities. To be more concrete, some part of each family's income must be spent to provide food, clothing, medical expenses and other 'necessities'. The change in the discretionary economic power of the family is the income the family has available to spend or save after meeting these non-discretionary expenses.

We believe that vertical equity is achieved when individuals and families pay taxes that are a constant proportion of their discretionary economic power.

Both horizontal and vertical equity would be achieved by the adoption of a tax system that embodied the following principles:

1. The family and the unattached individual should be recognized as the basic tax-paying units in the system. The family unit would consist of parents and their dependent children. Transactions and transfers between members of a family unit would have no tax consequences.

2. All resident individuals and families should be taxed on a base that measures the value of the annual net gain or loss in the unit's power, whether exercised or not, to consume goods and services. Such a base would ignore the form of the gain or what was done to obtain the gain. We call this the comprehensive tax base. We also refer to it as 'income' because this term is so commonly used. Income to us has, however, a much broader meaning than that ascribed to it under current law.

3. This comprehensive tax base should be subject to progressive rates of tax. The progressive rates would reflect the diminishing relative importance of non-discretionary expenditures for those with larger gains in economic power.

4. The tax burdens of those with particularly heavy family and other obligations and responsibilities should be reduced to reflect the non-discretionary expenditures required to meet them. This

would be done through the adoption of separate rate schedules, tax credits and deductions.

Combined with a government expenditure system that provides relatively greater benefits for the poor than for the wealthy, a tax system with these characteristics would redistribute some of the power to consume goods and services in favour of the lowest income groups. We are firmly convinced that this redistribution is necessary if we are to achieve greater equality of opportunity for all Canadians and make it possible for those with little economic power to attain a decent standard of living. However, we are also convinced that the rates of tax which are applicable at any level of income should not be so high as to discourage initiative and thereby reduce the production of goods and services for Canadians.

Significance of Equity Principles

Adoption of these equity principles is of profound significance for this *Report*. Some of the more important considerations are discussed below.

The taxation of people versus the taxation of organizations

All taxes are ultimately borne by people through the reduction in their command over goods and services for personal use. Taxes can, of course, be collected not only from people but also from corporations, trusts and co-operatives. But organizations as such cannot bear taxes. It is the people who work for, sell to, buy from, or are members, beneficiaries or owners of these legal entities who are made better off or worse off by taxes. It is the effect of taxes on the well-being of people that matters.

Taxes on the income of organizations

If it were possible to determine each year the change in the value of each individual's claims against all organizations, and if all those who had claims against Canadian organizations were residents, and if avoidance and evasion were not problems, Canadian organizations should not be subject to income taxes. The shareholder (to consider only one kind of claim against one kind of organization) should bring into his tax base the dividends received from corporations during the year and the gain he made or

145

could have made during the year by selling all of his shares. These two things together constitute the change in the shareholder's economic power from the ownership of shares.

Unfortunately, the foregoing conditions cannot be met. We must continue to collect income taxes from organizations, for reasons that are discussed later. But in so far as the income of these organizations accrues to the benefit of Canadian resident individuals, these taxes on organizations should be considered as withholding taxes collected on behalf of the individuals. Residents should be given full credit for income taxes collected from Canadian corporations, co-operatives and trusts. We have called the provision of a full credit to residents for the underlying corporation tax, the integration of corporation and personal income taxes. Under our proposal the present 20 per cent dividend tax credit would be withdrawn. The integrated system we recommend would provide for the grossing-up of a dividend (in cash or stock) received by a resident shareholder to its pre-tax amount. That grossed-up amount would be included in income. The shareholder would then be permitted a full deduction from the tax otherwise payable of an amount equal to the corporation income tax attributable to the dividend. Where the credit exceeded the amount of tax otherwise payable the taxpayer would receive a refund.

The integration proposal would be limited to resident shareholders in respect of dividends received from Canadian companies. A partial credit would be allowed for foreign taxes on dividends from direct investment in foreign companies.

Sales taxes

Rigid adherence to our equity principles would call for the complete abolition of all sales taxes. Any adverse effects which the abolition of sales taxes and the increased reliance on personal income taxes would have on the rate of saving and on Canada's international competitive position could be offset by changes in monetary and trade policies and the fairness of the system would be improved. We do not advocate such a course, in part because we think that virtually the same result could be achieved in a way that would be less disruptive. For reasons to be explained later, we recommend that the federal government abandon its manufacturer's sales tax and replace it with an indirect retail sales tax collected, if possible, by the provinces. Having taken this step the federal government should then seek to provide the provinces with sales tax room in exchange for provincial withdrawal from the imposition of corporation income taxes. This exchange would be ruled out if the federal government left the sales tax field unilaterally.

At some point in the future when virtually all Canadian individuals and families are submitting income tax returns, and suitable means of protecting the revenue have been devised, residents could be provided, in lieu of sales tax exemptions, with arbitrary credits against their personal income tax liabilities for a portion of the sales taxes paid. However, adoption of the sales tax rate and base that we propose would ensure that sales taxes would not be regressive. We therefore do not consider the adoption of sales tax credits to be urgent.

However, we would like to see a gradual reduction in the relative importance of sales taxes in the Canadian tax mix as a method of increasing the progressiveness of the tax system. This should not be difficult to achieve. As the economy grows, the revenues from income taxes increase more rapidly than those from sales taxes. Thus, if sales tax rates were held at present levels and income tax rates were maintained, the result we seek would be achieved.

We recommend an immediate, although small, reduction in the relative weight of sales taxes by proposing that initially the federal government should impose tax at a 7 per cent rate on the new retail sales tax base. This rate, when applied to the proposed base, which would include some services, together with the elimination of some of the special excise taxes on so-called 'luxury' goods, would reduce federal sales and excise tax revenues by about 8 per cent.

The Comprehensive Tax Base

We are completely persuaded that taxes should be allocated according to the changes in the economic power of individuals and families. If a man obtains increased command over goods and services for his personal satisfaction we do not believe it matters,

147

from the point of view of taxation, whether he earned it through working, gained it through operating a business, received it because he held property, made it by selling property or was given it by a relative. Nor do we believe it matters whether the increased command over goods and services was in cash or in kind. Nor do we believe it matters whether the increase in economic power was expected or unexpected, whether it was a unique or recurrent event, whether the man suffered to get the increase in economic power or it fell in his lap without effort.

All of these considerations should be ignored either because they are impossible to determine objectively in practice or because they are irrelevant in principle, or both. By adopting a base that measures changes in the power, whether exercised or not, to consume goods and services we obtain certainty, consistency and equity.

For the vast majority, adoption of the comprehensive base would not result in great changes. Most employees, for example, are now taxed on a comprehensive tax base. To the few, particularly property holders, it would involve a great broadening of the tax base.

A large part of our *Report* is devoted to the development of specific recommendations that would implement the comprehensive tax base. But before describing the major features of the comprehensive tax base for particular kinds of gains we should indicate why we have rejected consumption and wealth as tax bases.

Consumption and wealth as tax bases

To tax consumption expenditures rather than income would be to exempt saving. To tax wealth rather than income would be to exempt consumption. With one exception we see no merit in exempting either saving or consumption. Because most individuals and families spend everything they earn during their lives, to change from a system that taxed what was spent rather than what was earned would simply change the time pattern of taxes throughout life. Taxing consumption rather than income would increase taxes for the young and the old, since youth and old age are the periods when consumption is high relative to income. It would reduce taxes in middle age when saving is typically at its peak. We do not think this would be an improvement.

Taxing wealth rather than consumption would obviously put those who obtain their income from their human capital (e.g. intelligence, knowledge, strength and skill) at an advantage relative to those who obtain their economic power from the ownership of property. It would penalize those who save relative to those who consume. We do not believe that property holders should be able to escape, as they do at present, paying taxes on much of the economic power they derive from their property. But we also do not believe that they should bear a heavier tax burden than those who obtain the same economic power from human capital. It is what you get, not how you get it, that should count for tax purposes.

We would, however, make one important exception. Through the special deductions now available for contributions to retirement savings, individuals are encouraged to save for retirement. This is a worthwhile social objective that the tax system can help to achieve. We therefore recommend that within limits retirement contributions should continue to be deductible.

Adoption of a tax system with retirement savings deductible without limit would convert an income tax system into a modified consumption expenditure tax system. That far we are not prepared to go. We propose stringent limits on the amounts that could be deducted in computing income. These limits would be related to the pension that could be obtained at the age of sixty-five rather than to an amount that could be deducted in a given year. This, we believe, would put an end to the abuses of the present provisions by a few upper income individuals, and yet would permit flexibility in the timing of contributions.

Under our proposals the tax treatment of the earnings of pension funds would be liberalized, and there would be great flexibility in the investment of pension funds, so that retirement savings would become more attractive than they are now. The limits we suggest are sufficiently high that low and middle income individuals and families would be free to choose to be taxed on an income basis or an expenditure basis depending upon how much they wished to save for retirement.

Employment income

Adoption of the comprehensive tax base would have less effect on the taxation of employment income than on most other kinds of income. However, some benefits in kind are now escaping tax, and strong measures should be taken to stop this abuse. On the other side, the failure to allow the deduction of expenses of earning employment income should be corrected.

Relative to other kinds of taxpayers many employees have been overtaxed. Tax has been withheld at source and the deduction of virtually all the expenses of earning that income has been denied. Drawing the line between the expenses of earning income and personal living expenses is exceedingly difficult, but we think that the present treatment has been too severe for many employees and often too generous for the self-employed.

The prohibition against the deduction of the expenses of earning employment income should be withdrawn and employees should be entitled to deduct the expenses reasonably related to earning income, as are proprietors and partners. To reduce the administrative problem to manageable proportions, employees should be entitled to deduct the greater of an arbitrary proportion of their employment income or their actual expenses.

The administration has not been sufficiently stringent in bringing employee benefits in kind into tax. Faced with high taxes on money income on the one hand, and the possibility of no tax on non-cash benefits on the other, employers and employees have found it attractive to substitute the one for the other. Free or subsidized meals, trips, homes, discounts, insurance policies and so on, are being accepted as remuneration to the mutual benefit of the employer and employee and to the detriment of the revenue and of other employees whose taxes are correspondingly higher. To stop this trend we recommend that employers should either add the value of all non-cash benefits to the tax base of the employee or pay a high tax on the amount not allocated to employees.

The 'expense account living' problem may not be of great significance from a revenue point of view. The amounts involved in aggregate are probably not great. But the suspicion that some are enjoying exotic holidays, lavish food and drink and expensive entertainment out of untaxed income is demoralizing even if frequently ill-founded.

Seeking out new tax dodges becomes a game; boasting about 'getting away' with an outrageous abuse, a pleasure; hearing of the opportunities missed, a torment. To stop 'expense account living' we propose some arbitrary rules that undoubtedly will be castigated as unreasonable. We frankly admit that some of them are stringent. That is exactly what we intend. The problem of taxpayer morale is serious and the strongest measures are called for. We deny that the rules we propose are unreasonable, however, relative to the alternatives. This is an area where generalities are useless and specific – if arbitrary – rules are the only solution.

Property income

The decision to tax the annual changes in the economic power of each tax unit rather than 'income', as it is now defined, has dramatic consequences.

For adoption of the comprehensive tax base requires the taxation of not only income from property, but also 'capital' gains on the disposition of property. Almost everyone is familiar, at least in a general way, with the difference between 'income' and 'capital', even though the words seem to be incapable of precise definition. Capital is the source of income. By levying a tax on 'income' the distinction between the two concepts takes on great significance, for if the courts find a particular gain to be 'capital' the transaction is not now taxable. There is an enormous incentive for the taxpayer to try to transform 'income' gains into 'capital' gains. However, it is impossible to draw an unambiguous distinction between 'capital' gains and 'income' gains and the attempt to do so necessarily results in great uncertainty for the taxpayer because a particular transaction may or may not be found by the courts to fall on one side of the line or the other.

After the most careful and exhaustive consideration of this complex question, we have arrived at the conclusion that the present distinction between kinds of gain is inconsistent with our concept of what we believe 'income' is for the purposes of determining the individual's capacity to pay tax.

Because tax postponement can be so valuable, taxpayers may be induced to hold property for a longer period than they otherwise would to avoid realization. This 'locking in' can also have unfortunate economic effects. Therefore, we recommend that the legislation should be very definite in designating most transactions to be dispositions, and therefore realizations. Thus, virtually all exchanges of property should be treated as leading to realizations. More important, we feel it is imperative that a realization be deemed to take place at least once in each taxpayer's lifetime (or in the lifetime of his surviving spouse) to ensure that postponement does not become indefinite deferment. Therefore, for reasons of taxpayer equity, and to reduce the economic disadvantages of 'locking in', we recommend that when an individual makes a gift of property or gives up Canadian residence he should be deemed to have made a disposition of property, except in the case of a gift or legacy to a member of his family unit. When an individual dies a realization should also be deemed to take place, except in the case of property passing to a surviving member of his family unit. If a child comes of age and takes property from his former family unit, there should be a deemed disposition of the property by that unit. The net gain or loss on a deemed disposition or realization would be brought into the tax base of the individual who is deemed to have made the disposition. He would have the opportunity of availing himself of the averaging provisions which we will recommend.

While valuation and liquidity problems are posed by the taxation of unrealized property gains, it is essential to recognize that when we back away from this approach for administrative reasons other complications are created, particularly when the income is earned by an intermediary in which it can be retained in order to postpone personal income tax liabilities.

If the full taxation of property gains would result in dire economic consequences or hopelessly complex administrative questions, some backing away from equity principles could be justified. We are satisfied that neither result would come about.

Accordingly, we recommend the full taxation of realized property gains. To prevent unwarranted postponement, to minimize the 'locking-in' effect, and to stop residents from avoiding the tax altogether by leaving the country, property gains should be deemed to have been realized on the death of the owner (unless the property passes to a surviving spouse or other member of the family unit) or on his leaving the country. For administrative

152

reasons we recommend a lifetime exemption of $25,000 on realized real property gains on residences and farms.

Simply to adopt the full taxation of capital gains as a modification of the present system could be disastrous, as critics of the taxation of these gains assert. This is not what we are recommending. The effects of taxing capital gains in full can only be assessed as one feature of an entirely new system. The new system would have:

1. Much reduced marginal personal rates of tax.

2. Averaging provisions of unparalleled liberality.

3. Loss provisions that would remove any tax bias against risk taking.

4. Full credit to residents for Canadian corporation taxes.

5. More efficient incentives for new and small businesses.

When the taxation of capital gains is only one component of a package with these features, we can dismiss the claims that it would destroy initiative, reduce saving, and drive people out of the country.

We have no intention that the taxation of property gains should be retroactive. Accordingly, we propose that only gains accruing after the effective date of the legislation should be subject to taxation, with a liberal option to avoid the necessity of a multitude of valuations.

The charge that to tax capital gains would raise no revenue and create great complexity can also be readily disproved. Even with the taxation of capital gains at half rates, and no deemed realization on death, the taxation of capital gains in the United States provides a significant proportion of federal revenues. However, we wish to emphasize that, even if our proposals for taking capital gains and losses into account in computing income produced no revenue, we would nevertheless recommend that they be taken into account for the reasons that we have outlined. Administrative complexity would actually be reduced by the full taxation of capital gains, as it is the attempt to distinguish between capital and income gains, in order to tax the one at a different rate than the other, that creates the complexity and uncertainty.

The concept of economic power, as we have defined it, clearly calls for including in the tax base not only what the tax unit actually consumes or gives to other tax units, but also the change in the market value of the net assets retained by the unit. Therefore, it is our view that, in principle, unrealized gains should be brought into the tax base. But some rights to, or interests in, property are both unique and infrequently traded, so that it is difficult and expensive to estimate their market value at a particular point in time. Probably the most important and difficult valuation problems are posed by closely held businesses. In addition, taxing changes in the value of assets that have not been sold would in some cases create liquidity problems, for it may be necessary for the individual to dispose of part of his assets in order to obtain cash to meet the tax liability. In many cases this would not be practical, although this problem, to the extent it exists, could be reduced by allowing taxpayers time to pay their taxes. Although we do not believe that the valuation and liquidity problems are insoluble we recommend that at least initially gains should only be taken into the tax base upon realization.

It should be recognized that where only realized net gains and losses are taken into the tax base, it is possible for tax units to postpone taxes. Just as cash in hand is worth more than cash that will be received in the future, so are postponed taxes less costly than present taxes because the cash that would otherwise be turned over to the government can be invested to earn a return until the tax actually has to be paid.

Business income

We will not attempt to describe in detail the many changes we propose in the measurement of business income for tax purposes. They are, by their nature, highly technical. The most important are:

1. Elimination of the problem of 'nothings' (business expenses that cannot be deducted for tax purposes at any time).

2. Elimination of many arbitrary rules, and hence greater reliance on accounting practices, in the tax treatment of reserves.

3. Recognition of the last-in-first-out method as an acceptable method of inventory accounting under restricted conditions.

4. Adoption of less stringent limitations on the deduction, carry-forward and carry-back of business losses.

5. Provision of more stringent limitations on losses created by the deduction of personal expenses.

6. Introduction of a system of rapid write-offs of capital expenses as an incentive for new and small businesses. This incentive would be more efficient, and less open to abuse, than the low rate of corporation tax on the first $35,000 of corporate income. The low corporate rate should be withdrawn.

Gifts, inheritances and windfall gains

Consistent with the principle that all increases in economic power should be taxed without regard to kind or source, all gifts, inheritances, and windfall gains should be brought into the tax base. We would, however, ignore gifts, including inheritances, between members of a family unit (as defined below). Lifetime and annual exemptions for gifts received from outside the family would be provided to reduce the administrative problem to manageable proportions. These exemptions would mean that most people would never pay tax on any gifts. The proposed system would be much more effective than the present gift tax in bringing large gifts into the tax net. The present tax is often avoided.

Non-charitable gifts should not be deducted from the tax base of those who make them. Making a gift is an exercise of economic power and should be treated in the same way as any other personal expenditure. Gifts to charity should, however, be deducted from the tax base, subject to certain conditions and limitations.

Government transfer payments

The comprehensive tax base calls for the inclusion of all kinds of gains. We would not exempt from this rule government transfer payments, such as family allowances, old age security payments, unemployment insurance benefits and workmen's compensation payments. We would, however, allow the deduction of specific contributions to these transfer programmes. In recommending that these government transfer payments be brought into the tax base we do not prejudge the adequacy of the payments made under such programmes. The amounts of the benefits and contributions should be reviewed in the light of our recommendations. But we are convinced that the consistent application of the rule we suggest would remove many of the anomalies that now exist; for example, a man who works part of the year and obtains unemployment insurance part of the year may pay less tax than another man who receives the same income and works all of the year.

Families and Individuals as Tax Units

The present system recognizes only the individual and not the family as a unit for tax purposes. This has certain undesirable consequences. A couple with one income recipient often pay substantially more tax than another couple with the same aggregate income derived by both spouses. If a man with a substantial salary marries a woman with a substantial independent income, their aggregate tax is not changed by their marriage. Yet it is clear that their discretionary economic power is greater because of economies which can be realized by living together.

Because income splitting results in important and unwarranted tax savings, married business proprietors would find it advantageous to hire their wives at high salaries to perform nominal duties if this were not prohibited. The prohibition results in anomalies. If the proprietor's wife does in fact perform productive work for the business the proprietor and his wife would be better off, from a tax point of view, if the wife worked elsewhere and the proprietor hired another person to do the same work. The man who owns and manages an incorporated business can often circumvent the prohibitions by having 'the corporation' hire his wife.

We therefore recommend in this *Report* that the income of families should be aggregated and taxed as a unit on a separate rate schedule. The rules against income splitting could largely be withdrawn because splitting would have no significance.

The most serious consequence of the failure to accept the family as a taxable unit arises when wealth is transferred from one spouse to another. Although in most families wealth accumulated by a couple is the result of their joint efforts and decisions, the passing of property from one spouse to another is a taxable event. Exemptions provide some relief, but we believe that the taxation of these intra-family transfers is wrong in principle. On the other hand, we have expressed our belief that all increases in the economic power of the taxpayer, regardless of their source, provide the same increase in tax-paying capacity. Thus, all gifts or bequests received from outside the family unit should be included in the comprehensive tax base.

We are of the opinion that the present system of gift and death taxes, both federal and provincial, is an anachronism. Through the use of personal corporations, trusts and exemptions, it is possible to avoid and postpone substantial gift and death taxes. These taxes almost certainly are not effective in breaking up pockets of wealth held by family dynasties, as is sometimes believed. They can, however, make it extremely difficult for a man to maintain his widow in the style she enjoyed when he was alive by substantially reducing the amount of property left for her support, even though he could not have accumulated the property without his wife's help.

We recommend an entirely different system. The present gift and death taxes should be withdrawn and transfers of wealth within family units should have no tax consequences. Transfers of wealth from one family unit to another tax unit should be taxed at full progressive rates to the recipient tax unit, subject to small annual exemptions and a $5000 lifetime exemption. Transfers of wealth between husbands and wives and between parents and minor children would not therefore come within the purview of the tax system at all. However, when children leave home, all property taken from the family, with certain exemptions for administrative convenience, would be taxable to the child. Any subsequent transfers from the family to the grown-up son or daughter, or to anyone else for that matter, should be taxed to the recipient. The family would ordinarily cease to exist on the death of the last surviving spouse. Property passing to other individuals or families on the termination of the family unit would also be taxable to the recipients.

Progressive Rates of Tax

Should taxation be progressive or proportionate? This is one of the most contentious issues in taxation. Our answer is clear and unequivocal. The tax base of each family and unattached individual should be subject to progressive rates of tax. Because we believe that non-discretionary expenses absorb a much larger proportion of the annual additions to the economic power of those with low income than of the wealthy, in order to attain the pro-

157

portionate taxation of discretionary economic power, we recommend that a base that measures total economic power be taxed at progressive rates.

It is not possible to measure accurately the proportion of a family's income that is required to meet non-discretionary expenses. What constitutes a 'necessity' and what constitutes a 'luxury' is essentially subjective. The wealthy man's necessities are the poor man's luxuries; with a rising income what was once a luxury becomes a necessity. A progressive rate structure that attempts to reflect the diminishing relative importance of non-discretionary expenses as income rises can only reflect a judgement of what is fair and reasonable.

The personal income tax schedules we recommend do have one anchor point, however. The rate schedules have a top marginal rate of 50 per cent. We think there is psychological merit in a rate structure that would limit the state's claim against a man's additional income to one half. In our opinion, it is essential that the marginal rates of tax be kept low enough that the incentive to produce goods and perform services and invest funds is not destroyed.

There is also a more concrete reason for advocating this top rate of 50 per cent. A substantial part of the net economic benefit that Canada secures from foreign direct investment in Canada is the revenue derived from levying income and withholding taxes on non-resident-controlled Canadian corporations. To push the present rate of tax on corporations higher would deter foreign investment; to reduce the rate would transfer revenue from the Canadian treasury to foreign treasuries. The 50 per cent corporate rate, therefore, should not be changed.

As already indicated, we propose that resident shareholders should receive full credit for corporation taxes. With a corporate rate of 50 per cent, if personal marginal rates of more than 50 per cent were adopted, upper income individuals could postpone their taxes by retaining profits in the corporations they controlled. It is essential to recognize that the postponement of taxes is equivalent to the reduction of taxes; indefinite postponement is equivalent to the elimination of a tax. The possibility of postponement biases corporation decision making, puts great pressure on taxpayers to discover means of realizing the retained earnings at less than the full rate of personal tax, and provides upper income shareholders with an advantage relative to upper income individuals who obtain their income in other ways, for example, by working for a salary. These serious problems can be eliminated by adopting a top marginal rate of tax that is not significantly higher than the corporate rate of 50 per cent.

The top marginal rate is now about 80 per cent, and applies to income in excess of $400,000. In our opinion, rates as high as this are on the statute books only because they are readily avoided by most of the few wealthy people with incomes of this size. By transforming income into non-taxable forms and through a myriad of tax avoidance techniques, the 80 per cent rate can be effectively circumvented, so that the effective marginal rate is much lower. Indeed, the effective average rate of tax on all income, including property gains, is now probably no more for extremely wealthy people than it is for those with much lower incomes.

We have examined the weight of total taxes on groups of families and individuals with different incomes as well as the value of the government benefits they receive, and find that while most middle and upper income taxpayers are net contributors to government, many of those at the very top are not making net contributions that are sufficiently large relative to their discretionary economic power. Broadening the base as we recommend, and lowering the rates as we propose, would increase the weight of tax on many families and individuals because the lower marginal rates would be more than offset by the broader base.

The present tax system, combined with the present system of government expenditures, particularly the system of transfer payments, such as family allowances, old age pensions and unemployment insurance, redistributes goods and services in favour of those at the bottom of the income scale. This is as it should be. However, the present system of transfer payments has important gaps. While the indigent as a group are net beneficiaries of government, some unfortunate families and individuals who do not benefit materially from government programmes are net contributors to government rather than net beneficiaries. This inequity can be removed either by reforming the system of government transfer payments to fill the gaps or by reducing personal income tax liabilities for those who are wholly or partially dependent upon gifts or allowances for subsistence. Pending a review of the former matter, which is quite outside our terms of reference, we believe that most low income families should pay lower taxes. As we show later, we believe that the adoption of our recommendation would have this result.

Specific Non-Discretionary Expenditures

Through the progressive rate structure it is possible to reflect the reduced relative importance of non-discretionary expenses generally as income rises. There are, however, specific non-discretionary expenditures that should also be taken into account if equity is to be achieved.

We have already said that the system should recognize both families and unattached individuals as taxable units. This raises the question of the appropriate relationship between the taxes imposed on families and unattached individuals; on families with children relative to those with no children; and on families with one child relative to those with, say, ten children.

In our opinion a childless couple should pay lower taxes than an unattached individual with the same income. This difference would reflect the fact that two cannot live as cheaply as one. But when two people with incomes marry, and both continue to receive these incomes, their total tax should increase, because there are economies in living together. These tax differentials can be obtained by adopting two separate rate schedules: one to be applied to aggregate family income and another to be applied to the income of unattached individuals.

With separate rate schedules the present system of personal exemptions for the taxpayer and his or her spouse can be eliminated. The same result can be achieved in a simpler way by the use of a first income bracket taxed at a zero rate. This is what has been done in the proposed rate schedules. The significance of such a change is to bring closer together income and taxable income. Taken by itself it has no impact on the calculation of an individual's taxes.

The present system takes into account the non-discretionary expenses of raising children by providing parents with an exemption for each child. The size of the exemption is affected by the eligibility of the child for family allowances. This approach has two weaknesses. First, it does not recognize that the first child involves greater non-discretionary expenditures than subsequent children. The parents often must find different and more expensive accommodation, equipment must be bought and, most important of all, the mother must either stop working or hire someone to look after the child. Subsequent children involve additional costs, but they are not as great as for the first child. The second weakness is that the present exemptions for dependants provide a greater benefit to those with larger incomes.

These faults can be overcome by the use of tax credits for children, with a larger credit for the first child than for the others. This we have recommended.

Most medical expenses are clearly non-discretionary expenses. Taxes, therefore, should be lowered for those who have unusually heavy expenses of this type. The 3 per cent of income floor should be retained as a rough-and-ready dividing line between the exceptional and the 'ordinary' medical expense. Only out-of-pocket expenses in excess of this floor should be deducted and not, as at present, amounts reimbursed through insurance. The standard deduction for medical expenses should be withdrawn.

Working mothers with young children are faced with substantial non-discretionary expenses. A tax credit should be provided to taxpayers in this situation.

The present deductions for the costs of post-secondary education should be abandoned and a system of transferable credits adopted that would be of greater value to low income parents and students. Living costs of students taking such education should also be recognized.

The administrative procedure for granting deductions for charitable donations should be revised to protect the treasury.

Distorting Effects of the Tax System

The narrow tax base and some extremely expensive incentive or concessionary provisions built into the present system mean that, to raise the required revenue, tax rates have to be higher than would otherwise be necessary, and the tax burden on some is therefore correspondingly heavier. This has the effect of driving labour and capital away from activities that are heavily taxed and drawing them into tax-favoured activities. Unless these pressures nicely compensate for non-tax distortions in the market, labour and capital are less productively employed than they should be. Fewer goods and services are available for Canadians. Some features of the tax system that unduly narrow the base have already been described. Other incentive or concessionary provisions that have a high revenue cost are:

1. The low rate of corporation tax on the initial $35,000 of taxable income.

2. The depletion allowances for the mining and petroleum industries.

3. The three-year exemption for new mines.

4. Inadequate taxation of the business income of life insurance companies.

All of these concessions should be withdrawn. More effective incentives could be provided at much lower revenue cost. The extra revenues could be used to reduce rates on business income generally.

The present system also has a number of specific biases that can only have a detrimental effect on the allocation of labour and capital. Among the most important are those listed below:

1. The stringent treatment of business losses makes investment in risky enterprises less attractive because the government shares in the gains while the investor may have to bear all of the losses.

2. Inadequate averaging provisions make activities that produce 'bunched' income less attractive.

3. Inconsistent tax treatment of various forms of business organization (partnerships, proprietorships, corporations, trusts and co-operatives) penalizes some activities that are unable to adopt the most advantageous form of organization. This bias arises largely because of the so-called 'double' taxation of corporate source income.

4. Retained earnings of corporations are given a tax advantage and high rates of distribution are penalized by the 'double' tax on dividends and the failure to tax share gains. Tax considerations thus distort the pay-out policy of corporations.

5. Purchases of Canadian equities by Canadian financial institutions are discouraged because these institutions do not benefit from the dividend tax credit.

All of these biases can and should be removed.

The Use of the Tax System to Compensate for Market Distortions

At least in the present state of our knowledge the market usually provides the best mechanism for allocating productive facilities and services so that people obtain the largest output of the goods and services they want. We are anxious that the tax system interfere as little as possible with this allocation. However, the market does not work perfectly and can distort the allocation of the means of production just as the tax system can. In particular, we believe that the capital market is biased against new, small risky enterprises. The tax system can be used to offset that bias and we propose some incentives for that purpose. In addition to the full credit to resident shareholders for corporation taxes, there should be:

1. A more liberal treatment of losses, including the full write-off against all other income of any losses in the initial years of a new business.

2. An immediate write-off of capital costs for new businesses up to a specified limit.

3. Continuation of the immediate write-off of exploration and development expenses for mining and oil companies.

4. Continuation of the exemption from taxation of the income of qualified retirement savings funds (including capital gains) until it is distributed to individuals.

5. Continuation of the immediate write-off of research and development expenditures, possibly complemented by subsidies.

6. Tax credits for post-secondary education and training.

Together these incentives would provide a substantial inducement to greater technical progress, risk taking and initiative.

Integration of Personal and Corporation Income Taxes

As stated earlier, we believe that resident shareholders should be given full credit for Canadian corporation taxes. We believe this to be in the interest of Canadian consumers.

It is frequently argued that shareholders should not be given credit for underlying corporation taxes because corporations pass such taxes on, typically by charging higher prices for what they sell, sometimes by paying less for what they buy. We accept that this is often true, but do not think it is a valid objection to the full credit to shareholders.

163

Corporation taxes are 'passed on' in two ways: through immediate increases in prices or reductions in costs that quickly restore the after-tax rate of return to corporate assets; through gradual increases in product prices (relative to what they otherwise would be) resulting from reduced capital spending and hence output. In the former case the corporation tax is a crude and regressive sales tax. In the latter case the corporation tax is a crude and inequitable tax on wealth, because the tax is borne by those who happen to hold the 'wrong' shares at the time the tax is imposed. These shareholders bear the tax because it is capitalized in lower share prices.

Consumers are worse off in either case. Either their real purchasing power is reduced because prices are higher or wages are lower or there are fewer goods and services available.

The important issue is, of course, what would happen if full credit was allowed for corporation taxes now. Here again there are two possibilities. The tax reduction on corporate source income could be quickly passed on to consumers through lower prices or passed on to workers through higher wages. The tax reduction could be capitalized in higher share prices. Only when the corporation was completely insulated from the competition provided by the entry of new firms attracted by the higher after-tax rate of return to shareholders would the full amount of the tax reduction likely be capitalized in the price of the shares. Few corporations have such a monopoly position. Probably the rise in share prices would be relatively small. If the tax reduction was not shifted quickly through lower prices, the higher after-tax rate of return to shareholders would stimulate capital spending, increased output and lower product prices and hence push down after-tax rates of return toward earlier levels. This process of adjustment would take a substantial period of time.

Consumers would benefit from the corporation tax credit if the tax reduction was passed on in lower prices or brought about increased output or both. Consumers generally would not benefit from the corporation tax credit if the tax reduction was simply reflected in higher share prices without any increase in capital expenditures and output.

We are confident that the instances of full capitalization of the tax reduction without favourable price and output effects would be the exception rather than the rule. To deny the tax reduction because the shareholders of a few corporations would obtain windfall share gains would be to cut off our collective noses to spite our collective faces. We would be denying ourselves greater output from the economy generally to ensure that the few did not get what they did not deserve. There are other methods for dealing with corporations that have massive and persistent monopoly power. To design a tax system to suit the exceptional case would be to lose all perspective.

Another advantage of the integration of corporation and shareholder taxes and the full taxation of property gains would be the prevention of tax avoidance. Under this system profits of all kinds and from all sources would be taxable in the same manner. Accordingly, there would be relatively little incentive to arrange transactions in such a way as to change the form of payment. The basic inconsistencies in our law which have resulted in widespread 'surplus-stripping' and other abuses would be eliminated. This result is, in our view, further evidence of the fundamental soundness of the system we propose.

Full Taxation of Share Gains

While we believe that resident shareholders should be given full credit for Canadian corporation taxes, we also believe that share gains should be taxed in full. These proposals should be considered as two sides of the same coin and not as two separate and separable proposals. The integration of personal and corporation income taxes through the full credit device would substantially reduce the weight of tax on Canadian corporate source income for residents; the full taxation of share gains would have the opposite effect. We have satisfied ourselves that, with the rates of personal tax that we propose, the net effect of the two changes would be to reduce the weight of tax on most Canadian corporate source income attributable to residents. Only some shareholders, particularly those holding shares in the extractive industries and life insurance companies and companies in special circumstances, would be worse off.

With lighter taxes on corporate source income the cost of equity capital would be reduced. This would increase capital spending and provide Canadians with more goods and services in the future.

Foreign Ownership and Control

The integration of personal and corporation income taxes would have another important and valuable side effect. Because full credit for Canadian corporation taxes would be confined to residents, and because Canadians would find holding Canadian shares more attractive than they do now, we expect that Canadian share prices would rise despite the full taxation of share gains. The cost of equity capital in Canada would be reduced. Canadian corporations, including those controlled by non-residents, would be encouraged to offer more shares to Canadians. This would be as effective or more effective an incentive for Canadian ownership than the lower withholding tax that is now in effect for corporations that have the desired degree of Canadian ownership. It would not have the same drawbacks.

The tax system could be used, in conjunction with other policies, to reduce our dependence on foreign capital, but this would result in a reduced growth rate or require reduced current consumption. It is by no means obvious that Canadians would thereby achieve greater economic independence.

[. . .]

The Commission has reached the following conclusions:

1. The present system does not afford fair treatment for all Canadians. People in essentially similar circumstances do not bear the same taxes. People in essentially different circumstances do not bear appropriately different tax burdens.

2. Canadians are less well off than they could be because there are fewer goods and services available than could be provided with the more efficient use of labour, capital and natural resources. The present tax system has contributed to this unfortunate result in two ways:

(a) it needlessly distorts the distribution of productive goods and services;

(b) it fails to compensate where it could for some non-tax barriers to the efficient allocation of productive goods and services.

3. The fiscal system has not been used as effectively as it could have been used to maintain full employment, contain inflationary increases in the price level, and encourage Canadian ownership and control of Canadian industry.

4. In some tax fields compliance and collection costs have been needlessly raised because of duplicate federal and provincial administrations.

5. Federal tax administration is not sufficiently shielded from political influence and is too centralized for efficiency and convenience.

6. Federal procedures used to obtain and analyze new ideas prior to the introduction of new federal tax legislation are inadequate, as are the procedures for hearing the views of taxpayers and other interested parties on proposed legislation.

7. Federal administrative and judicial appeal procedures are deficient and require reforms.

We are fully aware that these conclusions constitute a severe criticism of the present tax system. They were not arrived at lightly nor are they the inevitable result of preconceived opinions. Our bias when we began our task was that the present system was basically sound and compared favourably with the systems of other countries. While we are still of the opinion that the present Canadian tax system is as good as most other systems, we are convinced that it falls far short of the attainable objectives. We therefore recommend many fundamental changes which, if adopted, would produce a complete transformation and, we believe, result in greater equity and efficiency.

We hope Canadians will accept the challenge implicit in our recommendations. And there can be no doubt that our recommendations constitute a great challenge. Preconceived opinions about taxation are deeply and firmly held. Many will find it extremely difficult to take a new look at old questions. Because some facts cannot be readily ascertained, honest differences of opinion are inevitable. There is a danger that the debate about these minor factual questions will divert attention from the major issues.

It seems unlikely that a similar close and objective inquiry into the tax system of any country in the world would find a more satisfactory state of affairs.

Part Two
The Choice between Private and Public Goods

There are certain objectives – the defence of the realm is the most obvious example – which if achieved for any one citizen are achieved for all; they may well be beyond the reach of an individual acting alone. Once this is recognized, taxes contributed to finance such government exhaustive expenditures take on something of the character of subscriptions to club membership or payment for value received. The existence of objectives which are attained for (and perhaps only attainable by) society as a whole raises an interesting allocation problem: how are the community's resources to be distributed between the satisfaction of public collective wants and the satisfaction of private wants? Many writers in the Anglo-Saxon tradition have avoided detailed consideration of this question to concentrate on the differential effects of particular ways of financing a (presumably politically) determined level of government expenditure. The great Pigou, whose *Economics of Welfare* is the *locus classicus* of the economic case for government intervention to improve the market-determined allocation of resources, deals summarily with the question of government expenditure in the excerpt from his *Public Finance* which is included in this part (Reading 8).

Clearly, a satisfactory general theory of public expenditure requires the simultaneous determination of the level of public goods provision and of tax payments. Professor Samuelson (Reading 9a), one of the leading contributors to the development of the 'new' welfare economics, in the article printed here [described by one reviewer as 'perhaps the best value for two and half pages in our subject' (Bliss, 1967, p. 344)] demonstrates beautifully the limits to the assistance economic theory affords in answering these questions. The concept of the pure public good is introduced and the Pareto-type equilibrium conditions for a mix of private and public goods are developed. Margolis' 'Comment' (Reading 9b) raises a number of important issues, and with Samuelson's further articles helps to provide clarification of the public goods concept. The second Samuelson paper (Reading 9c) contains a magnificent statement of the considerations from which public expenditure and regulation proceed.

Some perplexities are avoided if it is borne in mind that there is not necessarily a one-to-one correspondence between wants and the physical goods that satisfy them: a good may minister to a number of different wants – one has only to think of the multifarious uses of water. A prolonged search might well fail to disclose a distinct physical commodity which exactly conformed with the Samuelson concept of a public good.[1] It would then not be sensible to abandon the concept, any more than to abandon the concept of a pure private good because of uncertainty as to whether there is anything the production and/or consumption of which confers no benefits or costs on third parties. The importance of external economies and dis-economies which are the unpriced by-products of private sector activities is that in their presence the composition of private sector output may well be non-optimal. Now, while unpriced goods or services are underprovided when produced in association with others which can be priced, *they are separately not provided at all* in the private sector. Where the exclusion principle cannot be applied social wants are either not satisfied at all through the market or are satisfied only to a limited extent by some by-product of a profitable private sector activity. Deficiencies in private sector provision may be made good by public provision but it is characteristic of a situation in which exclusion is not possible that the tax financing system, while a good substitute for price financing in producing revenue, by contrast, automatically secures neither the revelation of preferences nor a determinate level of supply.

Real world goods which satisfy both private and social wants – compulsory education satisfies the private want of the individual *and* (perhaps) a public want that no individual should receive less than a minimum standard of education – are sometimes called 'merit' goods. In many such cases it seems that consumers' preferences are interdependent. If my utility is increased by the education of the children of others, I have a demand price for this education. The total demand for education is then the vertical summation of aggregated individual demands for own education and the aggregated demands of individuals for the education of others. Clearly the analysis used in the pure public goods case may be applied here;

1. This term may not be descriptively the best available, and *collective good* or *group consumption good* perhaps conveys better the nature of the phenomenon.

where such interdependence of preferences exists – to put it another way – where there are external economies of consumption an economic case exists for income redistribution, either in kind, through education subsidies, as indicated above, or in money. For a discussion of the case for money transfers, see Hochman and Rodgers (1969).

It is a simple but easily overlooked point that the whole analysis depends on the substitutability of private and public goods. It does not necessarily follow from the fact that public goods have a positive value to an individual that he will be prepared to pay for them by sacrificing some private goods:[2] the public goods may yield only a lower order utility to him. This point is relevant to the consideration of external economies of consumption and production. The mere existence of spill-overs from the activities of an economic unit is not sufficient evidence of a possible improvement by, for example, arranging a market in what is spilled over: the beneficiaries may not be prepared to buy at any positive price.

A class of cases which has attracted renewed attention since Samuelson wrote, is that characterized by freedom of access to a facility at zero marginal price. All roads in the United Kingdom are available for use by any motor car driver without charge.[3] As Pigou showed long ago the differential advantage of the better of two routes may be completely eroded if there is free access. (Pigou, 1920, pp. 193–4. On this see Knight, 1924, pp. 582–606.) Once this has happened welfare can be unambiguously increased by imposing a congestion tax. The case of roads is not a special one: wherever a facility, which may be a gift of nature, such as lakeland scenery or a safe beach, is freely available to all it is possible that the level of use will be greater than the welfare optimum. The gifts of nature and the heritage of the past not in private ownership may be conveniently analysed as public goods, for they are available to all at zero price (at least if transport costs are excluded) and enjoyment by one individual has zero social cost so long as congestion does not occur. If the level of use exceeds the welfare optimum various devices can be used to restrict consumption. The establishment of private property rights to be exploited so that profits are maximized is one; physical rationing is another. For the

2. The opposite view has been christened 'the *ordinalist fallacy*' by Professor Nicholas Georgescu-Roegen (1954).

3. A moment's consideration will show that the existence of road fund, petrol and purchase taxes do not affect the argument which follows in the text.

purpose of restricting consumption, the government-imposed congestion tax is equivalent to the private property owner's price. However, these solutions are only possible when citizens may be excluded from enjoying the facility and where this is administratively possible the most awkward characteristic of the pure public good is absent; moreover, when supply is fixed, the troublesome problem of deciding the level of provision does not arise.

It smacks of paradox that the decade which saw the demolition of many hopes raised by the 'new' welfare economics also saw an upsurge in the use of cost/benefit analysis. The aim of the new welfare economics – to provide objective criteria for analysing economic change in which efficiency and distributional factors would be separated – proved too ambitious; grandiose expectations were disappointed. However, practical problems, one species of which is referred to in the previous paragraph, remained to be solved. The genus to which these problems belong exists because the market mechanism does not always produce an optimal solution. Cost-benefit analysis – a technique for appraising projects the costs and benefits of which are susceptible to measurement – has obvious relevance, where the markets jibs or fails. As the survey by Eckstein (Reading 10) shows, there are many possible reasons for market failure to carry out projects yielding adequate net benefits. However, a thorny problem of income distribution is raised by the use of this technique. Various possibilities are open here: income distribution can be ignored, cost and benefits being measured where they fall and then aggregated; the distributional consequences for groups of individuals of alternative policies can be set out for the policy maker's consideration; income changes can be given weights for example by multiplying them by marginal personal tax rates, and so on.

The earmarking of tax revenues for particular expenditure purposes is unpopular with budget administrators and has for long been a neglected subject with public finance theorists. It can hardly be ruled out as a potentially useful technique in a voluntary exchange approach to public expenditure and has obvious possibilities in the field of social security and welfare service financing. Buchanan (Reading 11) deals with some interesting theoretical aspects of earmarking.

References
BLISS, C. (1967), 'Review of *The Collected Scientific Papers of Paul Samuelson*', *Economic Journal*, vol. 77.

GEORGESCU-ROEGEN, N. (1954), 'Choice expectations and measurability', *Quarterly Journal of Economics*, vol. 68, pp. 503–34. Reprinted in N. Georgescu-Roegen, *Analytical Economics*, Harvard University Press, 1966.

HOCHMAN, H. M., and RODGERS, J. D. (1969), 'Pareto-optimal redistribution', *American Economic Review*, vol. 59, pp. 542–57.

KNIGHT, F. H. (1924), 'Some fallacies in the interpretation of social cost', *Quarterly Journal of Economics*, vol. 38. Reprinted in G. J. Stigler and K. E. Boulding (eds.), *A.E.A. Readings in Price Theory*, Allen & Unwin, 1956.

PIGOU, A. C. (1920), *Economics of Welfare*, Macmillan.

8 A. C. Pigou

The Range of Government Expenditure

A. C. Pigou, 'The range of government expenditure', *A Study in Public Finance*, Macmillan, 1947, pp. 30–34.

1. In so far as government departments engage in the manufacture of goods and services to be sold for fees so arranged as to cover cost of production, the amount of resources which will be devoted to these purposes is automatically determined by the public demand. The main part of a modern government's activity is not, however, of this class. The bulk of its non-transfer expenditure is devoted to services of a general sort – defence, civil administration and so on – which cannot practicably be sold against fees to individuals; while the whole of its transfer expenditure is outside the range of fees altogether. Hence there is no automatic machinery to determine how far expenditure shall be carried; and some other method has to be employed.

2. At any given moment it is probable that large parts of current transfer expenditure will be regulated by practically irrevocable contracts. In Great Britain at the present time expenditure on the services of the debt, war pensions and old age pensions clearly belongs to this class. On the other hand, expenditure on subsidies to particular industries or particular classes of persons and expenditure on Poor Relief are optional, in the sense that the government is free, within fairly wide limits, to determine their amounts by present policy. With the exception of government payments in interest and sinking fund on foreign-held debt, practically all non-transfer expenditure is optional in this sense, so far as legal considerations go: but, as regards a great deal of it, economies could not be carried very far except at the cost of breaking away from deeply rooted traditions. The optional parts of expenditure – the only parts which are practically subject to control – ought plainly to be regulated with some reference to the burden involved in raising funds to finance them. This aspect of

Public Finance is an important one. But it is not a main theme of my present study, and can only be touched upon briefly.

3. As regards the distribution, as distinct from the aggregate cost, of optional government expenditure, it is clear that, just as an individual will get more satisfaction out of his income by maintaining a certain balance between different sorts of expenditure, so also will a community through its government. The principle of balance in both cases is provided by the postulate that resources should be so distributed among different uses that the marginal return of satisfaction is the same for all of them. Evidently this is true of the non-transfer expenditure of governments, so far as this is not already determined by past contracts. Among various forms of optional transfer expenditure the same principle evidently holds; and – though here the matter is more difficult to envisage clearly – it also holds between optional non-transfer expenditure in general and optional transfer expenditure in general. Expenditure should be distributed between battleships and Poor Relief in such wise that the last shilling devoted to each of them yields the same return of satisfaction. We have here, so far as theory goes, a test by means of which the distribution of expenditure along different lines can be settled.[1]

4. This method of approach suggests an analogous test for determining how large government expenditure in the aggregate ought to be. If a community were literally a unitary being, with the government as its brain, expenditure should be pushed in all directions up to the point at which the satisfaction obtained from the last shilling expended is equal to the satisfaction lost in respect of the last shilling called up on government service. This last, or 'marginal' shilling is, of course, to be regarded as made up of parts contributed by all of the separate contributors to government funds in proportion to their respective contributions, not as the last shilling taken from the poorest contributor. So interpreted, the above conception, though, as will be shown in a moment, it is not adequate to the conditions of real life, nevertheless enables some useful, if fairly obvious, deductions to be drawn.

5. First, it enables us to see that the *optimum* amount of government expenditure, whether for actual using-up or for transfer

1. For a criticism of the view that the concept of sacrifice can properly be used in this way and for a reply cf. part 2, ch. 1, para. 3 [not included here].

from relatively rich to relatively poor persons, is likely to be larger, the greater – the numbers of the population being given – is the aggregate income of the community. For, other things being equal, the marginal sacrifice involved in raising n shillings (assumed to represent a given real value) from any group will be smaller, the larger is the number of shillings constituting the public income. Immediately after a war, in which capital equipment has been allowed to run down and the organization of markets has become dislocated, real income will, in general, be diminished, and, with it, capacity to provide resources for government. Therefore, certain government expenditures, which it used to be worth while to undertake, a country may no longer be able to 'afford'. Secondly, other things being equal, if and when new opportunities for expenditure by government that would yield large benefits or obviate large evils, are opened up, and no corresponding opportunities for expenditure by private persons are opened up at the same time,[2] the balance between the marginal benefit and the marginal damage of raising revenue will be struck at a higher point; i.e. more revenue ought to be raised. Thirdly, when aggregate income and population are given, if a large part of the income is concentrated in the hands of a few rich persons, it is possible to frame a tax-scheme that will raise a given revenue with less *immediate* marginal sacrifice than would be imposed under any scheme if the income was spread evenly over the whole community.[3] Lastly, other things, including income-distribution, being equal, the *immediate* marginal sacrifice involved in the raising of a given revenue will be smaller the more progressive is the revenue-raising scheme. Thus, subject to what will be said in part 2, chapter 4 [not included here] on the relation between *immediate*

2. The purpose of this qualification is to exclude such things as the invention of new uses for capital (e.g., in railway building). These do not necessarily give ground for raising more revenue, even though government is fully competent to build railways; for private capitalists are also competent to do this.

3. When we speak of the distribution of income as a relevant factor in this connexion, we assume that the main part of an ordinary man's income (other than the part absorbed in taxation) is used for his own consumption and investment. Obviously, if all rich men were accustomed to give away income to such an extent that, after their gifts, everybody had equal amounts for consumption and saving, we should have a state of things equivalent for practical purposes to one in which all incomes are initially equal.

sacrifice and *total* sacrifice, a government may properly engage in larger expenditures (i) the less even is the distribution of income among its citizens and (ii) the more progressive is the revenue-raising scheme that it decides to employ.

6. The foundation of the foregoing analysis was the assumption, set out in paragraph 4, that the community is a unitary being for which the government acts as brain. In fact, of course, this is not so. If battleships were goods that people need for individual personal use, that would not, indeed, matter. There could still be the same sort of balancing at the margin between clothes purchased individually and battleships purchased through the government as there is between clothes purchased individually and coal purchased through a co-operative buying agency. But battleships are a collective good, to be used in the general interest by the government. Consequently, any taxpayer's desire to contribute towards buying them is dependent, not only on his desire that the country shall possess them, but also on the number of them which are being made available by the contributions of other people. The government is not, therefore, simply an agent for carrying out on behalf of its citizens their several separate instructions; it cannot simply balance at the margin each man's desire to buy battleships against his desire to buy clothes, in the way that an individual balances his desire for clothes against his desire for coal. As the agent of its citizens collectively, it must exercise coercion upon them individually, securing the funds it needs either by a contemporary tax or by a loan associated with a subsequent tax to provide for interest and sinking fund. Where, however, coercion intrudes there are introduced two new elements, of which the method of analysis so far described takes no account. The first of these is the cost of administration. This includes, not merely the costs of the government departments which have to collect and distribute the funds raised from the public, but also the costs thrown on the public themselves in the form of accountants' and solicitors' fees, together with the trouble to which taxpayers are individually put in filling up income tax forms and so on. The second element is less obvious but not less important. The raising of an additional pound of revenue necessitates increasing the rates at which taxation is imposed, either now or (if resort has been had to loans) subse-

quently. With some sorts of taxes this inflicts indirect damage on the taxpayers as a body over and above the loss they suffer in actual money payment. Where there is indirect damage, it ought to be added to the direct loss of satisfaction involved in the withdrawal of the marginal unit of resources by taxation, before this is balanced against the satisfaction yielded by the marginal expenditure. It follows that, in general, expenditure ought not to be carried so far as to make the real yield of the last unit of resources expended by the government equal to the real yield of the last unit left in the hands of the representative citizen. It follows, further, that the extent of the gap which ought to be allowed varies according to the methods available for raising extra funds; being greater where it is necessary to resort to methods that involve large indirect damage than where there is opportunity for comparatively harmless expedients.

9 A Pure Theory of Public Expenditure

(a) P. A. Samuelson

The Pure Theory of Public Expenditure

P. A. Samuelson, 'The pure theory of public expenditure',
Review of Economics and Statistics, vol. 36, 1954, pp. 387–9.

Assumptions

Except for Sax, Wicksell, Lindahl, Musgrave and Bowen, economists have rather neglected the theory of optimal public expenditure, spending most of their energy on the theory of taxation. Therefore, I explicitly assume two categories of goods: ordinary *private consumption goods* $(X_1, \ldots, X_n)$ which can be parcelled out among different individuals $(1, 2, \ldots, i, \ldots, s)$ according to the relations

$$X_j = \sum_1^s X_j^i$$

and *collective consumption goods* $(X_{a+1}, \ldots, X_{n+m})$ which all enjoy in common in the sense that each individual's consumption of such a good leads to no subtraction from any other individual's consumption of that good, so that $X_{n+j} = X_{n+j}$ simultaneously for each and every ith individual and each collective consumptive good. I assume no mystical collective mind that enjoys collective consumption goods; instead I assume each individual has a consistent set of *ordinal preferences* with respect to his consumption of all goods (collective as well as private) which can be summarized by a regularly smooth and convex utility index $u^i = u^i$ $(X_1^i, \ldots, X_{n+m}^i)$ (any monotonic stretching of the utility index is of course also an admissible cardinal index of preference). I shall throughout follow the convention of writing the partial derivative of any function with respect to its jth argument by a j subscript, so that $u_j^i = \partial u^i / \partial X_j^i$, etc. Provided economic quantities can be divided into two groups, *outputs* or goods which everyone always wants to maximize and *inputs* or factors which

179

everyone always wants to minimize, we are free to change the algebraic signs of the latter category and from then on to work only with 'goods', knowing that the case of factor inputs is covered as well. Hence by this convention we are sure that $u^i_j > 0$ always.

To keep production assumptions at the minimum level of simplicity, I assume a regularly convex and smooth production-possibility schedule relating totals of all outputs, private and collective; or $F(X_1, \ldots, X_{n+m}) = 0$, with $F_j > 0$ and ratios F_j/F_n determinate and subject to the generalized laws of diminishing returns.

Feasibility considerations disregarded, there is a *maximal* (ordinal) *utility frontier* representing the Pareto-optimal points – of which there are an $(s-1)$ fold infinity – with the property that from such a frontier point you can make one person better off only by making some other person worse off. If we wish to make normative judgements concerning the relative ethical desirability of different configurations involving some individuals being on a higher level of indifference and some on a lower, we must be presented with a set of ordinal interpersonal norms or with a *social welfare function* representing a consistent set of ethical preferences among all the possible states of the system. It is not a 'scientific' task of the economist to 'deduce' the form of this function; this can have as many forms as there are possible ethical views; for the present purpose, the only restriction placed on the social welfare function is that it shall always increase or decrease when any one person's ordinal preference increases or decreases, all others staying on their same indifference levels: mathematically, we narrow it to the class that any one of its indexes can be written $U = U(u^1, \ldots, u^s)$ with $U_j > 0$.

Optimal Conditions

In terms of these norms, there is a 'best state of the world' which is defined mathematically in simple regular cases by the marginal conditions

$$\frac{u^i_j}{u^i_r} = \frac{F_j}{F_r} \quad \begin{array}{l} (i = 1, 2, \ldots, s; r, j = 1, \ldots, n) \text{ or} \\ (i = 1, 2, \ldots, s; r = 1; j = 2, \ldots, n) \end{array} \qquad \mathbf{1}$$

$$\sum_{i=1}^{s} \frac{u_{n+j}^i}{u_r^i} = \frac{F_{n+j}}{F_r} \quad \begin{matrix} (j=1,\ldots,m;r=1,\ldots,n) \text{ or} \\ (j=1,\ldots,m;r=1) \end{matrix} \qquad \mathbf{2}$$

$$\frac{U_i\, u_k^i}{U_q\, u_k^q} = 1 \quad \begin{matrix} (i,q=1,\ldots,s;k=1,\ldots,n) \text{ or} \\ (q=1;i=2,\ldots,s;k=1). \end{matrix} \qquad \mathbf{3}$$

Equations **1** and **3** are essentially those given in the chapter on welfare economics in my *Foundations of Economic Analysis*. They constitute my version of the 'new welfare economics'. Alone **1** represents that subset of relations which defines the Pareto-optimal utility frontier and which by itself represents what I regard as the unnecessarily narrow version of what once was called the 'new welfare economics.'.

The new element added here is the set **2**, which constitutes a pure theory of government expenditure on collective consumption goods. By themselves **1** and **2** define the $(s-1)$fold infinity of utility frontier points; only when a set of interpersonal normative conditions equivalent to **3** is supplied are we able to define an unambiguously 'best' state.

Since formulating the conditions **2** some years ago, I have learned from the published and unpublished writings of Richard Musgrave that their essential logic is contained in the 'voluntary-exchange' theories of public finance of the Sax–Wicksell–Lindahl–Musgrave type, and I have also noted Howard Bowen's independent discovery of them in Bowen's writings of a decade ago. A graphical interpretation of these conditions in terms of *vertical* rather than *horizontal* addition of different individuals' marginal-rate-of-substitution schedules can be given; but what I must emphasize is that there is a different such schedule for each individual at each of the $(s-1)$fold infinity of different distributions of relative welfare along the utility frontier.

Impossibility of Decentralized Spontaneous Solution

So much for the involved optimizing equations that an omniscient calculating machine could theoretically solve if fed the postulated functions. No such machine now exists. But it is well known that an 'analogue calculating machine' can be provided by competitive market pricing, (a) so long as the production functions satisfy the neoclassical assumptions of constant returns to scale and generalized diminishing returns and (b) so long as the individuals' indifference contours have regular convexity and, we may add, (c) so long as all goods are private. We can then insert between the right- and left-hand sides of **1** the equality with uniform market prices p_j/p_r and adjoin the budget equations for each individual

$$p_1 X_1^i + p_2 X_2^i + \ldots + p_n X_n^i = L^i \qquad \textbf{1}'$$
$$(i = 1, 2, \ldots, s),$$

where L^i is a lump-sum tax for each individual so selected in algebraic value as to lead to the 'best' state of the world. Now note, if there were no collective consumption goods, then **1** and **1**' can have their solution enormously simplified. Why? Because on the one hand perfect competition among productive enterprises would ensure that goods are produced at minimum costs and are sold at proper marginal costs, with all factors receiving their proper marginal productivities; and on the other hand, each individual, in seeking as a competitive buyer to get to the highest level of indifference subject to given prices and tax, would be led as if by an Invisible Hand to the grand solution of the social maximum position. Of course the institutional framework of competition would have to be maintained, and political decision-making would still be necessary, but of a computationally minimum type: namely, algebraic taxes and transfers ($L^1, \ldots L^s$) would have to be varied until society is swung to the ethical observer's optimum. The servant of the ethical observer would not have to make explicit decisions about each person's detailed consumption and work; he need only decide about generalized purchasing power, knowing that each person can be counted on to allocate it optimally. In terms of communication theory and game terminology, each person is motivated to do the signalling of his tastes needed to define and reach the attainable-bliss point.

Now all of the above remains valid even if collective consumption is not zero but is instead *explicitly set* at its optimum values as determined by **1**, **2** and **3**. *However no decentralized pricing system can serve to determine optimally these levels of collective consumption*. Other kinds of 'voting' or 'signalling' would have to be tried. But, and this is the point sensed by Wicksell but perhaps not fully appreciated by Lindahl, now it is in the selfish interest of each person to give *false* signals, to pretend to have less interest in a given collective consumption activity than he really has, etc. I must emphasize this: taxing according to a benefit theory of taxation cannot at all solve the computational problem in the decentralized manner possible for the first category of 'private' goods to which the ordinary market pricing applies and which do not have the 'external effects' basic to the very notion of collective consumption goods. Of course, utopian voting and signalling schemes can be imagined. ('Scandinavian consensus', Kant's 'categorical imperative', and other devices meaningful only under conditions of 'symmetry', etc.) The failure of market catallactics in no way denies the following truth: given sufficient knowledge the optimal decisions can always be found by scanning over all the attainable states of the world and selecting the one which according to the postulated ethical welfare function is best. The solution 'exists'; the problem is how to 'find' it.

One could imagine every person in the community being indoctrinated to behave like a 'parametric decentralized bureaucrat' who *reveals* his preferences by signalling in response to price parameters or Lagrangean multipliers, to questionnaires, or to other devices. But there is still this fundamental technical difference going to the heart of the whole problem of *social* economy: by departing from his indoctrinated rules, any one person can hope to snatch some selfish benefit in a way not possible under the self-policing competitive pricing of private goods; and the 'external economies' or 'jointness of demand' intrinsic to the very concept of collective goods and governmental activities makes it impossible for the grand ensemble of optimizing equations to have that special pattern of zeros which makes *laissez-faire* competition even *theoretically* possible as an analogue computer.

Conclusion

To explore further the problem raised by public expenditure would take us into the mathematical domain of 'sociology' or 'welfare politics', which Arrow, Duncan Black and others have just begun to investigate. Political economy can be regarded as one special sector of this general domain, and it may turn out to be pure luck that within the general domain there happened to be a subsector with the 'simple' properties of traditional economics.

(b) J. Margolis

A Comment on the Pure Theory of Public Expenditure

J. Margolis, 'A comment on the pure theory of public expenditure', *Review of Economics and Statistics*, vol. 37, 1954, pp. 347–9.

In a recent article Professor Samuelson [see Reading 9a] proves anew the assertion that 'no decentralized pricing system can serve to determine optimally the levels of collective consumption' (p. 182). It is possible, he further states (p. 183), that

Utopian voting and signalling schemes can be imagined. . . . But there is still this fundamental technical difference going to the heart of the whole problem of *social* economy: by departing from his indoctrinated rules, any one person can hope to snatch some selfish benefit in a way not possible under the self-policing competitive pricing of private goods; and the 'external economies' or 'jointness of demand' intrinsic to the very concept of collective goods and governmental activities makes it impossible for the grand ensemble of optimizing equations to have that special pattern of zeros which makes *laissez-faire* competition even *theoretically* possible as an analogue computer.

The conclusion and the reasoning are familiar but never as cogently put.

Samuelson divides the budget into two sectors. The first sector presents no difficulties to him. It consists of 'algebraic taxes and transfers (of an income redistribution type) which would have to be varied until society is swung to the ethical observer's optimum' (p. 182). It is in the second sector, the provision of collective goods, that the difficulties arise. The contention of this note is that a decentralized pricing system for all public services is technically difficult for reasons other than those stated by Samuelson; but more important is the contention that his approach to a theory of public expenditures is unfruitful.

The heart of Samuelson's argument against a decentralized pricing system is the definition of collective goods. They are goods 'which all enjoy in common in the sense that each individual's consumption of such a good leads to no subtractions from any other individual's consumption of that good . . .' (p. 179). It follows from this that if both A and B desire an additional unit of a collective good, it would be advantageous to both that the other person 'pay', since each will receive the full benefits of the good no matter who pays. The good, because of its technological characteristics, cannot become private property. Since Samuelson claims that he is analysing 'the theory of optimal public expenditures' we must assume that he is asserting that there are public expenditures on services if and only if these services are collective consumption goods. A more sympathetic reading of the note might suggest that the author was only discussing the possibility of sole reliance on benefits taxation as a pricing mechanism for public services and was not explaining their genesis, or that he was even more modest and was suggesting the technical difficulties of benefits taxation in the case of a restricted set of public expenditures.

Are there collective consumption goods? Are they the typical public services? In defense of Samuelson there are a host of theorists who have begun their arguments the same way. Against Samuelson are the facts. He claims that collective goods are not rationed – that the use of a good by A does not involve any costs to B. Clearly this is not the case in such common public services as education, hospitals and highways, where capacity limitations and congestion are topics of the daily press. Would it be true of the more sovereign functions of justice and police? The crowded calendar of the courts certainly implies that the use of this function by A makes it less available to B. Similarly a complaint to the police ties up the officers in a maze of arguments, forms to be completed, and hearings to be attended, reducing their availability to others. Possibly the only goods which would seem to conform to Samuelson's definition are national defense and the aged lighthouse illustration. The lighthouse shines for all ships, when the lanes are not crowded; and everyone receives a full share of protection from the military machine.

The rejection of Samuelson's argument does not mean an acceptance of the feasibility of universal benefits taxation for public services. He could have developed the same conclusions with a less restrictive definition of collective goods. But of more importance, we would insist that his separation of the budget into a sociopolitical sector and a technical sector which falsely creates hopes for an 'economist's, *qua* economist, solution' to the problem of public expenditures is an error.

Essentially Samuelson's formulation of the domain of public services stems from an economic liberal's image of the state. Values are determined by the preferences of independent individuals. A private market economy is the 'natural' condition of society, and it will lead to a maximization of values produced. There are some goods which are desired but will not be produced in sufficient numbers since property laws can be applied to them only imperfectly. The more limited the ability of the individual to exercise ownership over a good, the less his profits in its production and the less efficient will be the 'natural' economy. Collective production therefore becomes necessary. In general, this argument follows along the same lines as that of the divergency arising between social and private benefits because of the existence of inappropriable benefits. An illustration is the restrictive zoning of billboards and roadside business alongside highways and public expenditures on landscaping. It would be foolish for a businessman to refrain from advertising along a right of way or to beautify his section of the highway unless he was assured that his competitors similarly would refrain or that all highway users would contribute to the improvements. (Note that with increased congestion and the accompanying increase in driving hazards individuals share less of the beauty.) This formulation is of no help at all to the understanding of most public expenditures.

The state, quite out of character with the above portrait, frequently makes the use of its 'services' compulsory, for example, national defense, elementary education, unemployment insurance. Other services may not be free to all who wish to partake of them but are rationed by price or other criteria. When 'free' the private costs associated with using them are a form of rationing. Often there is no technical reason why these goods could not be distributed on a private basis. They serve private ends and are divisible.

Education is a 'private consumption good which can be parcelled out among different individuals' (p. 179). But it is also true that education is one of the few ways in which those with little property can build up capital (human wealth) with which to enhance their productivity. The provision of public education is a reflection of the political power of the propertyless classes. Education becomes a government end, but its inclusion in this set is an outcome of a working compromise of relationships among conflicting social groups. If the individualistic model were appropriate to the state in the case of public education, we should have a demand by the propertyless for an income redistribution so that they could then purchase the amount and type of education they wish. (This may be the form of the future collective production of health services with the development of state subsidized insurance schemes.) Why isn't this pattern followed? Why are some forms of public services compulsory, free or rationed? The answers to these questions are vital to a theory of public expenditures, and unfortunately they require penetration into the murky waters of political sociology. A few lines indicating the general direction of the arguments are appropriate and should indicate the inadequacy of an individualistic model.

The money income redistribution necessary to realize the socially acceptable distribution implicit in public services would have far-reaching implications. It would necessitate a direct frontal attack on a vital institution of capitalism – the productivity principle as a basis for income distribution. This principle cannot be scrapped without a social revolution, but it can be compromised by a set of concessions to particular goals of aggressive social groups. The political structure, where power is differently distributed than in the market, is a favorite battlefield for these partial victories. Is the budget merely a treaty among warring social groups? No, it is more likely that there is a structure of existential social values, differentiated according to range, levels of legitimation, logical connectedness, and so forth,[1] which are the bases of alternative public activities. Genetically one might argue that these values are the results of compromises among competing groups where each tries to maximize its tastes, but this is not a sufficiently interesting statement. The values, whatever their origins, are existential and are instrumental to controlling group behavior.

What relation would this positive theory of the budget have to a normative theory which was the concern of the Samuelson note? Not only are the rules of behavior of individuals different according to whether they are operating in the everyday individualistic activities or as a conscious part of a social group but also the criteria that are applicable to these two situations are

1. See the work of E. C. Banfield, T. Parsons and E. Shils.

different. To explain the existence of public activities and to evaluate the efficiency of an allocation of the public budget we must refer to the structure of social values.

(c) P. A. Samuelson

Diagrammatic Exposition of a Theory of Public Expenditure

P. A. Samuelson, 'Diagrammatic exposition of a theory of public expenditure', *Review of Economics and Statistics*, vol. 37, 1955, pp. 350–56.

In the November 1954 issue of the *Review of Economics and Statistics*, my paper on 'The pure theory of public expenditure' [see Reading 9a] presented a mathematical exposition of a public expenditure theory that goes back to Italian, Austrian and Scandinavian writers of the last seventy-five years. After providing that theory with its needed logically complete optimal conditions, I went on to demonstrate the fatal inability of any decentralized market or voting mechanism to attain or compute this optimum. The present note presents in terms of two-dimensional diagrams an essentially equivalent formulation of the theory's optimum conditions and briefly discusses some criticisms.

A Polar-Case Model of Government

Doctrinal history shows that theoretical insight often comes from considering strong or extreme cases. The grand Walrasian model of competitive general equilibrium is one such extreme polar case. We can formulate it so stringently as to leave no economic role for government. What strong polar case shall the student of public expenditure set alongside this pure private economy?

One possibility is the model of a group-mind. Such a model, which has been extensively used by nationalists and by Romantic critics of classical economics, can justify any, and every, configuration of government. So there is perhaps little that an economic theorist can usefully say about it.

My alternative is a slightly more sophisticated one, but still – intentionally – an extreme polar case. It is consistent with individualism, yet at the same time it explicitly introduces the vital external interdependencies that no theory of government can do without. Its basic assumption is an oversharp distinction between the following two kinds of goods:

1. A *private* consumption good, like bread, whose total can be parcelled out among two or more persons, with one man having a loaf less if another gets a loaf more. Thus if X_1 is total bread, and X_1^1 and X_1^2 are the respective private consumptions of Man 1 and Man 2, we can say that the total equals the sum of the separate consumptions – or $X_1 = X_1^1 + X_1^2$.

2. A *public* consumption good, like an outdoor circus or national defense, which is provided for each person to enjoy or not, according to his tastes. I assume the public good can be varied in total quantity, and write X_2 for its magnitude. It differs from a private consumption good in that each man's consumption of it, X_2^1 and X_2^2 respectively, is related to the total X_2 by a condition of *equality* rather than of summation. Thus, by definition, $X_2^1 = X_2$, and $X_2^2 = X_2$.

Obviously, I am introducing a strong polar case. We could easily lighten the stringency of our assumptions. But on reflection, I think most economists will see that this is a natural antipodal case to the admittedly extreme polar case of traditional individualistic general equilibrium. The careful empiricist will recognize that many – though not all – of the realistic cases of government activity can be fruitfully analysed as some kind of a blend of these two extreme polar cases.

Graphical Depiction of Tastes and Technology

The first three charts summarize our assumptions about tastes and technology. Each diagram has a private good, such as bread, on its vertical axis; each has a public good on its horizontal axis. The heavy indifference curves of Figure 1 summarize Man 1's preferences between public and private goods. Figure 2's indifference curves do the same for Man 2; and the relative flatness of the contour shows that, in a sense, he has less liking for the public good.

The heavy production-possibility or opportunity-cost curve AB in Figure 3 relates that total productions of public and private goods in the usual familiar manner: the curve is convex from above to reflect the usual assumption of increasing relative marginal costs (or generalized diminishing returns).[1]

Because of our special definition of a public good, the three diagrams are not independent. Each must be lined up with *exactly the same horizontal scale*. Because increasing a public good for society simultaneously increases it for each and every

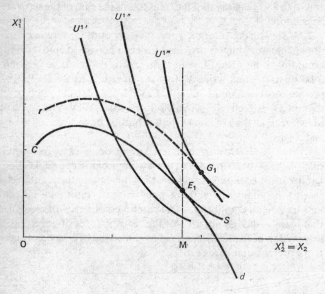

Figure 1   Indifference contours relating Man 1's consumption of public and private goods

man, we must always be simultaneously at exactly the same longitude in all three figures. Moving an inch east in one diagram moves us the same amount east in all.

1. Even though a public good is being compared with a private good, the indifference curves are drawn with the usual convexity to the origin. This assumption, as well as the one about diminishing returns, could be relaxed without hurting the theory. Indeed, we could recognize the possible case where one man's circus is another man's poison, by permitting indifference curves to bend forward. This would not affect the analysis but would answer a critic's minor objection. Mathematically, we could without loss of generality set $X_2^1 =$ any function of X_2, relaxing strict equality.

The private good on the vertical axis is subject to no new and unusual restrictions. Each man can be moved north or south on his indifference diagram independently. But, of course, the third diagram does list the total of bread summed over the private individuals; so it must have a larger vertical axis, and our momentary northward position on it must correspond to the sum of the independent northward positions of the separate individuals.

Tangency Conditions for Pareto Optima

What is the best or ideal state of the world for such a simple system? That is, what three vertically aligned points corresponding to a determination of a given total of both goods and a determinate parcelling out of them among all separate individuals will be the ethically preferred final configuration?

To answer this ethical, normative question we must be given a set of norms in the form of a *social welfare function* that renders

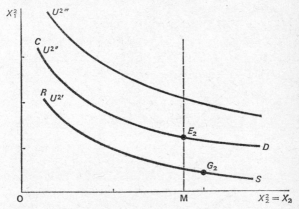

Figure 2 Indifference contours relating Man 2's consumption of public and private goods

interpersonal judgements. For expository convenience, let us suppose that this will be supplied later and that we know in advance it will have the following special individualistic property: leaving each person on his same indifference level will leave social welfare unchanged; at any point, a move of each man to a higher indifference curve can be found that will increase social welfare.

Given this rather weak assurance about the forthcoming social welfare function, we can proceed to determine tangency conditions of an 'efficiency' type that are at least necessary, though definitely not sufficient. We do this by setting up a preliminary maximum problem which will eventually necessarily have to be satisfied.

Holding all but one man at specified levels of indifference, how can we be sure that the remaining man reaches his highest indifference level? Concretely, this is how we define such a tangency optimum: Set Man 2 on a specified indifference curve, say his middle one CD. Paying attention to Mother Nature's scarcity, as summarized in Figure 3's AB curve, and following Man 1's tastes as given by Figure 1's indifference curves, how high on those indifference curves can we move Man 1?

The answer is given by the tangency point E_1, and the corresponding aligned points E_2 and E.

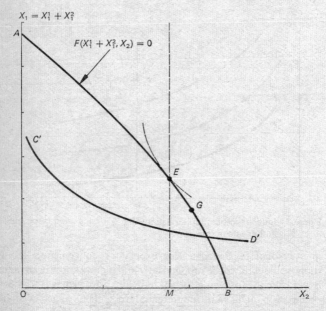

Figure 3   Transformation schedule relating totals of public and private goods

How is this derived? Copy CD on Figure 3 and call it $C'D'$. The distance between $C'D'$ and AB represents the amount of the two goods that are physically available to Man 1. So subtract $C'D'$ vertically from AB and plot the algebraic result as cd in Figure 1. Now where on cd would Man 1 be best off? Obviously at the tangency point E_1 where cd touches (but does not cross) his highest attainable indifference contour.[2]

How many such Pareto-optimal points are there? Obviously, for each of the infinite possible initial indifference curves to put Man 2 on, we can derive a new highest attainable tangency level for Man 1. So there are an infinity of such optimal points – as many in number as there are points on the usual contract curve. All of these Pareto-optimal points have the property that from them there exists no physically feasible movement that will make every man better off. Of course we cannot compare two different Pareto points until we are given a social welfare function. For a move from one Pareto point to another must always hurt one man while it is helping another, and an interpersonal way of comparing these changes must be supplied.

Figure 4 indicates these utility possibilities on an ordinal diagram. Each axis provides an indicator of the two men's respective indifference curve levels. The utility frontier of Pareto-optimal points is given by pp: the double fold infinity of 'inefficient', non-Pareto-optimal points is given by the shaded area; the pp frontier passes from northwest to southeast to reflect the inevitable conflict of interests characterizing any contract locus; the curvature of the pp locus is of no particular type since we have no need to put unique cardinal numbers along the indifference contours and can content ourselves with east–west and north–

2. The reader can easily derive rs and the tangency point G_1 corresponding to an original specification of Man 2's indifference level at the lower level RS rather than at AB. He can also interchange the roles of the two men, thereby deriving the point E_2 by a tangency condition. As a third approach, he can *vertically* add Man 2's specified indifference curve to each and every indifference curve of Man 1; the resulting family of contours can be conveniently plotted on Figure 3, and the final optimum can be read off from the tangency of AB to that family at the point E – as shown by the short broken-line indifference curve at E. It is easy to show that any of these tangencies are, in the two-good case, equivalent to equation 2 of my cited paper [Reading 9a]; with a single private good my equation 1 becomes redundant.

south relationships in Figure 4 without regard to numerical degree and to uneven stretchings of either utility axis.

The Optimum of all the Pareto Optima

Now we can answer the fundamental question: what is the best configuration for this society?

Use of the word 'best' indicates we are in the ascientific area of 'welfare economics' and must be provided with a set of norms. Economic science cannot deduce a social welfare function; what it can do is neutrally interpret any arbitrarily specified welfare function.

The heavy contours labelled U', U'' and U''' summarize all that is relevant in the provided social welfare function (they provide

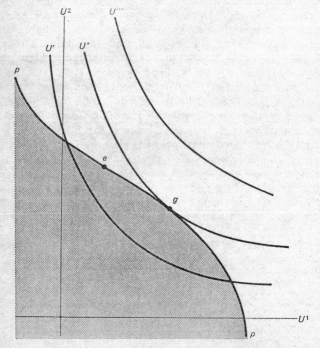

Figure 4   Utility frontier of Pareto-optimal efficiency points and its tangency to highest attainable social welfare contour

the needed ordinal scoring of every state of the world, involving different levels of indifference for the separate individuals).[3]

Obviously society cannot be best off inside the utility frontier. Where then on the utility frontier will the 'best obtainable bliss point' be? We will move along the utility frontier pp until we touch the highest social indifference curve: this will be at g where pp tangentially touches, without crossing, the highest obtainable social welfare level U''. In words, we can interpret this final tangency condition[4] in the following terms:

1. The social welfare significance of a unit of any private good allocated to private individuals must at the margin be the same for each and every person.

2. The Pareto-optimal condition, which makes relative marginal social cost equal to the sum of all persons' marginal rates of substitution, is already assured by virtue of the fact that bliss lies on the utility frontier.[5]

3. These social welfare or social indifference contours are given no particular curvature. Why? Again because we are permitting any arbitrary ordinal indicator of utility to be used on the axes of Figure 4.

An ethical postulate ruling out all 'dog-in-the-manger phenomena' will make all partial derivatives of the social welfare function $U(u^1, u^2, \ldots)$ always positive. This will assure the usual negative slopes to the U contours of Figure 4. However, without hurting the Pareto part of the new welfare economics, we can relax this assumption a little and let the contours bend forward. If at every point there can be found at least one positive partial derivative, this will be sufficient to rule out satiation points and will imply the necessity of the Pareto-optimal tangency condition of the earlier diagrams.

4. This tangency condition would have to be expressed mathematically in terms of numerical indicators of utility that are not invariant under a monotonic renumbering. However, it is easy to combine this tangency with the earlier Pareto-type tangency to get the formulation 3 of my cited paper [Reading 9a], which is independent of the choice of numerical indicators of U, u^1 or u^2.

5. A remarkable duality property of private and public goods should be noted. Private goods whose totals add – such as $X_1 = X_1^1 + X_1^2$ – lead ultimately to marginal conditions of simultaneous equality – such as $MC = MRS^1 = MRS^2$. Public goods whose totals satisfy a relation of simultaneous equality – such as $X_1 = X_2^1 = X_2^2$ – lead ultimately to marginal conditions that add – such as $MC = MRS^1 + MRS^2$.

Relations with Earlier Theories

This completes the graphical interpretation of my mathematical model. There remains the pleasant task of relating this graphical treatment to earlier work of Bowen (1943, pp. 27–49; 1948, ch. 18) and others.

To do this, look at Figure 5, which gives an alternative depiction of the optimal tangency condition at a point like E. I use the private

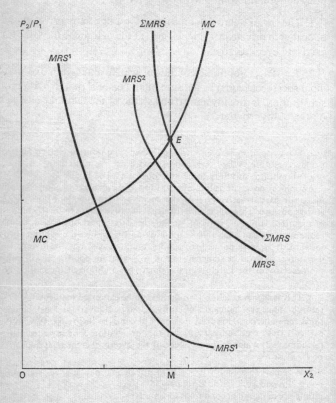

Figure 5   Intersection of public good's marginal cost schedule and the vertically-summed individual's marginal rates of substitution as envisaged by Lindahl and Bowen

good X_1 as numeraire, measuring all values in terms of it. The MC curve is derived from the AB curve of Figure 3: it is nothing but the absolute slope of that production-possibility schedule plotted against varying amounts of the public good; it is therefore a marginal cost curve, with MC measured in terms of the numeraire good.

The marginal rate of substitution curves MRS^1 and MRS^2 are derived in a similar fashion from the respective indifference curves of Man 1 and Man 2: thus, MRS^1 is the absolute slope of the $u^{1''}$ indifference curve plotted against varying amounts of the public good; MRS^2 is the similar slope function derived from Man 2's indifference curve CD. (All three are 'marginal' curves, bearing the usual relationship to their respective 'total' curves.)

These schedules look like demand curves. We are accustomed to adding horizontally or laterally the separate demand curves of individuals to arrive at total market demand. But this is valid only for private goods. As Bowen rightly says, *we must in the case of public goods add different individuals' curves vertically.*

This gives us the heavy ΣMRS curve for the whole community. Where is equilibrium? It is at E, where the community MC curve intersects the community ΣMRS curve. Upon reflection the reader will realize that the equality $MC = \Sigma MRS = MRS^1 + MRS^2$ is the precise equivalent of my mathematical equation **2** and of our Pareto-type tangency condition at E_1, E_2 or E. Why? Because of the stipulated requirement that Figure 5's curves are to depict the absolute slopes of the curves of Figures 1–3.

Except for minor details of notation and assumption, Figure 5 is identical with the figure shown on page 31 of the first Bowen reference, and duplicated on page 177 of the second reference. I am happy to acknowledge this priority. Indeed anyone familiar with Musgrave's valuable summary of the literature bearing on this area[6] will be struck with the similarity between this Bowen

6. Musgrave (1939), pp. 213–17. This gives citations to the relevant works of Sax, De Viti de Marco, Wicksell and Lindahl. I have greatly benefited from preliminary study of Professor Musgrave's forthcoming treatise on public finance, which I am sure will constitute a landmark in this area.

type of diagram and the Lindahl 100 per cent diagram reproduced by Musgrave.[7]

Once the economic theorist has related my graphical and mathematical analysis to the Lindahl and Bowen diagrams, he is in a position, I believe, to discern the logical advantage of the present formulation. For there is something circular and unsatisfactory about both the Bowen and Lindahl constructions: they show what the final equilibrium looks like, but by themselves they are not generally able to find the desired equilibrium. To see this, note that whereas we might know MC in Figure 5, we would not know the appropriate MRS schedules for *all* men until we already were familiar with the final E intersection point. (We might know MRS^2 from the specification that Man 2 is to be on the AB level; but then we wouldn't know MRS^1 until Figure 1's tangency had given us Man 1's highest attainable level, $u^{1''}$.) Under conditions of general equilibrium, Figures 1–3 logically contain Figure 5 inside them, but not vice versa. Moreover, Figures 1–3 explicitly call attention to the fact that there is an infinite number of different diagrams of the Lindahl-Bowen type, one for each specified level of relative interpersonal well-being.[8]

7. Musgrave, (1939) p. 216, which is an acknowledged adaption from Erik Lindahl (1919), p. 89. I have not had access to this important work. This diagram plots instead of the functions of Figure 5 the exact same functions after each has been divided by the MC function. The equilibrium intersection corresponding to E now shows up as the point at which all persons will together voluntarily provide 100 per cent of the full (unit? marginal?) cost of the public service. (If MC is not constant, some modifications in the Musgrave diagram may be required.)

8. The earlier writers from Wicksell on were well aware of this. They explicitly introduce the assumption that there is to have been a *prior* optimal interpersonal distribution of income, so what I have labelled E might better be labelled G. But the general equilibrium analyst asks: how can the appropriate distribution of income be decided on a prior basis *before* the significant problems of public consumptions have been determined? A satisfactory general analysis can resist the temptation to assume (i) the level of government expenditure must be so small as not to affect appreciably the marginal social significance of money to the different individuals; (ii) each man's indifference curves run parallel to each other in a vertical direction so that every and all indifference curves in Figure 1 (or in Figure 2) give rise to the same MRS^1 (or MRS^2) curve in Figure 5. The modern theorist is anxious to free his analysis from the incubus of unnecessarily restrictive partial equilibrium assumptions.

Concluding Reflections

I hope that the analytic model outlined here may help make a small and modest step towards understanding the complicated realities of political economy. Much remains to be done. This is not the place to discuss the wider implications and difficulties of the presented economic theory.[9] However, I should like to comment briefly on some of the questions about this theory that have been raised. (Enke, 1955, pp. 131-3; Margolis, 1955, p. 347.)

1. On the deductive side, the theory presented here is, I believe, a logically coherent one. This is true whether expressed in my original mathematical notation or in the present diagrammatic form. Admittedly, the latter widens the circle of economists who can understand and follow what is being said. The present version, with its tangencies of methodologically the same type as characterize Cournot-Marshall marginal theory and Bergson-Pigou welfare theory, should from its easily recognized equivalence with the mathematical version make clear my refusal to agree with Dr Enke's view that my use of mathematics was limited 'to notation'.

2. In terms of the history of similar theories, I hope the present paper will make clear relationships to earlier writers. (In particular, see the above discussion relating my early diagrams and equations to the Bowen-Lindahl formulation.) I shall not bore the reader with irrelevant details of independent rediscoveries of doctrine that my ignorance of the available literature may have made necessary. Yet is it presumptuous to suggest that there does not exist in the present economic literature very much in the way of 'conclusions and reasoning' that are, in Dr Margolis' words, 'familiar'? Except for the writers I have cited, and the important unpublished thoughts of Dr Musgrave, there is much opaqueness in the literature. Much of what goes by the name of the 'voluntary exchange theory of public finance' seems pure obfuscation.[10]

9. At the 1955 Christmas Meetings of the American Economic Association and Econometric Society, I hope to present some further developments and qualifications of this approach.

10. See Colm (1936), pp. 1-11 (1955), pp. 27-43 for an admirable criticism of the Graziani statement, 'We know that the tax tends to take away from each and all that quantity of wealth which they would each have voluntarily yielded to the state for the satisfaction of their purely collective wants' (p. 32).

3. Far from my formulation's being, as some correspondents have thought, a revival of the voluntary exchange theory – it is in fact an attempt to demonstrate how right Wicksell was to worry about the inherent political difficulty of ever getting men to reveal their tastes so as to attain the definable optimum. This intrinsic 'game theory' problem has been sufficiently stressed in my early paper so that it has not been emphasized here. I may put the point most clearly in terms of the familiar tools of modern literary economics as follows:

Government supplies products jointly to many people. In ordinary market economics as you increase the number of sellers of a homogeneous product indefinitely, you pass from monopoly through indeterminate oligopoly and can hope to reach a determinate competitive equilibrium in the limit. It is sometimes thought that increasing the number of citizens who are jointly supplied public goods leads to a similar determinate result. This is reasoning from an incorrect analogy. A truer analogy in private economics would be the case of a bilateral-monopoly supplier of joint products whose number of joint products – meat, horn, hide and so on – is allowed to increase without number: such a process does not lead to a determinate equilibrium of the harmonistic type praised in the literature. My simple model is able to demonstrate this point – which does have 'policy implications'.

4. I regret using 'the' in the title of my earlier paper and have accordingly changed the present title. Admittedly, public expenditure and regulation proceed from considerations other than those emphasized in my models. Here are a few:

(a) Taxes and expenditure aim at redistributing incomes. I am anxious to clear myself from Dr Margolis' understandable suspicion that I am the type of liberal who would insist that all redistributions take place through tax policies and transfer expenditures: much public expenditure on education, hospitals, and so on, can be justified by the feasibility consideration that, even if these are not 100 per cent efficient in avoiding avoidable dead-weight loss, they may be better than the attainable imperfect tax alternatives.[11]

(b) Paternalistic policies are voted upon themselves by a demo-

11. See Samuelson (1950, p. 18 ff.) for analytic discussion of this important truth.

cratic people because they do not regard the results from spontaneous market action as optimal. Education and forced paces of economic development are good examples of this.

(c) Governments provide or regulate services that are incapable of being produced under the strict conditions of constant returns that go to characterize optimal self-regulating atomistic competition.

(d) Myriad 'generalized external economy and diseconomy' situations, where private pecuniary interest can be expected to deviate from social interests, provide obvious needs for government activity.

I am sure this list of basic considerations underlying government expenditure could be extended farther, including even areas where government probably ought not to operate from almost anyone's viewpoint.

5. This brief list can end with the most important criticism that the various commentators on my paper have put forth. They all ask: 'Is it factually true that most – or any! – of the functions of government can be properly fitted into your extreme category of a public good? Can education, the courts, public defense, highway programs, police and fire protection be put into this rigid category of a "public good available to all"? In practically every one of these cases isn't there an element of variability in the benefit that can go to one citizen *at the expense* of some other citizens?'

To this criticism, I fully agree. And that is why in the present formulation I have insisted upon the polar nature of my category. However, to say that a thing is not located at the South Pole does not logically place it at the North Pole. To deny that most public functions fit into my extreme definition of a public good is not to grant that they satisfy the logically equally-extreme category of a private good. To say that your absence at a concert may contribute to my enjoyment is not to say that the elements of public services can be put into homogeneous additive packages capable of being optimally handled by the ordinary market calculus.

Indeed, I am rash enough to think that in almost every one of the legitimate functions of government that critics put forward there is to be found a blending of the extreme antipodal models. One might even venture the tentative suspicion that any function of government not possessing any trace of the defined public good (and no one of the related earlier described characteristics) ought to be carefully scrutinized to see whether it is truly a legitimate function of govern~ ~nt.

6. Whether or not I have overstated the applicability of this one theoretical model to actual governmental functions, I believe I did not go far enough in claiming for it relevance to the vast area of decreasing costs that constitutes an important part of economic reality and of the welfare economics of monopolistic competition. I must leave to future research discussion of these vital issues.

Economic theory should add what it can to our understanding of governmental activity. I join with critics in hoping that its pretentious claims will not discourage other economic approaches, other contributions from neighboring disciplines, and concrete empirical investigations.

References

BOWEN, H. R. (1943), 'The interpretation of voting in the allocation of economic resources', *Quarterly Journal of Economics*, vol. 58.

BOWEN, H. R. (1948), *Toward Social Economy*, Reinhart.

COLM, G. (1936), 'The theory of public expenditure', *Annals of the American Academy of Political and Social Sciences*, vol. 183. Reprinted in G. Colm, *Essays in Public Finance and Fiscal Policy*, Oxford University Press, 1955.

ENKE, S. (1955), 'More on the misuse of mathematics in economics: a rejoinder', *Review of Economics and Statistics*, vol. 37.

LINDAHL, E. (1919), *Die Gerechtigkeit in der Besteuerung*, Lund.

MARGOLIS, J. (1955), 'On Samuelson on the pure theory of public expenditure', *Review of Economics and Statistics*, vol. 37.

MUSGRAVE, R. A. (1939), 'The voluntary exchange theory of public economy', *Quarterly Journal of Economics*, vol. 53.

SAMUELSON, P. A. (1950), 'Evaluation of real national income', *Oxford Economic Papers*, new series, vol. 2.

(d) P. A. Samuelson

Aspects of Public Expenditure Theories

P. A. Samuelson, 'Aspects of public expenditure theories', *Review of Economics and Statistics*, vol. 40, 1958, pp. 332–8.

Economic theorists have done work of high quality and great quantity in the field of taxation. Public expenditure seems to have been relatively neglected. To illustrate this, let me turn to Professor Pigou. I do so with some diffidence, remembering what Ralph Waldo Emerson said to Oliver Wendell Holmes when Holmes showed him a youthful criticism of Plato. 'When you strike at a King', Emerson said, 'be sure you kill him'.

I have no wish to assassinate Professor Pigou. Nor even to criticize him. But immortality does have its price: if one writes an outstanding treatise such as Pigou's *A Study in Public Finance* (1928), one must expect other men to swarm about it, picking a nugget here and probing for a weakness there.

Of a book of some 285 pages, Pigou devotes most attention to taxes. At least 200 pages to taxes; of the rest, most are concerned with fiscal policy and its impact on the business cycle. What about the pure theory of public expenditure? I can find barely half a dozen pages devoted to the heart of this matter – specifically, pages 30–34 [reprinted here as Reading 8]. And even if we widen the category – to include Pigou's definitions of transfer and exhaustive expenditure and his discussion of pricing of state-operated public utilities – we still cannot bring the total of pages much beyond twenty.

Now it may be that this ratio of 200 on taxes to 20 on expenditure is the proper one. Perhaps there is really nothing much to say about expenditure, and so heavily overbalanced a page budget may be truly optimal. On the other hand, we must admit that fashion has a great influence in economics, which suggests that we ought periodically to survey the neglected areas of theory to make sure that they do deserve to be left in their underdeveloped and backward states.

I have previously published [Reading 9a] some thoughts on public expenditure theory, and in order to widen the discussion among economic theorists, I later gave a non-mathematical exposition [Reading 9c]. I do not propose here to give a detailed review of these theories. Rather, I'd like to think aloud about some of the difficulties with expenditure theory and with political decision-making. On these subjects, Richard Musgrave and Julius Margolis have done outstanding research and I must confess my obligation to them for much friendly counsel.

I

Let me first take a fresh look at the nature of government and of public finance from a purely analytical viewpoint. I must give warning: the result will be rather like a New Yorker's map of the United States, in which vast areas of the country are compressed into almost nothing and certain places – like Hollywood, Cape Cod and Times Square – are blown up far beyond their true proportions.

Similarly, I shall commit all the sins of those bad historians and anthropologists who recreate the history of the human race according to their *a priori* conceptions of the moment. To keep from getting caught, I'll imagine a planet rather like the earth.

Once upon a time men on this planet were all alike and very scarce. Each family hunted and fished its symmetrical acres; and each ended with the same production and real income.

Then men turned to cultivating the soil and domesticating animals. This left even more of the globe vacant, but did not disturb the symmetry of family incomes.

But finally population grew so big that the best free land was all occupied. Now there was a struggle for elbow room. According to the scenario as I choose to write it, the struggle was a gentlemanly one. But men did have to face the fact that recognizing squatter's rights and respecting *laissez-faire* did result in differences of real incomes among families.

Optimal transfer expenditure

Here then for the first time, government was introduced on this planet. A comprehensive program of redistributing income so as to achieve a maximum of the community's social welfare function was introduced. The budget was balanced at a non-zero level: taxes were raised in a non-distorting lump-sum fashion, and transfer expenditure was allocated among families so as to achieve the marginal conditions necessary to maximize the defined social welfare function.

Now here on earth, things don't seem to have worked out exactly according to such a timetable. In fact, look at Adam Smith's 1776 discussion of the three duties of government – protection against external aggressors, maintenance of order at home, and erecting those public institutions and works 'which though they may be in the highest degree advantageous to a great society, could never repay the expense to any individual'.

We could interpret the last of these in so broad and tautological a way as to be compatible with anything. But if we stick to a narrower non-empty interpretation, it would appear that our planet began with redistributional governmental functions that Smith had not even dreamed of and which would most surprise him if he were to come to life and revisit any modern nation.

Now why do I describe so bizarre a model? It is to underline this theoretical point: Given a social welfare function, and given the absence of all technological and taste externalities, and given universal constant returns to scale, there would be needed only one type of public policy – redistributive transfers. (Under some ethical assumptions, these might be from poor to rich rather than rich to poor; but only by chance alone would zero redistributions maximize a specified social welfare function that depends solely on real incomes.)

Minimal collective expenditure

But what about the neglected exhaustive elements of public expenditure that even the most thorough-going *laissez-faire* economy will want to make – e.g. courts of justice to enforce contracts or any of the other items under Smith's first two duties? Later I shall review a possible theory of such expenditure. But first let me mention why the problem of financing such expenditures is, so long as they remain small, secondary to that of transfers.

Even on other planets, perfectionist lump-sum taxes are rarely feasible. We tax the objects that we can feasibly tax. And this must introduce deadweight-theoretically-avoidable tax burdens in addition to the unavoidable real burden involved in having to use resources for public purposes. (This doesn't mean the public services aren't worth their costs; on well-run planets, they are.)

Years ago, when studying this problem, I encountered what was to me a surprising fact. It turns out that, so long as exhaustive expenditure is 'small', the deadweight burden is 'negligible' no matter what system of taxation is used. Only in the second approximation, so to speak, does it matter what tax structure we use to 'cover' the needed program. At least this would be the case if incomes were already distributed optimally. *If*, as is more likely, *incomes are distributed prior to taxation in a non-optimal manner* (not as determined by me but as determined by the relevant social welfare function), *then the manner of taxing is very important even at the first level of approximation; and it is the interpersonal distributive elements that are all important in defining an optimal tax structure*.

It is because of this conclusion that my planet had to start out with transfer taxation. As I have said, this result seemed odd to me at first; but having been led there by the invisible hand of mathematical logic, I was forced to draw my map in this way.

Sizeable exhaustive public expenditure

Once we admit the possibility of public collective services on our planet, we have to face the possibility that they will be large rather than small; and in any case they will be finite rather than zero or infinitesimal. So we do need an analysis of their logical nature.

We can approach this indirectly. What is our theory of *non*-public expenditure? So long as goods are producible at constant returns to scale and so long as each person's consumption of a good is measurably distinct from any other person's, the perfect-competition model of markets can be used as *an* optimal social computing device. If we deny constant returns to scale – and technology on this or any other planet may make this denial mandatory in many areas – an opening wedge for an alternative kind of social allocation arises. And if we deny that every good's consumption is purely individualistic, instead insisting on strong 'external effects', we will have still another reason why the ordinary private marketing calculus must be non-optimal.[1]

To handle one difficulty at a time, let's keep to a strict assumption of constant returns to scale in all production. But let's introduce important externalities ('neighborhood' effects, etc.) into the consumption sphere. Thus, the battleship that protects your rights and investments also protects mine.

I don't suppose that anyone, upon reflection, would try to build up a theory of public expenditure without bringing in some kind of externality. Yet it is surprising that Pigou, who above

1. There are still other basic reasons for governmental action or interferences: e.g., 'paternalistic' dissatisfaction by the electorate with the effective tastes that they will all display in their day-to-day market preference acts – leading to public policies in the field of education, capital formation, etc.; exercise of economic entrepreneurship and decision-making by public officials; and many more.

all welfare economists has reminded us of external diseconomies of the smoke nuisance type, should in his brief discussion of expenditure theory have left this externality element almost completely implicit.

Now remembering that we theorists like to work with extreme polar cases, what is the natural model to formulate so as to give strongest emphasis to external effects? I have long thought that this is best brought out by the following model.

Assume that some goods, like bread, are privately consumed: this means that the total of bread can be written as the sum of the bread consumptions of each separate individual. But along with such purely private goods, assume public goods – like national defense – which *simultaneously* enter into many persons' indifference curves. Then assuming no transcendental group mind, but only a set of individual tastes and an ethical social welfare function dependent upon these tastes and ranking them in order of deservingness, we can prove that the perfect-competition market model will not work optimally. We can prove that there exists an inefficient configuration from which all men can be made better off, and a frontier of efficient points from which no universally advantageous movements are possible; of all the infinity of such efficient points, a socially best one is definable in terms of a specified normative welfare function.

It is this model that I explored in the two cited papers [Readings 9a and c]. And it is also this model that Sax, Wicksell, Lindahl, Musgrave, Bowen and other economists of the last seventy-five years had considered under the 'voluntary exchange theory of public finance' name or some other. The principle conclusions of this analysis seem to be the following:

1. Efficient, inefficient and socially optimal configurations can be theoretically defined: a point on the efficiency frontier requires equality between the vertically-added marginal rates of substitution of all men for the public and private goods; and the best of such points requires lump-sum redistributions of the transferable private goods until they have equal marginal social significance.

2. Although the optimum is definable, rational people will not, if left to themselves, be led by an invisible hand to the bliss point. On the contrary, it will pay for each rational man to dissemble,

207

trying to mask his preference for the public goods and to engage in other game-strategy maneuvers which, when all do them, will necessarily involve deadweight loss to society.

Having called attention to the nature of the difficulty, I do not wish to be too pessimistic. After all, the world's work does somehow get done. And to say that market mechanisms are non-optimal, and there are difficulties with most political decision processes, does not imply that we can never find new mechanisms of a better sort. (Example: skillful use of the symmetry that prevails between individuals may enable us to find optimal computing algorithms. Example: Interrogate people for their tastes with respect to public goods in such large homogeneous groups as to give each respondent the feeling that his answer can be a 'true' one without costing him anything extra.)

Decreasing-cost phenomena

Once people have understood the above model, they are likely to object to its unrealism. Thus, Dr Stephen Enke and Dr Julius Margolis have both pointed out that many, if not all, government expenditures can be qualitatively varied so as to confer more benefit on one man at the expense of another man. This raises the question whether we cannot bring back the market pricing mechanism, charging fees for public services and letting their quantity and quality be determined by money voting of the supply and demand type.

Certainly, it should be possible for the theorist to go beyond the polar cases of (1) pure private goods and (2) pure public goods to (3) some kind of a mixed model which takes account of all external, indirect, joint-consumption effects. I shall not write down such a mathematical model. But if I did do so, would we not find – as Pigou and Sidgwick so long ago warned us is true of all external economies and diseconomies – that the social optimum could not be achieved without somebody's taking into account all direct and indirect utilities and costs in all social decisions?

Now in connexion with running a particular railroad, highway or concert, we might find just the right conditions of scarcity of space and of independence of consumptions so that ordinary market pricing could lead to the optimum. In such a case, we can really reduce matters to our first category of purely private goods, and self-policing perfect competition might be an optimal social signalling and computing device.

However, generally a mixed model that refuses to fall in my polar case of a pure public good, will not thereby obligingly go into the other polar case of a pure private good. The mixed case has elements of both in it. And while we cannot by pure logic alone deduce that the intermediate case must qualitatively be a blend of the properties of the two poles, we can by logic know that ordinary pricing will be non-optimal unless it happens to be able to pick up each indirect external marginal utility.

Here is a contemporary instance. The Federal Communications Commission is now trying to make up its mind about permitting subscription television. You might think that the case where a program comes over the air and is available for any set owner to tune in on is a perfect example of my public good. And in a way it is. But you would be wrong to think that the essence of the phenomenon is inherent in the fact that the broadcaster is not able to refuse the service to whatever individuals he pleases. For in this case, by use of descramblers, it is technically possible to limit the consumptions of a particular broadcast to any specified group of individuals. You might, therefore, be tempted to say: A descrambler enables us to convert a public good into a private good; and by permitting its use, we can sidestep the vexing problems of collective expenditure, instead relying on the free pricing mechanism.

Such an argument would be wrong. Being able to limit a public good's consumption does not make it a true-blue private good. For what, after all, are the true marginal costs of having one extra family tune in on the program? They are literally zero. Why then prevent any family which would receive positive pleasure from tuning in on the program from doing so?

Upon reflection, you will realize that our well-known optimum principle that goods should be priced at their marginal costs would not be realized in the case of subscription broadcasting. Why not? In the deepest sense because this is, by its nature, not a case of constant returns to scale. It is a case of general decreasing costs. So long as increasing returns prevail in the actual range of consumption, we know that perfect competition will not be self-preserving and market behavior is unlikely to be optimal.

The case of decreasing costs may be empirically very important. Certainly, when you try to analyze why public utilities are public utilities and why certain activities (like railroads, water supply, electricity and post offices) may fall into either the category of public or private enterprise, you will usually find that some significant deviation from strict constant returns to scale is involved. I cannot then be completely satisfied with Pigou's statement:

These are not problems of Public Finance, as I understand that term. I do not propose, therefore, to discuss at all the question over what classes of enterprise it is desirable that public operation should be extended, but to proceed on the assumption that this is already determined (Pigou, 1928, p. 24).

Considerations concerning waste thus enable us to say, with regard to several classes of goods and services [primarily those which do not have an inelastic demand], that, if the government decides to provide them, it should finance their provision by fees (ibid., 1928, pp. 27–8).

It is precisely in such cases that uniform average cost pricing will sin against the rule that prices should equal marginal costs. As Hotelling has insisted, there is here a *prima facie* case for government subsidy. To argue, as some economists have done, that the government budget is already so loaded with necessary expenditure as to make it undesirable for it to have to take on such subsidy expenditures, is to miss the point I am trying to make. This *is* one of the needed functions of government, and in making compromises because of fiscal necessities, there is no *a priori* reason why this function should be particularly neglected.

There is a related significant point that needs stressing. It is not enough in the decreasing cost case to come closer to marginal cost pricing in the Lerner-Lange manner, making up the deficits by general taxation. As soon as decreasing cost and diversity of product appear, we have the difficult non-local 'total conditions' to determine what finite mix of product is optimal. This involves a terrible social computation problem: we must scan the almost infinite number of possible products and select the best configuration; we cannot feel our way to the optimum but must make judgement at a distance to determine the *optimum optimorum*.

All this is familiar. But what I have to point out are the complications that arise when there are two or more people on the planet. I like my cider sour; you like it sweet. With constant returns we could both get what we want, or at least what we deserve. But with initial indivisibilities or other forms of increasing returns, what I get will depend on what you get. (This is true even if we pay in the form of fees the marginal costs of our separate consumption.)

Now, how can society decide on the product mix which will maximize a specified social welfare function? It must weigh in all the different individuals' utilities from each decision. And *this is a problem that is analytically almost exactly like my model of public expenditure.*

Given the individual indifference curves and the social welfare function compromising them, one could define the theoretical optimum. (In practice, finding the solution might be very tedious.) But now try to devise a system of 'benefit taxation' that will in some sense make people pay for what they get – either because justice or equity requires this, or, more subtly, because the necessity of having to make such payments is thought to be a way of helping to determine the proper place for society to arrive in the end. Instantly, you will discover that the same game-theory reasons that compel rational men to hide their desires for public goods will be motivating them to hide their consumers' surpluses from different product configurations.

II

Once again, in contemplating the dilemmas that most forms of political voting involve, we are reminded of the beautiful and special simplicities of the *laissez-faire* model. But, alas, the difficulties are those of the real world. And it would be quite illogical to conclude from all this that men and technology should be different, should be such as to make the competitive game all-sufficient. That would be as silly as to say that we should all love sawdust because its production is so beautiful.

Conclusion

Unfortunately, I have only gotten my planet started. Time hasn't permitted me to do more than describe its transfer expenditures, to relate them to the financing of small public services, and to formulate some of the analytic difficulties with a theory of public services. Though my model of pure public goods has turned out to be an unrealistic polar case, it turns out that almost all deviations from constant returns to scale and almost all externalities must inevitably involve some of the same analytic properties and dilemmas of my polar case.

We must leave to other times and other stars the exploration of those momentous coalitions of decision-making that are part of the essence of the political process. To the theorist, the theory of public finance is but part of the general theory of government. And at this frontier, the easy formulas of classical economics no longer light our way.

Appendix: Strotz and Tiebout Discussions

Distributional aspects of public goods

I should like to comment briefly on two papers that have grown out of the earlier discussion. In the present issue Professor Robert H. Strotz (1958, pp. 329–31) has pointed out a formal implication of my original equations **1** and **2**: they define a Pareto optimality frontier[2]

$$u^1 = f(u^2, u^3, ..., u^s); \tag{A}$$

and each point on that frontier will generally determine a set of all public goods

$$X_{n+j} = g^j(u^2, u^3, ..., u^s) \ (j = 1, 2, ..., m). \tag{B}$$

Now under what conditions can the left-hand variables in (B) be regarded as independent variables? If $s - 1 = m$ and the Jacobean matrix $[g_j^i]$ is well-behaved, (B) can be inverted. Or if $s - 1 > m$ and the Jacobean $[g_j^i]$ is of rank m, m of (B)'s right-hand us can be solved for in terms of the public goods ($X_{n+1}, ..., X_{n+m}$) and the remaining right-hand us. So the Strotz conclusion follows: Any public good configuration is optimal if only the 'distribution of income' is such as to get us to a point on the Pareto-frontier compatible with that public good configuration.[3]

In view of the modern trend to regard mere Pareto-optimality or efficiency as incomplete necessary conditions, what follows

2. I use my original notation, which is related to Strotz's by $X_{n+j} = S_j$, $s = I$, $m = K$, $L^i = s_i$, etc.

3. When you reflect that the degrees of freedom to *completely specify* a single post office exceed the number of people in the United States, the case where $s - 1 < m$ may seem most realistic. In such a case, or in case people's preferences for public goods are so alike as to lead to ill-behaved Jacobians, an arbitrary choice of (X_{n+j}) will be compatible with no Pareto-optimal point.

from the above conclusion? To me, this.

It is wrong to make, as some have made, a sharp separation between correct public-good decisions and correct redistributional-taxation decisions. Changing public goods *does* materially affect the distribution of income and all decisions have to be made *simultaneously*.

As Professor Strotz says, there is no disagreement between our analyses.

Local finance and the mathematics of marriage

A second paper of interest in the present connection is that of Professor Charles M. Tiebout (1956, pp. 416–24). He argues that the public expenditure theory simplifies itself at the local level – as people spontaneously join in forming homogeneous communities which will legislate what each (and all) want in the way of collective goods.

This attempted solution fits in under one or another of the 'symmetry' principles that I had referred to. That it goes some way toward solving the problem, few would doubt. As a solution, though, it raises a number of serious questions.

Thus, when you study in detail a supposedly homogeneous suburb, you find it riddled with conflicting desires. The old, with grown-up children, oppose the desire of the young for more school expenditure. And so it goes. It avails little for one group to say to another: 'If you don't like it here, go back where you came from.' Ours is a fluid society, with little respect paid to hard-to-identify charter members. People want to 'improve' their community, not abdicate from it.

Secondly, people often like heterogeneity even though it involves conflict. The old don't want to live in homogeneous ghettos with their own kind, and the same goes for many other groups. In an interdependent world, one man's privacy is another man's condemnation to loneliness.

Thirdly, there is the political and ethical question whether groups of like-minded individuals shall be 'free' to 'run out' on their social responsibilities and go off by themselves. At the national level, society respects no such freedom: e.g., migration control, compulsory taxation, etc.

A simple mathematical model will illustrate a few of the intricacies of the problem. If a group of men and women have each a preference rating for members of the opposite sex, who will end up marrying whom? This assignment problem – which is stated in biological terms only for concreteness – is also faced by colleges and students choosing each other, by clubs and fraternities, etc. In real life, it is solved by dynamic reconnoiter, contact, proposal, refusal or acceptance – in short, by general trial and error, which is not guaranteed to represent any optimum.

Consider the trivial case of 2 boys A and B and two girls 1 and 2. Each boy has an ordinal preference rating of the girls, which in this simple case must be either the permutations (1, 2) or (2, 1). Each girl's rating of the boys must be (A, B) or (B, A).

Now what are the possible preference configurations? In this simple case, they are essentially only the following (where the first row lists people, with their choices shown in the columns below them):

1	2		A	B
A	B		1	2
B	A		2	1

or

1	2		A	B
A	A		1	2
B	B		2	1

or

1	2		A	B
A	B		2	1
B	A		1	2

or

1	2		A	B
A	A		1	1
B	B		2	2

Of these four cases, the first fits Tiebout's attempt best. All the guinea pigs are in agreement: 1 and A want to marry; so do 2 and B; all get their first choices. The solution (1,A; 2,B) is Pareto-optimal; being the only Pareto-optimal solution, it is also

214

Bergson-optimal, maximizing *any* social welfare function that respects individual tastes.

But now turn to the last case. A and 1 are preferred by all of the other sex. If we give persons the 'property right' to form bilateral compacts, the favored ones will presumably marry each other with (1,A; 2,B) the resulting equilibrium.

However, given a social welfare function which respects tastes, this outcome is not necessarily optimal. The other possible outcome (2,A; 1,B) might be 'ethically better' (e.g. where 2 has a 'great' preference in favor of A but 1 is 'almost' indifferent, and 2 is 'ethically deserving' of great social respect). Or we can put the matter a little differently: (2,A; 1,B) is just as Pareto-optimal as is (1,A; 2,B). When you leave the former and go to the latter, you make two people happier and two people unhappier.

In the second case, there is likewise no unique Pareto-optimal point. Left to themselves with certain 'freedoms' and 'property rights' to make bilateral collusions, probably 1 and A will marry, ignoring 2 and B. And B will be glad. But 2 will not be glad, showing that the configuration (2,A; 1,B) is also Pareto-optimal. Of course, if you used a crude majority vote rule, (1, A; 2, B) would be the winning position. But – as Arrow, Black and others have shown – majority-rule devices are subject to many intransitivities and drawbacks.

Finally, the third case is like the last in that both outcomes are Pareto-optimal and in going from one to the other you sadden two people and gladden two. Whether the girls or boys are to be made glad cannot be decided except in terms of a given determinate social welfare function.

I conclude from all this that there remain many important analytical problems of public-good determination that still need investigation at every level of government.

References

Pigou, A. C. (1928), *A Study in Public Finance*, Macmillan, 3rd edn.

Samuelson, P. A. (1954), 'The pure theory of public expenditure', *Review of Economics and Statistics*, vol. 36.

Samuelson, P. A. (1955), 'Diagrammatic exposition of a theory of public expenditure', *Review of Economics and Statistics*, vol. 37.

Strotz, R. H. (1958), *Review of Economics and Statistics*, vol. 40.

Tiebout, C. M. (1956), 'A pure theory of local expenditures', *Journal of Political Economy*, vol. 64.

10 O. Eckstein

A Survey of the Theory of Public Expenditure Criteria

O. Eckstein, 'A survey of the theory of public expenditure criteria',
Public Finances, Needs, Sources and Utilization, Princeton University Press,
1961, pp. 439–94.

The theory of expenditure criteria has received a lot of attention in recent years, stimulated by the practical needs of the world. In the United States, the evaluation of public works, particularly in the field of water resource development, had led to the evolution of techniques and criteria for project evaluation. This work was largely pioneered within the federal government. The need for devising development plans for underdeveloped countries has led to extensive theoretical study of investment criteria for that particular economic context.

This paper presents the elements of the theory. Rather than propose or defend specific criteria, I try to indicate the issues about which assumptions must be made. First, possible objective functions are discussed – What, if anything, is to be maximized? There follow sections on constraints, interest rates, repercussion effects, and the treatment of risk and uncertainty. Finally, with the taxonomy of the problem in hand, most of the more important decision models that have been developed are surveyed and discussed.

Some limitations should also be mentioned. First, there is very little empirical work in this study, in particular, no real allocation-problems are presented or solved. In view of the scope of the problems to be covered at a theoretical level, intensive treatment of specific empirical situations was not attempted. Second, there is no treatment of the various technical maximization methods, such as Lagrangian techniques, linear and nonlinear programming, simulations, queuing theory, and game theory, since excellent treatments are now available. Third, the macro-economic decision models developed by Frisch, Tinbergen and Theil are not discussed, even though they are closely related conceptually. Nor is the theory of public expenditures, advanced by Wicksell and others, and developed further by Samuelson and Musgrave, treated here. This theory concerns itself with those expenditures for which conventional value theory breaks down completely. My concern is largely confined to public works and development projects of a sort for which measures of value can be established empirically.

The Objective Function

Introduction

The most fundamental consideration in a decision model is the choice of an objective function. Should the model seek to maximize (or minimize) some operationally definable measures? And if so, what should the measure be?

Typically, in economics, the analysis presupposes that we seek to maximize economic welfare, however this may be defined. The notion of maximization is perhaps the central analytical concept of economics. Recently, Simon (1957a, ch. 14; and 1957b, Introduction and chs. 4 and 5) has questioned this idea, and at least as a description of the real world has suggested that people and corporations merely seek to obtain a satisfactory state of affairs, rather than some optimum.

One could reconstruct prescriptive (or welfare) economics along Simon's lines, letting the analyst indicate what policies keep the state of affairs within the tolerance levels of the interest groups affected inside and outside government. The 'putting out fires' approach to policy, which frequently characterizes American political leadership, certainly suggests that politicians are also 'satisficers', in Simon's phrase. Nevertheless, the present study takes the view that economic analysis will play a more productive role if it seeks to maximize something. The extent to which policy makers decide to accept the economist's optimizing analyses will probably be decided by satisficing considerations.[1]

What should be maximized? Welfare economics

Assuming a maximizing approach, a yardstick which will define the optimum must be specified. Economic welfare is the usual

1. For a different view, that politicians are maximizers of votes, see Downs (1957).

objective, but there are a number of alternative ways of defining this broad concept.

First, in Western economics, economic welfare is almost always related to individual welfare; it is postulated that there can be no welfare other than what accrues to individuals. This is a rejection of the organic theory of the state: the state as an entity enjoys no welfare, only the people that compose it.[2]

Following Bergson (1938), the function for social economic welfare at any point in time can be written formally:

$$W = W(W_1, \ldots, W_n),$$

where W_i is the economic welfare of individual i. A change in economic welfare can be written

$$\Delta W = \Delta W(\Delta W_1, \ldots, \Delta W_n). \qquad \mathbf{1}$$

When can the change in social economic welfare caused by a policy be said to be positive? A definition of this positive change is needed for to strive to maximize welfare, all changes which serve to increase it must be undertaken. An optimum point is defined as a situation in which no further positive changes in social welfare can be accomplished.

Clearly, if all individuals are made better off ($\Delta W_i > 0$ for all i) economic welfare is improved according to any nonmalevolent standard. A somewhat weaker, although still very strong, requirement is this: Let no one be made worse off and let at least one person be better off. ($\Delta W_i \geq 0$ for all i, with at least one $\Delta W_i > 0$.)

There are few (or no) economic changes which could pass this test. Usually, some person is affected adversely, which is sufficient to preclude this criterion from ruling on the desirability of the change. A test which promised to yield an answer in a wider range of situations was introduced by Kaldor (1939, pp. 549–52) and Hicks (1940, pp. 105–24). They did not require that no one be made worse off, only that the gainers of any economic change be able to compensate the losers, though the compensations need not necessarily be carried out. In this way, it was hoped that the production features of economic policy could be separated from their distri-

2. For the view that economics only encompasses the case of individually based welfare, see Ellis (1950, pp. 1–12). For a reply, see Allin (1953a, pp. 362–79; and 1953b, pp. 605–14).

butional implications. Presumably, pure lump-sum transfers of income can achieve any distribution of output that is desired. If the total value of output minus the value of factor services is increased, presumably the gainers can compensate the losers, and economic welfare is increased. If the economic change is so small that prices are unaffected, this is a simple and unambiguous test. Where prices change, Hicks suggested use of the new prices, Kaldor of the old.[3]

An implicit assumption of this approach is that the economic welfare of any individual (or family) only depends on the goods and services consumed and supplied by him; his welfare is not affected by the welfare of his neighbors. For if there were such external effects of consumption, even an increase in total net value which made more goods and services available to everyone might reduce economic welfare – by causing envy, for example.[4] Of course, if all individuals were so noble as to derive only happiness from an increase in other people's consumption, this result would be ruled out.

The Kaldor–Hicks compensation criteria were subjected to much criticism. Scitovsky showed that if the economic change is large enough to cause prices to change, the criterion may become inconsistent; the gainers could compensate the losers after the change, yet the potential losers might be able to compensate the potential gainers prior to the change (Scitovsky, 1942, pp. 98–110). He found that an unambiguous increase in welfare required that the value of net output must increase both at the new and the old prices. Samuelson deepened this line of criticism, contending that all the potential distributions of welfare of any given production situation be considered relevant. One situation would be ruled superior to another only if every potential distribution of welfare possible under it is superior for at least one individual, and is inferior for none. This statement, which would be extremely difficult to implement empirically, eliminates some cases which would be ranked even under the Scitovsky double criterion.

3. This is the interpretation of Graaff (1968). For a different view, see Little (1957, ch. 6).
4. This phenomenon is stressed by Baumol (1952, pp. 88, 127). (Also see Graaff, 1968, pp. 43–5.)

Another line of criticism questions the use of potential compensation (Baumol, 1952, p. 123; Little, 1957, ch. 6; Kennedy, 1952–3; Baldwin, 1953–4, p. 154). Can one situation be considered to yield greater economic welfare if everyone could be made better off even though, in fact, the necessary compensation payments are not made? Hypothetical payments, according to most later writers, are not an adequate device to remove the distribution issue. On the other hand, actual compensation payments have not been accepted either, since they would attach particular desirability to the income distribution before the economic change. The most widely accepted modern view insists that the redistribution of income of any economic change be evaluated separately on the basis of specific ethical judgements. As formulated by Little (1957, p. 105), an appropriate criterion for the desirability of an economic change would be the following:

1. The gainers must be able to overcompensate the losers and/or the losers must not be able to overcompensate the gainers.
2. The redistribution of income must be good. This assumes that the option of making pure redistributions is excluded; otherwise different criteria apply.

The above criterion permits the comparison of any two situations on the basis of what is probably rather close to a minimum of restrictions that must be imposed on the economic welfare function.

As a theory of economic policy, this formulation leaves much to be desired, however. First, as Graaff has argued persuasively, the prevalence of external effects in consumption contradicts a necessary assumption of the theory. Second, analysis of real-world situations is usually ill-suited to be couched in terms of choices among two alternatives. Third, since most policies involve a loss of welfare to someone, a formal basis for interpersonal comparisons is needed, and since the economist has no particular right to attach social weights to individual welfare in the social welfare function, this is sufficient ground to rule out rigid prescriptions. Of course the economist can stop short of this judgement, leaving the evaluation of distributive effects to the politician. But even under this view the economist will find it very difficult to sidestep the distribution issue altogether. After all, he cannot conduct his analyses in terms of the names of the millions of people in his country, and grouping of population into categories – by income, class or geography or anything else – already prejudges the distributive issue.[5]

The complexity of the criteria, their inability to resolve most practical issues, and the inherently ethical problem of judging the distribution of income has brought many of the leading students of welfare economics to very pessimistic conclusions. Baumol, in his 'Epilogue: the wreck of welfare economics?' stresses the prevalence of interdependence effects which invalidate the use of market prices and rejects the standard marginal optimum conditions. Historically, the main use of welfare economics has been the derivation of these conditions and the proof that *laissez-faire* is the best economic system (Boulding, 1952, p. 24); thus, Baumol's stress on interdependence strikes at the heart of the theory. Other than as a means of exploding fallacious arguments, he writes, the fact that categories like 'external economies' and 'external diseconomies' remain largely empty economic boxes prevents any further applications of welfare theory as it now stands.

Is there any hope of further progress based on empirical investigation and analysis of the problem of the interdependence of activities of economic units? I cannot pretend to offer even tentative answers. It seems to me, however, that if the subject is to achieve primary importance for practical men, this question must be faced and answered (Baumol, 1952, p. 167).

Graaff's (1968, pp. 170–71) pessimism rests on two grounds. First, he does not believe that there will be agreement on the ends of policy. He is concerned not only with the distribution of income, but also with the attitude toward uncertainty, the time horizon, and the rate of progress. The external effects in consumption which he stresses also hopelessly complicate the problem. He concludes that economists had best devote themselves to factual studies of the functioning of the economic system, perhaps predicting the effects of policy on some index numbers, but attaching no prescriptive value.

A more modest role for welfare economics: the objective function

Its critics underestimate the usefulness of welfare economics. It is true that it has failed in the tasks which had been set for it:

5. For other difficulties of the concept of distribution of welfare, see Arrow (1951a, pp. 923–34, esp. 931–2).

it has not (i) proved the superiority of *laissez faire*; (ii) provided simple criteria for judging economic changes or economic optima, or (iii) provided a method of isolating the economic aspects of policy from ethical considerations. But the failure to accomplish these objectives is due to their grandiose nature. There are more modest objectives of analysis for which welfare economics must play a crucial role.

What I propose is this. First, the rather casually dispensed advice of the critics of welfare economics should be taken seriously. I follow Baumol and seek to establish what interdependence effects should be measured, and to indicate the methods that may be appropriate. I follow Graaff by emphasizing measurement rather than absolutist advice. But this should be no senseless retreat into hypothesis-testing unrelated to potential action, nor the collection of random sets of facts; rather it should be the establishment of decision-models which will reveal explicitly what actions will maximize the achievement of specified objectives.

I do not insist that the economist be given the objectives in polished, formal manner. Rather, the economist must interpret the desires of the policy people whom he is serving and express them in an analytical form as an objective function. He then seeks to maximize this function, given the empirical relations in the economy and the institutional constraints that may be appropriate to the analysis. In this manner, the economist can play the role of technician, of bringing his technical equipment to bear on policy problems, with maximum effectiveness.

The specification of the objective function thus is not primarily meant to let the economist play omnipotent being; rather, it is a device for bridging the gap between the positive quantitative research which is the main stock-in-trade of the economist, and the normative conclusions which policy requires.[6]

6. This is not to say that an objective function must always be specified when economics is used for policy purposes. Perhaps in most cases, particularly where the analysis involves few steps, such as the mere marshalling of figures, it would be excess theoretical baggage. But once the analysis takes on some complexity, an explicit objective function becomes more important if normative recommendations are to be derived. At the least, the function is a means of forcing the technician to state his normative assumptions; at its best, it is a powerful analytical aid, eliminating uninteresting areas of exploration, and permitting the ranking of alternatives.

Single v. multiple indicators

Individual and 'social' welfare: the problem of income distribution.
In formulating the objective function so as to express our notion
of economic welfare, there is a question about the number of
variables to be employed. From a theoretical point of view, the
ideal function would define at least one variable for each individual
measuring his welfare, and probably more than one, say, a measure
of expected gain in real income plus a measure of the probable
dispersion. Thus the objective function might take the form

$$W = W(\bar{y}_1, \sigma_{y_1}, \bar{y}_2, \sigma_{y_2}, \ldots, \bar{y}_n, \sigma_{y_n}), \qquad 2$$

where $\bar{y}_i$ is expected gain in real income of individual $y (i = 1, \ldots, n)$ and σ_i is the standard deviation of that gain. Were we given
individual preferences about risk, so that we could write $u_i = (\bar{y}_i, \sigma_{y_1})$, and perhaps of higher moments, 2 could be rewritten

$$W = W(u_1, u_2, \ldots, u_n). \qquad 3$$

But functions of this form are a counsel of perfection. Policy
problems rarely present themselves in a form suitable for such ideal
evaluation. Thus, W must be given some other form.

A particularly simple version weights a dollar of expected gain
(or loss) of different individuals equally and ignores risk.
Thus

$$W = (\bar{y}_1 + \bar{y}_2 + \ldots + \bar{y}_n), \qquad 4$$

this is the form of the function which stresses economic efficiency
to the exclusion of all else. The welfare theorists of the Kaldor–
Hicks school sought to give strong normative significance to 4
through the compensation tests. In more recent literature, 4 plus an
independent ethical judgement on the distribution of the incomes
$\bar{y}_i$ has found considerable favor and has been applied. This can be
written as

$$W = W(\Sigma_i \bar{y}_i, \bar{y}_1, \ldots, \bar{y}_n), \qquad 5$$

where the detailed list of individual incomes permits judgement
about the income distribution, a judgement to be rendered by the
policy-maker. This information cannot, in fact, be specified for
individuals since it would be an impossible statistical task. It can be
presented for income classes, however, either by size class or functional type of income, or the data can be developed by regions (for

an example, see Krutilla and Eckstein, 1958, chs. 7 and 8). This specializes 5 to

$$W = W(\Sigma_m \bar{y}_i, \Sigma_{r_1} \bar{y}_i, \ldots, \Sigma_{r_k} y_i), \qquad 6$$

where i in m includes all individuals in the nation (or world), i in r includes all individuals in region (or income class) i, and so on.

When the policy-maker uses the objective function, he can attach any weights he wishes to the national and regional groupings of income. The economist *qua* economist has no right to attach these social utilities to the incomes of individuals. But he usually cannot escape the task of defining the groupings for which income distribution data are to be constructed. The efficiency minded economist will stress the national (world?) grouping and no other. The regionally oriented economist may stress the regional breakdown, and so on. Certain objective functions could be identified as bad economics if labeled as serving the public interest, e.g., the case where weight is only attached to the income of a specific pressure group.

While 5 and 6 have found most common application, they do not exhaust the possibilities of dealing with the distributional question. The policy-maker may specify more detailed rules. He may impose distributional side conditions, insisting that any policy produce a certain pattern of gain, or alternatively, that a certain minimum accrue to some group, or perhaps that no group suffer a net loss.

The economist can also feel free to perform experiments in policy evaluation using specific objective functions, treating the results as free of absolute normative significance. For example, he can assume a certain shape for the marginal utility of income functions. He may assume some elasticity to this curve, or he may choose to use a form of the function that has been implicitly produced by the political process. The effective marginal rates of the personal income tax at different income levels can be interpreted as implying a marginal utility of income curve. If the government is assumed to act on the principle of equimarginal sacrifice, then marginal effective tax rates can be the basis for deriving a measure of the government's notion of marginal utilities of income.

The kind of question that could be posed when such a function is applied to the analysis of a policy is of the following form:

assuming the values placed by the government on marginal income of different income classes in its personal tax legislation, will a policy raise total national economic welfare?[7]

Single v. *multiple objectives*. Economic welfare can be viewed as a one-dimensional quantity for each individual or group, related presumably to the goods expected to be enjoyed, plus perhaps some allowance for the associated risk. The tools of economic analysis are not always designed to yield this type of answer; in practical work, the objective function has to be tailored to the analysis. For example, a public works program may produce certain outputs over a long period of time, generate a certain amount of economic growth, have a counter-cyclical potential, alleviate a pocket of local poverty, reduce some natural risks, create a potential for a future recreation facility, dot the landscape with beautiful monuments that have symbolic significance at home and abroad, and so on. Insistence on one-dimensional welfare indicators would either produce a meaningless hodge-podge, or a slighting of all objectives other than expected tangible output. In principle, the many outputs may be considered reducible to common units for each individual, assuming a scalar utility function to exist; in practice the many effects must be grouped into meaningful categories of objectives. These categories can be related to such factors as:

1 Economic circumstance; for example, full employment benefits, which may be measurable from market data, can be considered a separate objective from depression benefits, which are more critically related to timing and to the employment and purchasing power generated.

2 The tangibility of the effect: is it measurable in some objective manner, or is it a rather arbitrary valuation?

3 Reliability of the estimates – with outputs meeting clear demands treated separately from more conditional benefits which may depend on various repercussion effects.

4 The date of the benefits – with the usually more uncertain remote benefits treated as a different kind of benefit.

Policy people rarely view their problem as one-dimensional. A multiple objective function corresponds more closely to their view

7. When the technique is applied to actual policies on an *ex post* basis, it yields a kind of consistency test of government attitudes.

of the world. In particular, it leaves to them the all-important weighting of the various objectives, giving them the results of the technical analysis in the most usable form. The extent of elaboration of objectives is an issue that must be resolved between the policy maker and the technician. But in no event should the technician arrogate the weighting of objectives to himself by presenting a one-dimensional answer after burying the weighting process in a welter of technical details.[8]

What are the benefits?

Since the objective function must be suited to the problem and must often be multiple in nature, the definition of benefits is also a relative matter. On some assumptions, benefits are defined in a particularly simple way. For example, under full employment conditions, with the marginal utility of income the same for all individuals, and with perfect markets and no external economies or diseconomies in production and consumption, prices are perfect measures of benefit. If a project is so large as to affect the prices of its outputs, a simple result is obtainable if the marginal utility of income is assumed not only the same for all individuals, but also constant over the range of variation. The area under the output's demand curve then constitutes a measure of benefits, and if the curves are assumed linear, an arithmetic average of old and new prices multiplied by the number of units will measure benefit. Another interesting case is the following: if the underlying individual indifference curves are assumed hyperbolic, Fischer's 'ideal' index number constitutes an indicator of benefit.[9]

In other cases, benefit cannot be defined so simply. While in principle it is always possible to measure the change in utility of individuals (assuming some cardinal concept that can be identified with willingness to pay), in practice this is an enormous task and short cuts must be devised. Often there is the question of what chains of repercussion should be pursued in benefit estimation; this issue is treated in the section on 'Repercussion Effects' (p. 241 et seq.). And where public services are genuine collective goods, benefit estimation often becomes impossible.

8. Examples of this practice abound in the evaluation practices in the water resource field. See Eckstein (1958, ch. 7).
9. This special case is discussed in Marris (1957, pp. 25–40).

A special case: cost minimization to achieve fixed objectives

A case which has been found to have very wide applicability, particularly in the general field of operations research, is the case where the objectives are strictly fixed and the remaining economic problem is to minimize the real cost of accomplishing them. This is only an interesting economic problem where there are several alternative and quite different ways of achieving the objectives. The problem can be approached through the neoclassical theory of the firm, from which the theorem about marginal productivities can be drawn, through linear programing, through simulation, or through the other maximizing procedures. While this paper does not elaborate on these techniques, the importance of the case for public expenditure analysis must be stressed, since it provides at least some role for economics even where the nature of the collective goods precludes benefit estimation.

The Constraints

Introduction

Economic policy is rarely concerned with the attainment of the best of all possible worlds. Rather, it seeks to improve economic welfare in the face of constraints. The economist, in devising a policy model, must decide how many of the constraints he will build into his analysis. Just as in the case of the objective function, there comes a point where the assumptions are so specific that they produce 'bad' economics. Constraints can be assumed to rule out all solutions except one, which automatically is then justified. This procedure can be viewed as excluding the application of economics to the problem. On the other hand, to prohibit the use of constraints altogether is to confine economics to a very narrow – and usually Utopian – range of problems.

Some types of constraints

There are many different sorts of constraints, originating in various institutional or physical limitations. In a sense, they mold the analysis, giving shape to the problem under study and determining the general nature of the solution.

For the kinds of public expenditures to which our analysis is meant to apply, several types of constraints can be distinguished.

First, there are *physical* constraints. The most general of these is the production function, which relates physical inputs to outputs. There may also be absolute limits to the size of structures, or else such sharp discontinuities to the cost curves that any point beyond them can be considered beyond the domain of analysis.

Legal constraints also may need to be incorporated into the model. A program or project must be in accordance with laws, whether it be water laws, property laws, treaties, or whatever. In admitting legal constraints, care must be exercised not to assume laws as fixed which could be affected by the analysis. This is one of the areas where the economist is in peril of accepting so many constraints that he will exclude the interesting solutions.

Administrative constraints may be imposed by the capability of the agency. Limits on the rate of expansion of a program, caused by the need to expand personnel and to diffuse administrative know-how, is one example. Excessive complexity of the planning process, requiring consideration of too many variables, or perhaps requiring excessive centralization of decision-making, is another.

We have already considered *distributional constraints*, which may impose a fixed pattern on the distribution of benefits and costs, or which may impose side conditions of minimum benefits for different groups.

There can be constraints of many other forms. *Uncertainty* can be introduced via constraints; for example, the condition may be imposed that the net gain of a project be positive at some specified probability level. Political constraints can also be imposed, though the line between realism and bad economics is particularly hard to draw on this point.

The final type is *financial* or *budget* constraints. In general, they specify that the amount of money available from some source is limited. In deriving expenditure criteria, this is a critical matter because it is the limited kind of money which must be allocated optimally, and it is to the constrained kind of funds that expenditure criteria address themselves. Elsewhere (Eckstein, 1958, pp. 47–80), I have explored the effect of alternative financial constraints on the form of expenditure criteria. If there is only one constrained financial resource and one category of benefits, the criterion requires that the rate of net benefit per dollar of the constrained funds be maximized. This maximization is accomplished by computing ratios of benefit to constrained funds for each project (or smaller unit of choice where possible), ranking projects by these ratios and going down the ranked list to the point where the scarce funds are exhausted. Although the ranking is by ratios, it is not the maximization of the ratio which is the objective but rather the total net gain that is possible, given the constraint. Examples of the use of various constraints will be found in the discussion of various models on page 256 et seq.

Constraints and the theory of budgeting

Constraints are rarely an accurate description of an institutional reality. Budgets are not rigidly fixed except over very short periods – and even then there can be supplemental appropriations. Financial requirements, e.g., that an operation be self-liquidating, are rarely followed if circumstances change. Particularly if a constraint severely interferes with the achievement of economic welfare, the constraint is likely to give way.

Nevertheless, the use of budget constraints is a powerful analytical device. It freezes one (or more) financial resource(s) and then permits an answer to the question: What is the best use of this scarce resource? The analysis then allocates the scarce kind of money in the optimal way. This is a meaningful procedure where, in fact, it is possible to identify the resource which serves to limit the overall size of the program.[10] A government agency allocating a budget that has been determined at a higher level, or a planning commission in an underdeveloped country drawing up an investment plan subject to limited domestic capital and foreign exchange, can view its problem in these terms. Thus, in a fundamental sense, the theory of constraints is at the heart of the theory of budgeting.

Constraints and opportunity costs

The acceptance of a budget constraint removes the possibility of reaching the *optimum optimorum* solution. In particular, it prohibits solution of the problem of determining the optimal level of expenditure of the constrained financial resource. Thus, an analysis

10. If there were a high degree of substitutability among financial resources, no resource would serve as a limit, and it would make no sense to use a constraint. Thus the constraint approach presupposes that the unconstrained financial resources cannot be a perfect substitute for the constrained resource.

using a constraint is restricted to optimum allocation of a fixed 'second-best' budget level, but it cannot determine the level itself.[11]

The latter problem requires some notion of the cost of budget money. What are the opportunity costs in other sectors of the economy and in fields of the budget outside the particular one under analysis? The extent to which these costs can be measured is still an open question, though some types of opportunity costs can definitely be estimated.

But whatever the difficulties of measurement, it is important to distinguish between two different problems. Where an undertaking must be assumed to be financed out of extra funds made possible by the political process, it is incorrect to compare it to projects within some budget constraint. The relevant comparison is between the project and the opportunity cost of the resources in the sector out of which the resources are drawn, whether by taxation, borrowing, or inflation. On the other hand, if a budget is accepted as fixed, the comparison must be made within that budget.

Wherever possible, constraints should not be accepted blindly. Even if there is an upper limit to expenditures in a particular budget, not only should the scarce funds be allocated in an optimal way, but also, a further test, which assures that the marginal expenditures yield a benefit as great as they would if spent outside the budget, must be performed.

Interest Rates

A particularly difficult problem in specifying an objective function is the choice of an interest rate. With outputs accruing at different points in time, it is necessary to place relative values on them, depending on the date at which they occur. Similarly, the dates at which costs are incurred may affect the value they represent. In this chapter, some of the possible approaches to specifying interest rates are examined.

The interest rate as a measure of value of outputs at different points in time: planners' time preference

There are several bases on which the interest rate for valuing outputs can be chosen. Acceptance of consumer sovereignty is, in one

11. For a general discussion of the theory of 'second-best' see Lipsey and Lancaster (1956-7, pp. 11-32).

sense, most consistent with individualist welfare economics. It requires that the interest rate used by households in their saving-spending decisions be applied. Clearly the use of this particular rate (or rather rates) makes sense only if the consumers' decision about the amount of saving and investment is also accepted; with the time profile of future output dependent both on the interest rate used for planning and on the amount of investment, rejection of consumer sovereignty with regard to one of the two variables requires modification of the other, even if consumer sovereignty is given full weight. Thus consumer sovereignty must be judged with respect to both variables simultaneously.

There is a long literature of criticism of consumer sovereignty for intertemporal choices.[12] Pigou, Ramsey, Dobb, Baumol and others reject the rationality of time preferences which prefer consumption earlier rather than later simply by reason of the date. Strotz (1955-6, pp. 165–80) has recently shown that a series of decisions made under pure time preference for the present lead to a total history of individual experience which contains less total satisfaction than would be possible in the absence of such 'myopia'. As the period of comparison lengthens, there is also the problem of comparing the welfare of future generations. And what assurance can there be that present consumers will make adequate provision for unborn generations?

An alternative approach has the public decision-maker, whether congressman, budgeteer, or central planner, exercise his own time preference. In a democratic society, the preferences on which he acts presumably bear some relation to the population's desires, though in practice, judging by the interest rates used in planning in most countries, there is also a good deal of concern with remote payoffs.

A theoretical foundation can be provided for planners' optimal time preferences, based on the notion of the diminishing marginal utility of individual income. If we assume that this marginal utility falls, then the value of marginal output falls as *per capita* income rises. Since the interest rate is designed to reflect the relative value of marginal output at different points in time, this rate should be lower the smaller the expected increase in *per capita* output, and where a decline in *per capita* income is in prospect, possibly due to

12. For a summary see Holzman (1958, pp. 3–20).

Table 1

Interest Rates Based on Diminishing Marginal Utility of *Per Capita* Consumption and Growth Rate of *Per Capita* Consumption[13]

Elasticity of marginal utility of income function	Per capita growth rate of consumption			
	−2%	0	+2%	+4%
2·0	−4·0	0	4·0	8·0
1·5	−3·0	0	3·0	6·0
1·0	−2·0	0	2·0	4·0
0·7	−1·4	0	1·4	2·8
0·5	−1·0	0	1·0	2·0

excessive population growth, the interest rate can even be negative.[14] Given the kinds of empirical magnitudes that actually

13. The underlying model is the following:

Let $W = W(y_1, \ldots, y_t, \ldots)$, where y_t is *per capita* consumption in year t.

Let $\dfrac{\partial W}{y_t} = (y_t)-\epsilon$, where ϵ is the elasticity of the marginal utility of consumption.

Then

$$\frac{\partial W}{\partial y_t} \bigg/ \frac{\partial W}{\partial y_{t+1}} = \frac{y_t-\epsilon}{y_{t+1}-\epsilon} = \left(\frac{y_t}{y_{t+1}}\right)^{-\epsilon} = (1+r)\epsilon,$$

where r is the growth rate of *per capita* consumption.

But $\dfrac{\partial W}{\partial y_t} \bigg/ \dfrac{\partial W}{\partial y_{t+1}}$ is the ratio of marginal values of consumption, and thus equals the interest factor, $1 + i$. Therefore

$$1 + i = (1 + r)\epsilon.$$

This is the formula used for the table. If we decompose the growth rate of *per capita* consumption into the growth rate of population, π, and of consumption, ρ, we get

$$1 + i = \frac{(1 + p)\epsilon}{(1 + \pi)\epsilon}.$$

Recently, Samuelson has examined a similar problem and pointed to the relation between population growth and the interest rate. (Samuelson, 1958, pp. 467–82.)

14. For a formal model reflecting these notions, see Eckstein's 'Investment criteria' (pp. 76–8). An earlier model, which has some points of similarity, can be found in Harrod (1948, pp. 35–62). A model which derives the optimal rate of investment from utility functions is given in Tinbergen (1956, pp. 603–10); but see the important comment by Sen (1957a, pp. 745–50).

prevail in the world, the interest rates suggested by the model are relatively low, 4 per cent or less, even for fairly large elasticities of the marginal utility of income curves. Table 1, which is reproduced from an earlier study, summarizes these results.

One paradoxical result is suggested by the analysis: the lower the rate of growth, the lower should be the interest rate. Since, typically, the lowest rates of growth of *per capita* income are found in the poorest countries, low interest rates should be used in these countries. Yet these are the places where the pressure for early consumption is greatest. The resolution of the paradox is simple: the interest rate relates not to the absolute level of consumption, but to the relative changes over time. Thus, high-growth countries, whatever the present levels, can afford the luxury of high valuation of present consumption versus future consumption, since they will have higher levels in the future. The association of high interest rates with low income levels is based on other phenomena, particularly the scarcity of capital and pure preference of present over future consumption. Pure time preference has often been believed to be greater at low levels of income.

Should the objective function of the planner allow for pure time preference? Or should it be above such 'irrationality'? Even from the narrow point of view of economic efficiency, this question cannot be resolved without use of strong value judgements. Preference for experiences in the near future can be rational for individuals, given the uncertainty of the duration of life. A lifetime consumption plan which stresses early years is more certain of fulfillment than one which emphasizes later years, since the probability of survival to the expected consumption dates is greater. Even if rationality is defined to exclude aversion to risk there is room for pure time preference. The utility to be enjoyed at each future moment must be multiplied by the probability of being alive at the time, and since this probability falls with the remoteness of the period, a kind of pure discount factor emerges. This assumes individuals to be narrowly selfish, caring nothing about the wealth they leave behind when they die.

Numerical values for this discount factor can be computed from mortality statistics. For consumption one year after the present moment, the factor is equal to the probability of not surviving the next year; for longer intervals, it is a geometric average of annual rates.[15] Table 2 gives numerical values for the probability of surviving the next year at different ages. The figures, which are given for an advanced country, the United States, and an underdeveloped country, India, are based on mortality statistics compiled by the United Nations; similar tables could be computed for many other countries, for either sex, and for the mortality experience at different points in history.

Table 2

'Rational Individual Time Preference', Based on Survival Probabilities, United States and India (both sexes[a])

Age	United States (1950) (in %)	India (1941–50) (in %)
5–9	0·04	1·50
10–14	0·04	1·10
15–19	0·07	0·85
20–24	0·10	0·95
25–29	0·10	1·25
30–34	0·15	1·60
35–39	0·25	1·90
40–44	0·40	2·15
45–49	0·65	2·50
50–54	1·00	3·10
55–59	1·45	3·80
60–64	2·10	4·90
65–69	2·90	6·15
70–74	4·50	7·50
75–79	5·85	8·95
80–84	7·45	10·55
Life expectancy:	68	32

Source: United Nations, Department of Social Affairs, Population Branch, Population Studies no. 22, *Age and Sex Patterns of Mortality, Model Life Tables for Underdeveloped Countries*, New York, 1955, ST/TOA/ Series A/22, pp. 30–31.

[a] The figures are the average values for the five-year interval.

15. For the theory of deriving long-term interest rates from a structure of short-term rates, see Lutz (1950, pp. 36–63).

The figures for the United States turn out to be amazingly low. Up to age fifty the probability of not surviving the next year is less than 1 per cent, and below age forty-five less than 0·5 per cent. Thus, the pure time preference of the rational individual as I have defined him, should be less than 1 per cent a year up to age fifty. Or to cite a long-run figure, a twenty-year-old person looking ahead to a date fifty years away should discount at an average annual rate of 0·9 per cent. In old age the rate rises, of course, as the probability of survival diminishes.

The figures for India are considerably higher. Pure time preference based on rational mortality expectations never gets much below 1 per cent, and ranges up to 5 per cent even for moderate ages. For example, a rational Indian at age twenty, evaluating utility to be enjoyed fifty years hence, would discount it at an annual rate of 2·8 per cent. Thus, in underdeveloped countries, where life expectancy is short, even 'rational individuals' are governed by substantial pure time preference.

Two factors must be kept in mind in interpreting these figures. First, these pure time preference factors measure only one component of interest rates reflecting the intertemporal values of individuals. The time profile of expected incomes interacting with the shape of the marginal utility of consumption curve at different ages also affects the 'rational' interest rate. A person with a rising income stream will find the marginal utility of early consumption greater and will use a higher interest rate in his intertemporal choices. Conversely, an older person with a falling income stream will find it worth while to postpone marginal consumption outlays to a time when the marginal utility of consumption will be greater; his valuation of present versus future marginal consumption may involve an implicit negative rate of interest. The second factor, trends in the marginal utility of consumption with age, probably works in the same direction; the cost of rearing children makes consumption expenditures in the younger, more active, years of greater utility than later on, i.e. the marginal utility of consumption function drifts downward in the conventional diagram.

Besides considering the other factors that enter into the 'rational' marginal valuation of consumption at different points in time, the desire to leave an estate may modify intertemporal valuations. Thus the high time preference rates of old-age that would be derived from mortality expectations may be over-ruled by a desire to transfer wealth to a wife or to future generations.

Despite the significance of these motivations, our computations have some suggestive implications. First, for all countries, the uncertainty of survival leads to a purely rational preference of present consumption over future. Thus, the condemnation of all time preference as 'due to weakness of the imagination' (Ramsey) is based on the unrealistic view that individuals live forever. Second, in advanced countries, the pure time preference discount rate is very low over a wide range of ages. But in underdeveloped countries, this pure discount rate is considerably higher, though even in a country with as bad a mortality experience as India, the factor ranges only from below 1 to 5 per cent over a range of ages which encompasses most of the population.

Granting then the existence of perfectly rational preference of earlier consumption for individuals, the question remains whether a public planning body should take such preference into account. As has been pointed out in numerous places, the society goes on forever, and in the absence of thermonuclear war, there is almost certainty about the perpetual life of the population as an entity. If the social welfare function is a sum of utilities enjoyed by individuals, regardless of when they live, then mortality probabilities of specific individuals become irrelevant, and pure time preference is eliminated.

An interest rate can still be based on the diminishing marginal utility of income as *per capita* income rises, but rates based only on this mechanism are relatively low for plausible combinations of rates of increase of *per capita* income and elasticities of the utility curves.

A planner's welfare function which ignores individual time preference may well be in the long run interest of the society, but, strictly speaking, it is not a preference derived from individual desires, and hence falls into the category of dictatorial preference functions. Now a welfare function which adds up the utility of everybody, present and future, may be a defensible value judgement by which a policy-maker may choose to operate. Where government is democratic, the population may choose to operate by this value judgement through the political process; that is to say, its politicians may find decision-making according to low interest rates a successful component of their platform. But there is nothing in economic analysis *per se* which justifies this particular welfare function over all others.

What is more, there is growing and abundant evidence that the people of underdeveloped countries do place a considerable premium upon benefits in the early years of development projects. In India, for example, there has been some dissatisfaction with investment plans that yield little for quite a while, partly because of long periods of construction. Even in Russia there has been some revamping of investment plans, reducing the number of new projects being started for the sake of more rapid completion of the vast amount of work in progress;[16] there has also been some shift away from gigantic long-lived projects, such as huge hydroelectric dams, toward smaller, less durable and less capital-intensive projects, including steam plants.

The planner may feel that he is protecting the nation against its own shortsightedness by using low interest rates. But where this flies in the face of popular desire, he runs some risks that he may lose the chance of development on the Western model altogether. And even within the narrow perspective of economic analysis, early benefits may have morale effects which yield extra production and generally add momentum to the development effort.

Thus the choice of interest rates must remain a value judgement. I have discussed some of the elements that enter into the choice and have presented two models which derive elements of interest rates from empirical magnitudes, to show that there are some objective factors that can enter into the choice. But these must be combined with subjective judgements that cannot be value-free.

The rate of return v. present value computations

Since the selection of an interest rate requires subjective judgement, the ranking of projects by means of rate of return comparisons has been an attractive alternative. The interest rate issue could be side-stepped, since each project has an internal rate of return which can be computed. Given a limited amount of capital, projects could be ranked by their rates of return, and the projects with the highest rates could be undertaken. The rate of the marginal project, the cut-off rate, could then serve for technological choices in project design.

16. Reported in the *New York Times*, 12 June 1958, p. 14.

This procedure is meaningful only under a regime of perfect competition, in which the capital market contains no rationing and is equated by the interest rate serving as the price.

Hirshleifer has recently shown, that only in very peculiar cases other than perfectly competitive capital markets does the use of the rate of return criterion result in optimal results.[17] Once the marginal returns inside the budget being planned differ from returns elsewhere in the economy and from the rates being offered to suppliers of capital, the internal rate of return loses any normative significance. Hirshleifer's neat and exhaustive analysis, which shows the inexorable relevance of the subjective time preference of the planning agent, disposes, once and for all, I think, of the rate of return criterion.

Other attempts to escape the necessity of specifying an interest rate have been made, and some of them are discussed below (pp. 271-3).[18] It will be argued there that none of these attempts is satisfactory. Relative values on the outputs of different periods must be established, and only an interest rate can do this. Once interest rates are used, present values of benefits and costs can be computed and utilized in decision criteria.

One of these present-value criteria is closely related to rates of return, and has sometimes not been sufficiently distinguished from it. This is the S.M.P., or social marginal product of capital criterion,[19] proposed by Chenery (1953, pp. 76–96). The S.M.P. of a project is the rate of present value of net benefit per dollar of capital cost. It applies where capital is a constraining factor on a budget, the case where the rate of return criterion might appear to apply. But while focusing on a rate on capital, it differs from the rate of return in the crucial respect that it requires an interest rate to be specified for the computation of the present value of net benefit. Thus the S.M.P. is one of a family of present value criteria, while the rate of return is not.

The opportunity cost of capital and the interest rate

Just as some form of social time preference is required for planning

17. Hirshleifer (1958, pp. 329–52). Also see Eckstein's 'Investment criteria' (p. 64), where the same point is made.

18. See the discussion of the model of Sen below.

19. For example, in Eckstein (1958, p. 61), I mislabel the S.M.P. criterion a rate of return criterion.

within the expenditure field, it is also needed for measuring opportunity costs. For efficient resource allocation, the capital in a specific use must yield as much satisfaction as in the opportunity which is foregone. But this cost must be expressed in terms comparable to the benefits. The foregone flow of satisfaction must be reduced to a present-value concept by means of a social rate of discount.

Elsewhere (Krutilla and Eckstein, 1958, ch. 4), I have measured the opportunity cost of capital raised by federal taxation in the United States, and expressed it as an interest rate. This rate proved to be 5 to 6 per cent. It is no more than an empirical approximation to the desired magnitude, since it does not employ a social discount rate.[20] To convert this opportunity cost rate to a present value concept, the chosen rate of social discount must be used in the following manner: suppose the opportunity cost rate is 6 per cent; as measured in my empirical study, this is a perpetual stream of 0·06 cents per dollar of capital. Assume that the chosen rate of social discount is 3 per cent, i.e. that the benefits of a project are reduced to a present value by discounting at that rate. Then in order to compare the benefits of the project with the foregone benefits of the opportunities in the private economy, the perpetual stream of 0·06 cents per dollar must also be valued at 3 per cent. In the present example, the present value of a dollar invested in the private opportunity is $2, since a perpetual stream of 0·06 discounted at 3 per cent has a present value of 2.[21] As an expenditure criterion, assuming the above numbers, this implies that public projects should only be undertaken if the ratio of present value of net benefits to capital cost is 2·0.

The particular notion of opportunity cost which was measured, the cost of capital raised by a particular tax system, is only of relevance in models which link expenditures to taxes, rather than to reduced other expenditures, inflation, foreign borrowing, tighter monetary policies, or whatever other method the government may devise to raise the capital. Each method has its own opportunity cost which must be measured, and valued with a social rate of time discount.

20. Peter O. Steiner first saw this point. See Steiner (1959).

21. If the opportunity cost is not expressed as a perpetual stream, for example, if the time profile of returns of the private opportunities can be identified, a present value has to be computed explicitly.

Thus both opportunity cost and an interest rate must be specified for expenditure models. For example, in conventional benefit-cost analysis, a present value of benefits must be computed, using some interest rate. The rate at which costs result in present value of benefit, that is, the marginal benefit-cost ratio, must then be compared with the rate at which present value is foregone elsewhere, i.e., the opportunity cost. A correctly constructed criterion will pass a project only if the rate of present value of benefit per dollar exceeds the rate of present value per dollar of opportunity cost. Even if a low rate of interest is chosen, this does not mean that projects which yield low rates of return can be built or that scales of development can be pushed to a point where increments yield a low return. It only means that the present values, both on the benefit and the cost side, are computed using a low interest rate.[22]

The necessity for measuring opportunity costs springs from the fact that there is no perfect market mechanism which measures the cost of resources from the private sector. In the perfectly functioning market economy, opportunity cost of resources is fully measured by the price of factors of production purchased for a project, and there is no need to worry about the concept separately. It is because there are imperfections in the private economy, particularly in the capital market, that opportunity cost must be measured and utilized as a criterion in determining public budgets, and must be valued at a social rate of interest.

22. The procedure proposed in my book (1958), corresponds to this logic. A low interest rate is coupled with marginal benefit-cost ratios sufficiently in excess of 1·0 to assure that the project exceeds its opportunity cost.

The procedure of the Hell's Canyon study (in Krutilla and Eckstein, 1958) takes the short-cut of comparing opportunity cost with a rate of return of alternative plans. None of the results would have been affected by going through the intermediate step of revaluing the alternatives and the opportunity costs at a social rate of interest and then comparing the present values.

An alternative interpretation of the latter study, the interpretation given in the theoretical derivation of the opportunity cost concept, is the following: the proper social rate of interest is stated to be the rate which the taxpayers who are forced to finance the project choose to be their marginal rate of time preference. That is, the time preference of individuals is accepted for the government. This model is certainly closer to the strict concept of economic efficiency based on individual tastes. The upshot of the present discussion is this, however: even if individual time preference is rejected for public decision-making, opportunity cost, including foregone consumption, is a critical parameter that must be in the model.

Repercussion Effects

Introduction: prices v. *interdependence recognized*

In devising an analytic framework for maximizing any given objective function, there is an important choice in the selection of the chain of effects which should be pursued, both on the benefit and on the cost sides. The proper circumscription of the analysis is one of the critical points in the economics of public expenditures. It is all too easy to find myriad favorable effects of a social nature, both tangible and intangible; it is equally easy to lapse into such rigid acceptance of the rationale of the perfect market mechanism that the broader public viewpoint is lost altogether.

So far in economic science, only one approach has been developed for defining the proper area of analysis. It uses the perfect competition scheme as a point of departure; as is well known, under perfect competition, with price ratios equal to marginal rates of transformation in production and marginal rates of substitution in consumption, prices are precise indicators of value, and there is no need to pursue any repercussion beyond the most immediate market; the market mechanism produces an efficient allocation of resources. Because the real world is not perfectly competitive, some repercussions ought to be pursued, but in this approach each instance is justified by showing how the specific situation fails to conform to the competitive ideal. As will be seen in what follows, the range of repercussion effects that can occur is very wide, and while the use of perfect competition as a point of departure may impart some conservative bias against measuring them, it is a small bias and a shrinking one, as economists concerned with the problems of underdeveloped countries discover more and more cases in which the repercussions count. Further, the need to justify inclusion of repercussions improves the quality of the analysis and provides a framework for empirical measurement; it gives specific meaning to the 'social' effects within an individualist welfare economic point of view.

We shall assay no comprehensive treatment of repercussion effects, since they vary from case to case. But we shall list the major categories, and give some indication of the techniques which would measure them.

A list of local effects

Local, including some regional, effects involve simpler considerations than overall national repercussions; they are listed first, not necessarily in the order of their importance.

Physical interdependence. If a project has off-the-site physical effects, a particularly common phenomenon in water resource projects, their economic implications clearly require inclusion in the analysis. Where off-the-site effects are small, it may be possible to make simple allowances for such benefits and costs. For example, when an upstream storage reservoir is added to a system, its incremental benefits to projects downstream can be computed directly. But as the number of projects increases above one and the interrelations become more complex, centralized planning must be applied to the river basin as a whole. The Harvard Seminar in Water Resource Planning is experimenting with various planning techniques, including elaborate simulations, programing, and marginal analysis; actual physical interdependence relations turn out to be very complex, involving mixtures of competitive and complementary relationships. From the researches of this Seminar it is clear that the problem is soluble for the water resource case – which is perhaps the most complex – but that it tests the analytic and computing technology of modern engineering and economics.

Economic interdependence; investment co-ordination. Where a project produces outputs that are producers' goods, the value depends on the existence of industrial markets. If the growth of industry in a region is rapid, additional outputs cannot be considered to be incremental, and must be evaluated as part of an overall investment plan.[23] In this field, too, planning techniques have not been perfected, but linear and nonlinear programing, utilizing input-output data, offer considerable hope of solution.[24]

Large changes in inputs and outputs. If a project is so large that it changes the prices of its outputs and inputs, market prices cease

23. For more detailed discussion of these matters, see Nurkse (1953, pp. 1–24), where they are treated as part of the problem of balanced growth. Also see Scitovsky (1954, pp. 143–51); and Stockfish (1955, pp. 446–9).

24. See the forthcoming book by Chenery; and Chenery and Uzawa, (1958, pp. 203–29).

to be unambiguous indicators of value. This is a matter we have touched upon in the section on 'The Objective Function' (p. 217) where we saw that reasonable approxmations, such as arithmetic or geometric means of old and new prices, are readily at hand. In some cases, such as large power projects, finer approximations are possible by analyzing separate segments of the demands.

Local unemployment. Where part of the factors of production, including labor, are un- or under-employed, their market price overstates their opportunity costs. If their opportunity cost is zero, their real cost for purposes of project planning may also be zero. Should their employment generate other costs, however, such as large food consumption or urbanization costs, these need to be considered, of course.

Social overhead. All productive enterprises require certain complementary investments in public facilities, such as police and fire protection, public health services, schools, workers' housing, etc. These are all real costs, of course, whether the project is charged a price for them or not.

Local monopoly and monopsony. If the project deals with monopolists, either in selling its outputs or in purchasing its factors of production, market prices may not measure value; the project then generates monopoly profits, which after all, are also part of national income (though they might be given a weight of zero in some objective functions). For example, if the profits in the processing of output include a monopsony element, then the price is below the value of output. Measurement is very difficult in this case, since accounting profits include normal profits and the regular return on equity capital.

Effects on the economy as a whole

Repercussion effects on the economy as a whole should properly be measured and included in the analysis to the extent that there are specific imperfections in the economic system. Unemployment, capital shortage, foreign exchange imbalance, and excessive population growth are some of the items that fall in this category. We treat a few of the more important.

Keynesian unemployment. In a situation of general unemployment, the conventional multiplier measures the repercussion effects on national income which are caused by the increase in purchasing power. Recent empirical studies suggest that the total multiplier in the American economy is on the order of $1 \cdot 4$ or so (Duesenberry, Eckstein and Fromm, 1960), when all the various leakages, including taxes and retained earnings, are taken into account.[25] Of course the multiplier differs from project to project, depending on the marginal propensities to consume of the income recipients; but the recent work of Strout, using input-output techniques, implies that the differences, at least as far as off-the-site purchases of goods and services are concerned, are extremely small.[26]

Whether multiplier effects should be incorporated in the analysis depends, in part, on administrative policy. Past experience with investment projects suggests that their time-table makes them rather ineffective in counteracting the swift disturbances that have characterized the postwar period in advanced economies. Some speed-up of work in progress does appear feasible in recession, but this does not require that original investment plans need reflect this possible repercussion; symmetry would also suggest that if multiplier effects in potential recessions be included in the analysis, similar effects in inflation also be measured. In underdeveloped economies, on the other hand, Keynesian lack of effective demand may not be the critical dimension of the unemployment problem.

Structural unemployment and underemployment. Where an underdeveloped economy simply has an inadequate number of jobs for its population, or where many people are in occupations in which their productivity is very low or zero, the expenditure decision

25. If it is assumed that government expenditures are limited by revenues, i.e. that the government has a marginal propensity to spend equal to $1 \cdot 0$, the multiplier becomes much larger. Also, if the impact on inventory fluctuations is included – an impact that has to come quickly because of the speed with which inventory fluctuations occur – the multiplier becomes larger.

26. Strout (1958, pp. 319–28). Strout analyzes employment multiplier effects, but since differences in marginal propensities to consume largely relate to differences between wage-earners and others, his conclusions carry over to income-multipliers.

model must take some cognizance of this state of affairs. From the point of view of maximizing national income, money-wages are not likely to be reasonable measures of opportunity costs, and so some 'adjusted' wage, possibly equal to zero, may be needed. In addition, employment-creation may be an important part of the objective function; separate quantitative analysis may be needed to measure the performance of projects on this scale, including the employment generated in subsequent stages of production; input-output analysis appears the logical quantitative technique.

Capital and foreign exchange scarcity. In many countries, the desired rate of economic development is limited by the scarcity of capital and of foreign exchange. This can be introduced into the expenditure model in at least two ways: first, the two sources of finance may be treated as budget constraints, determining the choice of criterion. Second, the repercussion effects of projects in this regard can be measured, including the indirect effects caused in other industries and in the purchases of consumers. The generation of reinvestible capital out of the income payments of projects is a particular instance of these repercussion effects.

Population effects. If it can be shown that some expenditures change the environment of workers in such a manner as to reduce the rate of population growth, and if the objective function is expressed in terms of *per capita* income, expenditure analysis must include population repercussions. This factor is often cited as making investment in urban areas relatively more attractive.[27]

Concluding comment

These lists of possible repercussions that ought to be measured in certain cases are far from complete. Each situation has peculiarities of its own, which make different repercussions of relevance. The only analytically valid principle that has been advanced so far for determining their inclusion or exclusion is the technique of comparison of the actual case to the perfectly competitive model.

27. This factor, as well as the importance of generating reinvestible capital, was put into the center of discussion by Galenson and Leibenstein. They also stress the effect of projects on the skills of the workers (Galenson and Leibenstein, 1955, pp. 343–70).

The Treatment of Risk and Uncertainty

Introduction

Expenditure criteria must take some cognizance of the risky and uncertain nature of the economic world. Unfortunately, welfare economics has no complete apparatus for dealing with risk, no applicable optimum conditions from which decision criteria can be derived.[28] Nevertheless, it can easily be shown that for many reasonable objective functions, some account must be taken of risk, and some approaches will be indicated.

In evaluating these various adjustments for risks and uncertainty, it must be borne in mind, however, that something is being given up in exchange for the greater security, and that from the point of view of the country in the long run, short-run adjustments may not prove to be optimal. For example, if there is an empirical foundation for the idea of a risk premium, i.e. that risky investments have to have a relatively higher expected gain, then the national income will rise more if risky investments are undertaken, even though more risk is being experienced. It is possible that a series of risky, high-return investments not only give the country a higher national income, but also will put it in a more secure position in the long run than safe, low-return investments. Thus, even though there is a strong case for various adjustments in the direction of secure actions, the sum of a lot of adjustments may have the opposite effect of what is desired.

Some crude adjustments

The traditional adjustment for risk is simply to be conservative. In expenditure analysis, this has often taken three forms: (i) contingency allowances, which arbitrarily raise certain categories of costs by a certain percentage or reduce benefits through price assumptions which are below expected prices; (ii) a limit to economic life shorter than physical life but also shorter than expected economic life; and (iii) a risk premium in the interest rate. The first of these adjustments, which in many instances is a part of standard engineering practice, may simply be an allowance for errors in

28. But see Arrow (1952, pp. 41–7), where an interesting model which seeks to incorporate risks, gambling, and insurance into the competitive model is presented. Also see Allais (1953, pp. 269–90).

forecasting which past experience suggests will recur. Contingency allowances for costs are particularly of this character, since some unexpected costs always occur in construction. Thus, in a sense, they simply improve the quality of forecasts by allowing for expected errors.

A limit on economic life, which is particularly significant for projects like dams which have no definite terminal date, partly serves to standardize analysis of different projects. It also is an adjustment for technological progress, since it implicitly assumes that the economic value of the project goes to zero at some future date; this is clearly a very crude adjustment. The risk premium in the interest rate accomplishes the same purpose more delicately, since it discounts remote benefits progressively more heavily. The risk premium can have a precise basis where the probability of failure is known and remains constant over time. For example, if the probability of failure, defined as an economic value of zero after some date, is equal to 0·04 per year, the risk premium should be approximately 4 per cent.[29] But this precise application is only possible in connexion with credit risks on securities with which there is lots of experience; for physical projects, there is, so far, no empirical method for determining the premium.

These crude adjustments are intellectually not very satisfying, and one should try to derive better adjustments from explicit objective functions and from the specific probabilistic nature of benefits. But where the probability distributions are unknown or based on very little information, or where it is difficult to specify an objective function that can fully value the effects of risk or uncertainty, the crude adjustments are appropriate and important; at least there is some cognizance of the problem.

The case of pure risk: putting risk attitudes into the objective function

Following conventional terminology, we call 'risk' the state of affairs in which a probability distribution can be specified without error. Strictly speaking, the evidence is never complete and the

29. It is only an approximation because the proper risk premium is $\sum_t (1 - p)^t$, where p is the probability of loss in a period. This expression is only approximated by $\sum_t \dfrac{1}{(1 + p)^t}$, the expression in the text. I owe this point to Donald Farrar.

parameters of the probability distribution are given with some error. But when such error is small, good results can be obtained by treating the problem as one of pure risk. While events which can be characterized as risky are rarely encountered in the analysis of public expenditures, the water resource field is replete with them because of the dependence of projects on hydrology; flood control benefits depend on the probabilities of flood events; irrigation benefits depend on stream flow probabilities. Social insurance is another field subject to risk, actuarial risk in this case.

There are several different ways of handling risk in the analysis.[30] With probability distributions of outcomes known, means, variances, and possibly even higher moments can be put into the objective function.[31] In the most general form, the objective function can be written

$$W = (\mu, \sigma, \dots). \qquad 7$$

If we confine ourselves to the first two moments, this can be represented by an indifference map with the mean on one axis and the standard deviation on the other.[32] If there is aversion to risk, the indifference curves will slope away from the origin, with an increase in expected gain offset by an increase in the standard deviation.

Maximization of expected utility. Following Bernoulli[33] a utility function can be specified for which the expected value is maximized. Unless that function is linear, implying a constant marginal utility, it will result in the utilization of the probability distribution of outcomes in the optimizing analysis. This maximization of expected utility has been argued widely to be the rational form of behavior under conditions of risk. As a descriptive hypothesis, it can be tested empirically,[34] and is certainly not a perfect descrip-

30. The need to include risk attitudes in the objective function was impressed on me by Harold Thomas in the Harvard Water Resource Seminar. See his paper discussed below.

31. For a survey of authors who have made this suggestion, see Arrow (1951b, pp. 269–90).

32. This is drawn, for example, in Lutz and Lutz (1951, p. 190).

33. See Bernoulli (1954, pp. 23–46) for the original statement. For a summary of the literature see Arrow (1951b, pp. 404–37).

34. Early tests provide some support, but at this time the evidence must still be considered mixed. See Arrow (1951b, p. 12), for a survey and further references.

tion of human behavior. But in normative welfare economics, as a prescription of what the rational consumer ought to do, it may serve the same purpose as the conventional theory of the consumer under certainty.

A particular problem in applying the approach to public expenditures is the choice of the person(s) whose utility function is to apply. Is it the utility function of the planner or of the affected individuals? This is a problem analogous to the choice of interest rate. From a strictly individualist ethical point of view, the functions of the individuals should be used and weighted in some way. But in connexion with the loss of utility due to risk, as with the loss of expected utility due to mortality risks, the group as a whole may suffer less than the individual. The variance of the total outcome may be relatively smaller than for each individual because of pooling.

An example: flood control design. This example is a highly simplified illustration of the effect of introducing utility functions on flood control design. It will be shown that for a broad class of utility functions, utility maximization leads to more flood control than income maximization. The latter is equivalent to minimizing the expected cost of damages plus the cost of control works.[35]

Suppose utility is related to income by

$$U = F(y), \qquad\qquad 8$$

and let $F'(y)$ be strictly decreasing with increasing y. Let s be the height of floods in the absence of control, expressed in feet of flood stage, and let r be the number of feet by which flood stage is reduced through control works such as a dam. Let

$$x = s - r \qquad\qquad 9$$

be the number of feet of flood stage after control works are installed (s is determined by rainfall and other hydrological factors). The probability of occurrence of any particular value of s is described by the probability distribution $p(s)$, where s takes on only integral values.

35. The following argument is due to E. C. Schlesinger of the Department of Mathematics, Wesleyan University.

Income is affected by a flood of x by an amount $g(x)$, measured by damages. Thus

$$\Delta U(x) = F\left(y_o + g(x)\right) - F(y_o) = h(x), \qquad 10$$

where y_o is the level of income without flood.

We wish to minimize the expected value of this loss of utility due to floods, where r is the policy variable. The loss comes from two sources, the flood damages and the cost of control works. Let $\delta(r)$ be the cost of r. Thus the function to be minimized is

$$p(r) = \bar{h}(r) + F'(y_o) \times \delta(r), \qquad 11$$

where $\bar{h}(r)$ is the expected value of $h(r)$ if control works serve to cut flood stage by r, and where $F'(y_o) \times \delta(r)$ is the marginal utility of income multiplied by the cost of r.

We must set

$$p'(r) = 0,$$

i.e.

$$\bar{h}'(r) + F'(y_o) \times \delta'(r) = 0. \qquad 12$$

But

$$\bar{h}(r) = \sum_{s=r+1}^{\infty} p(s) h(s - r),$$

so that

$$\bar{h}'(r) = - \sum_{s=r+1}^{\infty} p(s) h'(s - r) \qquad 13$$

Hence the condition which minimizes the loss of utility is

$$\sum_{s=r+1}^{\infty} p(s) h'(s - r) = F'(y_o) \times \delta'(r), \qquad 14$$

which must be solved for r.

Next, suppose we seek to maximize income, i.e. minimize the loss of income caused by floods. We substitute $g(r)$ for $h(r)$. Then we must minimize

$$\Phi(r) = \bar{g}(r) + \delta(r), \qquad 15$$

the expected damages plus the cost of control. This requires

$$\bar{g}'(r) + \delta'(r) = 0,$$

or

$$\sum_{s=r+1}^{\infty} p(s) g'(s - r) = \delta'(r), \qquad 16$$

which is to be solved for r.

We now contrast the two solutions **14** and **16**. Suppose r_o satisfies **16**, the minimum cost solution, and that **14** has only one solution. It will be shown that

$$p'(r_o) < 0,$$

from which we can conclude that the optimal value of r for **14** is larger than that for **16**.

The proof is based on **10** and on the assumption of the decreasing nature of $F'(y)$. From **10** we obtain

$$h'(x) = F'(y_o + g(x)) \times g'(x),$$

and from the assumption about the utility function we obtain that

$$h'(x) > F'(y_o) \times g'(x), \text{ since } g(x) < 0 \text{ for } x > 0. \text{ **17**}$$

We substitute **17** in **14**. This yields

$$- p'(r_o) = \sum_{s=r+1}^{\infty} p(s)h'(s-r_o) - F'(y_o)\,\delta'(r_o).$$

The right side is greater than

$$F'(y_o)\left\{ \sum_{s=r+1}^{\infty} p(s)g'(s-r_o) - \delta'(r_o) \right\},$$

which equals zero by our assumption that r_o satisfies **16**. Hence $p'(r_o) < 0$, as asserted.

This shows that utility maximization leads to more flood control than income maximization. This is no more than an application of the theory of insurance. It is interesting that the procedures actually applied in the design of flood control works reject income maximization, requiring substantially more control. The extent to which a utility-maximizing solution exceeds the income-maximizing result depends on the distribution of flood probabilities and the elasticity of the marginal utility of income curve. The more frequent and routine the flood losses, the smaller will be the deviation between the two solutions. An optimal set of flood-control design principles can be derived from a model which maximizes expected utility.

Models utilizing means and standard deviations of outcomes.[36] In the general case, the maximization of expected utilities requires

36. This section has benefited from my reading Don Farrar (1958), which discusses the models by Roy and Thomas, as well as an interesting model by Steindl.

knowledge not only of the utility functions, but also of the complete probability distribution of outcomes. Decision criteria which require less knowledge have long had practical appeal. Several theoretical bases have been found for criteria that employ only the mean and standard deviation of outcomes.[37] Cramer (1930, pp. 7–84, cited in Arrow, 1951b, p. 423) derived such a criterion in connexion with insurance companies from the idea that the probability that income would fall below a certain level be minimized. A similar idea was applied by Roy (1952, pp. 431–49). He writes the objective function $W = f\left(\dfrac{\bar{B} - D}{\sigma_B}\right)$, where $\bar{B}$ is expected gain and D is the disaster level of outcome, the occurrence of which is to be minimized. The specification of the disaster level, which is a critical parameter for the ranking criterion, is a problem which appears to be of the same order of difficulty as specifying the utility functions. And the use of the standard deviation to measure the probability of failure is appropriate only if the probability distribution is normal, if it is of some other form that can be fully characterized by mean and standard deviation, or if all the alternatives have the same form of probability distribution.

A model of the same general type has been advanced by Thomas (0000)[38] for ranking water-resource projects. He argues that a project should have a positive pay-off over its life at some pre-specified probability level. He suggests that an insurance fund be set up of such size that it is capable of making up the losses in any specific year, and that it have a positive balance at the end of the undertaking. It turns out that if the outcomes are normally distributed, the size of this insurance fund depends on the mean and standard deviation of outcomes and the specified probability level that the fund be adequate. With the fund considered part of costs, the objective function takes the form $W = \bar{B} + a\sigma$, where a depends on the probability level at which the success of the insurance fund is to be guaranteed. Where Roy minimizes the probability of disaster, Thomas maximizes net gain, including an insurance charge against failure. As in the previous model, the

37. The indifference curves which correspond to this criterion are a series of parallel lines on a plane which has mean on one axis, standard deviation on the other.

38. For an empirical application see King (1958).

determination of this probability level is a problem akin to the specification of utility functions.[39]

The models of this type have a greater ring of concreteness than the maximization of expected utility. Yet except for those rare cases where there is an institutional basis for specifying the disaster level of outcome or the even rarer cases where the acceptable probability level of failure can be empirically determined, they are arbitrary adjustments to risk, perhaps not as crude as the 'crude adjustments' discussed earlier, yet considerably removed from modern optimizing criteria. They stand in the same relation to expected utility maximization as the classical theory of statistical inference stands to modern decision theory (see Luce and Raiffa, 1957, pp. 318–24).

Further comment on utility maximization. If we insist on the specification of utility functions, we must be prepared to give some empirical implementation to this idea. While this is not an easy problem, it is an unavoidable one, since even in the classical models the specification of disaster levels of income or of confidence levels of probability presumably would need to be derived from implicit estimates of utility functions. Certain elements of these functions can be derived from objective data. For example, in irrigation and hydroelectric power the money losses of shortage of stream flow are a crucial variable, and similarly in navigation and low flow control. Thus the derivation of these loss functions is a necessary and empirically feasible first step toward deriving optimal criteria. In addition, the shapes of individual utility of income functions must be specified, admittedly a heroic task. But reasonable assumptions about their general shape can be made, which, if not derived from experimental data, may be in the nature of value judgements (see section on 'The Constraints', p. 227). To fail to specify them is not to solve the problem, but simply to leave its resolution to the random process of picking the function which is implicit in the selection of values of other, more 'pragmatic' parameters.

The case of uncertainty [40]
By uncertainty we mean the case where information about the

39. L. Telser has employed the same model as Thomas in an analysis of hedging behavior (see Telser, 1955–6, pp. 1–17).

40. A critical survey of the relevant literature can be found in Luce and Raiffa (1957).

probability distributions of outcomes is incomplete, that is, that their parameters are not known precisely. Strictly speaking, this includes all empirically derived probability distributions; but in this section we are concerned with that range of cases in which it is not a reasonable assumption for policy purposes to treat the distributions as known.

Even for individual action there are few settled conclusions about what constitutes rationality under conditions of uncertainty. In a few cases, considerable theoretical progress has been made. The most important of these are games of strategy involving at least two players. Here the Von Neumann-Morgenstern theory and subsequent developments (including bargaining theories) provide principles of decision. Public expenditures for national defense clearly require this type of analysis, as may expenditures which are primarily part of domestic political games.

Leaving genuine games aside, there still remain stubborn problems where decisions must be made with imperfect information. For example, no empirical probabilistic description can be given to the problem of price projection or to the forecasting of floods so extreme that the historical record contains only one or even no instance. Several principles have been advanced that might be applied. From the theory of games, the minimax principle has been drawn, which would require that course of action which would minimize the losses which would occur if the worst possible circumstance arose. Where no rational opponent is involved, this is too conservative a principle. In flood control or irrigation design, for example, it would make decisions depend exclusively on the worst possible event that human imagination could visualize for the project, regardless of how remote the possibility. A somewhat different principle is the 'minimax regret' criterion,[41] suggested by Savage. In choosing between two alternatives, it minimizes the difference between what would happen in the better outcome and in the worse outcome. Choices among more alternatives would be made by a series of comparisons among pairs. It is doubtful that this concept of regret is a desirable principle of action in the areas with which we are concerned; this criterion also suffers from

41. Besides Luce and Raiffa, there are several other interesting surveys of these criteria. See Arrow (1958, pp. 1–23); Radner and Marschak (1954, pp. 61–8); and Milnor (1954, pp. 49–59).

excessive influence of very unlikely extreme values and has the additional fault that the optimum choice can be altered by the introduction of irrelevant alternatives. Hurwicz has suggested a third criterion, a weighted average of the best and the worst possible outcomes, with the weights left to the inherent pessimism or optimism of the decision-maker. This criterion, while it has the advantage of introducing both good and bad possible outcomes into the decision, still suffers from excessive influence of the extreme values.[42]

I can only echo Arrow's conclusion 'that we do not really have a universally valid criterion for rational behavior under uncertainty. Probably the best thing that can be said is that different criteria are valid under different circumstances'. For the range of decisions that is our concern, expenditure decisions that are not strictly strategies in a game, there is one important property that the decision criterion ought to reflect: while the probability distributions are not known, there is some experience, some knowledge which ought to aid in the decision. Typically the uncertainties are cases of difficult forecasting of prices, of rare floods, of industrial location patterns in the case of transportation facilities, and of other events the underlying mechanism of which is not fully understood.

The use of *a priori* probabilities is one possibility, in which the qualified 'expert' attaches subjective probabilities on the basis of the evidence and of his intuition. Given these probabilities, including the joint probability distributions of the various dimensions of output, the problem can then be treated like a problem in risk. Since the subjective probability mechanism is no more than a method of utilizing a combination of evidence and intuition, there is a question as to whether it is the best method. This is a matter of personal taste; some may find the mechanism natural to their thinking processes; others may find it an encumbrance.

Another possibility is to use some sort of contingency approach, in which the major hazards are identified to which the undertaking is subject and which have some minimum *a priori* probability of occurrence. Strategies can then be devised which will reduce the maximum possible loss caused by each contingency to some bear-

42. Luce and Raiffa criticize this criterion on other grounds.

able level. Within these constraints, some maximization of expected values might then be carried out. Alternatively, striking a completely defensive posture, the probabilities of certain loss levels might be minimized, with the weights given to the prevention of different contingencies determined from some preference function. The similarity of contingency planning to the models of Thomas, Roy and others discussed above will be seen.[43] It also has some strong similarities to Simon's 'satisficing' analysis.[44]

I am sure enough has been said to indicate that this particular problem is far from a solution. In the meantime, judgement methods must be used, whether verbal or formal, with the identification of the major contingencies and some provision being made against them constituting a minimum program for the design of reasonable decision procedures in the face of uncertainty.

A Survey of Some Recent Models

Introduction

Having set up a taxonomy of the problem of public expenditure criteria, I shall now use it to classify the various models that have been advanced in recent years. No attempt will be made to present each model in full detail; in particular, the algorithms that have been advanced for the numerical solution of some of them will not be given. But the taxonomy should permit us to give the essence of each model, and to show the interrelations between them. The models designed for projects of water resource development are presented first, followed by a model for transportation, and concluding with more general models for economic development planning.

U.S. Government practice in evaluation of water resource projects

The federal government evaluates water resource projects by means of benefit-cost analysis. There is no single model which is employed by all agencies;[45] one of the problems in evaluation

43. For discussion of contingency planning, see Kahn and Mann (1957, pp. 85–113). For a similar view, applied to research and development decisions, and stressing the resultant need for preserving flexibility, see Klein and Meckling (1958, pp. 352–63).

44. See 'The objective function', p. 217.

45. A detailed account of actual practices can be found in Eckstein (1958).

practice has been the lack of uniform methods among agencies. But there are certain characteristics from which an 'ideal' model of federal practice can be derived.[46]

The objective function of this model has two kinds of benefits; 'direct' benefits which are largely net additions to individual incomes, and 'indirect' benefits which are miscellaneous repercussion effects. At least in principle, the difference between benefits and costs is to be maximized in determining the scale of projects, while project ranking is to be based on the ratio of total benefits to total cost, the crude benefit-cost ratio. Except for the inconsistency between pursuing the scale of individual projects to a point where marginal benefit equals marginal cost while the benefit of marginal projects has to exceed costs at a rate equal to some benefit-cost ratio greater than one, this procedure corresponds to a model in which benefits minus costs are maximized subject to a constraint on cost. A dollar of benefit is given the same weight, no matter 'to whom it may accrue', suggesting an objective function of the form 4 in the section on 'The Objective Function' (p. 217).

The constraint is not applied to the same concept of cost by all agencies. *Proposed Practices* ... suggests project costs as the proper denominator of the ratio, and hence implicitly as the proper constraint. These are all the costs incurred on the project itself and are contrasted with associated costs, the costs of associated enterprises. The Corps of Engineers follows this concept. The Bureau of Reclamation uses federal cost, the cost borne by the federal government. The constraint is applied to costs occurring in all periods, present and future, discounted by the interest rate.

The interest rate needed to discount benefits and costs to derive present values[47] is specified independently and related to government borrowing costs. Since the funds for projects are rarely borrowed but rather raised by taxation, the government borrowing rate is irrelevant. Being rather low, it may be a reflection of social time preference however.

Repercussion effects are measured in the form of 'indirect' benefits. These include profits created in processing and in sales to

46. The classical statement of the general approach of the government can be found in Federal Interagency River Basin Committee (1950).

47. In actual practice annual equivalents are employed. These correspond to present value concepts, expressed as an annual average figure.

the project, in increased production and wage payments made possible by eliminating floods, and in several other ways. Most of these 'indirect' benefits cannot be derived from any reasonable objective function unless a particularly heavy weight is attached to the income – and particularly to the profits – earned in the immediate proximity of the projects, and no weight at all is attached to the offsetting losses elsewhere in the economy.

There is relatively little adjustment for risk and uncertainty. Benefits that are particularly uncertain, usually only expected to begin to accrue in the future, are to be discounted at a higher rate of interest, injecting a slight risk premium. Also, there is general use of engineering contingency allowances in cost estimation. In flood control, some provision is made to stress control of rare 'disaster' floods.

Without seeking to subject the federal techniques to systematic critique, five points should be made:

1. The objective function is consistent with the traditional individualist welfare economics and can fairly be interpreted as representing the national interest.

2. In the ranking procedure, there is recognition of the existence of a budget constraint, though the resultant implications for project design are not followed. Some ambiguity remains about the concept of cost to which the constraint is applied.

3. The opportunity cost of budget money is not brought into the analysis; no test is performed to assure that benefits on marginal outlays exceed these opportunity costs.

4. Measurement of repercussion effects largely seeks to measure irrelevant effects.

5. The model presented is an 'ideal', with actual practice rarely utilizing the rankings by the benefit-cost ratio; the analysis is primarily used as a test by which projects with ratios less than 1·0 are rejected, with the scores above 1·0 having only a minor influence in project selection. Also, marginal principles are frequently not followed in project design, particularly in choice of scale.

A model for benefit-cost analysis

In my book, *Water Resource Development: The Economics of Project Evaluation*, I present a decision model which was designed to be appropriate to the budgeting problem of the federal water resource programs. This model maximizes the increase in real national income, assuming equal marginal utilities for individuals, subject to a constraint on federal cost. This constraint applies to both capital and operating and maintenance costs; in particular, it applies to the present value of these costs, measured with the interest rate of the analysis. This constraint was chosen over several others. A constraint only on capital was rejected because operating and maintenance costs represent a serious drain on the federal budget in several fields, particularly flood control and navigation; and in the others, e.g. irrigation, these costs are borne by local interests, and hence would automatically fall outside the constraint as far as appropriate. It was also chosen over separate constraints applicable to the funds used in different periods because there was no evidence to suggest drastic changes in the future pattern of availability of funds, and so a perennial constraint equal to present conditions was selected; this assumes that project opportunities are generated at the same rate as funds become available. Finally, while there is some exploration of constraints that include the funds generated by the reimbursable portions of a project, I reject this constraint, because, in actual federal practice, revenues of projects go into general treasury funds, and not into further expenditures for water resource programs.

The interest rate is to be chosen as an expression of social time preference. To bring the opportunity cost of budget money into the analysis, the marginal benefit-cost ratios which correspond to the opportunity costs of budget money raised by taxation are given. In the event that the benefit-cost ratio of marginal projects that can be undertaken within the budget constraint falls below this opportunity cost rate, the latter rate serves as a cutoff, and not all of the available budget money is to be spent.

Repercussion effects are limited in the model, because it is assumed to be applied in full employment conditions and in the mature market economy of the United States, where prices are, on the whole, adequate indicators of value. Where there are genuine external economies, largely of a physical nature, these should be measured, of course. Also, in the case of decreasing cost transportation industries, marginal costs rather than actual freight rates measure value.

The treatment of risk and uncertainty is confined to 'crude adjustments', particularly risk premiums in the interest rate. In connexion with flood control, some recognition is taken of the effect of diminishing marginal utility of income, justifying departure from minimizing the expected total cost of floods in the direction of paying more attention to 'disaster-type' floods, but no specific criteria are advanced.

Multiple purpose river development

Some closely related models were used in a volume of empirical studies.[48] Four investigations were undertaken; (i) the opportunity cost of tax-raised budget money was estimated; (ii) an economic analysis of alternative plans of development of the Hell's Canyon project was prepared, using the social cost of capital, as measured by opportunity cost; (iii) the extent to which private development is likely to produce the potential nonmarketable outputs of multipurpose projects was investigated through a case study of the Coosa River, Alabama, and (iv), the income distribution effects of a project in the Pacific Northwest were measured under the alternative conditions of private and local, and federal development, with both costs and benefits allocated to regions and income classes. The fourth of these studies seeks to implement an objective function of the form 6 of the section on 'The Objective Function' (p. 217), identifying distribution of gains and costs by region and of federal costs by income class. No effort is made to rank the alternatives, a task left to the political process; but the necessary data for judgement are presented. It turns out that federal development redistributes income toward the region, compared with other places. The distribution of federal costs by income class depends on the assumed tax changes, but under some likely assumptions falls heavily on the lower income groups. The third study determines the flood control and other nonmarketable benefits that could be produced by the project of the case study, compares them with the incremental costs, and then analyzes the private plan of development. It turns out that the private plan provides virtually none of the nonmarketable benefits.

48. Krutilla and Eckstein (1958). Also see Reuber and Wonnacott (1961), where the opportunity cost of funds raised by borrowing is estimated.

The remaining two studies are interrelated. The opportunity cost of tax-raised funds is measured from what Musgrave calls the differential incidence of taxation; if the level of expenditures is changed, what tax changes would accompany it, assuming that stabilization policy requires some offset and that fiscal policy is the device chosen? Specific assumptions are made about these tax changes, based on judgement, the tax burden is traced to its ultimate incidence, and insofar as it falls on investment, the foregone rates of return are estimated. Foregone consumption is valued at the time preferences of the affected consumers, as revealed by their saving-borrowing behavior. The resultant average cost of marginal tax funds turns out to be on the order of 6 per cent. This rate is then applied to the Hell's Canyon case, and using it as a test, it turns out that a two-dam plan that costs less than the actual private three-dam plan of development but produces more output is the best choice. The incremental investment required for the one large dam, the public proposal, yields less than 4·5 per cent, assuming fully integrated operation. With opportunity costs at 6 per cent, this increment is rejected.

This model uses rate-of-return comparisons, though they are applied through a benefit-cost terminology. A strict efficiency point of view is taken, in which the interest rate of the analysis is based on individual time preference of the people who are taxed. Had a social time preference been used, perhaps including a lower interest rate, the results would have been the same. The opportunity cost would have had to be revalued into a present-worth concept at the preferred interest rate, and compared to the incremental benefit-cost ratios of the alternative plans. The empirical conclusions would have been identical, since the benefit-cost ratio of the foregone opportunities would have been on the order of 2·0, assuming an interest rate of 3 per cent, while the incremental investment of the large dam plan has a ratio of only 1·5; the two-dam plan would have continued preferable to the private plan, since it has lower costs and greater benefits.

This analysis assumes no budget constraints. This is justified because Hell's Canyon was not a question of choosing the best public projects, but rather to compare competing private and public plans. A victory for the public plan would have meant that the additional budget money would have been voted; in fact, such a victory would have resulted in a general expansion of public power programs, since it was a symbolic showdown between public and private power advocates. To have used a budget constraint might have condemned the public plan on the grounds that it prevented other good public undertakings, a line of reasoning which was contradictory to the institutional reality of the situation.

There was no concern with risk and uncertainty, and repercussion effects were limited to physical downstream power benefits. Much of the difference in benefits among the plans proved to be in these repercussions, which are nonmarketable for a private developer and which therefore are not considered in private decisions.

The study by McKean

A recent book by McKean devotes a great deal of attention to the theory of expenditure criteria (McKean, 1958, esp. pp. 25–150). I cannot summarize the entire discussion, much of which is devoted to practical problems of implementation, to saving the innocent from fallacy, and to setting out the fundamental principles of selecting criteria – a discussion which to some extent parallels this paper, but from a rather different conceptual point of view. I present only the bare outline of McKean's argument with regard to the criteria he considers appropriate. McKean stresses the many objectives of policy, and the limited weight that is to be attached to criteria that reflect only economic efficiency. In the economics, he seeks to maximize the expected gain of real income, though he also stresses the need for consideration of intangibles and of adjusting to uncertainty.

McKean takes the maximization of the difference of the present values of benefits and costs as the ultimate objective (p. 76). The interest rate he would use to compute present values is the marginal internal rate of return. As McKean points out, this is tantamount to a strict rate of return criterion, though there is still an open question about the interest rate to be used in the design of supramarginal projects. McKean makes clear the assumptions that are required for this to be the correct criterion. Either of two sets of assumptions suffices: (i) funds are available without constraint at an interest rate equal to the marginal rate of return – an assumption which makes many criteria, including benefit-cost ratios, come to the same result; (ii) there is a constraint on investment funds, public and private, and the net returns can be reinvested at the marginal rate of return when they accrue (p. 85). McKean makes the necessity of the reinvestment assumption abundantly clear. He is concerned with the sensitivity of the results to the rate of return at which reinvestment occurs, and in view of the necessary arbitrariness on this matter, he proposes that supplementary data be submitted as part of the analysis which give some idea about the time profile of benefits and costs. By giving this profile, the need for any interest rate is eliminated, and the decision-maker, whether Congress or President, is forced to apply his own time preference. Recognizing the need for simple criteria, however, McKean ultimately does propose the internal rate of return as the best simple decision-rule.

McKean rejects benefit-cost ratios (pp. 113–18). He correctly seizes on the critical issue: What are the financial constraints which limit the program? McKean argues that the constraint only applies in the immediate future when the investment costs are incurred, that operating and maintenance costs are financed out of revenues generated by benefits – including the revenues recaptured through taxation. He also feels no need to distinguish between federal costs and other costs. Finally, he prefers to treat the benefits as being reinvested. In my own work, I have preferred other assumptions on these matters. First, I believe budget money will remain scarce for a long, long time, and operating costs a decade from now will prove as much a drain on a scarce financial resource as current investment outlays. Second, since it is the preparation of a federal program which is at stake, I prefer to treat only federal cost as the constrained financial resource. Third, I assume that there is no reinvestment, partly because the benefits of projects and the institutional arrangements in this particular field are such that there is very little direct revenue generated, and what there is does not return to the water resource field; as for benefits recaptured through taxation, in fields such as flood control and irrigation virtually no taxes are created, while in power and navigation it is not clear that the resultant taxes are more than the taxes that would have been paid by the alternative private investments that might have occurred.[49]

49. This controversy repeats some of the issues of the Lutz-Hildreth exchange of the 1940s. Lutz rejected the internal rate of return in favor of a

On analytical grounds, I believe there are no contradictions between the study of McKean and my own. Different assumptions are made, but these are matters on which reasonable men can disagree.

The Steiner pre-emption model

Steiner has extended models of this general type in an important way (Steiner, 1959). He employs the same general objective function as the models discussed above, maximizing the difference between present value of benefits and costs. He stresses the need for specifying an interest rate, not only to compute present values of benefits and costs of projects, but also to compute present values of opportunity costs. There is no treatment of risk and uncertainty. The novelty of his approach lies in a combination of constraints and of sectoral analysis which brings out some interesting features of public development in a predominantly private economy.

Steiner defines four sectors of the economy: (1) the public sector the budget of which is being allocated; (2) the private sector which would contain private alternative developments of the particular public projects being considered; (3) the broader public sector in which funds left over from the particular budget would be spent; and (4) the general private sector containing marginal opportunities into which private funds displaced by public projects are pushed.

The total outlay for projects in sector (1) is limited by a budget constraint. This outlay has certain direct benefits in sector (1) of course, but in addition, it leads to repercussions in the other sectors. Sector (3), the general public sector, may receive some funds from the budget of sector (1). This comes about in two ways: first, some funds may be diverted because the marginal returns in sector (1) fall below the opportunities in sector (3). Thus the introduction of public sector (3) assures that marginal projects yield benefits at a rate equal to the opportunities elsewhere in the public sector.

---

strict present-value concept, though he did not select the constraint issue as the critical one. Hildreth, in reply, used an illustration which had the re-investment property which validates the internal rate of return.

See Lutz (1945, pp. 56–77), and Hildreth (1946, pp. 156–64). Also see the later and much extended discussion which resolves some of the issues in Lutz and Lutz (1951, pp. 16–48).

Second, funds spill over into (3) because Steiner employs discrete projects and a fixed budget, and so a small amount of money is likely to be left over because the project costs do not exactly equal the constraint.

The other repercussion effect which emerges is the change in benefits earned on private investments because an investment opportunity has been pre-empted by the government. This forces private funds from the pre-empted opportunity into a marginal investment, or in the terminology of Steiner, from sector (2) to sector (4). This creates a loss in the private economy.

Steiner also explores the case where there is no budget constraint, the case where funds are drawn from the private economy and where opportunity costs play a key role. He brings the pre-emption problem into this case as well.

To summarize his model, Steiner writes a general equation

$$y_{ij} = (G_{ij} - a_1 k_{ij}) - (G_j - a_2 1_j) - a_3 m_{ij},$$

where y_{ij} is the net gain from the ij^{th} project, G_{ij} is the present value of benefits minus costs of the project, a_1 is the opportunity cost in the general public sector (2), k_{ij} is the project's drain on the limited public budget, G_j is the present value of the pre-empted private opportunity, a_2 is the opportunity cost in marginal investments in the private sector (4), 1_j is the capital cost of the pre-empted private project, a_3 is the opportunity cost of funds transferred from the private sector by taxation, borrowing, inflation, or whatever method is actually employed, and m_{ij} is the amount of such funds actually transferred for project ij. This equation can assimilate combinations of budget constraints and transfers of funds from private to public sectors, can assure full recognition of opportunity costs elsewhere in the public and private sectors as far as this proves appropriate, and can reflect the losses caused by pre-emption of private opportunities.

The empirical magnitudes necessary to implement the model, other than the usual benefit and cost data for each project, include the three constants a_1, a_2 and a_3 (the three opportunity costs) and a rate of interest. Steiner does not advocate any particular interest rate, nor does he propose any specific method of measurement of the opportunity costs. As an empirical matter, in the general public sector, where many outlays do not produce outputs that can be measured with prices, it is extremely difficult to place a value on alternatives which would be comparable to the values attached to the projects being analyzed. The private opportunity cost of marginal investments could presumably be valued; in fact, in a market economy, money costs should be such a measure and no explicit treatment needed. The opportunity cost of funds transferred from the private sector to augment the public budget is measured by computations of the sort discussed above in connexion with the Hell's Canyon study, or by similar computations applied to funds raised by public borrowing, or perhaps even by inflation. Thus Steiner's emphasis on the opportunity costs in the general public sector, sector (3), is likely to remain a counsel of perfection, but the rest of the analysis could probably be implemented empirically.

Tinbergen's transportation model

Tinbergen has devised a model designed to measure the change in national income due to projects which improve the transportation system of a country (Tinbergen, 1957. Also see Bos and Koyck, 1961). This model consists of a set of geographical points in which production and consumption are carried on. For each product, supply and demand equations are determined, as well as the transportation costs for each product among all points. Each supply function contains the price of the product and of the other products in the geographical point; the demand functions contain the product's delivered price, and hence reflect transportation costs. Given these functions, it is possible to determine what will be produced in each place, and hence what its total production and income will be.

A transportation project will change some of the transportation costs in the model. The equations can be solved again assuming the new, lower transportation costs, and the change in total production and income can be seen from the difference between the two solutions.

This model is a technique for estimating benefits of transportation projects. It allows for the repercussions on production caused by broadening the markets in which the output of a place can compete. This increase in production and of income leads to further increases in demand and production. The resultant estimate of the impact on national income is greater than the estimate produced by conventional benefit-cost analysis, where the impact on national income is limited to the savings in transportation cost. The extent of the difference depends particularly on the supply elasticities, high elasticities implying large increases in production.

To apply the model as an expenditure criterion, a symmetrical analysis must also be carried out for the cost side. Presumably, repercussion effects on production and income would also result from alternative uses of the resources. Some assumptions would also have to be made about interest rates and budget constraints.

Chenery's S.M.P. model

H. B. Chenery has advanced an expenditure model designed to aid in the planning of investment budgets for economic development.[50] The objective is to maximize the present value of benefits minus costs, i.e. to maximize the present value of the real national income. In the closed-economy model, a constraint is applied to capital funds, with the resultant criterion, the Social Marginal Product (S.M.P.), consisting of incremental ratios of present values of benefits minus operating costs divided by the requisite increment of capital. This criterion can be applied to the design of projects, and to project selection, with individual projects treated as increments in the determination of a program. Thus the technique is similar to the use of incremental benefit-cost ratios, except that the denominator contains only capital costs.

The criterion requires an interest rate. Chenery avoided this issue by confining his criterion to projects within the same field and with very similar capital intensities, so that the rankings of projects would be unaffected.

Chenery also applied the model to an open economy where foreign exchange has a higher opportunity cost than the nominal exchange rate. The S.M.P. in this case consists of two terms.

$$\text{S.M.P.} = \frac{B - M}{K} + f \frac{E}{K},$$

where B is present value of benefits, M of operating costs, f is the premium on foreign exchange, E the total effect of the project on the balance of payments, and K is the capital cost. Chenery has a

50. Chenery (1953, pp. 76–96). There is an earlier literature by N. S. Buchanan, A. E. Kahn and J. J. Polak, which is discussed by Chenery. Kahn introduced the S.M.P. criterion.

very sophisticated repercussion analysis to estimate the balance of payment effect, including direct foreign exchange needs of the project, import savings made possible, as well as the import demands generated by the increase in the national money income caused by the multiplier effects of the project. These models are applied to development planning in several countries.

Chenery's programming models

More recently, Chenery, in collaboration with others, has used programing techniques to solve the same type of problem. The practical advantage of programing is the great potential of empirical implementation. While some simplifying assumptions must be made to make the problem fit the apparatus of linear (and non-linear) programing, complete solutions of the investment allocation problem of rapidly changing economies are possible. The marginalist approach, based on Lagrangean multipliers, is fundamentally a partial equilibrium approach (though in principle it could of course be applied to centralized planning of an economy as well).[51] When applied to expenditure decisions, it usually requires, at the least, that prices be projected. In advanced economies, particularly where the programs being planned are a small part of the economy, such projections can be made and are likely to be more accurate than prices which emerge from a programing computation. But where an economy is being transformed by rapid development, the supply and demand relations are so strongly modified by the development program itself that prices cannot be assumed. Even prices for planning must emerge from the planning computations; the programing technique produces such prices, in addition to solving for the overall quantities.

Without seeking to present the results of the programing approach, the key characteristics of these models will be presented, particularly the assumptions made about objective functions, constraints, interest rates and the other matters with which we have dealt above.

51. At a high level of abstraction, linear programing and the quadratic programing problems used by Chenery are logically equivalent to a Lagrangean problem, following the Kuhn-Tucker Theorem. See Arrow, Hurwicz and Uzawa (1958, chs. 1, 3, 4 and 5).

In a study of development planning for Southern Italy, Chenery and Kretschmer (1956, pp. 365–99) employed the following model: the economy is divided into fourteen sectors, each of which is an industry aggregate. The sectors are divided into subsectors which have the property that they have the same input-output structure except for differences in capital inputs. A set of targets is specified, a list of goods, which is derived from demand projections based on income elasticities. The objective of the program is to meet these targets at a minimum total investment, with the total availability of labor and of foreign exchange acting as constraints. The production relations of the economy consist of two parts: first there is the input-output matrix of the fourteen sectors (applied also to the subsectors). This matrix, together with the capital coefficients, defines one method of production for each subsector. Purchase from abroad, at a given import price, is an alternative method. The good of each subsector also has an export demand curve, relating the price the good can command abroad to the amount being sold. This foreign demand curve, assumed to be a declining straight line, introduces a nonlinearity into the model and makes it a case of quadratic programing.[52] When solved, the model reveals what demands should be met by production in domestic subsectors as well as their total outputs, what and how much should be imported, and how much of various goods should be exported. It also reveals the total amount of investment that is required and in what subsectors it has to be placed. In the event more capital is available than is needed, the targets can be raised, of course.[53]

Models of this type clearly have an enormous potential for expenditure analysis in many areas. In water resource planning, for example, the most efficient program of meeting specified needs

52. In a subsequent paper, this is generalized to declining demand curves both at home and abroad. See Chenery and Uzawa (1958, ch. 15).

53. In a paper to be published in the *Essays in Honor of E. S. Mason*, Chenery applies a similar model to illustrate several problems in development planning. He shows, with realistic empirical magnitudes, how much is gained (1) by using cost figures that reflect real costs rather than money costs, (2) by using a changing price structure suggested by the programing solution rather than constant prices, and (3) by including urbanization costs in the analysis. He also shows (4) how programing can be used to measure the value of generating reinvestible funds in a dynamic (three-period) program.

could be derived. Similarly in planning regional development, the most economic means of raising, say, the average income of substandard regions could be approximated.

Re-investment models

Galenson and Leibenstein (1955, pp. 343–70) proposed that several sets of repercussion effects which had not been considered previously in formal analysis ought to be given an important place in decision models. They stress three effects: first, education of the labor force on the job is considered a benefit of some projects; second, if *per capita* growth of income is in the objective function, differential effects of projects on population growth should be included in the criteria. Finally, if a government finds it impossible to achieve an optimal level of investment, the capability of projects to generate further capital out of benefits should be considered, and a marginal reinvestment coefficient is advanced as a measure. All three of these repercussion effects, it is argued, would favor industrial projects in urban locations as opposed to agricultural or handicraft investments in the countryside. Galenson and Leibenstein do not propose a formal criterion;[54] they make their points by illustrative example.

In a subsequent model, I sought to incorporate the reinvestment factor in a formal decision model. The present value of benefits minus costs, or real national income, is maximized subject to a capital constraint. Each alternative has a re-investment co-efficient which states what fraction of its benefits is re-invested, either through private saving or through taxation. The resultant criterion has two components: an efficiency term indicating the present value of benefit minus operating cost per marginal dollar of investment, plus a term which places a premium on that portion of the output which is to be re-invested. This premium has to be derived from the productivity of the reinvestible capital. Because of the long perspective over time, the resultant criterion is very sensitive to the choice of interest rate, and it was in this connexion that the analysis of planner's time preference in the section (on 'Interest Rates', p.230) above was worked out.

54. Subsequent criticism interprets the reinvestment coefficient as a decision criterion, and shows it to be wrong or incomplete. But I think this interprets their position too broadly.

The models of A. K. Sen

A. K. Sen (1957b, pp. 561–84) has advanced a series of theoretical models designed to illustrate the problem of development planning in an underdeveloped country. These models are not meant to be used in practical planning, but to provide the theoretical underpinning for rules-of-thumb that are empirically feasible.

Sen is particularly interested in exploring the right degree of capital intensity for development, particularly when viewed in relation to the level of re-investment that might be generated and to balance-of-payments effects. He sets up a simple sectoral model for an underdeveloped country, and by means of it evaluates the alternative strategies of development.

There are two sectors, a backward sector containing lots of unemployment, which can supply labor in any amount without loss of output, and an advanced sector which contains two departments, one producing capital goods, the other 'corn'. Two techniques can be employed to add to the output of 'corn', one requiring relatively little capital, with labor having relatively low productivity, the other being more capital intensive but having a higher productivity. Following Ricardo, all of wages are consumed, all of profits constitute a surplus and are re-invested. In order to maximize the rate of growth, the rate of re-investment per dollar of original investment is to be maximized, and this requires that the technique be chosen which produces the greatest surplus. With labor productivity greater under the capital-intensive technique, the rate of surplus per unit of output will also be greater. But there will be less output per unit of investment. The empirical question, which can only be answered by getting magnitudes for the parameters of the model, then becomes this: is the extra surplus per worker made possible by the more capital-intensive technique sufficiently great to offset the loss of total surplus caused by the smaller output which results from sinking the capital into intensive uses?

In a second model, Sen adds foreign trade to this scheme. He assumes that the capital-intensive technique requires imports of foreign machinery, which can be purchased by means of the export of some of the corn being produced. The rate of surplus of corn still needs to be maximized, but in addition to the corn going into

271

wages, the corn absorbed by exports must be subtracted from the total to derive the reinvestible surplus.

Maximization of the rate of growth of output is an odd objective function, and in realistic cases with alternative time profiles, it is ambiguous. However, in Sen's model, if the parameters are assumed to remain unchanged, the growth rate remains constant unless there is a switch in technique. And so, assuming the target date is chosen far enough in the future, the higher growth rate will always dominate short-run losses of output. Maximization of the rate of growth is considered by Sen to be a polar case in which only the economic situation at a remote point in time is considered.[55] Sen views simple turnover criteria, which only takes the first period into account, as the other polar case.

To bring time discount back into the analysis, Sen employs the concept of a 'recovery' period. If it is true that the capital-intensive technique produces less output in the early years but more later on, the only case in which there is a real problem of choice, then there must be some number of years over which both techniques produce the same amount of output. It is up to the government to decide how many years of output it wishes to consider in its objective function, and by comparing the 'recovery' period of the capital-intensive technique with the government's time horizon, a choice of technique can be made.

These models allow the analyst to bring certain important empirical features of underdeveloped countries into the analysis. Particularly where broad strategic choices are concerned, such as the concentration on urban industry or rural cottage industries, empirical evaluation of models of the type proposed by Sen may prove valuable. It is my feeling, however, that whatever can be done by means of these explicit sectoral models, which must simplify reality enormously in order to keep the mathematics from getting out of hand, can be done more easily and more completely by means of programing techniques.

In Sen's particular illustrative models there is a weakness, I think, in the choice of objective function. Maximizing the rate of growth will, among interesting choices, bury more detailed time preferences of the objective function; the decision-maker will not be applying sufficient judgement to the issue, and will essentially

55. He identifies Galenson-Leibenstein with this particular case.

leave it to chance. Similarly, the 'recovery' period, which is the same as the 'pay-out' period of private investment criteria, is arbitrary, placing equal value on output at any time within the period, and a zero value on any output thereafter.

Concluding Comments

Since this paper is a commentary on the problem of expenditure criteria and models, little further remains to be said. I have tried to bring out the major issues on which the choice of economic criteria turn. A deliberately narrow economic point of view has been taken, not because non-economic factors are unimportant, but rather because we ought to be clear about things about which we can be clear. I would also pass the judgement that there is no excessive preoccupation with the economic aspect in public expenditures decisions, and that improvement of the economics of government activities can be justified by higher criteria.

References

ALLAIS, M. (1953), 'L'extension des théories de l'équilibre économique général et du rendement social au cas du risque', *Econometrica*, April.

ALLIN, B. W. (1953a), 'Is group choice a part of economics?', *Quarterly Journal of Economics*, August.

ALLIN, B. W. (1953b), 'Replies', *Quarterly Journal of Economics*, November.

ARROW, K. J. (1951a), 'Little's critique of welfare economics', *American Economic Review*, December.

ARROW, K. J. (1951b), 'Alternative approaches to the theory of choice in risk-taking situations', *Econometrica*, October.

ARROW, K. J. (1952), 'Le rôle des valeurs boursières pour la répartition la meilleure des risques', *International Colloquium on Econometrics*, Centre National de la Recherche Scientifique, Paris; reprinted as Cowles Commission Paper, new series 77.

ARROW, K. J. (1958), 'Utilities, attitudes, choices: a review note', *Econometrica*, January.

ARROW, K. J., HURWICZ, L., and UZAWA, H. (eds.) (1958), *Studies in Linear and Nonlinear Programing*, Stanford University Press.

BALDWIN, R. (1953–4), 'A comparison of welfare criteria', *Review of Economic Studies*, no. 55.

BAUMOL, W. J. (1952), *Welfare Economics and the Theory of the State*, Harvard University Press.

BERGSON, A. (1938), 'A reformulation of certain aspects of welfare economics', *Quarterly Journal of Economics*, February.

The Choice between Private and Public Goods

BERNOULLI, D. (1954), 'Exposition of a new theory on the measurement of risk' (1738), translated by L. Sommer in *Econometrica*, January.

BOS, H. C., and KOYCK, L. M. (1961), 'The appraisal of investments in transportation projects: a practical example', *Review of Economics and Statistics*, vol. 43.

BOULDING, K. E. (1952), 'Welfare economics', in B. Haley (ed.), *A Survey of Contemporary Economics*, vol. 2, Irwin.

CHENERY, H. B. (1953), 'The application of investment criteria', *Quarterly Journal of Economics*, February.

CHENERY, H. B., and KRETSCHMER, K. S. (1956), 'Resource allocation for economic development', *Econometrica*, October.

CHENERY, H. B., and UZAWA, H. (1958), 'Nonlinear programing in economic development', in K. J. Arrow, L. Hurwicz and H. Uzawa (eds.), *Studies in Linear and Nonlinear Programing*, Stanford University Press.

CRAMER, H. (1930), 'On the mathematical theory of risk', *Forsakringsaktiebolaget Skandias Festskrift*, Stockholm.

DOWNS, A. (1957), *An Economic Theory of Democracy*, Harper.

DUESENBERRY, J. S., ECKSTEIN, O., and FROMM, G. (1960), 'A simulation of the U.S. economy in recession', *Econometrica*, vol. 28.

ECKSTEIN, O. (1958), *Water Resource Development: The Economics of Project Evaluation*, Harvard University Press.

ELLIS, H. (1950), 'The economic way of thinking', *American Economic Review*, March.

FARRAR, D. (1958), 'The investment decision under uncertainty', *Harvard Water Resource Seminar Paper*, September.

FEDERAL INTERAGENCY RIVER BASIN COMMITTEE (1950), Subcommittee on Benefits and Costs, *Proposed Practices of Economic Analysis of River Basin Projects*, May.

GALENSON, W., and LEIBENSTEIN, H. (1955), 'Investment criteria, productivity and economic development', *Quarterly Journal of Economics*, August.

GRAAFF, J. de V. (1968), *Theoretical Welfare Economics*, Cambridge University Press.

HARROD, R. F. (1948), *Toward a Dynamic Economics*, Macmillan.

HICKS, J. R. (1940), 'The valuation of social income', *Economica*, new series, vol. 7.

HILDRETH, C. G. (1946), 'Note on maximization criteria', *Quarterly Journal of Economics*, November.

HIRSHLEIFER, J. (1958), 'On the theory of optimal investment decision', *Journal of Political Economy*, August.

HOLZMAN, F. D. (1958), 'Consumer sovereignty and the rate of economic development', *Economia Internazionale*, vol. 11.

KAHN, H., and MANN, I. (1957), *Techniques of System Analysis*, RAND Corporation, RM–1829–1, ASTIA Doc. No. AD133012, June.

KALDOR, N. (1939), 'Welfare propositions and interpersonal comparisons of utility', *Economic Journal*, vol. 49.

KENNEDY, C. F. (1952–3), 'The economic welfare function and Dr Little's criterion', *Review of Economic Studies*, no. 52.

KING, J. S. (1958), 'A method for consideration of risk and uncertainty in water resource project evaluation', *Harvard Water Resource Seminar Paper*, September.

KLEIN, B., and MECKLING, W. (1958), 'Application of operations research to development decisions', *Operation Research*, May–June.

KRUTILLA, J. V., and ECKSTEIN, O. (1958), *Multiple Purpose River Development: Studies in Applied Economic Analysis*, Johns Hopkins Press.

LIPSEY, R. G., and LANCASTER, R. K. (1956–7), 'The general theory of second-best', *Review of Economic Studies*, vol. 24 (1), no. 63.

LITTLE, I. M. D. (1957), *A Critique of Welfare Economics*, Oxford University Press, 2nd edn.

LUCE, R. D., and RAIFFA, H. (1957), *Games and Decisions*, Wiley.

LUTZ, F. A. (1945), 'The criterion of maximum profits in the theory of investment', *Quarterly Journal of Economics*, November.

LUTZ, F. A. (1950), 'The structure of interest rates', *Quarterly Journal of Economics*, November.

LUTZ, F. A., and LUTZ, V. (1951), *The Theory of Investment of the Firm*, Princeton University Press.

MARRIS, R. L. (1957), 'Professor Hicks' index number theorem', *Review of Economic Studies*, October.

MCKEAN, R. N. (1958), *Efficiency in Government through Systems Analysis, with Emphasis on Water Resource Development*, RAND Corporation Research Study, Wiley.

MILNOR, J. (1954), 'Games against nature', in R. M. Thrall *et al.* (eds.), *Decision Processes*, Wiley.

NURKSE, R. (1953), *Problems of Capital Formation in Underdeveloped Countries*, Oxford University Press.

RADNER, R., and MARSCHAK, J. (1954), 'Note on some proposed decision criteria', in R. M. Thrall *et al.* (eds.), *Decision Processes*, Wiley.

REUBER, G. L., and WONNACOTT, R. J. (1961), *The Cost of Social Capital in Canada*, Johns Hopkins Press.

ROY, A. D. (1952), 'Safety first and the holding of assets', *Econometrica*, July.

SAMUELSON, P. A. (1958), 'An exact consumption-loan model of interest with or without the social contrivance of money', *Journal of Political Economy*, December.

SCITOVSKY, T. (1942), 'A note on welfare propositions in economics', *Review of Economic Studies*, vol. 10.

SCITOVSKY, T. (1954), 'Two concepts of external economies', *Journal of Political Economy*, April.

SEN, A. K. (1957a), 'A comment on Tinbergen's "The optimal rate of saving"', *Economic Journal*, December.

SEN, A. K. (1957b), 'Some notes on the choice of capital-intensity', *Quarterly Journal of Economics*, November.

SIMON, H. (1957a), 'A behavioral model of rational choice', *Models of Man*, Wiley. Reprinted from *Quarterly Journal of Economics*, 1955.

SIMON, H. (1957b), *Administrative Behavior*, Collier-Macmillan, 2nd edn.

STEINER, P. O. (1959), 'Choosing among alternative public investments', *American Economic Review*, December.

STOCKFISCH, J. A. (1955), 'External economies, investment and foresight', *Journal of Political Economy*, October.

STROTZ, R. (1955–6), 'Myopia and inconsistency in dynamic utility maximization', *Review of Economic Studies*, vol. 23.

STROUT, A. (1958), 'Primary employment effects of alternative spending programs', *Review of Economics and Statistics*, November.

TELSER, L. (1955–6), 'Safety first and hedging', *Review of Economic Studies*, vol. 23.

THOMAS, H. A., Jr, 'A method for accounting for benefit and cost uncertainties in water resource project design', *Harvard Water Resources Seminar Paper*.

TINBERGEN, J. (1956), 'The optimal rate of saving', *Economic Journal*, December.

TINBERGEN, J. (1957), 'The appraisal of road construction: two calculation schemes', *Review of Economics and Statistics*, August.

11 J. M. Buchanan

Earmarked Taxes

J. M. Buchanan, 'The economics of earmarked taxes',
Journal of Political Economy, vol. 71, 1963, pp. 457–69.

Economists do not agree on the effects of earmarking. For example Julius Margolis and Walter Heller suggest that the earmarking or segregating of fiscal accounts tends to reduce the willingness of taxpayers to approve expenditures on specific public services.[1] By contrast, Earl Roplh and George Break, along with Jesse Burkhead, discuss earmarking as one device for generating taxpayer support for expansion in particular services.[2] The staff of the Tax Foundation, in a more comprehensive study, have expressed views in accord with the latter position (Tax Foundation, 1955).

This paper develops a theory of earmarking that 'explains' the divergent predictions and also suggests certain hypotheses, the implications of which should be testable through the observation of political processes. In order to construct this theory, it is necessary to introduce models of the political-decision process that are not consistent with those that have been implicitly assumed in the orthodox normative evaluation of earmarking. The near-universal condemnation of the institution by experts in budgetary theory and practice is familiar and need not be summarized here.[3] This

1. Margolis, in his stimulating paper, provides empirical support for this hypothesis in the case of expenditures for education. See Margolis (1961, esp. pp. 261–6).

Heller criticizes the institution of the attached mill-levy because it serves to restrict unduly the willingness of taxpayers to support mosquito control programs and the like. See Heller (1957, p. 650, esp. n. 39).

2. In both cases here, the argument is applied to the financing of special functions in underdeveloped countries. See Rolph and Break (1961, p. 62), and Burkhead (1956, p. 469).

3. For statements of the argument in standard works see Slade Kendrick (1951, p. 331); Schultz and Lowell Harriss (1959, p. 107); Taylor (1963, p. 28); Groves (1958, p. 500).

'Classical' statements of the standard position are to be found in Bastable (1895, p. 689); Leroy-Beaulieu (1906, p. 30 ff.); Jeze (1922, pp. 82–103).

position cannot be supported on the basis of the efficiency considerations that may be derived from the models emphasized in this paper.

'Earmarking' is defined as the practice of designating or dedicating specific revenues to the financing of specific public services. It is discussed under such headings as 'special funds', 'segregated accounts', 'segregated budgets', 'dedicated revenues'. Normally, earmarking as a term is used with reference to the dedication of a single tax source to a single public service within a multitax, multiservice fiscal unit, but the identical effects are produced by the creation of special-purpose fiscal units, such as school districts, fire districts, and sanitation districts, each of which is granted independent, but restricted, taxing powers. Quantitatively, earmarking is important in the overall United States fiscal system. At the local government level, the special-purpose units remain predominant in the financing of important services, education being the notable example.[4] At the state level, one study suggested that one-half of all state collections in 1954 were earmarked (Tax Foundation, 1955). At the federal level, the modern growth of the trust-fund accounts, such as that for highways, suggests that, proportionately, earmarked or segregated revenues are assuming increasing significance.

I

The standard normative 'theory' of earmarking adopts the reference system of the budget-maker, the budgetary authority, who is, by presumption, divorced from the citizenry in the political community. An alternative working hypothesis of political order is the individualistic one in which the reference system becomes that of the individual citizen. In this model, the only meaningful decision-making units are individual persons, and the state or the collectivity exists only as a means through which individuals combine to accomplish collective or jointly desired objectives. The state is not an independent choosing agent, and 'collective choice' results from separate individual decisions as these are processed by constitutional rules. The analytical device of the social welfare function, which guides the judgements of an independent budgetary

4. Independent school districts account for almost four-fifths of tota school enrolment in the United States (see Margolis, 1961, p. 263).

authority, has no place in this model. The earmarking of revenues must be re-examined in the context of individual participation in the formation of collective decisions. When this approach is taken, it becomes apparent that the restrictions that such practices as earmarking may impose on the independence of a budgetary authority need not produce 'inefficiency' in the fiscal process. Some such segregation of revenues may provide one means of insuring more rational individual choice; under some conditions, earmarking may be a 'desirable' rather than an 'undesirable' feature of a fiscal structure.

Institutionally, earmarking provides a means of compartmentalizing fiscal decisions. The individual citizen, as voter-taxpayer-beneficiary, is enabled to participate, *separately*, either directly or through his legislative representative, in the several public expenditure decisions that may arise. He may, through this device, 'vote' independently on the funds to be devoted to schools, to sanitation, and so on, given the specified revenue sources. Only in this manner can he make 'private' choices on the basis of some reasonably accurate comparison of the costs and the benefits of the specific public services, one at the time.[5] By contrast, general-fund budgeting, or non-earmarking, allows the citizen to 'vote' only on the aggregate outlay for the predetermined 'bundles' of public services, as this choice is presented to him by the budgetary authorities.[6]

The appropriate market analogue to general-fund financing (non-earmarking) is a specific tie-in sale, as opposed to independent quantity adjustment in each market, the analogue to earmarking. Independent adjustment is characteristic of privately

5. The necessity of relating decisions on public expenditures explicitly to decisions on taxes through the political process, and of assigning a definite revenue category to each single expenditure was stressed by Wicksell in his classic statement of the individualistic theory of public finance (see Wicksell, 1896, pp. 72–118, but esp. p. 94).

6. Control over the budgetary allocation, at one stage removed, does exist through the voter's ultimate power to remove public officials through electoral processes. And, even for the budgetary allocation as presented, legislative power to modify the allocation of funds among the separate public service outlays is normally exercized. However, these powers to change the uses to which general-fund revenues may be put do not modify the basic 'tie-in' features of the model until and unless the tax structure is simultaneously considered in the same decision processes.

organized markets for goods and services. The individual is not normally required to purchase goods and services in 'bundles' of complex heterogeneous units. Insofar as some tie-ins are observed to persist in competitive markets, these reflect the advantages of superior efficiency to the purchaser. In the absence of genuine cost-reducing aspects of marketing separate goods in 'bundles', any restrictions that are placed on the ability to adjust quantities independently must move the purchaser to some less preferred position on his utility surface. For example, any requirement that one stick of butter be purchased with each loaf of bread would surely produce 'inefficiency' in choice, and could be implemented only through the exercise of monopoly power.[7]

II

The model of individual fiscal choice that is required must remain extremely simplified. It is necessary to abstract from the complexities of alternative political decision rules and at the same time to retain for the model some relevance for collective results. To accomplish this, the 'median' voter-taxpayer-beneficiary is introduced. 'Median' here characterizes the individual's preference structure as typical of that describing his fellows in the group. With single-peaked preferences the 'median' individual becomes decisive under simple majority voting rules (see Black, 1958). Hence, the behavior of the single 'median' individual mirrors that of the effective decision-making group in the community. Through this device, collective results can be discussed in terms of the behavior of the single individual. The conception is similar to, although somewhat broader than, the community-of-equals assumption that has been employed frequently in fiscal analysis.

I shall assume that the goods or services provided publicly utilize a sufficiently small share of total community resources to allow income effects to be neglected in the behavior of the individual. Collective goods are assumed to be produced at constant marginal costs, and, finally, the costs of reaching collective decisions are neglected. Initially, I shall assume that the collective goods, whether supplied singly or jointly, are to be financed

7. For recent statements of the theory of tie-in sales see Burstein (1960a, pp. 68–73, and 1960b, pp. 62–95); see also Bowman (1957, pp. 19–36).

through the imposition of a particular form of lump-sum tax. This tax is designed so that the 'terms-of-trade' between the individual and the fisc cannot be affected by the behavior of the former. The 'tax price per unit' of the collective good made available to him is invariant over quantity, although the total tax bill is, of course, dependent on the quantity chosen by the community. This relatively pure model allows us to discuss the behavior of the individual free from any elements of strategic bargaining with his fellows that might be present were the terms of trade subject to influence by his own actions.

The choice calculus of the individual can now be analyzed in familiar terms. He is confronted by a fixed 'supply price'; the supply curve, to him, for the collective good, singly or in a bundle, is horizontal at some predetermined 'tax price'. This tax price, to the individual, is some share of the total supply price or cost price of the good to the whole community. The quantity of collective goods made available to one person is assumed equally available to everyone else in the group. The distribution of taxes among the separate individuals is assumed to have been determined outside the model. In a world-of-equals model, an individual share might be taken simply as a pro rata part of total unit cost. In this more general setting, any distribution of taxes is possible so long as this distribution is independent of the particular choice analyzed.

Consider first a single collective good. We can think of an individual marginal evaluation schedule or curve, which in this instance is equivalent to a demand curve, for this good in the same manner that we think of such a schedule or curve for a privately marketed good or service. Individual or private 'equilibrium' is reached at a point where the demand price equals the individual supply price or tax price. In this collective good case, there is no opportunity for the individual, acting alone, to adjust quantity purchased to price. Hence, the attainment of his 'equilibrium' position is possible, even for the 'median' consumer, only through 'voting for' or 'voting against' extensions or contractions in public goods supply. The construction enables us to depict the voting choices of the individual with respect to the collective good in a manner analogous to the standard treatment of market choice, so long as we assume that marginal adjustments in public expenditure programs are possible. If marginal adjustments are not possible, and the voter is presented with a final choice of voting for or against specific expenditure proposals, elements of all-or-none offers enter his calculus, and the treatment requires modification.

The analysis is straightforward when we consider a single collective good or service. Since, however, we want to introduce the tie-in 'sale' that general-fund financing implies, a two-good model becomes the simplest one that is helpful. For descriptive flavor, think of a community that supplies both police protection and fire protection services collectively. We seek to determine the possible differences between financing these two services separately, through a system of earmarking where each service is supported by revenues from a tax of the sort indicated above, and financing them jointly, with revenues from a general-fund budget derived from only one tax. In either case, the total amount of public expenditure is assumed to be determined by the rationally motivated choice of the voter-taxpayer. Will general-fund financing result in a larger or a smaller provision of one or both public services than that produced under an earmarked revenue scheme? Will total public outlay, on both services, increase, decrease, or remain the same as an institutional change from one revenue system to the other is made?

The answers to these, and other, questions must depend upon the particular form that a general-fund budgetary tie-in takes. It would be possible to define this tie-in with respect to physical units of service, such as, for example, the requirement that the same number of policemen and firemen be supplied. It will, however, be descriptively more realistic and analytically more convenient if we define the tie-in with respect to a budgetary allocation between the two services. In other words, general-fund financing takes the form of a specific proportion of the total budget devoted to each of the two services. There will always exist one budgetary allocation that will insure identity of solution as between the two institutions. That is, there is always one budgetary ratio that will cause the median individual to 'vote for' the same relative quantities of the two services and the same public outlay with or without earmarking. This unique solution, which I shall label 'full equilibrium', provides a starting point for a more careful analysis.

It is convenient to illustrate the analysis geometrically. In Figure 1 quantity units are measured along the horizontal axis, but these units are defined in a special way. Under the tie-in arrangement, a unity of quantity is defined as that physical combination of the two services available for one dollar, one hundred cents. Thus, the number of dollars expended is directly proportional to the distance along the horizontal axis. Now assume that the 'full equilibrium' budgetary mix prevails, and that this is defined by the forty-sixty

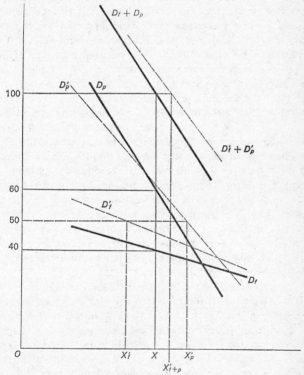

Figure 1

ratio. Forty cents out of each budgetary dollar is devoted to providing fire protection and sixty cents to providing police protection; each service is supplied at constant cost. We may now derive demand curves for fire protection services, D_f, and police protection services, D_p, respectively. These demand curves must be defined with respect to the dimensions indicated by the budgetary ratio. A unit of fire protection is defined as that quantity available to the individual for an outlay of forty cents, and a unit of police services is defined as that quantity available for an outlay of sixty cents. For expositional simplicity, I shall use linear demand functions. The vertical summation of the two demand curves, $D_f + D_p$, represents the demand for the bundle of services, available for one dollar per unit, when the forty-sixty ratio prevails. By definition of 'full equilibrium', this composite demand curve cuts the tax-price curve, drawn at the one-dollar level, along the same vertical line measuring the independently chosen equilibrium quantities of fire protection and police protection respectively. The elements of circularity that are present in this whole construction are not damaging since the purpose is illustrative only.

Given the conditions of demand shown in Figure 1, there is no differential effect as between earmarking and general-fund financing of the two services at the forty-sixty budgetary ratio. The individual will choose, will vote for, the same quantity of services and the same overall public outlay under either one of the two institutional forms. If separately presented, he will vote for an amount, OX, of fire services, defined in forty-cent units, which can, of course, readily be translated into any other physical dimension. Similarly, he will choose an amount, OX, of police services defined in sixty-cent units. Or, if forced to take these two services in bundles, defined by the forty-sixty ratio, he will choose an amount, OX. In either case, he will vote for a total budget outlay that is directly proportional to the horizontal distance, OX.

Differential effects arise only when some budgetary ratio other than that required for 'full equilibrium' is introduced. Assume now that the budgetary ratio is exogenously determined, and that a proposal is made to shift from a system of segregated financing to general-fund financing under, say, a fifty-fifty ratio, with underlying demand conditions for the two services remaining as depicted in Figure 1. It is necessary to translate the demand curves, D_f and D_p, into the modified dimensions, with physical units now being defined as the quantities available at fifty cents. The new demand curves, drawn in the fifty-cents dimensions, are shown as D_f' and D_p'. The effects of general-fund financing at this nonequilibrium ratio, which has been shifted in favor of fire protection services, can be clearly indicated. As might be expected, more fire protection is demanded and less police protection than under earmarking. In the new dimensions, OX_f' represents the 'full equilibrium' or earmarking quantity of fire protection services, and OX_p' the corresponding quantity of police services. In other words, OX, in the old dimension, is equivalent to OX_f' in the new; both represent the same physical quantity of fire protection services. General-fund financing under the new, fifty-fifty budgetary ratio will produce a 'tie-in equilibrium' at a quantity measured by $OX_{f'+p}'$, which is determined by the intersection of the newly drawn composite demand curve, $D_f' + D_p'$, with the composite supply curve.[8]

Any shift in the budgetary ratio away from that required for 'full equilibrium' will insure that general-fund financing introduces some distortion in the choice pattern of the individual. Forcing him to purchase the two services in a bundle, rather than separately, will move the individual to some less preferred position on his utility surface, given our framework assumption that decision-making costs are zero. Since, under independent quantity adjustment, he could always, should he desire, select quantities of fire and police services indicated by the second solution, the fact that he does not do so in the first solution suggests that such a combination must be less preferred than the initial combination chosen. The distortion produced by the non-equilibrium budgetary ratio will take the form of an expansion in one of the two services beyond the 'full equilibrium' quantity and a contraction of the other to some less than 'full equilibrium' quantity. Relatively, the service expanded will be that one that is differentially favored by the ratio. The analysis remains incomplete, however, until and unless further questions are answered. Will overall public outlay tend to increase or decrease, and under what conditions? What are the characteristics of those services most likely to be substantially increased as a result of favorable-ratio general-fund financing?

Total public outlay need not remain the same under earmarking and non-earmarking when a non-equilibrium budgetary ratio prevails, and the direction of change will depend on the configuration of the demand functions. Examination of the model produces

8. The geometrical constructions in both Figure 1 and Figure 2 are drawn on the basis of a specific numerical model that will be supplied upon request.

the following conclusions: If the ratio turns in favor of the service characterized by the more elastic demand at the full equilibrium quantity (as in the example), total public outlay will be expanded as earmarking is replaced by general-fund financing. Conversely, if the ratio shifts in favor of the service characterized by the less elastic demand at the full equilibrium quantity, total public outlay will be reduced as a result of a similar shift in institutions. These results hold, however, only for limited shifts in the ratio away from the full equilibrium one. As the construction of Figure 1 suggests, the relative elasticities of demand may change as the 'tie-in equilibrium' quantity changes. When and if relative elasticities change, the direction of change in total expenditure is reversed. Utilizing the linear demand curves of Figure 1, this point may be illustrated readily. As the ratio shifts initially in favor of fire protection, characterized by the more elastic demand at the initial quantity, total outlay will be increased by the tie-in scheme. However, beyond some critical value, the elasticity of demand for fire protection, at the tie-in quantity, becomes less than that for police services, and, total public outlay diminishes as the budgetary ratio continues to shift in favor of fire protection.[9]

Several of the relevant relationships are illustrated in Figure 2. On the horizontal axis is measured the percentage of fire protection services in a tie-in budgetary mix, from zero to one hundred. On the vertical axis is measured total outlay, on both and on each service, as determined by the demand pattern of the individual and the assumed cost conditions for the two services. Specifically, Figure 2 is derived from the same configuration as Figure 1, which embodies linear demand functions, although a similar set of relationships could be readily derived from any postulated initial

9. Note that these conclusions can be stated in terms of relative elasticities only in the model that allows the quantity dimensions to shift as the budgetary ratio changes. This shifting of quantity dimension insures that, for both services, the quantity taken is the same. This, along with the additional requirement that the absolute changes in price for the two services must be precisely offsetting, allows shifts along two separate demand functions to be evaluated in terms of relative elasticity coefficients. Without these constraints, shifts along two separate demand functions could not be compared with respect to changes in total outlay solely in terms of relative elasticities. The latter would remain important, but some relative price factor would have to be added.

conditions of demand. The full equilibrium ratio, defined previously as the forty-sixty one, must involve a total public outlay equal to the sum of the spending on the two services when 'purchased' separately. If a ratio with zero fire protection services is introduced, total spending will be on police services alone; conversely, if a one hundred per cent ratio is present, all spending will be for fire protection. Thus, income effects being neglected, the vertical distance, E, at full equilibrium, must equal the sum of the

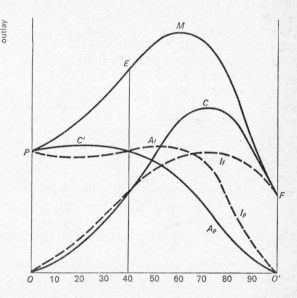

Figure 2   Percentage of general-fund outlay devoted to fire protection

distances, OP, and $O'F$. As the ratio shifts in favor of fire protection services, total outlay expands, as shown by the rising portion of the top curve to the right of E. Total outlay reaches a maximum at M, and then falls sharply to F as the ratio becomes more and more favorable to fire protection. As the ratio shifts in favor of police protection services, total outlay falls, as is indicated by the top curve to the left of E. It continues to fall to P where no part of the budget is devoted to providing fire protection.

The additional curves in Figure 2 break down this total outlay as between the two services and into actual and imputed components. Actual outlay is, of course, computed by taking the indicated percentage of total outlay as shown by the ratio on the horizontal scale. 'Imputed outlay' on a service is defined as that part of total outlay on a bundle that is attributed to the service by the individual at each particular tie-in equilibrium. Imputed outlay on a service equals actual only at the full equilibrium budgetary ratio. For all other ratios, imputed outlay differs from actual, and the difference reflects the degree of 'exploitation', negative or positive, that non-equilibrium ratios can generate. Imputed outlay falls below actual outlay on the service that is favored in the budgetary mix; it exceeds actual outlay on the remaining service. This is shown in Figure 2. To the right of 40 per cent, imputed outlay on fire protection services, I_f, falls below actual outlay, A_f. To the left of 40 per cent, the opposite relationship holds. And, of course, the relationships for police services are the inverse of those for fire services.

Maximum total outlay is reached at M. As the ratio shifts beyond this point, total expenditures fall although the share of this total devoted to fire protection continues to increase. At some point, C, to the right of M, these two factors become mutually offsetting, and some maximum outlay on fire protection services alone is reached. Increasing the share in the budget beyond this 'critical ratio' will result in fewer resources devoted to fire protection, always on the assumption that the voter-taxpayer retains the basic power of determining the level of total spending.

As the ratio shifts in favor of police services, in our model, total outlay falls continuously. However, because of the increasing share, the quantity of police services supplied increases to some critical ratio, C', where actual outlay reaches a maximum.[10]

10. The rising portion of the I_p curve at the left in Figure 2 requires some explanation. As the budgetary mix shifts in favor of police services, imputed expenditures on both services fall, as indicated. However, as a smaller and smaller share of the budget is allotted to fire protection, the degree of exploitation that consumers of police services can attain reaches some maximum. Beyond this point, the 'relative price reduction' that the tie-in involves is progressively diminished.

The derivation of this construction is clarified in the numerical example upon which both Figures 1 and 2 are based. It should be emphasized,

III

The analysis, to this point, has been based on the choice calculus of the single median individual. Even before generalizing this analysis, we are able to draw some interesting implications for political group behavior. In any community specific individuals and groups will find particular interest in the performance of one or the other public services provided. Using the two-service model we can examine the predicted behavior of groups organized in support of either fire protection or police protection services. If both services should be initially financed through independently designated taxes, that is, if earmarking prevails, then groups in support of either service would have some incentive to attempt to secure a general-fund budgetary scheme favorable to its own service. Conversely, either group would try to retain earmarking if it predicts an unfavorable budgetary allotment under general-fund arrangements.

The characteristics of demand, however, make for considerable differences in the expected gains to be secured under favorable general-fund ratios. Relatively, the group that is organized in support of the service characterized by the more elastic demand stands to gain more by favorable tie-ins. In this way, sizable amounts of 'taxpayers' surplus' can be captured from the relatively less elastic demand service that is tied into the budgetary bundle.[11] Not only will the favored service be allotted a larger share of each budget dollar, but also total spending on both services increases. By comparison, the pressure group organized to support the relatively inelastic-demand service will not be able to secure so much

---

however, that the general results do not depend upon the particulars of the example or on the shapes of the curves derived therefrom.

11. This is, in general, consistent with the conclusions of Burstein with respect to the tie-in sales of the monopolist. As he suggests, the monopolist, selling a product that is necessarily price elastic, will seek to tie in the sales of an inelastic-demand product. The monopolist can, of course, control the relevant ratio (see Burstein, 1960a).

The analysis of earmarking, as developed here, is simpler than the comparable analysis of monopolistic tie-in sales. In the earmarking model, the unit cost of supplying services, either jointly or separately, is always equal to the 'tax price' charged to 'purchasers'. In other words, the government does not seek to make profits. With the monopolist, the difference between unit cost and price is a central variable that the fiscal model need not include.

advantage even from comparably favorable shifts in the budgetary ratio. A higher share of the budgetary dollar will be advantageous, but the degree of exploitation from 'taxpayers' surplus' on the other service is severely limited. This group therefore, stands to gain less and possibly to lose more from a general change in institutions leading away from segregated revenue sources. It will be much more likely to opt for the continuation, or the introduction, of segregated budget accounts.

Note that *both* pressure groups could never be observed to approve a shift from segregated to general-fund financing or vice versa if the budgetary ratio is known in advance, and known to be a non-equilibrium one. If the model has predictive value at all, observation should reveal that some groups support one financing arrangement and some the other. There is an appropriate market analogue. Rational monopolists producing two separate goods could never be observed to join in a mutually agreed tie-in sale without the pooling of revenues. Any particular tie-in, other than the full equilibrium one, must benefit one and harm the other.

As mentioned, Margolis refers to data that suggest somewhat larger expenditures on education under general-fund than under segregated financing schemes. If the analytical model presented here is valid, these facts suggest that education is favored in general-fund budgetary ratios. It seems probable, also, that total municipal spending is larger in those cases where education is included in the general-fund budget. This supplementary hypothesis, if confirmed by observation, would imply that, over the relevant ranges, educational services are characterized by a relatively higher demand elasticity than companion services in the budget. There is independent evidence to support this implication. Public services, like education, that provide differentially higher benefits to particular subgroups in the community (in this case families with children) will tend to be relatively more demand elastic than services that are more 'general' in benefit incidence (say, police protection). By requiring taxpayers who do not secure direct benefits from publicly provided educational services to purchase general community services such as police only through a tie-in arrangement with education, some 'taxpayers' surplus' is captured, as Margolis has suggested. The bachelor who might vote against additional school district taxes (and expenditures) may vote for additional taxes to finance a bundle of services that includes education. The analysis does not imply, however, even if further research should confirm fully the hypotheses involved, that school superintendents and P.T.A. groups take no chances in pushing for the abolition of segregated financial sources. Such plans would, of course, backfire unless favorable budgetary ratios are secured.[12]

The behavior of subgroups in the political community that are not organized to support specific expenditures may also be noted briefly. Taxpayer groups, those whose primary objective is that of reducing the level of tax rates independently of any consideration for public spending levels, will tend to favor earmarking schemes if they expect that general-fund budgeting implies shifts in favor of the more elastic-demand services. For the same reason, these groups would desire general-fund financing in the converse case. Since, however, the gain to be expected in the latter institutional arrangement is likely to be slight, taxpayer groups normally might be predicted to support earmarking.

By comparison and contrast, the 'bureaucracy', whose objective is primarily that of expanding the size and importance of the public sector, independently of costs, will directly oppose the taxpayer groups. If voter-taxpayer response is presumed, ultimately, to determine the total public expenditure level while the bureaucracy chooses the budgetary mix, the model that seems to be implicit in much of the orthodox discussion emerges. Here the budget-makers 'should' try to select a mix that approximates the full equilibrium ratio. If, however, these officials include consideration of bureaucracy objectives in their decisions, they will be biased toward shifting general-fund allocations in favor of the relatively elastic-demand services, and, in this way, toward insuring some over-all expansion in public spending.

IV

The first step toward generalizing the model involves the extension to more than two public services. Basically, the same propositions

12. As W. C. Stubblebine has pointed out, the analysis here seems appropriate to the behavior of certain charitable organizations. The model 'explains' why the Boy Scouts seek to be included in general-fund Community Chest revenue-raising drives, while the Red Cross and the Cancer Society prefer independent (earmarked) financing.

hold. The departures from independently determined or 'optimal' levels of provision for particular services become larger as more services are included in the budgetary bundle. Partial segregation of fiscal accounts, with each including several services that are commonly financed, can be shown to be more 'efficient', from the reference system of the voter-taxpayer-beneficiary, than overall integration into a comprehensive budgetary system, given the restrictions imposed on the model. Similar conclusions apply to the effects of segregated budget accounts created by special-purpose governmental units. Incorporation of decision-making costs into the model could, of course, modify these initial conclusions.

In the model discussed the separate services were assumed to be wholly independent. Extension of the analysis to cover those cases where services are either close substitutes or close complements will not affect the results. Services were also assumed supplied at constant cost, but this simplification does not affect the conclusions.

A major step toward generalizing the analysis is that which relaxes the specific tax assumptions. The individual, whose decision processes are examined, is confronted with a fixed 'tax per unit'. Only a form of lump-sum tax satisfies this requirement. Under most real-world taxing institutions, the tax price per unit at which collective goods are made available to the individual will depend, at least to some degree, on his own behavior. This element is not, however, important under the major tax institutions such as the personal income tax, the general sales tax, or the real property tax. With such structures, the individual may, by changing his private behavior, modify the tax base (and thus the tax price per unit of collective goods he utilizes), but he need not have any incentive to conceal his 'true' preferences for public goods. His own tax liability, per unit, is to such a small extent modified by his own choice for public goods that he will not normally include this factor in his decision for or against public spending proposals. His behavior in participating in collective choice can remain broadly analogous to his behavior as a purchaser of goods and services in the market place.

In the formal model, it was assumed that the distribution of taxes among separate persons is in some way determined independently of the particular fiscal choices analyzed. The tax price per unit that the individual confronts does not depend on the outcome of the choice. This, in itself, seems 'realistic'. Local communities, for example, make decisions on expansions and contractions in public spending programs in the expectation that costs will be placed on the ratepayers, and the distribution of these costs does not normally depend on the pattern of public services chosen. Similarly, assemblies at higher governmental levels vote on appropriations measures independently of the given tax structure. Conversely, tax reform does not imply change in budgetary allocation. The model employed can, therefore, apply equally to the calculus of the low-income citizen who, presumably, is required by the tax structure to pay a differentially low tax price for units of collective good and to the high-income citizen who is required to pay a differentially high tax price for the same good.

Complications produced by distributional elements must be faced when the results of the individual-behavior model are applied to fiscal experience. In the normal order of events, collective goods and services are 'priced' to individuals in a discriminatory fashion. This fact makes it necessary that we interpret the conclusions concerning the relative elasticities of demand for public services quite carefully. In ordinary market analysis, when the demand for a good is classified as relatively elastic over a relevant price range, this conveys specific meaning since, presumably, all buyers confront the prevailing price. If, however, separate consumers buy at different prices, as they do in the case of collective goods, the elasticity of total demand depends on the pattern of discrimination that happens to be present. It becomes impossible to classify public services, even at known relative cost levels, into elastic and inelastic demand categories independently of the tax structure.

A further reference to Margolis' interesting evidence on educational spending illustrates this point. As suggested above, the data indicate that education secures favorable ratios in general-fund budgeting arrangements. If, in addition, municipal spending on all goods is higher when general-fund financing is adopted, the demand for educational services, *at the prevailing tax structures*, is relatively more elastic than that for companion services. But a shift or change in the tax structure can modify this relative demand elasticity, since any change in the distribution of costs among individuals amounts to a shifting of relative prices, as these are confronted by the separate individuals in the group. Margolis suggests that a shift to general-fund financing for education may be needed in many localities in order to generate political support for expanded expenditures. However, this expansion would be secured at the expense of some additional distortion in individual fiscal choice, along with a necessary contraction in accompanying services. A more fruitful, and more 'efficient', means of securing the same objective may lie in some modification of the structure of taxes imposed by special-purpose governments, some change in the pattern of discriminatory rates.

V

The theory of earmarking presented in this paper may be criticized on many grounds. Any formal model based on individual behavior in collective choice processes must remain remote from real-world political experience. Even when compared with models of market behavior, a high degree of abstraction remains in this approach to political decisions. Testable implications of the theory are difficult to derive, and testing itself presents serious problems. Defense of the approach comes down, quite simply, to the faith that 'some theory is better than nothing'.

The analysis developed is intended only as a first step toward understanding this important fiscal institution. A more complete and more complex treatment may lead to normative conclusions that would be somewhat more in conformity with ruling opinion. The most important element omitted has been that of decision-making costs, in its various institutional manifestations. If this is given due weight, the basic individualistic model may indicate that the segregation of revenues remains 'inefficient' relative to consolidated revenue schemes. The point to be stressed here is only that, if this conclusion should be forthcoming, the added features must be demonstrated to outweigh the distortions upon which the model of individual fiscal choice focuses attention.

References

BASTABLE, C. F. (1895), *Public Finance*, Macmillan, 2nd edn.

BLACK, D. (1958), *The Theory of Committees and Elections*, Cambridge University Press.

BOWMAN, W. S., Jr (1957), 'Tying arrangements and the leverage problem', *Yale Law Journal*, vol. 67.

BURKHEAD, J. (1956), *Government Budgeting*, Wiley.

BURSTEIN, M. L. (1960a), 'The economics of tie-in sales', *Review of Economics and Statistics*, vol. 42.

BURSTEIN, M. L. (1960b), 'A theory of full-line forcing', *Northwestern University Law Review*, vol. 55.

GROVES, H. M. (1958), *Financing Government*, Henry Holt.

HELLER, W. (1957), 'CED's stabilizing budget policy after ten years', *American Economic Review*, vol. 47.

JEZE, G. (1922), *Cours de Science des Finances: Théorie Générale du Budget*, Marcel Girard, 6th edn.

LEROY-BEAULIEU, P. (1906), *Traité de la Science des Finances, II*, Guillaumin, 2nd edn.

MARGOLIS, J. (1961), 'Metropolitan finance problems: territories, functions and growth', *Public Finances: Needs, Sources and Utilization*, National Bureau of Economic Research, New York.

ROLPH, E., and BREAK, G. (1961), *Public Finance*, Ronald Press.

SCHULTZ, W. J., and LOWELL HARRISS, C. (1959), *American Public Finance*, Prentice-Hall, 7th edn.

SLADE KENDRICK, M. (1951), *Public Finance*, Houghton Mifflin.

TAX FOUNDATION (1955), *Earmarked State Taxes*, Tax Foundation, New York.

TAYLOR, P. E. (1963), *The Economics of Public Finance*, Macmillan, rev. edn.

WICKSELL, K. (1896), 'A new principle of just taxation' (originally *Finanztheoretische Untersuchungen*, Gustav Fischer, 1896), in R. A. Musgrave and A. T. Peacock (eds.), *Classics in the Theory of Public Finance*, International Economic Association, 1958.

Part Three **Taxes v. Loans**

The simplest way in which the government can provide itself with finance is by printing money. If resources are idle this method is uniquely efficient. Governments may also charge fees (prices), raise loans or impose taxes. If a rational choice is to be made among the possibilities any differences in their effects must be known. To raise revenue by increasing the price of a government-provided good or service is no different from imposing a tax on that good or service and may be compared to other tax alternatives. This point seems to have been incompletely appreciated in the discussions of the U.K. Electricity Council's decision substantially to raise electricity prices in 1967. Part of the problem was to finance higher than expected unit capital costs incurred in an investment expansion geared to the (as it turned out) optimistic 1965 National Plan. Borrowing was ruled out by the government. Many commentators then seemed to think the issue was increased electricity prices *or* increased taxes, failing to see that the price increase was in fact a tax – almost certainly a highly regressive one.

Recently, considerable controversy has raged around the question of government borrowing. Rather unfortunately it centred on the so-called 'burden' of the national debt. Although the 'burden' discussions were essentially a matter of semantics – whether it exists and, if so, its location depends on how the 'burden' is defined – the controversy served to clarify the question of the differential effects of taxes and internal loans. It may be helpful to set out the circumstances in which, in a closed economy, there will be no difference between the two methods of finance.

People will be indifferent between tax finance and loan finance if the present value of discounted future tax liabilities under the loan scheme is equal to the value of present taxes under the tax scheme. For this to be the case it is required not only that the capital market be perfect so that those who prefer to pay taxes in the future rather than the present can do so by raising personal loans at the government's borrowing rate, but also that *either* people expect to live for ever, paying known taxes, *or* that they treat the known liabilities of taxpayers in the future as their own. If, compared on a present value basis, tax liabilities differ under the two schemes, their economic consequences may differ.

The foregoing analysis assumes that the *level* of taxation at a point in time is of no importance. This is unlikely to be so if taxes have 'announcement' effects, that is they distort the choice between, for example, work and leisure, which will generally be the case if the marginal rate of tax is not zero. It is the alleged disincentive effects of high marginal tax rates on the supply of effort, saving and risk bearing that are usually taken as the justification for war-time borrowing. However, in this case, the present value of future tax liabilities for present tax payers implied by borrowing is likely to be less than the value of the same sum contributed in present taxes. One reason is that the future tax paying population, including returned servicemen, will be larger than the present, so taxes will be spread more thinly. Clearly equity considerations may arise here which could also affect the choice between borrowing and taxation and, as in other cases, equity and efficiency objectives may conflict.[1]

The background discussion for these conclusions is given in the many contributions to the recent debate on the consequences for futute generations of government borrowing, some of which are reprinted here. The dialogue of Bowen, Davis and Kopf with Lerner (Reading 13, a–c) sets out the main issues, while Carl Shoup's survey (Reading 14) provides a summing up. The rather neglected question of foreign borrowing is elegantly dealt with by Buchanan in Reading 15.

1. The equity issues raised here are discussed in a way which has not, I think, been improved on in Sprague (1917).

Reference

SPRAGUE, O. M. W. (1917), 'Loans and taxes in war finance', *American Economic Review, Proceedings*. Reprinted in A. Smithies and J. K. Butters (eds.), *Readings in Fiscal Policy*, Irwin, 1955, pp. 107–21.

12 A. P. Lerner

The Burden of the National Debt

Excerpts from A. P. Lerner, 'The burden of the national debt',
in L. A. Metzler *et al.* (eds.), *Income, Employment and Public Policy:
Essays in Honor of Alvin H. Hansen*, Norton, 1948, pp. 255–61.

Millions of people are now taking time off from worrying about
the prospects of atomic warfare to do some worrying on account
of the burden of a growing national debt. But there are many quite
different concepts of the nature of this burden. The purpose of this
article is to examine the most important of these worries and to
see to what extent they are justified and to what extent they are
about imaginary burdens which only confuse the real issues.

Imaginary Effects of National Debt

By far the most common concern about the national debt comes
from considering it as exactly the same kind of thing as a private
debt which one individual owes to others. Every dollar of an
individual's indebtedness must be subtracted from his assets in
arriving at a measure of his net wealth. Indebtedness is impoverishment. It places the debtor in the hands of the creditor and threatens
him with hardship and ruin. To avoid indebtedness as far as possible is undoubtedly an eminently well-established rule of private
prudence.

The simple transferability of this rule to national debt is denied
by nearly all economists. But nearly everybody who has ever
suffered the oppressions of private indebtedness is tempted to
apply the analogy directly, and the primary orthodoxy of the
editorial writers, the dogma that sound government finance means
balancing the budget, has no other basis.

One of the most effective ways of clearing up this most serious
of all semantic confusions is to point out that private debt differs
from national debt in being *external*. It is owed by one person to
others. That is what makes it burdensome. Because it is *inter-*

personal the proper analogy is not to national debt but to *international* debt. A nation owing money to other nations (or to the citizens of other nations) *is* impoverished or burdened in the same kind of way as a man who owes money to other men. But this does not hold for national debt which is owed by the nation to citizens of the *same* nation. There is then no external creditor. 'We owe it to ourselves.'

This refutation of the validity of the analogy from *external* to *internal* debt must not be interpreted as a denial that any significant problems can be raised by internal national debt. When economists are sufficiently irritated by the illegitimate analogy they are liable to say that the national debt does not matter at all. But this must be understood in the same sense as when a man who finds that rumor has converted a twisted ankle into a broken neck tells his friends that he is perfectly all right.

A variant of the false analogy is the declaration that national debt puts an unfair burden on our children, who are thereby made to pay for our extravagances. Very few economists need to be reminded that if our children or grandchildren repay some of the national debt these payments will be made *to* our children or grandchildren and to nobody else. Taking them altogether they will no more be impoverished by making the repayments than they will be enriched by receiving them.

Unfortunately the first few times people see this argument destroyed they feel tricked rather than convinced. But the resistance to conceding the painlessness of repaying national debt can be diminished by pointing out that it only corresponds to the relative uselessness of incurring it. An *external* loan enables an individual or a nation to get things from others without having to give anything in return, for the time being. The borrower is enabled to consume more than he is producing. And when he repays the external debt he has to consume less than he is producing. But this is not true for *internal* borrowing. However useful an internal loan may be for the health of the economy, it does *not* enable the nation to consume more than it produces. It should therefore not be so surprising that the repayment of internal debt does not necessitate a tightening of the belt. The internal borrowing did not permit the belt to be loosened in the first place.

Many who recognize that national debt is no subtraction from national wealth are nevertheless deeply concerned about the interest payments on the national debt. They call this the *interest burden* almost as if the interest payments constituted subtractions from the national income.

This involves exactly the same error. The interest payments are no more a subtraction from the national income than the national debt itself is a subtraction from the national wealth. This can be shown most clearly by pointing out how easy it is, by simply borrowing the money needed to make the interest payments, to convert the 'interest burden' into some additional national debt. The interest need therefore never be more onerous than the additional principal of the debt into which it can painlessly be transformed.

Borrowing money to make the interest payments sounds much worse than simply getting into debt in the first place. Popular feeling on this score seems so strong that economists who are themselves quite free from the erroneous analogy have felt themselves constrained by the power of the prejudice to assume that the interest payments on national debt are never borrowed but raised by taxes.[1]

The strict application of such a secondary orthodoxy would mean much more than these economists intend to concede to the popular prejudice. It would mean nothing less than the prohibition of all borrowing, and a meticulous adherence to the primary orthodoxy of balancing the budget at all times. For as soon as there is any national debt at all on which any interest has to be paid, *any* further government borrowing is indistinguishable from borrowing to pay the interest – unless we are taken in by book-keeping fictions of financial earmarking which say that the money borrowed goes for other purposes so that the particular dollars used to pay the interest come from taxation.[2] [. . .]

1. e.g., Domar (1944, p. 799). 'This assumption (that all funds for payment of interest charges are to be raised by taxation) is made both to simplify the argument and to protect the reader from a shock. To many, government investment financed by borrowing sounds so bad that the thought of borrowing to pay the interest is simply unbearable.' (Reprinted by permission.)

2. If we did permit ourselves to indulge in such make-believe, the secondary orthodoxy would be reduced to declaring that everything is all right as long as the interest paid on the national debt does not exceed the total tax revenue. It could then be declared that the interest payments all come out of taxes even if all other expenditures are financed by borrowing!

Real Effects of National Debt

Since the interest payments on the national debt increase private spending, a fiscal program which would have led to the right level of total spending in the absence of the national debt and the interest payments on it would now result in too much spending. Any increase in national debt (which increases money income and therefore also the spending out of income) must therefore be accompanied by a decrease in government spending or by an increase in taxation (or both). If this involves the abandonment of useful government undertakings or the enactment of harmful taxes, we really have a bad effect or 'burden' of national debt.

This looks somewhat like the secondary orthodoxy which says that the money to make interest payments on the national debt must be raised from taxes, but the resemblance is only superficial. Since Functional Finance is interested only in total spending, it does not care whether the additional revenues from the taxes are equal to the interest payments. If more than an additional dollar is collected from the taxes needed to offset the extra spending due to an additional dollar of interest payments, tax revenue will have to be increased by more than the additional interest payments. On the other hand, if the efficiency of a dollar of tax revenue in reducing spending is greater than the efficiency of a dollar of interest payment in increasing spending, no increase in total spending will occur even though additional tax revenues are less than the additional interest payments.

But it is not really satisfactory to speak of tax revenues at all. Spending is affected by the tax *rates*, not by the tax *revenues*. The revenues are themselves effects of the taxes, and the efficiency of a tax in reducing spending is only indirectly connected with its efficiency in raising revenue. An increase in sales taxes which sharply diminished spending, for instance, might actually reduce the tax revenue. Functional Finance would then be served by additional taxes which offset the spending induced by the interest payments, even though tax revenues would actually be diminished just when the interest disbursements are increased.

In attempts to discredit the argument that we owe the national debt to ourselves it is often pointed out that the 'we' does not consist of the same people as the 'ourselves'. The benefits from interest payments on the national debt do not accrue to every individual in exactly the same degree as the damage done to him by the additional taxes made necessary. That is why it is not possible to repudiate the whole national debt without hurting anybody.

While this is undoubtedly true, all it means is that some people will be better off and some people will be worse off. Such a redistribution of wealth is involved in every significant happening in our closely interrelated economy, in every invention or discovery or act of enterprise. If there is some good general reason for incurring debt, the redistribution can be ignored because we have no more reason for supposing that the new distribution is worse than the old one than for assuming the opposite. That the distribution will be *different* is no more an argument against national debt than it is an argument in favor of it.

The growth of national debt may not only make some people richer and some people poorer, but may increase the inequality of distribution. This is because richer people can buy more government bonds and so get more of the interest payments without incurring a proportionately heavier burden of the taxes. Most people would agree that this is bad. But it is no necessary effect of an increasing national debt. If the additional taxes are more progressive – more concentrated on the rich – than the additional holdings of government bonds, the effect will be to *diminish* the inequality of income and wealth.

There are also effects on investment. Additional taxes reduce the net yield from investment, after taxes, and make socially useful investments unprofitable to the investor.

This effect is cancelled whenever there is the possibility of balancing losses against profits for tax purposes. If such offsetting were universally possible the taxation would not discourage investment at all.[3] But the opportunity of loss offset is not universal, so that the interest payments on the national debt, by making more taxation necessary for the prevention of inflation, interferes with the efficiency of the economy by discouraging useful investments.

3. See Lerner (1943, 1946). On the assumption of perfect loss offset, taxation might even *encourage* investment by impoverished investors willing to take more chances in attempts to maintain their standards, but this does not invalidate the general argument that a social loss is involved. See Musgrave and Domar (1944).

References

DOMAR, E. D. (1944), 'The burden of the debt and the national income', *American Economic Review*, December.

LERNER, A. P. (1943), 'Functional finance and the federal debt', *Social Research*, February. Reprinted in *International Postwar Problems*, October 1945.

LERNER, A. P. (1946), 'An integrated full employment policy', *International Postwar Problems*, January. Reprinted in A. P. Lerner and F. Graham, *Planning and Paying for Full Employment*, Princeton University Press, 1946.

MUSGRAVE, R. A., and DOMAR, E. D. (1944), 'Proportional income taxation and risk taking', *Quarterly Journal of Economics*, May.

13 A Burden on Future Generations?

(a) W. G. Bowen, R. G. Davis and D. H. Kopf

The Public Debt: A Burden on Future Generations?

W. G. Bowen, R. G. Davis and D. H. Kopf, 'The public debt: a burden on future generations?', *American Economic Review*, vol. 50, 1960, pp. 701–6.

> Personally, I do not feel that any amount can be properly called a surplus as long as the nation is in debt. I prefer to think of such an item as a reduction on our children's inherited mortgage.
>
> President Eisenhower, *State of the Union Message*,
> 7 January 1960

Two things are certain. The first is that, whatever else this quotation from President Eisenhower's *State of the Union Message* may imply, the President appears convinced that the costs of debt-financed public projects can be passed on to future generations. The second is that the popular economics textbooks of our day are nearly unanimous in their rejection of this 'naïve' view of the public debt. The purpose of this brief note is to suggest that in this instance it is the President who is – in at least one highly important sense – right.[1]

The basic question at issue seems simple indeed: Can the 'real burden' of a public project financed by a privately held internal

---

1. J. M. Buchanan (1958) is one of the few contemporary economists to argue in favor of the proposition that the real burden of a public debt *can* be shifted to future generations. It was Buchanan's stimulating book that started the train of thought that has resulted in the argument contained in this paper. The reason for the present paper is that while Buchanan has arrived at essentially the same conclusion, he has apparently not succeeded in convincing very many people that he is right – at any rate, he has not convinced several reviewers of his book; see, for example, the reviews by Rolph (1959, pp. 183–5), Lerner (1959, pp. 203–6), and Hansen (1959, pp. 337–8). Perhaps the reason these reviewers have not accepted Buchanan's conclusion on this point is that Buchanan: (1) does not always define 'real burden' in a sufficiently clear manner; (2) defines 'generation' in such a manner that the same person can be considered a member of many different generations (1958, pp. 33–4) and (3) relies on what Rolph (1959, p. 184) has called a 'proof by indirection'. We have tried to avoid these pitfalls.

debt be shifted from one generation to another? The usual economics textbook answer to this question is that the burden can *not* be shifted to future generations because government spending must drain real resources from the community at the time the government project is undertaken (assuming full employment of resources) regardless of whether the project is financed by borrowing, taxes, or money creation. As Samuelson puts it: 'To fight a war now, we must hurl present-day munitions at the enemy; not dollar bills, and not future goods and services.'[2]

What is wrong with this by-now-standard argument? Absolutely nothing, if the real burden of the debt is defined as the total amount of private consumption goods given up by the community *at the moment of time the borrowed funds are spent*. Under this definition of real burden, the cost of the public project simply must be borne by the generations alive at the time the borrowing occurs.

There is, however, another definition of real burden which permits, under certain circumstances, present generations to shift the burden to future generations. And this definition, we submit, is a more accurate representation of the everyday notion of burden and is a more sensible concept for deciding if the real cost of a certain project can or cannot be postponed to future generations. Let us define the real burden of a public debt to a generation as the total consumption of private goods foregone *during the lifetime* of that generation as a consequence of government borrowing and attendant public spending. (For the moment, we are not taking into account the benefit that may result from the public expenditure, and so we are talking about a 'gross burden'.) Our preference for the lifetime of a generation as the unit of account is based on the proposition that people can and do forego consumption at a moment of time in order to be able to consume more later, and that to use the amount of consumption foregone at any one moment of

2. Samuelson, (1958, p. 351). Among the widely used elementary texts, C. L. Harriss' book (1959, pp. 689–97) seems to come the closest to accepting the line of argument presented here. However, Harriss' exposition is badly impaired by an unclear distinction between 'real costs' and 'money costs'. All writers seem to agree that the so-called 'transfer payments' necessitated by a public debt involve real burdens in the sense that taxes used to meet interest payments may impair incentives to work and save. Neither this aspect of the debt problem nor the relationship between the public debt and economic stabilization are discussed in this paper.

time as some sort of index of the overall sacrifices made by a generation is misleading.

Let us now consider the following situation. Assume a full-employment economy. Assume further that there is within the society an identifiable 'generation' of people, all of whom are, let us say, twenty-one years old. Suppose that at a given moment of time the government sells bonds to the private sector of the economy in order to finance public project X[3] and that all of these bonds are voluntarily purchased by the group of twenty-one-year-olds, whom we shall refer to as Generation I.

To determine the allocation of the burden of public project X between generations, consider a point of time forty-four years later when all members of Generation I are sixty-five years old and the rest of the community is made up of a Generation II, whose members are all twenty-one years old. Suppose that at this moment of time all the members of Generation I who own the still outstanding government bonds sell these securities to members of Generation II and use the proceeds for the purchase of consumer goods during retirement.

In this case it is clear that the lifetime consumption of the members of Generation I has not been reduced even though the total subtraction from the production of private goods due to the carrying out of public project X took place during their lifetime. The reason is simply that the saving represented by Generation I's original purchase of the bonds has been matched by the dissaving resulting from the later sale of the bonds to Generation II and the subsequent spending of the proceeds. Conclusion: Generation I has not assumed any of the burden entailed in financing public project X by the issuance of government bonds. (For the time being, we ignore the interest charges on the debt.)

Let us now examine the situation of Generation II. If the government makes no effort to retire the debt during the lifetime of Generation II, and if Generation II sells its bonds to Generation III, then Generation II also escapes the burden of paying for the public project, and so on. To make a potentially long story short, suppose, however, that during the lifetime of Generation II the government

3. At this juncture, the precise characteristics of the government project are best left unspecified. The relevance of the particular type of government project undertaken will be considered shortly.

decides to retire the debt by levying a general tax in excess of current government spending and using the surplus to buy up the bonds that are now held by members of Generation II. The inevitable outcome of this decision is a reduction in the lifetime consumption of Generation II. The taxpayers of Generation II forego consumption in order to retire the debt and yet the bondholders of Generation II do not experience any net lifetime increase in their claims on consumption goods since they are simply reimbursed for the consumption forgone at the time when they (Generation II) bought the bonds from Generation I. Conclusion: the burden of public project X rests squarely on Generation II, and not on Generation I.

The skeleton of our argument is now complete: While the resources consumed by a debt-financed public project must entail a contemporaneous reduction in private consumption, the issuance of government bonds permits the generations alive at the time the public project is undertaken to be compensated in the future for their initial sacrifice. Generation I merely makes a loan of its reduced consumption, and the real reduction of consumption is borne by the generation(s) alive at the time this loan is extinguished. Consequently, even though the real private consumption of the community as a whole need not be altered by the growth of the public debt, it is still possible for the distribution of the community's private consumption *between generations* to depend on whether or not public projects are debt-financed.

One other form in which the general argument that no burden can be passed on to future generations often appears is the 'we owe it to ourselves' or 'assets equal liabilities' version.[4] No burden can be passed on because corresponding to every asset in the form of a government bond outstanding there is an equal liability in the form of liability for taxes to meet the interest charges and to repay the principal of the debt. Since there are always these two offsetting sides to the debt instrument, the argument proceeds, future generations cannot be handed any burden since when our taxpayer-children inherit the tax liability our bond-holder children will acquire an equal asset.

The difficulty with this argument is simply that the asset and

4. For a fuller exposition of this line of argument, with references to the literature, see Buchanan, 1958, pp. 4–14 and *passim*.

liability sides of the public debt are 'passed on' in significantly different ways. Insofar as the government bonds are acquired by Generation II by purchase rather than bequest, the recipients of the bonds have only received a *quid pro quo*. On the other hand, the members of Generation II who are handed the tax liability are not reimbursed for accepting this liability. From the vantage point of Generation I, the bondholders in this generation received claims on consumption in exchange for the asset (bonds) which they sold to Generation II; at the same time, the members of Generation I as liability-holders passed on their tax liability to Generation II by the simple expedient of dying, and thus did not have to give up consumption goods to get rid of the liability. Consequently, unless Generation II can in turn pass its assets on to Generation III by sale while at the same time passing on its liability without making a compensating payment, the burden of the debt will be borne by Generation II.

We come now to the question: How about interest payments? We shall argue that the interest payments on the debt represent some burden on each and every generation that must pay taxes to make such payments.

To show why this is so it is necessary to reconsider the meaning of our definition of real burden – namely, 'the total consumption of private goods foregone during the lifetime of a generation'. Thus far we have implicitly assigned all amounts of consumption enjoyed during the generation's lifetime equal weights in arriving at total lifetime consumption, and have disregarded entirely the stage in a generation's lifetime at which various amounts of consumption were enjoyed. Consequently, we were able to argue that a generation which gave up a certain amount of consumption early in life to buy bonds and then was able, by selling the bonds later in life, to enjoy the same amount of consumption during retirement years had avoided all of the burden involved in the debt financing of project X. The difficulty with this treatment is obvious. So long as people have a positive rate of time preference (that is, prefer present consumption to future consumption), they will feel that they have made a sacrifice if they give up a certain amount of consumption in their youth and then receive back exactly the same amount of consumption in their old age.

If we assume that the interest rate on the government bonds

309

approximates the generation's rate of time preference, then the interest payments on the national debt serve to compensate the owners of the debt for their willingness to forgo consumption early in life, and thus (along with the recapture of the principal late in life) serve to make the discounted value of the lifetime consumption of the bondholders the same as it would have been if project X had never been contemplated.

Turning now to the tax side of the interest transaction, it is clear that the tax payments needed to make interest payments represent a real reduction in the lifetime consumption of the people paying the taxes. Furthermore, since any given year's debt service is paid out of approximately contemporaneous tax payments, the same generation that receives the interest payments will be making a large part of the tax payments. The inescapable conclusion is that while the interest payments (along with the repayment of the principal) do not increase the discounted lifetime consumption of a generation, the tax payments do decrease lifetime consumption. Consequently, the discounted lifetime consumption of the generation is, on balance, reduced by the existence of debt service. This burden represents the real loss of welfare incurred by the generation as a consequence of the fact that it postponed its consumption but did not – because it received in interest payments only what it paid in taxes – receive any compensation for this distortion of its preferred consumption pattern.

The reason that in our discussion of interest payments we have spoken of 'a' generation or 'the' generation is that this burden (measured now in terms of the reduction in the discounted value of the generation's lifetime consumption) is borne, of course, by each generation that pays a service charge on the debt. Consequently, even if the principal value of the debt is continually passed on, each generation bears a burden in the form of an uncompensated distortion of its preferred pattern of consumption.

So far we have avoided consideration of the type of government project financed by the initial borrowing. Actually, whether the government funds are spent wisely or foolishly is largely irrelevant to the question at issue here; for we are concerned solely with the allocation of the real *cost* of debt-financed government spending between generations and not with the allocation of the benefits of the government spending over time. Consequently, our conclusion that it is possible to shift at least a part of the cost to future generations does not imply that the absolute well-being of the future generations has been worsened by the combined borrowing and spending operation. If the borrowed funds were spent on a project whose benefit stream extends far into the future (for example, on fighting a 'war-to-end-wars'), then the generation that assumes the main burden of the debt may still be much better off than if the debt had never been incurred. Our point is simply that the use of borrowing – as opposed to taxation or money creation – has improved the lot (measured in terms of lifetime consumption) of the first generation relative to the lot of succeeding generations.[5]

There is one final qualification to our argument. We have constructed a somewhat simplified case by assuming that all the bonds held by Generation I are sold to Generation II and that the proceeds are used entirely to increase consumption during the remaining years of Generation I's life. If, for example, all the members of Generation I were to will their bonds to Generation II, all real sacrifice of consumption would be borne by Generation I. Nevertheless, in spite of this simplification, the argument undoubtedly contains a large measure of relevance for the real situation. Purchasers of bonds, during a war for example, lose current consumption and receive marketable securities which surely are at least in part intended for conversion into spending on consumables in later years. The resulting claims upon consumer goods are realized at a time when they draw against the productivity of new members of the community who would otherwise enjoy a higher level of consumption. The existence of the marketable bonds undoubtedly makes possible at least some transfer of real income between generations.

5. There is a second, closely related reason for not tying the argument of this paper to a particular government expenditure, whether it be the construction of public schools or the giving of an enormous fireworks display. If, at the time public debt is issued, the government is spending money for many activities and financing these activities by taxes (and perhaps by money creation) as well as by borrowing, then it is hard to see how one can impute any specific project to any specific method of finance. The fact that we cannot solve this version of the imputation problem is irrelevant to the basic proposition that the cost of debt-financed government projects can be passed on to future generations, and thus cannot be used to disprove this proposition.

Our conclusion that the real cost of debt-financed government spending can (at least in part) be transferred to future generations does not, of course, establish any *prima facie* case against deficit financing or in favor of the prompt retirement of the national debt. For one thing, to the extent that public projects undertaken today aid future generations, it may be fairer to let these future generations help pay the cost of these projects than to put the entire burden on present generations. Furthermore it is obvious that many considerations other than the location of the debt burden – such as the employment situation, the needs of the country for collective consumption, and the effect of taxes on incentives – are relevant in determining budget policy. However, at the present moment, there seems to be less danger that economists will forget the importance of these other considerations than that they will deny the possibility that the public debt can be used to shift a part of the real cost of public projects on to later generations.

References

BUCHANAN, J. M. (1958), *Public Principles of Public Debt*, Irwin.

HANSEN, A. H. (1959), 'The public debt reconsidered: a review article', *Review of Economics and Statistics*, vol. 41.

HARRISS, C. L. (1959), *The American Economy*, Irwin, 3rd edn.

LERNER, A. P. (1959), 'Review of Buchanan's *Public Principles of Public Debt*', *Journal of Political Economy*, vol. 47.

ROLPH, E. R. (1959), 'Review of Buchanan's *Public Principles of Public Debt*', *Journal of Political Economy*, vol. 49.

SAMUELSON, P. A. (1958), *Economics: An Introductory Analysis*, McGraw-Hill, 4th edn.

(b) A. P. Lerner

The Burden of Debt

A. P. Lerner, 'The burden of debt', *Review of Economics and Statistics*, vol. 43, 1961, pp. 139–41.

'But look,' the Rabbi's wife remonstrated, 'when one party to the dispute presented their case to you you said "you are quite right" and then when the other party presented their case you again said "you are quite right," surely they cannot both be right?' To which the Rabbi answered, 'My dear, you are quite right!'

Messrs Bowen, Davis and Kopf have shown [Reading 13a] that the real burden of a project using up resources in the present can be shifted to future generations by internal borrowing, providing one defines 'generation' in a particular way. It is just as easy to prove that all politicians are economists or that all economists are dunces, provided one defines 'economist' in a particular way. But even if I call the tail of a sheep a leg that will not turn sheep into quintapeds. The issue is of course terminological rather than substantive. It is nevertheless one of the utmost importance because the conclusion reached by Bowen *et al.*, although not incorrect on their own definitions, is bound to be misinterpreted as meaning what it seems to be saying in English and as indeed implying that most politicians understand economics better than the economists – most, if not all, of whom are dunces.

Bowen, Davis and Kopf are absolutely right when they agree that there is 'absolutely nothing' wrong with the standard argument of modern economists that the real burden of a debt can *not* be shifted to future generations if it is defined as 'the total amount of private consumption goods given up by the community *at the moment of time the borrowed funds are spent*'. But President Eisenhower 'appears convinced that the costs of debt-financed public projects can be passed on to future generations'. Like the Rabbi in the story, Bowen *et al.* want to say that he too is right, but in their enthusiasm they even say that the purpose of their note 'is to suggest that in this instance it is the President who is – in at least one highly important sense – right',[1] thus clearly implying that the economists are wrong.

To make the President appear right, Bowen *et al.* redefine 'present generation' to mean the people who lend the money to finance the project, and they redefine 'future generation' to mean the people who pay the taxes that are used to repay the principal and the interest on the loans. The perversity of the redefinitions is obscured by supposing that the lenders ('this generation'), are all twenty-one years old at the time of the execution of the project when they lend the money and by supposing that they are repaid forty-four years later, on their sixty-fifth birthday, with funds

---

1. W. G. Bowen, R. G. Davis and D. H. Kopf (1960, p. 701), where President Eisenhower is quoted as saying, 'Personally, I do not feel that any amount can be properly called a surplus as long as the nation is in debt. I prefer to think of such an item as a reduction on our children's inherited mortgage', in his *State of the Union Message*, 7 January 1960.

obtained at that time from twenty-one-year-old taxpayers ('the next generation'). The burden is thereby shifted from 'this generation' to 'the next generation'.

What has been proved, if we obstinately insist in expressing the conclusion in English, is that it is possible to shift the burden from the Lenders to the Taxpayers or, we might say, from the Lowells to the Thomases. The Lowells are better off and the Thomases are worse off than if the Lowells had been taxed to raise the money for the project in the first place.

The 'red herring' nature of having the Lowells lend the money now (so that we can call them the present generation), and having the Thomases pay the taxes in the future (so that they can be called the future generation), jumps to the eye if we note that the shifting of the real burden of the project from the Lowells to the Thomases, (or indeed of any other burden), could take place just as well at the time of the project (or at any other time) by simply taxing the Thomases instead of the Lowells.

No economist, so far as I am aware, has ever denied the possibility of borrowing or of lending or of taxing some people instead of others, or of any combinations of such operations. And if we redefine Mr Eisenhower's words so that they mean only that such operations are possible, then indeed the words used by the President constitute a true statement. But there is no reason for supposing that the President was trying to use any language other than English, and what the President said is simply wrong (in English), unless indeed all the economists (including Bowen *et al.*, as well as J. M. Buchanan, who plays similar linguistic tricks (1958)) are absolutely wrong.

The real issue, and it is an important one, between the economists and Mr Eisenhower is not whether it is possible to shift a burden (either in the present or in the future) from some people to other people, but whether it is possible *by internal borrowing* to shift a real burden from the present generation, in the sense of the present economy as a whole, onto a future generation, in the sense of the future economy as a whole. What is important for economists is to teach the President that the latter is impossible because a project that uses up resources needs the resources *at the time that it uses them up*, and not before or after.

This basic proportion is true of all projects that use up resources.

The question is traditionally posed in terms of the burden of a *public* project financed by *privately* held internal debt; but the proposition is quite independent of whether the project is public or private as well as of whether the debt is private or public. The proposition holds as long as the project is financed *internally*, so that there are no outsiders to take over the current burden by providing the resources and to hand back the burden in the future by asking for the return of the resources.

It is necessary for economists to keep repeating this basic proposition because one of their main duties is to keep warning people against the fallacy of composition. To anyone who sees only a part of the economy it does seem possible to borrow from the future because he tends to assume that what is true of the part is true of the whole. It *is* possible for the Lowells to borrow from the Thomases, and what this borrowing does is to shift a burden from the Lowells to the Thomases in the present, and then to shift an equal burden from the Thomases to the Lowells in the future when the loan is repaid. To the Lowells (and to anyone else who sees only the Lowells) the combination of these two shifts looks like the shifting of a burden from the present into the future or the shifting of resources from the future into the present. To the Thomases, of course, the transactions will look like the opposite, namely, the shifting of a burden from the future into the present or the shifting of resources from the present into the future. But the borrowing and the repayment do not make a Time Machine. There is no shift of resources or of burdens between different points in time. It is possible for a *part* of the economy (the Lowells) to shift *its* burden into the future only as long as *another part* of the present economy (the Thomases) is ready to take it over for the intervening period. It is not possible for *the whole* of the present generation to shift a burden into the future because there are no Thomases left to play the magician's assistant in the illusion.

This is not to say that there is no way at all in which the present generation can shift a burden onto future generations. Our proposition is only that this is not done by internal borrowing. We can impoverish the future by cutting down on our investment in capital resources (or by using up or destroying natural resources) that would have enabled future generations to produce and enjoy higher standards of living. There is even a possible connexion between internal debt financing and this way of really impoverishing future generations. If full employment (or some other level of employment) is somehow being maintained, and if the conditions of the borrowing and the kinds of people from whom the borrowing is done are such that they reduce consumption by less than consumption would have been reduced if the money had been raised instead by taxes, then there will be more consumption and there will therefore have to be less investment. The borrowing will then have reduced the real resources inherited by future generations.

But there is no *necessary* connexion. It would almost certainly not work this way in the conditions of 1960. Whether the borrowing increases or decreases consumption depends on the nature and on the conditions of the borrowing on the one hand and of the alternative – the taxation – on the other hand. Furthermore, at the present time, when we have considerable unemployment and unused capacity, an increase in consumption is more likely to lead to *more* investment (out of unutilized resources) and therefore to an *increase* in the productive resources inherited by future generations. And it is quite certainly not these complicated considerations that are responsible for the President's belief that internal borrowing increases and repayment reduces 'our children's inherited mortgage'. In any case even the *possibility* of a genuine impoverishment of future generations by an induced reduction in investment is *explicitly* ruled out by Bowen *et al.* when they say that the resources consumed by the project '*must* entail a contemporaneous reduction in private consumption' (Bowen *et al.*, 1960, p. 703).

Any genuine impoverishment of future generations must be the result of *not* reducing private consumption by the full amount of the resources used up in the project so that some of these resources must come out of alternative investment (if we rule out the use of unemployed resources). It is only the curtailed alternative investment outside of the project that can tend to impoverish future generations (although this might be more than made up for them by the benefits that these same future generations will derive from the project in question).

We can also impoverish the future by using up in the production of armaments too much of the resources that would have gone into investment; and we can equally impoverish the future by an over-economy in armaments, or by skimping in our contribution to the building of a healthy world, so that we invite aggression or foster resentments and revolutions. But both of these possibilities are completely independent of whether we borrow or tax.

Semantic playfulness like that of Bowen *et al.*, seriously sabotages economists in their important task in educating the public to the appreciation of an important truth. By their ingenious redefinition of 'generations' they have made it more difficult to point out just where the fallacy of composition is perpetrated. It is perpetrated when a part of the economy (as in their definition of this or that generation) is taken for the whole (as in the usual meaning of a generation as *all* the people living at a certain date); and this is exactly what Bowen *et al.*, do when they say that President Eisenhower (speaking English) is right.

They have taken a true proposition – i.e. that some people can shift a burden into the future by borrowing from other people – and rewritten it in such a manner that almost everyone will read in it the false proposition that the nation as a whole can filch resources from the future by internal borrowing (public or private), thereby impoverishing future generations. It is unfortunately the false proposition that is implied in the statement by the President, and believed by many people in positions to make vital decisions. The false belief may well contribute to a failure of the free nations to take the steps necessary to maintain and extend freedom in the world. There is even a clear and present danger that because of a baseless fear of impoverishing future generations by leaving them with a larger internal debt (which they will owe to themselves), we may fail to protect them from nuclear war and /or totalitarian domination; the confusion sown by Bowen *et al.*, tends to increase that danger. It is to be hoped that these authors will tell the President that they were using a special language of their own and didn't mean what they seemed to be saying when they seemed to be denying a proposition with which, as they themselves declare, there is 'absolutely nothing' wrong.

References
BOWEN, W. G., DAVIS, R. G., and KOPF, D. H. (1960), 'The public debt: a burden on future generations?', *American Economic Review*, vol. 50.
BUCHANAN, J. M. (1958), *Public Principles of Public Debt*, Irwin.

(c) W. G. Bowen, R. G. Davis and D. H. Kopf

The Distribution of the Debt Burden: A Reply

W. G. Bowen, R. G. Davis and D. H. Kopf, 'The distribution of the debt burden: a reply', *Review of Economics and Statistics*, vol. 44, 1962, pp. 96–100.

It is almost a pleasure to be denounced in prose as delightful as that employed by Lerner in his critique of our public debt article – even in view of his somewhat alarming suggestion that the publication of our paper has increased the danger of nuclear war [see Reading 13b]. However, our pleasure would have been less mixed if he had not misunderstood the point of our argument and confused some of the basic issues. In an effort to clarify the situation, we offer the following comments.

First, no amount of 'linguistic playfulness' on the part of anybody should be allowed to obscure the substantive point of our argument: that debt finance can be used to alter the lifetime distribution of claims against consumption goods between people alive at the time borrowing takes place and people not yet born. The basis for this argument is spelled out in our first paper on this subject and amplified in a subsequent rejoinder [see Reading 13a, and Bowen, Davis and Kopf (1961, pp. 141–3)]. Since Lerner offers no substantive criticism of this argument, there is no need to repeat it here.

The word 'generation', which causes Lerner so much anxiety, has been omitted altogether from the above summary statement to emphasize that *this is not a terminological dispute*, as Lerner implies. The essence of Lerner's criticism seems to run as follows: Bowen, Davis and Kopf obtain their result by using a trick definition of 'generation' so as to make what is in fact simply a redistribution of burden among existing taxpayers look like a shift in burden over time. We deny the validity of this criticism.

With regard to our definition of 'generation', we are willing to agree that this word, like so many other words, can be used in a variety of ways. Nevertheless, we thought that it was clear from the whole context of our original article that the essential point of our definition of generation was to distinguish between different groups of people born at different times, so as to enable us to trace through the effects of a given fiscal action on the *lifetime* consumption of groups of people born at different points of time. We still fail to see anything 'perverse' in this use of words.

However, we are more interested in making sure that the substance of our argument is clear than in arguing for any particular terminological trappings. Consequently, we are glad to have this opportunity to try to remove any vestiges of semantic confusion. In this connexion, it may be helpful to refer to all persons alive at the particular moment of time when the borrowing occurs (t_0) simply as 'Set I.'[1] As each year passes, the total size of Set I will diminish steadily as more and more Set I persons die and are replaced in the population by persons born after t_0. As this change in the composition of the population takes place over the years, the Set I persons who bought bonds at t_0 will sell at least some of these bonds to the newcomers. Some bonds will also, no doubt, be exchanged among Set I persons, but transactions of this sort are of no lasting significance in the context of this discussion. Eventually, of course, we shall reach the year in which not a single member of old Set I is still alive; by this time we can be sure that all of the bonds originally purchased by Set I will have been sold (ignoring bequests, which modify the problem quantitatively, but not qualitatively) to persons born after t_0. Our proposition is that the use of debt finance permits, by the process described in our original paper, a relative improvement in the lifetime economic position of Set I persons *vis-à-vis* a situation in which taxation was employed at t_0.

It must be emphasized that the lifetimes of persons born in different years do overlap at points in time, and that recognition of this basic fact of life is essential to an understanding of the logic of our argument. Any transfer of real resources must take place at some point in time and obviously can take place only between persons alive at the same point in time. Indeed, this is just the process by which the burden is transferred from persons alive at t_0 to persons born later. But this transfer of real resources does not

1. How the bonds are distributed among different age-groups within this Set is of no consequence from the standpoint of the question to which our analysis is addressed. In our original paper we assumed that all bonds were sold to persons twenty-one years old at the time of the borrowing. This artifice was designed solely to simplify the exposition; we could just as well have assumed that the bonds were sold to all persons alive at t_0, regardless of age.

take place at the time the debt is issued; nor is it true, as Lerner suggests, that what is gained at one point of time must be lost in the future. ('It is possible for the Lowells to borrow from the Thomases, and what this borrowing does is to shift the burden from the Lowells to the Thomases in the present, and then to shift an equal burden from the Thomases to the Lowells in the future when the loan is repaid.' [Lerner, 1961, p. 140.]) To use Lerner's terminology, the Thomases will end up with the burden, or they may pass it on to the Lowell's children, but they will obviously be unable to pass it back to the Lowells if the Lowells have all died by the time the debt is repaid.

In short, Lerner misleads the reader when he suggests that the redistribution of burden we are talking about is nothing more than a redistribution among taxpayers alive at the time the borrowing occurs. A redistribution of lifetime real income between people alive at the time the borrowing occurs and people born later can take place even if all people alive at the time the borrowing occurs buy bonds in amounts exactly equivalent to their taxpayer liabilities for the public debt. Regardless of the distribution of bond holdings among the working population alive at the time of the First World War, there is little doubt but that some part of the goods and services foregone by these persons during the First World War was recouped as the bond-holders subsequently exchanged their bonds for claims against consumption goods produced in later periods – goods produced in part by individuals not alive at the time the original debt was incurred. And this process is still going on. It seems clear that had the First World War been financed entirely by taxes, the lifetime consumption of the 1917–18 population would have been lower, apart from any effects of debt finance on the consumption-investment mix.

We wish to stress that we are not suggesting that the First World War was fought with shells still being produced. In our analysis it is individuals, with their claims against consumption goods, who move through time, not real resources. Our analysis is concerned with the effects of debt finance on the *distribution* of lifetime consumption between persons alive at the time the borrowing occurred and persons yet to come, not on the level of output of the economy as a whole at different points in time.

Lerner, on the other hand, seems unwilling to speak of the 'burden of the debt' in terms of any measure other than induced changes in the level of national income. This is the way in which economists have become accustomed to defining the burden of the debt, it is *one* useful way of looking at the effects of debt finance, and we of course agree with Lerner that debt-financing produces a burden in this sense only if there are effects on the investment-consumption mix. We submit, however, that it is also meaningful to ask if the use of debt finance alters the distribution of lifetime consumption between persons alive when a debt is incurred and persons born later. The answer to this question is 'yes', and in this sense debt finance does improve the relative economic position of the 'present' populace *vis-à-vis* the future populace. Given these two ways of looking at the effects of debt finance, Lerner's rabbi was, after all, a very wise man.[2]

Finally, we wish to re-emphasize a point made (we thought) very clearly in our original article but ignored by Lerner. There are many considerations relevant to the choice among alternative methods of financing government expenditures in any given situation. Under many (probably most) circumstances, such issues as effects on employment, effects on price stability, and effects on incentives will outweigh any consideration of equity in the inter-generation distribution of income. Our only concern is that many economists have explicitly or implicitly denied the very existence of such a consideration. In so doing, they have been in error.

2. It may be noted in passing that the effect of debt finance on the investment/consumption mix (and thus on the relationship between present and future levels of national income enjoyed by society as a whole) and on the distribution of lifetime income between persons born at different times are not, however, completely unrelated. To the extent that debt finance makes the populace alive at the time of the borrowing better off, it is reasonable to expect some derived effects on the volume of saving, consumption, and investment.

References

BOWEN, W. G., DAVIS, R. G., and KOPF, D. H. (1960), 'The public debt: a burden on future generations?', *American Economic Review*, vol. 50.

BOWEN, W. G., DAVIS, R. G., and KOPF, D. H. (1961), 'The burden of the public debt: a reply', *American Economic Review*, vol. 51.

LERNER, A. P. (1961), 'The burden of debt', *Review of Economics and Statistics*, vol. 43.

14 C. S. Shoup

Comment on the Burden of the Debt
and Future Generations

C. S. Shoup, 'Debt financing and future generations', *Economic Journal*,
vol. 72, 1962, pp. 887–98.

The question, whether debt financing shifts the burden from
present to future generations, has been raised again, by what
appear to be dissents from a received doctrine.[1] These dissents
have stimulated comments to the effect that the dissenters are in
error.[2] But the comments do not, I think, meet the dissenters (if
they really are dissenters) on their own grounds, though they do
strengthen our understanding of the relation of government borrowing to capital accumulation. I shall therefore attempt to hold
strictly to the issue: what is it that Bowen–Davis–Kopf, Buchanan
and Musgrave are charging, or implying, is wrong with the earlier
analysis? Have they, in fact, discovered an analytical error? If not,
how have they reached conclusions that appear to differ from the
older doctrine?

The first question to be settled is, what is the doctrine from
which B D K, Buchanan and Musgrave are apparently dissenting or
departing? It is not the simple argument that since resources are
used up at the time of government expenditure, the generation
living at the time of expenditure will bear the burden. What the
new analyses are opposing, or bypassing as unimportant or ir-
relevent, or supplementing, is the more sophisticated view that the

1. See Bowen, Davis and Kopf (1960, 1961, 1962); Musgrave (1959, pp.
562–5, 571–3); Buchanan, (1958, esp. chs. 2–4). Meade (1958, 1959) is not
discussed here, since it does not contradict flatly, or ignore, the classical
conclusion regarding the conditions under which a debt burden can be
shifted to a future generation.

2. See Lerner (1959, 1961); Modigliani (1961); Neisser (1961); Ratchford
(1958), a review article of Buchanan's book; Rolph (1959); Vickrey,
Scitovsky and Elliott (1961).

burden can be passed on to future generations, but only insofar as the present generation responds to the Government's action by reducing its rate of saving. An excellent statement of this view is to be found in the second edition of Pigou's *Public Finance*, but its essentials had been set out long before by Ricardo.[3] It is this assertion, that the burden can be shifted only through a reduction in the rate of investment, that is attacked explicitly by Bowen, Davis and Kopf, and more or less implicitly by Buchanan, or is supplemented by Musgrave.

The Ricardo-Pigou thesis is as follows: If the government expense is financed by taxation the first generation hands on to the second nothing but tax receipts; if by bond issue, the first generation bequeaths the bonds to the second generation, but, along with them, a tax liability represented by the annual charge on the debt for interest, and, if the bonds are not perpetuities, for redemption or amortization. The members of the second generation, like those of the first, pay the interest to themselves, and hence cannot gain by holding bonds rather than their forbears' tax receipts. The welfare of the second generation depends, not on whether it inherits tax receipts or government bonds, but on what it inherits in the way of real stock of capital; and this latter inheritance depends on the reaction of the first generation to the taking away of real resources by the Government. The first generation may well cut its consumption more and its investment less, if it receives only tax receipts

3. See Pigou (1929, pt 3, ch. 1) and Ricardo, (1951a; 1951b, pp. 187–8). See also Shoup (1956, ch. 11). Ricardo said that whether financing is by taxes or by government borrowing, the real resources used by the Government are lost to society at the time of use; but I do not think he can be interpreted as meaning that the present generation always bears the burden (cf. Modigliani, '. . . Ricardo's famous conclusion that the cost of government expenditure is always fully borne by those present at the time', p. 746, note 1), in view of the fact that he concluded that private capital accumulation would be less under borrowing, because of a failure by the present generation to reckon the present value of future taxes needed to pay the interest, when deciding whether to cut their consumption or their saving ('The war-taxes, then, are more economical; . . .', Ricardo, vol. 4, 1951, p. 187). This result reflected, in Ricardo's view, irrationality, or at least shortsightedness: '. . . but if he leaves his fortune to his son, and leaves it charged with this perpetual tax, where is the difference . . . ?' (ibid.); this statement reflects his own rational view, not the irrational view that he regretfully concluded held the stage (but cf. Neisser, 1961, p. 228).

from the Government, than if it receives bonds, because it fails to give full weight to the task ahead of servicing the bonds. The failure is perhaps understandable, if only because no one individual can be sure of the amount of tax he will have to pay towards bond servicing each year in the future. Almost every individual may therefore pursuade himself that he is richer with bonds, plus an undefined future tax obligation, than he would be with tax receipts and no such future obligation. Feeling richer, he may cut his consumption less. Moreover, 'large subscribers have good reason to hope that the interest on their holdings will exceed the contribution in taxes which they will have to make to provide this interest' (Pigou, 1929, p. 244).

Now the less the first generation decreases its consumption, the smaller is the capital stock handed down to the second generation. In this sense, and only in this sense, says the classic (Ricardo–Pigou) doctrine, can financing by bonds lay a burden on the second generation, relative to financing by taxes. The burden consists of inheriting a smaller stock of capital instruments than otherwise.

The Bowen–Davis–Kopf Thesis

Bowen, Davis and Kopf postulate that under debt financing the community's private consumption falls, by the amount of the financing, from the level it would have reached in the absence of the government expenditure and financing. The fall occurs in the period when the government expenditure and financing occur, let us say in Year 100. This assumption, that subscriptions to the bond issue come entirely out of consumption, is not realistic, but it is appropriate, in view of BDK's analytical aims. It presents them with their most difficult case.[4] If they can show that under bond financing a part of the burden is shifted to a future generation, even in the event that the financing comes entirely out of current consumption, then indeed they have raised an issue that the traditional analysis must meet head-on.

BDK further postulate that forty-four years later (a 'generation' later) there occurs, within the economy, a simultaneous increase in consumption by one group and decrease by another group: in-

4. That this is the reason BDK make their assumption seems not to have been recognized in any of the comments cited in note 3 above.

crease or decrease from what each group's consumption would have been if the government expenditure and financing had never occurred. The increase and the decrease are each of the same size as the initial decrease in consumption forty-four years earlier. Another pair of simultaneous changes takes place after another forty-four years and so on. The increase in consumption is always by the older generation, the one just about to leave the stage; the simultaneous decrease in consumption is by the just-emerging newer generation. Thus in Year 144 Generation I increases its consumption and Generation II decreases its consumption by exactly the amount that Generation I had decreased its consumption in Year 100.

Meanwhile, during the forty-three-year interval, in Years 101–43, Generation I has been consuming no more and no less than it would have consumed if the government expenditure and financing had not occurred.

If the debt is retired in Generation II's lifetime the taxes to retire the debt come out of consumption, by BDK assumption. Even if the bond redemption proceeds are spent at once on consumption, Generation II will have experienced a net decrease in lifetime consumption, and it is in terms of a decrease in lifetime consumption that BDK test for the existence of a 'burden'.

Since the community's private consumption decreases in Year 100, the year of government expenditure, by an amount equal to that expenditure, and does not alter in any subsequent year, total private investment is in no year any different from what it would have been if the government expenditure had not been incurred. Each year there exists just as much capital equipment as there would have existed, had the Government not made the expenditure. Yet, assert BDK, part of the burden of the Government's expenditure rests on Generations II, III, etc. The following seems to me to be the heart of their thesis: it is 'the otherwise unrecognized fact that even if loan finance fails to dampen private investment [that is to say, even if loan finance is met entirely by reducing consumption], the present generation can still shift at least a part of the burden of government spending to future generations.' (BDK, 1961, p. 141). Only 'a part', because the deferment of consumption by Generation I from Year 100 to Year 144 is a sacrifice that this generation never recoups; similarly, Generation II never makes up for the delay in its consumption, from Year 144 to Year 188; and so on. The sacrifice represented by the deferment of consumption runs on, through generation after generation, until the bonds are redeemed. The generation that redeems the bonds restricts its consumption in its opening year, say Year 144, and never in any later year increases its consumption above the level it would have enjoyed if the government expenditure and financing had never taken place.

This thesis may at first appear to run counter to the older analysis, which asserted that a future generation could be burdened only if its patrimony were impaired by the generation during whose lifetime the government expenditure was incurred. Under the BDK scheme, to repeat, Generations II and following possess just as much capital equipment as they would have possessed if no government expenditure and financing had occurred; yet BDK conclude that they are bearing part of the burden.

If we look at this conclusion closely we see that it does not contradict the traditional analysis. In real terms, and disregarding the paper transactions that evidence them (whether bonds, tax receipts, or what not), BDK's Generation I does impair the capital of the economy. It does pass on to Generation II a smaller amount of capital equipment than would have been in existence if the government expenditure had not been made. Generation II makes good this impairment, right away, by restricting its own consumption in the very year that Generation I is enjoying its increment of consumption. Generation II thereupon *possesses* the same stock of capital that it would have possessed if there had been no government expenditure; but its does not *inherit* the same stock.[5] Suppose, for simplicity, that the capital stock consists entirely of growing timber. In Year 100 let the Government cut *j* units of timber and use it up in war, or reparations. Generation I responds at once to this government action by cutting *j* fewer units for private consumption than it would have done. Consumption in the remaining years to Year 144 remains as it would have been otherwise, and the capital stock at the start of Year 144 is just what it

5. This distinction between possession and inheritance of real capital is not drawn explicitly in any of the comments on BDK cited in note 3 above. Vickrey, Scitovsky and Elliott (1961, p. 139) perhaps come closest to doing so.

would have been if the Government had not made the expenditure of Year 100. Generation I dies off in Year 145, after having gone on a consumption spree in Year 144, consuming j units more than normal. It bequeaths to Generation II j units less than it would have bequeathed if no government expenditure had been made. To this estate there is at once added the j units that Generation II is postulated to save, above what it would have saved if no government expenditure had been made in the first place. Thus Generation II, by cutting its consumption in Year 144, brings the capital stock back up; there is no impairment of capital stock resulting from the Government's expenditure.

Accordingly, no conflict exists between the findings of BDK and the traditional theorem that future generations can be burdened only if, and to the extent that, they inherit a smaller stock of real capital than otherwise.

Generation I, in the BDK illustration, bears part of the burden by deferring its consumption. By reminding us of this possibility, BDK make a significant contribution. Had Generation I not deferred its consumption at all, had it gone on consuming in Year 100 just as it would have done otherwise, and also not expanding its consumption in Year 144, a still smaller stock of real capital would have been passed on to Generation II. Fewer trees would have been growing in the period, Years 101–43.

The mechanism by which the inheritance is impaired can be any one of several. For example: if the Government finances the expenditure in Year 100 by taxation Generation I may possibly react in just the same way as is postulated for the bond case: they may cut their consumption by the full amount of the government expenditure in Year 100, maintain their consumption as it otherwise would have been in Years 101–43 and decide to make up for their earlier deprivation, in Year 144, by increasing their consumption by the amount of the decrease in Year 100. They pass on to their heirs, Generation II, j units of timber less than otherwise and a tax receipt. The tax receipt is no less and no more valuable to Generation II than would have been a parcel of bonds of the same face amount, for the bonds would have yielded only interest that would have had to be paid to Generation II by levying taxation on itself.

For purposes of policy we need to know, of course, whether tax-payers will react differently from lenders, whether, at the moment of finance, it is consumption or investment that is reduced, and whether a backlash, or reverse reaction, follows in a later year. BDK consider it an 'important point that, regardless of whether loan finance reduces C or I, loan finance can result in intergeneration transfers of burden'. (BDK, 1961, p. 141). This statement is, of course, correct, if 'reduces C or I' refers to the reaction in the year of finance, and if the word 'can' implies that we may add, 'but also may not.' The next sentence, however, seems more positive, and hence in error, in predicting the actual outcome. 'No matter what happens to C and I, Generation I (the present generation) is going to enjoy a higher level of lifetime consumption relative to the consumption of future generations if government expenditures are financed by issuance of debt instruments than if taxes are employed.' (BDK, 1961, p. 141). The phrase 'is going to' seems a little too strong. The BDK argument is that, with more financial assets in its hands, Generation I is going to be more able to step up its consumption towards the end of its life. But when one thinks of the mass of capital instruments that Generation I owns, and which it can sell to Generation II in exchange for consumption goods that Generation II was going to consume, does the existence of an extra block of financial assets – assuming that interest rates are not driven so high by the issuance of debt that the total value of all debt does not increase – really make an appreciable difference? Perhaps it does; Vickrey attaches some importance to this point:

. . . the reverse option, i.e. that of taking individual action, where the project is tax-financed, which would impose a burden on the future generations [Presumably: stepping up consumption in the later years by the generation that has foregone consumption in the first year], is less completely available: it is often difficult to arrange to leave a negative estate when the estate was originally zero or very small (Vickrey, Scitovsky and Elliott, 1961, p. 136).

But Elliott puts it well:

The older members of any economy which incorporates the principles of private property and the right of transfer are always free to sell their creditor claims. The sale may be made to other members of Generation I or to those of Generation II. If, during the lifetime of Generation I, there had been no deficit finance, they would still be free to liquidate *other* forms of creditor claims – life insurance, industrial bonds, common stock, etc. (Vickrey, Scitovsky and Elliott, 1961, p. 139).[6]

The Musgrave Inter-Generation Example

Although Musgrave explicitly recognizes the validity of what is here called the Ricardo–Pigou argument, in the setting that they assumed (Musgrave, 1959, p. 559), he goes on to construct a case in which, regardless of the reaction of Generation I to tax finance or loan finance, loan finance always divides the cost among generations, and tax finance never can do so. Evidently, there must be some special assumptions here; as it turns out, the most important assumption is largely implicit.

In this case, Musgrave is concerned with a long-lived government facility, the cost of which is to be distributed equitably among those who make use of it. He has in mind chiefly the problem that arises from shifting residence; not all those who are in a certain city when the facility is financed will be there to enjoy the services of the project throughout its life, and others, not in the city in the year of finance, will move in later, and enjoy some years of service from the facility. But Musgrave also speaks of 'life span', and implies that his argument applies equally to successive residency spans and life spans.

His assumptions about the reactions of lenders and tax-payers differ radically from those of BDK, but the point at issue remains the same: can the burden be shifted among generations by the method of financing, without reference to the traditional analysis that looks to stock of capital inherited by one generation from its predecessor? Musgrave's answer is, yes. Let us see what makes this affirmative answer possible.

The project has a life of three 'periods', which for Musgrave can evidently be as short as a year, or as long as a decade or more; at least, he does not suggest how long a period may be. Each

6. BDK restate their thesis in their reply to Lerner: 'Our proposition is that the use of debt finance permits, by the process described in our original paper, a relative improvement in the lifetime economic position of Set I persons, *vis-à-vis* a situation in which taxation was employed at t_0 [when the government expenditure was incurred] . . . had World War I been financed entirely by taxes, the lifetime consumption of the 1917–18 population would have been lower, apart from any effects of debt finance on the consumption-investment mix' (BDK, 1961, pp. 98, 99).

generation has a life span (or residency span) of three periods. As period I opens, Generation I, already in its last period, is on the scene; so also is Generation II, with one more period to go, and Generation III, in its initial period. In the second period there exist Generations II, in its last period, III and IV. In the third period we find Generations III (in its last period) and IV (in its second period), and a new Generation V.

The problem is: how to take from Generation I just one-ninth of the cost of the project; from Generation II, just two-ninths; Generation III, just three-ninths; Generation IV, just two-ninths; and Generation V, just one-ninth. Musgrave's solution is to require Generation I to pay one-ninth of the cost in taxation and so on. As to financing the project in its year of construction, six-ninths must be covered by loan; but no part of the loan can be demanded from Generation I, since it is already in its last period, and thus could never be repaid. We may think of Generation I as vanishing at the end of the first period. At least this seems to be what is behind Musgrave's stipulation that 'loans advanced by any one generation must be repaid within its life span.' (1959, p. 563.) So, the six-ninths is financed by loans from Generations II and III, who are repaid before they vanish. Thus everybody gets his money back, except to the extent that he is required to pay tax, and the tax is distributed over time in accordance with degree of service use.

Musgrave stipulates that the loan finance comes completely out of private capital formation (at the opposite pole from the BDK assumption), and that each tax dollar comes 75 per cent from consumption and 25 per cent from private capital formation (BDK: 100 per cent from consumption). But Musgrave could vary these percentages without at all affecting his conclusions about how the burden is distributed among the generations.[7] Evidently, the economic position of Generation II depends not at all on how Generation I reacts to the finance measure. It does so depend, of course, in the BDK analysis, and in the traditional analysis. Musgrave, in effect, abstracts from the fact that Generation I may

7. In the 'compensatory system', where private investment is a fixed amount, all of the tax or loan must come out of consumption; here, distribution of the burden among generations according to use must be accomplished by taxation, of a kind that discriminates among the coexisting generations (Musgrave, 1959, pp. 572–3).

pass on part of its real capital to Generation II; there is no passage of property from one generation to a later one in this part of his analysis.[8] The implicit assumption of no inheritance is the key to this analysis.

This assumption seems to be quite reasonable as long as the analysis is confined to frequently shifting groups of residents. A San Franciscan, let us say, is spending his last period in New York before returning home; an earlier Chicago resident, perhaps the same age as the San Franciscan, has come to New York to stay two periods; he is Generation II, even if he is the same age as Generation I (the San Franciscan); a third man of, say, the same age, is starting the first of three periods of residence in New York – and so on. We have no grounds for supposing that the ex-Chicagoan will benefit if the returning San Franciscan possesses more capital, by the time he leaves for home, under one plan of financing than he would under another. Musgrave, indeed, stipulates that 'each generation consumes its assets while still present' (1959, p. 563); perhaps this somewhat cryptic condition is just another way of saying that in his model there shall be no passage of property from one generation to another.

Generation I pays its 11·1 per cent tax (out of the total 100 per cent needed for finance), 8·3 per cent by cutting consumption and 2·8 per cent by cutting its saving below the levels they would otherwise have reached. It 'dies', or leaves, 2·8 per cent the poorer; but none of the other four generations is held to be affected by this fact. Consequently, Musgrave's analysis has no application to the ordinary case of intergeneration equity, where the generations are connected by inheritance. What Musgrave has done is to state, more explicitly than has been done before (cf. Haig and Shoup, 1953, ch. 14, pp. 539–41), the case for loan finance in a geographic area marked by considerable immigration and emigration over the life span of the project that is being financed.

Even here, as Vickrey has reminded us in his discussion of the BDK thesis (Vickrey, Scitovsky and Elliott, 1961, p. 135), Generation I may find its net worth impaired by more than the tax it pays, less its restriction of consumption, for if it owns property in

8. So far as I am aware, no comments on Musgrave's debt analysis have called attention to the fact that, in the case here considered, he allows no inheritance.

the taxing city the promise of higher property tax over the life span of the project may result in a fall in value of that property as of the start of Period Two, relative to what it would have been if the project had been completely tax financed in Period One. But of course the owners of property in the taxing city may be anyone, in or outside the city. The burden may fall on some who will never benefit from the project, unless, in turn, we assume that the project gives off services of a kind that enhance property values. Indeed, once we begin dealing in a wide-open economy, the possible variations on the burden theme become numerous.

The Buchanan Thesis

In his *Public Principles of Public Debt*, Buchanan argues that debt financing, as compared with tax financing, does shift the burden from the present generation to a future generation. The argument runs as follows. In the year of financing, the year when the resources are diverted from the private sector of a full-employment economy to public use, no individual can be found who feels that he is undergoing a sacrifice, whereas in the future year, when the bonds are redeemed by taxes, it is very easy to discover someone (the tax-payer) who is experiencing real sacrifice, while no one can be found who is thereby experiencing a gain. Since the sacrifice of a generation can exist only through the sacrifice of one or more of the individuals who comprise it, we must conclude that bond financing postpones the sacrifice to a future generation. The nature of the government expense is not relevant to the argument, but to remove any doubts, Buchanan is willing to talk in terms of a wasteful expenditure.

Buchanan, in the initial stages of his argument, assumes that 'the funds used to purchase government securities are drawn wholly from private capital formation' (Buchanan, 1958, p. 32). As we shall see, this assumption is not central to his argument. He does not expressly stipulate that, if taxes were used instead, the funds would be drawn wholly from private consumption, so we cannot be sure that in his community the use of debt finance will burden the future generation, relative to tax finance, in the sense of causing them to inherit a smaller stock of capital goods. But let us assume that, if taxation were employed, the tax would come wholly out of consumption.

To centre on the point at issue, let us also assume that the Government's expenditure does not create an asset of value to anyone in the economy.

At the time of withdrawal of resources for government use, Generation I must make a decision, a decision that has important consequences for Generation II. Shall Generation I reduce its lifetime consumption below the level it would have reached if there had been no such withdrawal of resources for governmental use? Or shall Generation I reduce (in the same sense) its capital equipment?

Whichever decision Generation I makes, it makes voluntarily. No one decrees that it must take the one road or the other. Each individual in Generation I makes up his own mind. Consider first the case where the Government finances by a bond issue. Each purchaser of a bond decides for himself whether, upon receipt of the bond, he shall restrict his consumption spending or shall divest himself of an asset (or, for that matter, shall work harder). Suppose, in contrast to Buchanan's assumption, that each bond purchaser decides to meet the cost by restricting his consumption spending. In the spirit of Buchanan's analysis, we may still say that this reaction to the bond issue represents no sacrifice to anyone in Generation I. No one in that Generation is moved to a lower indifference surface than if he had not participated in the financing by restricting his consumption. Note that the Government's withdrawal of resources is here a datum, and so is the issuance of bonds. The Government offers the bonds for purchase, but does not compel anyone to buy them. The bonds are so attractive, and (we assume) the desire to maintain one's other assets so strong, that the individuals of Generation I willingly cut their consumption in order to buy the bonds. By doing so, they move, indeed, to a higher indifference surface than if, in the face of this bond issue, they had continued to consume and had not bought the bonds – this must be so, by our assumptions about their preferences. In Buchanan's sense there is no sacrifice by any member of Generation I, given the fact of the Government's withdrawal of resources, and the offering of bonds.

Yet it is equally clear that Generation II now inherits a capital equipment larger than it would have inherited if Generation I's voluntary decision had gone the other way, that is, if Generation I had decided to pay for the bond issue by lowering the rate of capital formation during the lifetime of that generation instead of restricting consumption. By restricting consumption, Generation I voluntarily sacrifices in favor of Generation II, if by sacrifice we mean simply: enjoy less consumption. Whichever way Generation I's decision goes, that decision imposes no burden on it in Buchanan's terminology, for Generation I makes that decision freely.[9] But Generation II is obviously better off, in some economic sense, if Generation I decides to restrict consumption than if it decides to restrict capital formation. This apparent asymmetry arises from the fact that among the factors that influence Generation I's welfare (the shape of its indifference surfaces) is the fate of Generation II, a fate in which Generation I may well take a lively interest, whereas Generation II's attempts to maximize its welfare cannot take into consideration the fate of Generation I; time cannot run backward. Thus Generation I can gain, in a welfare sense, by sacrificing, in the consumption sense, thus leaving Generation II on as high an economic level as if the Government had never diverted resources to a wasteful purpose.

Let us suppose that during the lifetime of Generation II the bonds are redeemed by taxation.[10] In Buchanan's sense a sacrifice

9. None of the commentators in note 2 above explicitly recognizes that Buchanan is dealing with sacrifice in terms of freedom of choice of the individual, except Modigliani, in passing (1961, p. 734, and p. 746, note 1), and Ratchford, who remains unpersuaded (1958, pp. 214–15). As Modigliani interprets this argument (1961, p. 734), the existence of a net burden on society from taxes to service the debt depends on an assumption that subscriptions to the government bonds come out of private investment. As I understand the free-choice argument, a net burden on society exists because of the debt-service taxes, no matter what is assumed about the source of the bond subscriptions. Scitovsky (Vickrey, Scitovsky and Elliott, 1961, p. 138) uses the free-choice argument in commenting on BDK, but this is not the point they are making. Ratchford, agreeing that 'Taxes are more readily identified and thus psychologically more burdensome [than the interest charges on investment, paid by consumers in the prices of goods]', discerns that 'the major question is whether these differences in psychological behavior and financial practices constitute a real economic burden. In my opinion they do not' (1958, p. 215). But Buchanan would presumably reply that taxes are not only more easily identifiable, they are compulsory.

10. On this point, see Pigou (1929), p. 238: 'Thus, though it is true, as Professor Seligman asserts, that the bondholder gets no benefit from debt repayment, it is also true that the taxpayer suffers no loss'.

has occurred, because somebody has been forced to do something; those who pay tax in Generation II do not voluntarily hand over cash to the bond-holders of Generation II in order that the bonds may be torn up. If the debt is not redeemed a smaller sacrifice, taxation to pay the interest, is repeated indefinitely.

If we view Generation I as holding a town meeting, in which everyone agrees that he prefers to have bonds issued, although knowing that in this case he and those who come after him will have to contribute taxes towards the interest, rather than paying for the resource diversion by a big tax effort at once, we are pushing Buchanan's type of analysis, viz., welfare as influenced by free choice, back and up one level, to government. The annual tax payments for the interest now impose no sacrifice, for they are but part of a package deal agreed to by all. And if the town meeting's decision had been to the contrary, i.e. that heavy taxes should be levied at once to pay for the resource diversion, these taxes, too, would not be said to impose a sacrifice (given, always, the fact of government diversion of resources), for each person would be placing himself on a higher indifference surface by choosing to pay heavy taxes now rather than accept the less-attractive alternative of light annual taxes to be paid forever by him and those who were to come after him. But Buchanan's analysis, perhaps more realistically, does not carry the free-choice assumption back to those levels. Anyone who is required to pay taxes is moved thereby to a lower indifference surface. The Government is a force external to him, requiring him to surrender something.

The fact that Generation II is better off, materially, if Generation I has saved rather than consumed is of no interest to Buchanan's analysis. But it is of overwhelming interest to the traditional school. To them, the fact that nobody in Generation I is forced to do anything, while somebody in Generation II is forced to do something, is of no consequence. Or perhaps we must say that the traditional view implies that there is no forcing at all, in the taxing process; that there is implied a collective agreement on the financial policy selected. The bond issue plus the annual tax for interest is selected, by the individuals, acting through their political representatives, because it is preferred to no-bond plus heavy immediate taxes – or vice-versa. Without this implication, indeed, the traditional view is in an embarrassing position *vis-à-vis* Buchanan and welfare economics. With this implication, they escape this embarrassment, if we can assume that Generation I can act for those who come after them.

Buchanan, who deems of no consequence for the argument on sacrifice the fact that Generation II possesses greater material wealth if Generation I reacts one way to the bond issue rather than another, does seem thereby to be in a somewhat difficult position *vis-à-vis* the traditional view. It seems awkward to disregard the material inheritance of Generation II when speaking of burden.

Summary

In conclusion: if, although capital is never impaired, inheritance is impaired; or if inheritance is not allowed; or if freedom of choice rather than level of consumption is the test of well being – then the traditional conclusion, that the burden is passed on to a future generation only insofar as the government outlay is not met at once by increased saving, is either incomplete, or not applicable, or irrelevant. But it is still to be judged correct, in the setting its formulators assumed for it, which is probably the setting that most of us have inferred as we studied it.

References
BOWEN, W. G., DAVIS, R. G., and KOPF, D. H. (1960), 'The public debt: a burden on future generations?', *American Economic Review*, vol. 50, pp. 701–6.
BOWEN, W. G., DAVIS, R. G., and KOPF, D. H. (1961), 'The burden of the public debt: a reply', *American Economic Review*, vol. 51, pp. 141–3.
BOWEN, W. G., DAVIS, R. G., and KOPF, D. H. (1962), 'The distribution of the debt burden: a reply' (to Lerner), *Review of Economics and Statistics*, vol. 44, pp. 96–100.
BUCHANAN, J. M. (1958), *Public Principles of Public Debt*, Irwin.
HAIG, R. M., and SHOUP, C. S. (1953), *The Financial Problem of the City of New York*, Columbia University Press.
LERNER, A. P. (1959), 'Review of Buchanan's *Public Principles of Public Debt*', *Journal of Political Economy*, vol. 47, pp. 203–6.
LERNER, A. P. (1961), 'The burden of debt', *Review of Economics and Statistics*, vol. 43, pp. 139–41.
MEADE, J. E. (1958), 'Is the national debt a burden?', *Oxford Economic Papers*, vol. 10, pp. 163–83.
MEADE, J. E. (1959), 'Is the national debt a burden?: correction', *Oxford Economic Papers*, vol. 11, pp. 109–10.

MODIGLIANI, F. (1961), 'Long-run implications of alternative fiscal policies and the burden of the national debt', *Economic Journal*, vol. 71, pp. 730–55.

MUSGRAVE, R. A. (1959), *The Theory of Public Finance*, McGraw-Hill.

NEISSER, H. (1961), 'Is the public debt a burden on future generations?', *Social Research*, Summer, pp. 225–8.

PIGOU, A. C. (1929), *A Study in Public Finance*, Macmillan, 2nd edn.

RATCHFORD, B. U. (1958), 'The nature of public debt', *Southern Economic Journal*, vol. 25, pp. 213–17.

RICARDO, D. (1951a), *On the Principles of Political Economy and Taxation*, vol. 1 in P. Sraffa (ed.), *Works and Correspondence*, Cambridge University Press.

RICARDO, D. (1951b), *Funding System*, vol. 4 in P. Sraffa (ed.), *Works and Correspondence*, Cambridge University Press.

ROLPH, E. R. (1959), 'Review of Buchanan's *Public Principles of Public Debt*', *American Economic Review*, vol. 49, pp. 183–5.

SHOUP, C. S. (1956), *Ricardo on Taxation*, Columbia University Press.

VICKREY, W., SCITOVSKY, T., and ELLIOTT, J. R. (1961), 'The burden of the public debt: comment', *American Economic Review*, vol. 51, pp. 132–41.

15 J. M. Buchanan

Internal and External Borrowing

Excerpt from J. M. Buchanan, *Public Principles of Public Debt*, Richard D. Irwin, 1958, pp. 75–84.

I shall assume, only for two paragraphs, the role of an advocate of the currently accepted views.

If a debtor community should be faced with two alternative situations identical in all respects save that in one of these the public debt instruments are internally held while in the other such instruments are externally owned, the first of these alternatives would clearly be preferable. This conclusion would follow whether we conduct our analysis in terms of social aggregates or in terms of individual components. The external debt would require that interest payments be made to foreigners, and such payments would represent deductions from income otherwise disposable. The interest payments on the internal debt represent no such deductions. While taxpayers are no better off, there are now bond-holder interest recipients, and the interest payments are mere transfers. The external debt is more burdensome to the community, and to the individuals within it, than an internal debt of comparable magnitude.

This remains true regardless of the relative rates of interest which the two loans might carry. On this logic, the external debt carrying an interest payment of no more than one per cent would be more burdensome than an internal debt carrying a rate of ten per cent. The relative rates of interest do not enter into the argument, and, by implication, into the original choice between the two debt forms. So ends the statement of the ruling conception.

The analysis by which the above conclusions are reached exposes the methodological fallacy already discussed in chapter 3 [not included here]. Alternatives of the sort mentioned cannot exist either in the real or in the conceptually real world. The relevant comparison for meaningful debt theory is not between two situations

338

which are identical in *every other respect* than debt ownership. Situations like these could never be present, and could never be constructed except as isolated and unimportant cases. Some *other respects* than debt ownership must be different, and any analysis which overlooks or ignores the other necessary differences must embody serious error.

In order to define properly the relevant, and realizable, alternatives it is necessary to examine these at the moment of initial decision or choice, that is, at the moment when the creation of the public loan is only one among several alternative actions which the community could adopt. In such a moment the community faces three broadly defined alternatives. First, it may borrow and in this way finance a public expenditure program. Secondly, it may tax currently to finance the expenditure, and, thirdly, it may neither borrow nor tax, nor spend. Inflation of the currency may be construed as a tax for our purposes here. Within each of these broad categories there are, of course, many possible sub-alternatives. We are concerned here only with those within the first. We shall assume that the community has made the decision to undertake the expenditure and to finance it by the borrowing method. Financing by means of ordinary taxation or by inflation has been ruled out. The only remaining decision concerns the form which the loan shall take.

Shall the government debt instruments be marketed domestically or shall they be sold in foreign countries?

If the first alternative is chosen, and the loan funds are secured from internal sources, the public expenditure project will be financed out of current domestic savings which presumably could have been, and in this model would have been, invested productively in the private domestic economy. Let us disregard for the time being the whole question of the productivity or the unproductivity of the public expenditure project. The creation of the internal public debt will act so as to reduce the community's privately employed capital stock by the amount of the loan. Future private income streams for the community are correspondingly lowered, with the precise amount of such reductions depending on the rate of return on private capital investment.

In the contrary case in which the community chooses to float the public loan externally rather than internally, the public expenditure will be financed from foreign savings. The incremental addition to domestic privately employed capital stock is not affected by the process of public debt creation. Therefore, as compared with the internal loan situation, the private income stream in subsequent time periods is higher. To this higher income stream there must, of course, be attached some drainage sufficient to allow the external loan to be serviced and eventually amortized.

It cannot be over-emphasized that the internal and the external debt *cannot* legitimately be compared on the assumption of an equivalent gross income stream in the two cases. The gross income of the community in any chosen future time period cannot be thrown into the *other respects* which are assumed identical in the two cases and thereby neglected. The external debt alternative must allow the community to receive a higher gross income in the future, quite apart from any consideration at all of the productivity of the public expenditure.

Criteria for Choice

Once this simple fact is recognized, the choice between the two debt forms is somewhat more complicated than the new orthodoxy implies. The community must compare one debt form which allows a higher income over future time periods but also involves an external drainage from such income stream with another form which reduces the disposable income over the future but creates no net claims against such income. The choice must hinge on some comparison between the rates at which the required capital sum originally may be borrowed. The choice between the internal and the external loan should, at this level of comparison, depend upon the relative rates at which funds may be secured from the two sources.

The community should be indifferent between the two loan forms if the external borrowing rate is equivalent to the internal borrowing rate, and if we may neglect the frictional or second-order effects of making the interest transfers. This latter neglect obscures important aspects of the problem here, and we shall discuss it at length later, but it is useful to proceed at this stage on the 'equal ease of transfer' assumption. We shall temporarily assume that the making of international transfers is no more difficult than the making of internal transfers.

If the two rates are equivalent under these assumptions, the internal loan would reduce domestic private investment which would, in turn, reduce the future income in any one period by an amount indicated by the magnitude of the loan multiplied by the internal rate or net yield on capital, which is assumed to be the rate at which the government borrows. The external loan would not cause such a reduction in private investment; income in a future period would be higher than in the internal loan case by precisely the amount necessary to service the external loan. Net income after all tax payments and interest receipts are included will be equivalent in the two cases.

The analysis is readily extended to the other possible situations. If the internal or domestic productivity of capital investment exceeds the rate at which funds may be borrowed externally, the community will be better off if it chooses the external loan form. Net income after all debt service charges are met will be higher than it would be if the alternative internal public loan were created.

In the third possible case in which the internal rate of return on capital investment falls short of the external borrowing rate, the community will be worse off with the external than with the internal loan. Net income of the community after debt service will be lower, and the external debt will impose a 'burden' in a differential sense. But it must be noted that the 'burden' imposed by the external debt in this case is no different from that imposed by the internal debt in the converse situation. The differential burden, or pressure, arises, not at all from the locational source of the loan funds, but from the fact that the community has not chosen the most 'economic' or 'efficient' source. The borrowing operation is not rational in either case, and the differential burden arises from the irrationality in community choice, not from the 'externalness' or 'internalness' of the debt.

The Transfer Problem

In reaching the above conclusions, we have employed the 'equal ease of transfer' assumption. We assumed that the making of internal transfers and international or external transfers are equivalent in effect. This simplifying assumption may appear to remove the fundamental elements of the internal-external debt comparison. That this is not really the case may be illustrated by reference to the problem of state and local debt. Such debts are normally classified as 'external'. Yet there is no apparent 'transfer problem' in the Keynes–Ohlin sense involved in making the interest payments on these obligations. Such interstate and interregional transfers are presumably effected as smoothly as are the purely 'internal' transfers required for servicing the internally held national debt. These results stem, of course, from the existence of the common monetary system and the comparatively free resource mobility among the separate regions of the country. For the individual state, the choice between the external and the internal debt should be dictated purely by market criteria.

This illustration should suffice to indicate that the problem of transfer is a second-order one when the distinctions between the external and internal debt are considered. No attempt need be made, and none is made here, to minimize the possible differences in the two cases when the genuinely international debt is compared with the internal debt. But the point is that such differences stem solely from the institutional framework imposed by the separate national monetary and economic structures. There are, of course, differences between the two loan forms when we introduce these institutional problems. But these differences are not the ones which the new orthodoxy has employed in making the external-internal debt distinction. The fact that the external debt involves a drainage out of a domestic income stream is not the reason that the external debt may be burdensome. And this is the clear implication of the new orthodoxy as the earlier citations prove.

Let us now examine the transfer problem in somewhat more detail and see how it might cause us to modify our conclusions reached above. A transfer problem is created by the necessity of servicing either the internal or the external debt. In so far as the purchase pattern of those taxed to pay the debt interest differs from that of the domestic bondholders in the first case and from foreigners in the second, some shifting of resources must take place. The issue concerns the differences in the two cases.

Some assumption must be made about exchange rate flexibility. In a world characterized by free flexibility in exchange rates, the international and the internal transfer problems would be substantially identical. For example, if Canada should decide to undertake a large-scale borrowing program, it would make little difference whether the bonds are sold in the United States or at home. The guiding principle in this case should be the comparative rates of interest. Similarly, if the world economy were characterized by some accepted international monetary system with fixed exchange rates but each economy in the system enjoyed internal price flexibility, the international transfer need be no more difficult than the internal transfer. To be sure, the debtor community will find it necessary to impose domestic deflation in order to surmount the balance-of-payments problems created by the necessity of transferring interest payments abroad. The point to be emphasized here is that the servicing of an internal debt requires that a similar deflationary effect be automatically imposed on the 'taxpayer' sector of the domestic economy (cf. Lösch, 1958).

It has been advanced as a conceptual possibility that, either under fixed or flexible exchange rates, extreme values for the elasticities of demand for imports and exports could prevent any transfer of income abroad which is consistent with international equilibrium in balances of payment. Much has been made of this possibility in recent years, but its existence may be questioned (see Sohmen, 1957). Even if the existence of this possibility is accepted, however, it should be noted that similar extreme values for certain elasticity coefficients in the various sectors of the domestic economy could produce similar results in reference to the internal transfer.

The current world economy is not, of course, characterized by either flexible exchange rates or an international monetary standard. Therefore, certain differential problems are created when 'international' loans are considered in this setting. The transfer problem in its classical form may arise, and some premium may be placed on the internal loans. This becomes especially true when the borrowing country obligates itself to service its debt in some international unit of account. In this case, the borrowing or debtor country no longer can retain control over the amount of real income transfer necessitated by the debt service. Action taken in foreign creditor countries can modify the size of the real income transfer.

The point to be made here is not that of minimizing the importance of the transfer problem. Rather it is that of stating that differences in the transfer difficulties provide the only *valid* reason for making a sharp conceptual distinction between the two debt forms. At the more fundamental level of comparison with which we are concerned here, this transfer difference is an adjustment factor only. It should not be allowed to obscure the essential truth, namely, that in basic respects the internal loan and the external loan are identical.

Sources of Error

What are the sources of the fallacious idea that the external loan and the internal loan differ in fundamental respects? There appear to be two. The first source of the error is found in the general assumption of the classical economists that all public expenditure is unproductive. If this assumption were true, then the external loan would always make future generations worse off than they would be without the loan. But again the relevant alternative must be considered. Similar conclusions would follow when the internal loan is considered. But the failure to see this may have been based on an oversight of the proper capital-income relationship. With the internal loan, the present value of the community's future income stream is directly reduced because of the direct usage of a portion of its current capital stock in an unproductive manner. This present value is not affected, in the aggregate, by the future interest charges which take the form of internal transfers. But with the external loan, the net present value of the community's income stream is reduced, not by any current using-up of resources, but by the necessity of making the future interest payments. The gross value must be adjusted downward by the present value of the interest payments. This adjustment may not be made explicitly, and, therefore, the external loan may appear to carry with it a greater burden.

The second source of the error lies in the failure of the new economics to make a distinction between the real and the monetary aspects of public debt. The 'new' approach to the public debt was related directly to the budgetary aspects of the new economics. Discussion was conducted almost wholly in terms of monetary debt obligations, and little attempt was made to separate the real and the monetary sides of the problem. This aspect of debt theory will be thoroughly discussed in chapter 9 [not included here] when we introduce the Keynesian assumptions.

References
LÖSCH, A. (1958), 'A new theory of international trade', *International Economic Papers*, no. 6, pp. 50–65.
SOHMEN, E. (1957), 'Demand elasticities and foreign exchange rates', *Journal of Political Economy*, vol. 65, pp. 431–6.

Part Four The Economic Effects of Taxes

Who pays taxes and how do taxes modify the behaviour of economic
agents? Suppose the government increases its consumption of real
resources in a full employment situation: however this is financed,
its cost is the reduction in resources available to the private sector.
The resulting change in the distribution of income available for
private use, or incidence, will be different according to the method
of finance used. The expenditure/revenue raising operation may well
alter the level of total output if it causes changes in factor supplies.
A satisfactory treatment of public expenditure requires a full general
equilibrium analysis. In the absence of such, it is still possible to
show that the theory that taxes are paid by those on whom they are
levied is, despite its popularity, a naïve theory. Suppose a tax is
imposed on a certain kind of worker in a single industry. With
perfect competition in the labour market this kind of labour will
move out to other industries unless its wages are raised to cover the
tax. If wages rise so, profits must fall unless prices are raised
sufficiently. If demand for the product of this labour has zero
elasticity prices will so be raised. Consumers' expenditure on this
good will be raised and expenditure on other goods will fall. If the
pattern of expenditure reductions elsewhere exactly matches that of
the increased government spending there will be no further repercussions. The tax/expenditure operations then will have reduced the real
consumption of other private sector goods of those who consume
the commodity produced by the taxed labour. Quite different results
can easily be achieved by different assumptions about demand and
supply relationships. The full effects of the government operation
may extend over a large part of the economy. The effects will be
different in different institutional settings: the power of trade
unions, the existence of government price controls and the kind of
monetary policy that is pursued are all clearly important
determinants of the final outcome.

Problems of economic welfare arise from the possibility that taxes
have what Pigou called 'announcement effects', that is, distorting
effects on behaviour. If the object of the tax plan is within the control
of the tax payer – if he can affect his tax bill by modifying his
behaviour – it may be possible to achieve a welfare improvement by

substituting a tax with zero announcement effects which produces the same revenue. A tax which drives a wedge between prices paid and received in an otherwise Pareto-optimal world, reduces welfare below the theoretically attainable maximum.[1] The literature on the excess burden of taxes with announcement effects is surveyed in Walker (Reading 16); although the controversy which is his subject was, as he said, sterile, it served to illuminate a number of dark corners in tax/welfare analysis.

The theoretical conclusion that partial taxes (taxes with announcement effects) may impose excess burdens does not mean that the use of such taxes is to be condemned. For one thing, there are probably no practically useful taxes of importance which do not have announcement effects. Moreover, tax systems do not operate in Pareto-optimal worlds. It is a property of partial taxes that they may be used to correct welfare reducing divergences between marginal social cost and marginal social valuation. One of the most striking examples has been referred to above: the congestion tax.

The analysis of the economic effects of income, sales, and profits taxes is well developed, most of it taking the form of applications of standard microeconomic theory. Stout (Reading 18) gives a succinct theoretical analysis of the highly topical tax on value added. The fragility of the theoretical foundation for the popular belief that income taxes cause a reduction in the supply of effort is clear from Walker (Reading 16). Such empirical work as exists on this subject is inconclusive – its most striking finding for the United Kingdom is the widespread ignorance concerning personal tax rates.[2] The effects of the income tax on risk bearing are analysed in the classic article by Domar and Musgrave (Reading 17) which is extensively referred to in other articles in this volume. The awkward problem of the effects of taxes on business income is covered in two chapters from a recent work by Krzyzaniak and Musgrave (Reading 19): they provide a neat survey of earlier analytical work and an introduction to their pioneering econometric study of the subject. Empirical work of this kind is scarce in the public finance field.

1. This statement is strictly too strong. If economic agents behave in exactly the same way after a price has been distorted by a tax as they would had the same revenue been raised by a lump sum levy, no excess burden is imposed. This is the basis of the proposition for taxing commodities with low demand elasticities.

2. Previous studies are reviewed and the results of an investigation into taxpayer knowledge are reported in C. V. Brown, 'Misconceptions about income tax and incentives', *Scottish Journal of Political Economy*, vol. 15, 1968, pp. 1–21.

16 D. Walker

Direct *v*. Indirect Taxes

D. Walker, 'The direct-indirect tax problem: fifteen years of
controversy', *Public Finance*, vol. 10, 1955, pp. 153–77.

In a recent issue of *Public Finance* I wrote as follows:

Economists (in the past) have argued against outlay taxes and in favour
of income taxes on the ground that outlay taxation distorts consumers'
choices as between goods and therefore imposes an excess burden upon
the individual tax payer or upon the community as compared with that
imposed by raising the same amount of money by an income tax. This
view has been exploded and the best opinion on these matters is that
purely theoretical reasoning cannot demonstrate the superiority of income taxes and the empirical knowledge about individuals' indifference
maps that would be needed to establish a correct view is obviously
unobtainable.[1]

This present article is essentially a defence and justification of
that claim and a discussion of its importance and implications.

We begin by indicating what is meant by the 'direct–indirect tax
problem'. Then – and this is the main part of the paper – we set out
and examine the recent contributions of a number of economists
who have discussed the 'problem'. Finally, we comment on the
value and importance of this work from the point of view of a
Chancellor of the Exchequer concerned with raising money in an
equitable manner to finance the business of government.

No very great originality is claimed. The author feels, however,
that this part of public finance is at present almost completely
shrouded in mystery to all except the narrow specialist and that the
time is ripe for a survey of the present state of the debate and an
assessment of the arguments and contributions of the various
debators.

1. Walker (1955). In support of this view I cited Stigler (1946, pp. 81–2),
Scitovsky (1951, p. 67), Little (1951) and Rolph and Break (1949).

Introduction

Two separate but related problems are discussed under the general heading of the 'direct–indirect tax problem'. Firstly there is a question which may be put as follows: Given that it is desired to raise a certain sum of money from a particular individual, will greater or less hardship be caused if the money is raised by a direct tax or by an indirect tax? The second problem poses the same issue from the point of view of the community as a whole: Given that it is desired to raise a certain sum of money from the general public, will direct taxes or indirect taxes impose the greater burden?[2] The first problem is the more simple and straightforward one and I shall discuss it first. Before we proceed, however, it is necessary that we make quite clear the meaning we intend to attach to the words 'direct' and 'indirect' respectively.

The grouping of taxes into two classes, direct and indirect, and the principles upon which the classification is made goes back a long way in the literature. The main guide as to the appropriate category has tended to be whether the person who actually pays the

2. It is important not to confuse the 'direct-indirect tax problem' in either of its forms with the subject primarily associated with the name of A. C. Pigou (though Marshall in his *Principles*, 1948, originated it and many recent writers have discussed it) who summarized his views on the matter (examined at length in pt 2 of *The Economics of Welfare*, 1932 edn) in a chapter in *Public Finance* (ch. 7, 1947) entitled 'Taxes and bounties to correct maladjustments'. The main maladjustment, of course, being that for certain goods the return at the margin to the various factors of production may be greater or less than the return to the community; private costs differing from social costs. Under this heading are discussed such familiar problems as that of smoke and the general problems of increasing and decreasing supply price industries. Now Pigou argues that such maladjustments can be corrected by imposing outlay taxes on industries which are over expanded in this sense and paying bounties on those which have not expanded sufficiently and he believes that there is an optimum level of bounties and taxes.

The above, interesting and important though it no doubt is, has little or no relevence to the problem we are discussing. Indeed as Professor Pigou put it when dealing with the closely associated problem of the relative merits from a welfare point of view of different sorts of outlay taxes: 'we assume that either no corrections are required or alternatively that whatever corrections are required have been made. We thus postulate that a certain revenue over and above whatever may have been necessary for the tax-bounty system is required' (Pigou, 1947, p. 101).

money over to the tax collecting authority suffers a corresponding reduction in his income. If he does then – in the traditional language – impact and incidence are upon the same person and the tax is direct; if not and the burden is shifted and the real income of someone else is affected (i.e. impact and incidence are upon different people) then the tax is indirect.[3]

This distinction between direct and indirect taxes is not entirely satisfactory for our purposes. Firstly, we are concerned in the 'direct–indirect Tax Problem' only with the taxation of personal incomes whereas the broad direct–indirect classification is applicable to personal and non-personal incomes (e.g. the undistributed income of companies) alike and indeed to capital taxes. Secondly, the development during the last decade or so of the practice of taxing wage and salary incomes at the source (the P.A.Y.E. system in the United Kingdom and the withholding system in the United States) make it difficult to include the income tax as a direct tax within the traditional definition as the employer pays the money to the tax collecting authority, whereas the burden is upon the employee. Thirdly, though the impact and incidence of taxes such as local rates and the motor vehicle duties are upon the same person, it is surely more appropriate that these taxes should be linked with taxes upon commodities rather than with the income tax, as would be the case if the traditional classification was followed.

Mrs Hicks' distinction between income taxes and outlay taxes (Hicks, 1948, ch. 4, and see also Hicks, 1946) approximates much more closely to our requirements than the traditional classification for it brings out very clearly the fundamental difference that is so important when discussing the 'direct–indirect tax problem', that is the distinction between those taxes whose burden depends upon the way in which individuals spend their incomes and those that do not. Or in the case of a no-saving world between tax structures the burden of which varies depending upon *how* one spends one's income and those that do not.

For our problem it has to be remembered that we are not interested in taxes levied upon the income of companies or in outlay taxes upon investment, government or export expenditure. In

3. See Mill (1965, ch. 3). For a similar treatment three-quarters of a century later see Dalton (1936, p. 33).

this paper we shall adopt Mrs Hicks' classification but we shall keep the words direct and indirect and use them as synonyms for personal income taxes on the one hand and outlay taxes that fall upon personal consumption expenditure on the other.[4]

In my discussion of the 'tax problem' I shall assume that all income is spent. If there was saving this would strengthen the case for the agnostic claim which began the paper, for an income tax (at any rate an orthodox income tax) discriminates against saving. If there is no saving a proportional income tax becomes identical in its operation and effects to an equal *ad valorem* outlay tax on all commodities. In a two commodity world assuming no saving the 'direct–indirect tax problem' in its simplest form becomes a discussion of the relative merits from an economic welfare point of view of an outlay tax at an equal *ad valorem* rate on the two commodities and outlay taxes of different *ad valorem* rates on them.

A difficulty arises, however, when we come to consider income and outlay taxes as methods of taxing personal property income, for, as is well known, it is just as feasible to raise money by taxing the capital value of the property as it is by taxing the income that the property produces. In the literature the two problems rightly or wrongly have grown up in isolation. On the one hand there is discussed the advantages and disadvantages of income taxes and capital taxes as methods of taxing property income and on the other hand there is the rather more general controversy – our problem – which is a discussion of the advantages and disadvantages of income and outlay taxes as methods of taxing personal income whether it be earned or investment income. I shall follow tradition and in this paper will ignore the income tax/capital tax problem. Indeed, my remarks will be mainly directed to considering the 'tax problem' with respect to earned income rather than property income. This enables me to neglect complications associated with entrepreneurship.

The Individual Consumer

Introductory

Recent discussion of the problem stems from the similar treat-

4. When I write 'income tax' I mean a proportional income tax. I will use the adjectives 'progressive' and 'regressive' before 'income tax' when I want to make reference to tax formulas possessing these qualities.

ment of it by Miss Joseph and Professor Hicks respectively[5] in 1939, the gist of which is as follows. A single economic man who spends his income on two goods is assumed. In Figure 1, Q_0 is the equilibrium tax free position. When a proportional income tax which is equivalent to an equal *ad valorem* outlay tax on the two goods is imposed, Q_1 represents the consumer's new position of equilibrium. The same sum of money could have been raised by an outlay tax upon Y only which would have resulted in the consumer

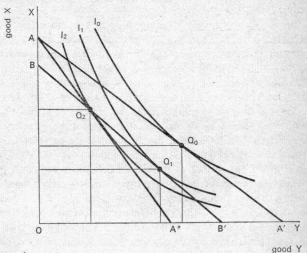

Figure 1

good Y

5. See Joseph (1939) and Hicks (1939, p. 41). It has been pointed out by A. T. Peacock and D. Berry (1951), and by D. Berry in a chapter entitled 'Modern welfare analysis' (1954), that E. Barone as long ago as 1912 in the *Giornale degli Economisti* had used indifference curve analysis to prove that an individual would be equally happy paying a larger sum of money by an income tax as a smaller sum by outlay taxes and that Miss Joseph's and Professor Hicks' special claim that a given revenue yield would leave the taxpayer better off under an income tax had been demonstrated in a similar manner by Gino Borgatta in 1921 in the same journal. Peacock and Berry give credit to Gerard Dehove (1947) for this discovery.

Even in the light of the above remarks it still seems to me correct to date the start of the modern discussion from the publication of the cited works by Miss Joseph and Professor Hicks. Later on I will comment on the role played by Marshall.

moving to a position such as Q_2. From the usual convexity assumptions it follows that Q_1 is preferable to Q_2.

This demonstration of the superiority of direct taxes – similar demonstrations occur in many textbooks (Stigler, 1946, pp. 81–2; Scitovsky, 1951, p. 67) – is open to objection on two fundamental grounds and we shall show that it is only if certain very special, restrictive and unrealistic assumption are made that the Joseph–Hicks demonstration can be accepted as a true and correct proof of the proposition that income taxes impose smaller burdens than outlay taxes.

Before looking at these objections it is useful and perhaps even necessary to insert a few words of caution as regards the applicability of indifference curve analysis in this field. Such analysis assumes that the indifference map does not alter and in particular that the indifference map is completely unaffected by changes in tax rates. This assumption does not seem to be a realistic one.

Another and more serious objection is whether a move to a higher indifference curve really means that people are better off! A move from a lower to a higher indifference curve can only signify an increase in total welfare if we define it as such. Above we have drawn our picture as though we believed that people feel themselves better off if they are taxed directly rather than indirectly. This may not be so; paradoxically though it may seem, people can move to a higher indifference curve (of the conventional type) and yet be worse off. This is a reflection of the Pigouvian distinction between economic welfare and total welfare; the two may not always move in the same direction. A person may just not like paying income tax. He may suffer, for example, a real loss of happiness in handing over money to the tax collector which is not counter-balanced by the fact that he loses less economic surplus with the direct tax. Or again, a person may think that it is not right to tax commodities essential to life and therefore suffers pain because of a sense of injustice when such a tax is imposed as it might be if equal *ad valorem* outlay taxes were imposed on all commodities. These examples are instances of additional losses to total welfare and it is possible that losses of this type may be greater than the gains in economic welfare that an indifference curve diagram might reveal; therefore in terms of total welfare the conclusions shown by the normal indifference curve analysis would be wrong.

It is possible, no doubt, to introduce these considerations into the indifference curve presentation of the problem but this has not so far been done in the literature.

At this stage in our discussion we notice these objections but ignore them and pass on in the conventional way. We shall, however, return to them in our concluding section.

The first objection to the Joseph–Hicks proof is that it implicitly assumes that the pre-tax income of the individual in question is the same whether an income tax is imposed or whether goods X or Y are taxed separately. Put more formally it is assumed that the supply of work is completely inelastic with respect to changes in the rates of income or outlay taxes. When this assumption is removed the simplicity and the correctness and the certainty of the so-called proof disappears.

The second objection is pertinent even if we accept the above-mentioned hidden premise of the Hicks–Joseph proof for their arguments also implicitly assume what has come to be called 'ideal initial conditions'; that is to say, that when considering the 'tax problem' they conveniently start from a position in which there are no taxes in existence.

Modifications are required in the analysis when considering the more realistic problem of raising a given amount of additional revenue by direct or indirect taxes when there are already certain taxes in operation bringing in revenue.

Broadly speaking, then, the Joseph–Hicks theoretical demonstration of the superiority on welfare grounds of direct or indirect taxation is only a satisfactory proof on the twin assumptions of a completely inelastic supply of labour with respect to income and outlay taxes and 'ideal initial conditions'. In the remaining sections of this part of the paper I propose to show what happens when these assumptions are removed.

Supply of labour permitted to vary[6]

Professor Lionel Robbins gave a pretty full account of the effects of an income tax on the supply of effort in his (1930) *Economica* article and Professor J. R. Hicks reached the same conclusion – that *a priori* analysis cannot tell us whether the supply curve of

6. In this section we assume 'ideal' initial conditions.

abour will be backward bending or forward rising – in *Value and Capital* using indifference curves (Hicks, 1939, p. 36). This conclusion arises, of course, from the well-known fact that on the supply side the income and substitution effects of a change in the net rate of return normally work in opposite directions.

When a man's income is reduced he usually wants less leisure. There are two main reasons for this. Firstly, since leisure is usually complementary to other goods, one would expect a reduction in the availability of these goods (which is what a reduction in income means) to lead to a reduction in the demand for leisure. Secondly, it can be argued that a reduction in income (say by a poll tax) will make the marginal disutility of work less than the marginal utility of income and therefore stimulate work.

An income tax also alters the reward for each marginal unit of work thus making every hour's work less attractive than it would be in its absence.

The income and substitution effects work in opposite directions and purely theoretical reasoning cannot establish which is likely to be the stronger – though common sense and what organized empirical data we possess would suggest that the income effect will prove more important than the price effect in most cases and that as income increases the demand for leisure will increase and *vice versa*.

We can push this a little further. For the above mentioned reasons we would expect the amount of work done to increase when a poll tax is imposed as compared to a no-tax position for in this case the income effect alone is at work; there is no change in the gain from each additional hour of work. We would also expect that the amount of work done would vary depending upon the kind of income tax imposed. For instance we can rank progressive, proportional, regressive and poll taxes in that order with respect to the amount of work done with taxes of that type bringing in the same revenue; poll taxes being associated with the least leisure and progressive income taxes with the most. In all cases the income effect is identical but whereas there is zero substitution effect with a poll tax there can be a marked one with a progressive income tax and so on in diminishing importance for proportional and regressive income taxes (see Pigou, 1928, ch. 5; Paish, 1941; Phelps Brown, 1951, ch. 4).

Both the writers mentioned in the first paragraph of this section (and indeed almost all the writers on this topic up to Haskell P. Wald (1944–5)) seem to take the view that a bad effect of an income tax might be that it reduced the amount of work performed. It was appreciated that an income tax could increase the amount of work done but this was not regarded as bad! Wald, however, in the article already cited pointed out that a proportional income tax imposed an excess burden on an individual as compared with a poll tax no matter whether the supply of labour increased, decreased or remained the same, and claimed that this excess burden was essentially similar to the excess burden of an indirect tax as shown in the Joseph–Hicks type of diagram.

It is interesting to note that the welfare ranking of the different forms of income tax is the same as the incentive ranking. This was pointed out by Professor Pigou (1928, pt 2, ch. 5) and Professor Boulding (1955, pp. 773–5) has given an elegant demonstration of the proposition with the use of indifference curves. The rationale of this, of course, is that the magnitude of the excess burden of these taxes in relation to a poll tax depends upon the extent to which an individual's actions are different with these taxes in operation than with a poll tax – which is really the incentive effect again.

It is important to remember that these excess burdens depend upon the extent to which individuals (a) have the freedom to choose the number of hours they work, and (b) are affected by taxes in so making up their minds. Many economists do not think that individuals have such freedom or temperaments.[7]

Wald's argument runs as follows. In Figure 1 let the X axis represent leisure and the Y axis income. Then the line AA' represents the pre-tax opportunities as regards income and leisure open to our individual, and Q_0 has preferred combination of these things. The government wish to take from AB ($A'B'$) in taxation. This it can do by a poll tax which gives a new set of opportunities BB' and a new position of equilibrium Q_1. It is also possible to raise the same sum of money by imposing a proportional income tax. Such a tax formula would present our individual with a new

7. See Pigou (1928 [1947 edn], pp. 69–71); Schwartz and Moore (1951). For some recent empirical evidence see the *Second Report of the Royal Commission on the Taxation of Income and Profits*, 1954.

budget line AA'' and he would choose the combination of income and leisure represented by position Q_2. From the usual convexity assumptions it follows that Q_1 is superior to Q_2 and that raising AB by an income tax imposes an excess burden upon the consumer as compared with raising the money by a poll tax.

In our example the individual is taking less leisure with an income tax than with no taxes in operation (i.e. he is working harder). The same conclusion would follow, however, if our individual's indifference map with respect to leisure and income had been such that the income effect had been less important than the substitution effect so leading him to work less hard with an income tax in operation as compared with the no-tax position.

The conclusion that Wald drew from his analysis was that though it could be demonstrated that a poll tax was superior to an income tax and that a poll tax was superior to an outlay tax *such theoretical studies could throw little light on the magnitudes of the excess burdens and, therefore, upon the relative merits from a welfare point of view of income taxes and outlay taxes respectively.* Wald did of course appreciate the conditions under which an outlay tax and an income tax are not associated with a loss of surplus and have exactly the same effect as a poll tax. For instance he writes as follows: 'A commodity tax will satisfy the criterion when income-elasticity and price-elasticity of demand are zero. In these circumstances the elasticity of substitution between income and the taxed commodity must be zero.'[8]

Though we shall see later that objection can be taken to the italicized portion of the summary above, I do not wish to take up that point at the moment. I want, however, to draw the reader's attention to the fact that Mr Wald's approach to the problem is not entirely satisfactory. His argument suggests that an identical diagram and argument is required for both the poll tax/income tax and the poll tax/outlay tax discussion. This is not correct as this would be assuming that the individual has the same pre-tax income with an outlay tax as with an income tax. Wald does, quite correctly, show that an income tax involves an excess burden on the payer as compared with a poll tax but he does not satisfactorily deal with the burden of an outlay tax as his discussion is still im-

8. Wald (1944–5, p. 596). For an income tax to be identical with a poll tax the same elasticity conditions have to be satisfied.

plicitly (and surely wrongly) based on the assumption that there is no relationship between the price of commodities and the demand for leisure. This is clearly an unreasonable position. Even if it is thought that outlay taxes do not have any substitution effects on the demand for leisure, it is not possible to deny the existence of income effects.

Professor A. M. Henderson fell into the same trap as Mr Wald (Henderson, 1948). In an article published in 1948 he tried to demonstrate that Wald's argument was unsatisfactory and misleading (as indeed it was in certain respects) and that the traditional Joseph–Hicks view was correct (which it was not). The essence of his argument was that an income tax structure and an outlay tax structure of equal progressiveness would have identical distorting effects on the supply of work as compared with a poll tax and, therefore, on that count would cause an equal loss of surplus but, in addition, he thought that outlay taxes would cause an additional loss of surplus as compared with an income tax when the income came to be spent.

Thus the traditional conclusion was correct. Now Professor Henderson is correct in that with a given income an outlay tax imposes a greater burden than an income tax (on our assumption of 'ideal initial conditions') – this, after all, is the traditional claim which I supported given these assumptions. But this is not the point. The point is that an individual faced with an income tax function and an outlay tax function of equal progressiveness will not in fact earn the same income.

To make this point quite clear we shall have to consider in rather close detail the meaning of 'equal progressiveness' in this context. The concept of progressiveness is quite clear-cut in relation to the income tax and let us here assume that we are dealing with a tax structure such that if an individual earns £ x he will pay y per cent of it in taxation. (For simplicity we could deal with a proportional income tax which on our general assumptions would be equivalent to an equal *ad valorem* outlay tax at y per cent on all commodities.) The interesting and complicated case is what is meant by an outlay tax structure of equal progressiveness to this income tax. In the case of an individual it must mean that system of unequal *ad valorem* tax rates which taking into account his tastes would ensure that if he had an income of £ x he would so allocate his expenditure as to spend y per cent taxation. Now the important point is this: our individual is faced not with a specific demand for cash but with a series of alternative tax formulae and he is perfectly free to vary his hours of work and his consumption of particular commodities. Our suggestion is that a consumer faced with the alternative direct and indirect tax possibilities noticed above will in fact choose to work a different number of hours in each case and in the *ex post* sense the tax systems would not be of equal progressiveness. It therefore becomes impossible to make the sort of statement that Henderson made with respect to the superiority of direct to indirect taxes.

One might think there was a way out of this by defining progressiveness in a rather different way. For instance one could define an indirect and a direct tax system of equal progressiveness as systems in which the tax rates were such that the individuals paid the same amount of money to the government even if – as they would be – the hours worked and the pattern of consumption spending were different. If it was possible to demonstrate that in such a situation income taxes imposed less hardship upon the consumer than outlay taxes one might be in a position to make out a case for the superiority of direct taxes. This is not possible. Indeed, as we shall see later, it is possible to establish a good case for the contrary view.

Without in any way disparaging the good work done by Wald and Henderson, it can I think be stated quite definitely that they did not grasp the intimate relationship between income taxes and the demand for commodities on the one hand and the prices of goods and the demand for leisure on the other. It is to I. M. D. Little (1951) that we owe the first specific statement of these important inter-relationships.

Instead of treating the poll tax /income tax and the poll tax /indirect tax problems as two distinct and separate problems, Mr Little treated them as aspects of the same problem. A consumer is assumed free and able to choose between different combinations of three goods A, B and L (leisure). If he wants more he can have more A and B at the expense of leisure; if he wants A and L he must have little B, and so on. If a poll tax is imposed upon this consumer his choices will be influenced by its income effect, but there will be no substitution effects. (We would expect his demand for L to fall.) If a tax is imposed upon A or B or L to bring in the same amount of money, there will be distorting effects and it seemed to

Little that there was complete symmetry from the theoretical point of view with respect to the distorting effects and therefore as regards the loss of welfare with any of these taxes and he felt able to conclude his justifiably famous article with the following sentences: 'If any general conclusion can be risked it is simply that the best taxes are those on goods for which the demand is least elastic. The same holds true for subsidies. Income tax which is a subsidy on leisure is not exceptional. Only in so far as the demand for leisure is highly inelastic is it a good tax. The purely theoretical case against indirect taxation is an illusion' (Little, 1951, p. 584).

The upshot of the Joseph–Wald–Henderson–Little discussion then was that purely theoretical reasoning cannot establish the inferiority (or superiority) of excise taxes to income taxes and that the question as to which form of taxation would impose the smaller loss of surplus in any given situation was, therefore, an empirical one, the result being determined by the particular shape of the demand curves for the commodities and leisure respectively. This was the flavour I wished to convey in my original article. Due to the recent researches of Messrs Corlett and Hague (1953–4, pp. 21–30) it is now possible to arrive at a slightly less agnostic conclusion (but *only a slightly less* one), namely that 'some indirect tax structure will be superior to direct taxation if individuals are able to decide how much they work' (Corlett and Hague, 1953–4, p. 30).

Three goods A, B and L (leisure) are assumed to exist. A proportional income tax is in operation and our consumer has chosen the combination of A, B and L that yields him the most satisfaction. If now the rate of income tax is reduced and a small outlay tax sufficient to raise an equivalent amount of revenue is imposed upon A or B, this change will have an effect upon the amount of L chosen by our consumer. Generally, either A or B will be more complementary with leisure than the other.[9] If A is more com-

9. Corlett and Hague (1953–4, p. 24) define what they mean by this expression as follows: 'A greater or smaller degree of complementarity could easily be defined if it were possible to measure the quantity of leisure as could be done if there were a maximum to the income which could be earned however hard an individual were to work. The quantity of leisure could then be measured by the difference between this maximum income and his actual earnings. In that case our condition would be that the elasticity of complementarity between one good and leisure should be higher than the elasticity of complementarity between the other good and leisure.'

plementary with leisure and the tax is imposed upon A our individual will work harder. If B is more complementary with leisure and a tax is imposed upon A then he will work less hard in the new tax situation than with the equal *ad valorem* tax rates on A and B of the first position.

This is not a surprising result. We have seen that an income tax always leads an individual to work less hard than he would paying the same money to the exchequer in the form of a poll tax. A poll tax may (in our model) be regarded as a tax levied at an equal *ad valorem* rate on all three goods, A, B, L. An income tax distorts choices in favour of leisure as compared to a poll tax and a change in the tax system, therefore, that tends to correct this distortion – for instance increased taxation upon the good complementary with leisure – will lead an individual to work harder. Again, as we might expect from our discussion above, such a change will reduce the loss of welfare and our individual will move to a higher indifference surface, though this, of course, only follows if he is in a position to alter his hours of work or if his supply curve of effort is not of zero elasticity.

The main contribution – and it is an important one – of the Corlett–Hague article is to demonstrate that in a three commodity world (one of which is leisure) in which individuals are in a position to vary their hours of work, a change from an equal *ad valorem* tax upon the two goods to a structure of non-equal *ad valorem taxes* will *reduce* the amount of leisure consumed and *increase* the individual's economic welfare if the higher tax rate is upon the good more complementary with leisure and *vice versa*. It follows also, given the previous assumptions, that some form of indirect taxation will always be superior to direct taxation.[10] These are theoretical conclusions and, as such, are important ones. As a guide to action in the field of practical public finance, however, they would seem to possess little value as at present and, indeed, in the foreseeable future, our knowledge of the particular shape of demand curves and of the relationship between an individual's demand for goods and demand for leisure is completely inadequate for such a purpose.

10. A similar conclusion follows if one relaxes some of the assumptions and takes into account the existence of more than two commodities in addition to leisure, more than one individual and the fact that income taxes may be progressive or regressive as well as proportional.

Other taxes in existence[11]

All the writers which we discussed in the previous section of the paper implicitly assumed what we have called 'ideal initial conditions'.[12] As in the real world, 'ideal initial conditions' are the exception rather than the rule, it is surely important to have some idea of the significance of this assumption and the implications of its removal.[13]

In the case of a single individual and assuming a two commodity world (A and B) four different initial conditions can be distinguished; no taxes at all; an income tax (equivalent to an equal *ad valorem* outlay tax on both goods); an outlay tax on A; an outlay tax on B.[14]

The traditional (Joseph–Hicks) conclusion that an income tax is preferable to an outlay tax on A bringing in the same revenue is applicable except in the last mentioned initial position; though the argument, particularly when there is already an outlay tax on A, is pretty complicated (Davidson, 1952–3, pp. 211–12). An income tax is always preferable to an outlay tax on A except when there is already an outlay tax on B.

There is an obvious commonsense reason for this conclusion. As we have seen above the reason why a poll tax is such a good tax from an economic welfare point of view is that it does not have any substitution or distorting effects upon an individual's behaviour. A poll tax does not directly alter relative prices. The only effect it has on prices – and this is only important when there are many individuals – is due to the new distribution of purchasing power it brings about and the corresponding changes in the demand for particular commodities. Now prices to an economist are

11. In this section we assume that the supply of labour is fixed.

12. Of the writers mentioned in the text or in footnotes Messrs Stigler, Wald and Scitovsky explicitly state that there is no tax on one of the commodities they are considering.

13. The analysis that follows is based upon a recent article by R. K. Davidson (1952–3). Mr Davidson's analysis of this problem is entirely satisfactory though – in my judgement – he does not seem to realize how all his conclusions are dependent upon the assumption of zero elasticity in the supply curve of labour nor to appreciate that certain writers (in particular Rolph and Break (1949) and Friedman (1952a)) had made substantial contributions to his problem – though in a much less elegant manner.

14. There might also be a combination of these.

relative prices or price ratios and a tax system that leaves relative prices or price ratios unchanged is equivalent to a poll tax; and a tax system that approximates to such a situation will tend to leave individuals on higher indifference curves than a tax system that does not. In our model let us assume no-tax prices of 4 and 2 for A and B respectively and a price ratio, therefore of $2:1$. Neither a poll tax nor an income tax will alter these prices. A tax upon A or B, however, will alter them and therefore they are inferior methods of raising money as compared with a poll tax or an income tax.

Now let us assume there is already an *ad valorem* tax of 50 per cent upon good B. In this initial position, then, the relative prices of A and B are 4 and 3 and the price ratio $1\frac{1}{3}$. If now an income tax is imposed the price ratio will remain at $1\frac{1}{3}$ and there will be distortion as compared with the no-tax initial position price ratio of 2. A further tax upon B bringing in the same total revenue as the previously mentioned combination of outlay tax on B and income tax will make the distortion worse. A tax on A however will reduce it. Let us assume that a 50 per cent outlay tax on A will bring in, in combination with the existing 50 per cent outlay tax on B, the same revenue as the first combination of outlay tax on B and income tax. With such a tax system the relative prices become 6 and 3 and the price ratio 2. In this case then an indirect tax upon A would be preferable to an income tax.

In our example the new outlay tax on A is at the same rate as the old outlay tax on B. Other situations can be distinguished. If the old tax on B was at a higher rate than the new one on A, the same conclusion follows. If, however, the new rate on A is greater than the old rate on B it is clearly possible for the second state of distortion with respect to the original pre tax position to be worse than the first and, therefore, for an income tax to be better than an outlay tax on A even when there is already an outlay tax on B in existence.

Marshall

Many of the writers we have mentioned have stated that Marshall attempted to demonstrate by consumer surplus arguments the superiority of direct to indirect taxation. Miss Joseph[15], Mr

15. Joseph (1939, p. 226). Here Miss Joseph footnotes Marshall (1948, p. 467).

Wald[16] and Professor Henderson[17] all make statements of this sort.

If we examine the cited portions of Marshall we find that in fact he does not deal with the 'direct–indirect tax problem' at all. To begin with the cited discussion is a footnote one and it is primarily designed as an illustration of the effects which a change in the conditions of supply have on consumers' surplus rather than as a considered view on taxation matters. Secondly, Marshall's discussion is designed to show the relative loss of surplus involved in raising the same amount of money by different sorts of outlay tax. There is no mention of income taxes in the footnote or the text and his conclusion is as follows: 'If therefore a given aggregate taxation has to be levied ruthlessly from any class it will cause less loss of consumers' surplus if levied on necessaries than if levied on comforts; though of course the consumption of luxuries and in a less degree of comforts indicates ability to bear taxation.'

Now it is true that this conclusion is open to objection because of the neglect of income effects, effects upon the supply of work and the fact that there may already be taxes in operation but, broadly speaking, it is a correct view and certainly Marshall makes *no* attempt to try and show that direct taxes are preferable to indirect.

With Marshall's implicit assumptions of a given supply of effort (or amount of income) and a no-tax initial position it can be shown that his claim that a smaller burden is imposed upon a tax payer by taxing the commodity for which he has a relatively inelastic demand should be that the commodity should be taxed which has a low elasticity of substitution. This alternative expression takes care of income effects; elasticity of demand will vary with the elasticity of substitution unless the good is an inferior good.

It might be thought that one could object to Marshall's formulation of the problem even if income–effect–complications etc. are ignored. Marshall argued that the tax payments that the individual makes cause the consumer a greater loss in terms of money than the financial payment to the exchequer owing to the loss in consumer surplus but – and this is important – he accounts the gain to the government to be equivalent to the tax payment. Now if one

16. Wald (1944–5, p. 578). Wald also footnotes Marshall (1948, p. 467).

17. Henderson (1948, p. 538). Henderson makes the same reference as Miss Joseph and Professor Wald.

takes into account utility equivalents on one side one ought to take them into account on the other; that is to say, take into account the utility increases due to the spending of the tax revenue which may well give rise to a form of consumers' surplus.

This objection, however, only arises when considering the *absolute* loss of surplus involved in raising money by a tax. It does not arise when considering the relative loss of surplus involved with different taxes as in this case it can be assumed that the same expenditure and therefore the same utility gains are involved and it becomes reasonable to compare the magnitude of the individual losses of surplus. The identical problem arises when using in-difference curves.

It is very difficult to understand why the writers cited fell into the error of ascribing to Marshall a view on the 'direct–indirect tax problem'. It is particularly odd, as Professor Pigou in all editions of his *Public Finance* (1928, 1929, 1947) went out of his way to point out that Marshall did not attempt to prove the proposition and that not even an extension of his analysis could be used to discuss the problem (Pigou, 1947, ch. 9).

Conclusion

As we are primarily interested in the relevance of recent discussion of the 'tax problem' to the practical tasks of Chancellors and Ministers of Finance, and as from that point of view the community aspects of the 'problem' are obviously of more importance than the 'tax problem' with respect to the individual consumer, we shall not attempt at this stage to develop a set of conclusions. What seems to follow from the analysis so far is that there is no straight-forward and unique proof of the superiority of income taxes or outlay taxes in the individual consumer 'tax problem' that has practical significance even on grounds of economic welfare. In the real world the supply of labour may not be completely fixed and 'ideal initial conditions' may not exist and our statistical know-ledge of the shapes of demand curves and the state of initial position *must* be inadequate.

The superiority on welfare grounds of a poll tax with respect to all other taxes can be established (though not a poll tax imposed in addition to an existing outlay tax) by theoretical reasoning, but no such case can be made out with respect to income and outlay taxes.

The Community

Introductory

The earlier writers that we noticed in the preceding part,[18] though in fact they only dealt explicitly with the problem of the relative effects of raising a given sum of money from an *individual* by direct or indirect taxes, implied that the same arguments and the same solution were adequate in relation to the problem of raising a given sum of money from the community as a whole.

We have seen that the Hicks–Joseph proof is open to a number of objections even when related to an individual consumer. Before considering these objections with respect to the community problem, it will be convenient to consider how far the simple proof is valid in this new context whilst making the assumptions that render the traditional proof correct in the old – that the supply of labour is completely inelastic and that there are no other taxes in operation.

We have to consider two complicating factors. Firstly, we have to deal with what is essentially a problem of interpersonal comparisons. On the one hand the fact that individuals have different tastes and on the other that they have different incomes. Secondly, we have to take into account the fact that it is the level of real government expenditure rather than the level of taxation that reduces the amount of goods available for private consumption and investment and that it is the reduction in private expenditure rather than the raising of revenue that is – in this context – the main purpose of taxation.[19]

Interpersonal comparisons

The determination of the burden of taxation that should be carried by people in different income groups is a political and not an economic question. Even if we assume that people have identical

18. Miss Joseph and Messrs Hicks, Wald and Henderson.

19. I write 'in this context' as taxation may also be used for other purposes, for instance to bring about a more equal distribution of income or to reduce the consumption of some particular commodity, etc.

tastes and make the commonsense assumptions that people in the same income group and with the same responsibilities should pay the same amount of tax and that the marginal utility of income falls continuously as income increases, we are not able to be at all specific about the percentage of his income that a £1000 a year man and a £2000 a year man respectively should pay over to the Chancellor of the Exchequer.

The role of the economist in this field is a minor one – though not a completely unimportant one. His main task is to point out the effects that are likely to follow the introduction of tax schemes of various degrees of progressiveness; effects on savings, work, entre-preneurship and the like. The politician, in the light of this and other expert information, has to choose the form of tax structure which seems to him to be the best; or that will lose least votes; or that is the best that is practicable in the light of administrative possibilities. Now the information that the economist should be in a position to supply to the politicians concerning the effects of different degrees of progressiveness is clearly of considerable im-portance but the point we have to emphasize here is that the economist as such is never in a position to lay down as law, as a matter of scientific truth, that such and such a tax structure of particular progressiveness is either the optimum one or even is better than some other tax structure of a different degree of progressiveness.

If people have different tastes and if it is not accepted that people in the same financial position should pay the same taxes then the problem becomes even more complicated.

In order to make progress in our discussion of the community aspects of the 'direct–indirect tax problem' it is necessary to assume that a government or a priest has laid down a rule of progression. Given this minor 'social welfare function' we are able to proceed.

If we assume that it has been decided by some non-economist decision-taker what the revenue contributions of particular income groups or individuals should be our problem becomes that of dis-cussing the relative burden of raising these various revenue contri-butions by a direct tax or by an indirect tax. This is a manageable problem. On our present assumptions of a constant supply of labour and ideal initial conditions it is clear that this problem is essentially the same as the problem of the individual consumer on the basis of the same set of assumptions. We are in the fortunate position of being able to argue that as for each and every person in the community a direct tax is better than an indirect tax, a similar conclusion must be applicable to the community as a whole.

We must beware of attaching too much significance to this conclusion. In particular we have to remember that though in each case the burden upon individual tax payers is less with a direct tax than with an indirect tax, the magnitude of the gain for the various tax-payers will be different – unless of course each tax-payer has the same tastes.

Object of taxation[20]

When considering the case of an individual tax payer it was reasonable to take his payments to the Exchequer as a good measure (except for the distorting effects) of the burden of government finance upon him. When we come to consider the community, however, we have to modify this approach.

With our assumptions of a constant amount of work and a two commodity world and with the additional assumption of perfect competition we can draw a transformation curve or production-possibility curve representing – in the absence of any government expenditure – the consumption possibilities open to a country's inhabitants. In Figure 2 we have commodity A on the X axis and commodity B on the Y axis. The transformation curve AB represents the various combinations of goods A and B that the society can produce with its given resources of labour, capital and technical knowledge (all assumed constant). I_0, I_1, I_2 are a set of community indifference curves[21] and in the absence of taxation and government expenditure and with perfect competition in the factor and goods markets the community will choose the combination of goods A and B represented by the position P_0 on the transformation curve. The slope of the transformation curve and the community indifference curve at P_0 will be the price ratio at which A and B will

20. This section is based upon the following contributions: Rolph and Break (1949), Little (1951) and Friedman (1952a and 1952b, pp. 334–6). See also Phipps (1952, pp. 332–4).

21. This procedure is meaningful provided each consumer has the same tastes.

exchange in the market. Behind the scenes not revealed in our diagram are the many complicated equalities of a *Paretian Optimum*. For instance we know that the ratios of marginal physical productivities of the factors of production involved in producing A are equal to those involved in B, and so on.

If the government now decides to utilize some of the community's resources for its own use the consumption possibilities open to the private sector of the economy will be reduced. If the government employs for its own uses – say in defence – resources that previously were capable of producing either AA^1 of A or BB^1 of B or the combination of A and B represented by the width of the band AA^1 or BB^1 at any point on AB, then the consumption possibilities of the private sector become A^1B^1. It follows that the private sector of the community will be worse off as it would be possible to have more goods in the first position than in the second.

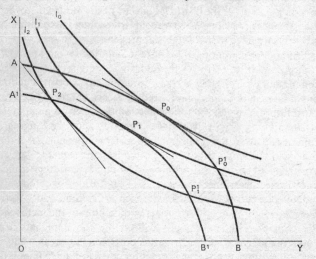

Figure 2

Now the point we are making is that it is the fact that the government has increased its real expenditure, has employed resources, that has shifted inwards the consumers' consumption possibility curve. Taxation has had nothing to do with it.

In a frictionless world of perfectly flexible prices and money wages in which there is always full employment an increase in taxation with no corresponding increase in government real expenditure will be deflationary; prices and money wages will fall but employment will be maintained. Similarly an increase in government real expenditure will reduce the real goods and services available to the private sector. Such a reduction associated with no increase in taxation will be brought about by a change in the relationship between earnings and prices.

With a given change in real government expenditure taxation is important if it is desired to avoid a change in the price level. An increase in real government expenditure accompanied by tax changes that reduce private expenditure by the same amount will leave the general price level unaltered.

In our diagram A^1B^1 represents the new set of consumption possibilities. It is important to note that this curve will represent the consumption possibilities whether the government obtains its revenue by direct or indirect taxes or by an increase in the quantity of money. What is influenced by the tax structure is the exact point on the new consumption possibility curve at which a new equilibrium position is established. If the revenue is raised by a poll tax or an income tax the new position will be P_1 and the relative prices of the two goods will again be the slope of the transformation curve and the indifference curve at P_1 which will be a 'Paretian Optimum'. If, however, the required revenue is raised by an outlay tax, say on B, the position of equilibrium might be P_2. In this case the relative prices of A and B will not be the same as the slope of the transformation curve (this price ratio could be represented in the figure by a straight line drawn tangental to the indifference curve I_2 at P_2) and P_2 which is clearly not a 'Paretian Optimum' is inferior to P_1. In this case the direct tax is preferable to the indirect tax.

This conclusion cannot however be generalized. It only follows if the first position was a 'Paretian Optimum'. If we relax our initial assumption of Perfect Competition it is possible that our zero-government-expenditure position was P_0^1 and not P_0 due to the existence of monopolistic elements in the industry producing A. If the government now carries out its expenditure and if revenue is raised by an income tax or a poll tax, we might move to a position such as P_1^1 on A^1B^1, whereas if an outlay tax had been levied on commodity B we might have moved to a position such as P_1 on

A^1B^1. In this situation an outlay tax would have imposed a smaller burden than an income tax.

The reader will have noticed how similar this last point is to the discussion in the previous part concerning the case for outlay taxes on, say, good A when there is already a tax on good B. Even with the very restrictive assumptions under which we are at present operating, there is no theoretical case in favour of direct taxation unless we know that the initial position was a 'Paretian Optimum'.[22]

Conclusion: a sterile controversy?

We have so far been considering the community aspects of the 'tax problem' under very restrictive assumptions. If we keep the concept of a 'minor social welfare function' but relax the assumption of constant factor supply, we can reach by reasoning very similar to that in the second section of this part of the paper the same conclusion that we reached with respect to the individual consumer. In that case it was suggested that though it could be demonstrated by theoretical reasoning that some indirect tax structure was better than a direct tax structure, one could not be sure which were the appropriate commodities to tax unless one possessed a much greater knowledge about the shape of demand functions than is possessed at the present time.

The value of the theoretical conclusion is even less in the community case. Unless the somewhat foolish assumption that everyone has identical tastes is made it is quite likely that for different consumers different outlay taxes would be necessary as the commodities most complementary with leisure might vary from person to person. In the real world it would not be possible to have such a complicated tax structure. It follows, therefore, that in the com-

22. It is interesting to note that many of the points that we have noticed as having been made during this controversy: the stressing of the importance of initial conditions both with respect to other taxes in operation and with respect to the presence or absence of monopolistic elements, and the suggestion that income taxes impose an excess burden as compared with a poll tax, were made during the well-known Hotelling–Frisch controversy in the 1938 and 1939 volumes of *Econometrica* arising out of Hotelling's presidential address to the Econometric Society in December 1937 (Hotelling, 1938). This, presumably, is yet another illustration of Kenneth Boulding's judgement about 'the fine English tradition that it is much easier to think of something than to look it up' (Boulding, 1952, ch. 1).

munity case even if one knew the shape of the demand functions (which is hardly likely) it would not be possible to take advantage of this knowledge, so as to minimize the burden of government finance.

Similar arguments are applicable when considering the burden of different sorts of direct taxes or the relative magnitudes of the burdens imposed upon different individuals in the same income group but with different tastes by direct and indirect taxes.

With respect to the initial position problem, we have seen that in the community case it becomes even more complicated because of the very likely divergence between prices and marginal costs due to elements of monopoly – the gap of course being different in different industries – and it becomes unreasonable to think that conclusions based on the assumption of ideal initial conditions have any general application or value in the real world.

Even if, owing to the development of our knowledge concerning demand curves and initial positions, it became possible to apply the various theorems concerning the 'direct–indirect tax problem' would this knowledge be of any use? In the real world there are many important issues and conflicts concerning tax policy between political parties and individuals but these issues and conflicts have very little to do with the problems that our disputants have been considering. The effects of different forms of taxation upon saving, work and entrepreneurship; the permissible extent of post-tax income inequality and the proper differentation between earned and unearned income; the appropriateness of particular taxes with respect to administrative costs, extent of possible avoidance or evasion; the extent to which the fiscal system should discriminate against the consumption of particular goods and services: all these are important problems upon which economists have something to contribute and upon which they will be heard with tolerance and interest by the public and politicians. But one cannot see anything likely to interest politicians and the public in the 'direct–indirect tax problem' controversy – even if the above mentioned descriptive and statistical knowledge existed – because these other considerations in the tax field overwhelm so completely the welfare implications – and of course the descriptive and statistical knowledge does not exist. And one cannot blame the public or the politicians for their lack of interest; it is not easy to see any purpose to which this knowledge could be put. We must also remember the doubts we cast – in the introduction to the first part of the paper – upon the value of arguments based solely upon considerations of economic welfare. Tax policy is part of economic policy and economic policy is to do with politics. Other much more general considerations enter into the formulation of tax policy and there is little value in arguing that such and such a tax structure is 'best' merely from a consideration of the economic welfare implications.

Without any hesitation, therefore, I would call the discussion with which I have been dealing a sterile controversy. It is true that recent work has shown that the 1939 views of Miss Joseph and Professor Hicks were not entirely satisfactory and, no doubt, this is important to economists in their role as members of a professional caste, but the practical importance of this is slight.

It seems to me unfortunate that such a barren topic as the 'direct-indirect tax problem' has occupied such an important place in Public Finance discussions in recent years as there is so much information needed (and, in principle, obtainable) in this field of study. Our knowledge of what Mrs Hicks (1948, ch. 9; see also Musgrave, 1953a and b) has called the formal and effective incidence of different taxes and of changes in these taxes is rudimentary, whereas such information is essential if the non-economist decision-taker is to perform his task efficiently.

References
BERRY, D. (1954), in A. T. Peacock (ed.), *Income Redistribution and Social Policy*, Cape.
BOULDING, K. (1952), in H. S. Ellis, (ed.), *Survey of Contemporary Economics*, vol. 2, American Economic Association.
BOULDING, K. (1955), *Economic Analysis*, Hamilton, rev. edn.
CORLETT, W. J., and HAGUE, D. C. (1953–4), 'Complementarity and the excess burden of taxation', *Review of Economic Studies*, vol. 21.
DALTON, H. (1936), *Public Finance*, Routledge, 9th edn.
DAVIDSON, R. K. (1952–3), 'The alleged excess burden of an excise tax in the case of an individual consumer', *Review of Economic Studies*, vol. 20.
DEHOVE, G. (1947), *Impôt, Economie et Politique*, vol. 1, Presses Universitaires de France.
FRIEDMAN, M. (1952a), 'The welfare effects of an income tax and an excise tax', *Journal of Political Economy*, vol. 60.
FRIEDMAN, M. (1952b), 'A reply', *Journal of Political Economy*, August.
HENDERSON, A. M. (1948), 'The case for indirect taxation', *Economic Journal*, vol. 58.

HICKS, J. R. (1939), *Value and Capital*, Oxford University Press, 2nd edn.

HICKS, U. K. (1946), 'The terminology of tax analysis', *Economic Journal*, vol. 56.

HICKS, U. K. (1948), *Public Finance*, Nisbet.

HOTELLING, H. (1938), 'The general welfare in relation to problems of taxation and of railway and utility rates', *Econometrica*, vol. 6.

JOSEPH, M. F. W. (1939), 'The excess burden of indirect taxation', *Review of Economic Studies*, vol. 6, no. 3.

LITTLE, I. M. D. (1951), 'Direct versus indirect taxes', *Economic Journal*, vol. 61.

MARSHALL, A. (1948), *The Principles of Economics*, ch. 12, Macmillan, 9th edn.

MILL, J. S. (1965), in J. M. Robson (ed.), *Principles of Political Economy*, vol. 5, University of Toronto Press.

MUSGRAVE, R. A. (1953a), 'On income', *Journal of Political Economy*, vol. 61.

MUSGRAVE, R. A. (1953b), 'General equilibrium aspects of lucidence theory', *American Economic Review* (supplement).

PAISH, V. F. W. (1941), 'Economic incentive in war-time', *Economica*, vol. 8.

PEACOCK, A. T., and BERRY, D. (1951), 'A note on the theory of income redistribution', *Economica*, vol. 18.

PHELPS BROWN, E. H. (1951), *A Course in Applied Economics*, Pitmans.

PHIPPS, C. G. (1952), 'Friedman's welfare effect', *Journal of Political Economy*, August.

PIGOU, A. C. (1932), *The Economics of Welfare*, Part 2, Macmillan.

PIGOU, A. C. (1928, 1947), *Public Finance*, Macmillan.

ROBBINS, L. (1930), 'On the elasticity of income in terms of effect', *Economica*, vol. 10.

ROLPH, E. R., and BREAK, G. F. (1949), 'The welfare aspects of excise taxes', *Journal of Political Economy*, vol. 57.

SCHWARTZ, E., and MOORE, D. A. (1951), 'The distorting effects of direct taxation', *American Economic Review*, vol. 41.

SCITOVSKY, T. (1951), *Welfare and Competition*, Irwin.

STIGLER, G. J. (1946), *The Theory of Price*, Macmillan.

WALD, H. P. (1944–5), 'The classical indictment of indirect taxation', *Quarterly Journal of Economics*, vol. 58.

WALKER, D. (1955), 'Some comments on the taxation of personal income and expenditure in the United Kingdom', *Public Finance*, vol. 9, no. 2, pp. 191–213.

17 E. D. Domar and R. A. Musgrave

The Effects of Income Taxes on Risk Taking

E. D. Domar and R. A. Musgrave, 'Proportional taxation and risk-taking',
Quarterly Journal of Economics, vol. 58, 1944, pp. 387–422.

The effects of income taxation on investment have been discussed
in economic literature with varying emphasis. Prior to the debacle
of the late twenties the detrimental effects of taxation upon the
volume of savings were stressed. During the thirties economic
thinking and experience indicated that the decision to invest
constitutes a crucial link between the setting aside of savings
and the flow of funds into actual investment. Accordingly, the
emphasis of the discussion was shifted to the effects of taxation
on the investment of available funds, particularly on investment in risky ventures. In this paper we examine the basic
aspects of this problem, which will be of vital importance after
the war.

An investment involves the possibility of a loss. It will not be
undertaken unless the expected return appears sufficiently
promising. In every investment decision the investor must weigh
the advantage of a greater return, or *yield*, against the disadvantage of a possible loss, or *risk*. These two variables serve as
tools for the analysis of the problem.

The effects of taxation upon risk taking are analyzed in two
steps: first, we consider how the imposition of a tax, under varying
conditions, affects the yield and the risk of an investment (or more
correctly, of a whole combination of various assets); second, we
inquire how the investor will react to these changes. That the tax
reduces the yield, is entirely evident and has been much emphasized;
but the equally important fact that the tax may also reduce the
degree of risk has received little attention. Its significance has

recently been pointed out by A. P. Lerner, to whom this paper owes a considerable debt.[1]

By imposing an income tax on the investor, the Treasury appoints itself as his partner, who will always share in his gains, but whose share in his losses will depend upon the investor's ability to offset losses against other income. Three cases may be distinguished:

1. If losses cannot be offset, the investor carries the entire burden of the loss. The tax reduces the yield (and even by a higher percentage than the tax rate), but leaves the degree of risk unchanged, so that the compensation per unit of risk taking is reduced. This is the case most frequently discussed in the literature.

2. If a complete offset of losses is possible, the result is very different. Suppose the investor receives an income of $1000, which is independent of the investment in question, so that after a 25 per cent tax he retains $750. If he now makes an investment and suffers a loss of $200, this loss can be fully deducted from his other income, so that only $800 remains subject to tax. Accordingly, the tax is reduced to $200 and his total income remaining after the loss, net of the tax, is now $600, as compared with $750 before the investment was made and the loss suffered. The net loss is thus only $150, the remaining $50, or 25 per cent, having been absorbed by the Treasury in the form of a reduced tax bill on the investor's other income. The yield *and* the risk of the investment have been reduced by the rate of the tax, so that the return per unit of risk taking remains unchanged.

3. If only a partial offset of losses is possible, the yield is reduced by a greater percentage than the degree of risk, and the results fall between those of cases 1 and 2.

How will the investor react to these changes in yield and risk, which the tax has produced? Prior to the tax, he was in an equilibrium position, which gave him the most advantageous combination of yield and risk available. After one or both of these variables are

1. See Lerner (1943). A similar point was also made by Simons (1938, p. 21). Also see Twentieth-Century Fund (1937, p. 292) and Bowman and Bach (1943, p. 768). As far as we are aware, the argument is neglected in the standard texts on Public Finance.

An empirical study of some phases of our problem has appeared since this paper went to print. See Butters and Lintner (1944).

changed, he may wish to change his position, that is, take more or less risk. We again consider the same three cases:

1. Since, without loss offset, the yield is cut, while risk is unchanged, the compensation for risk taking is reduced. Risk taking has become less attractive, so that the investor will want to take less risk. But the reduction in yield also means a lower income from his investments. To restore his income, the investor will try to take more risk, since risky investments can be expected to have a higher yield. These two forces are operating in opposite directions. Theoretically the result is uncertain; practical evidence would indicate that the investor is likely to shift in the direction of less risk.

2. If losses can be offset, and the Treasury assumes part of the risk, as well as of the yield, a distinction must be drawn between *private* risk (and yield), which is carried by the investor, and the *total* risk (and yield), which includes also the share borne by the Treasury. It is the private risk (and yield) of an investment that is reduced by the tax; the total risk (and yield) remains, of course, unchanged. Since the private risk and yield are reduced by the same percentage, risk taking has not become less attractive. The inducement to take less risk, which was present in the first case, has disappeared. The investor's income, however, has been reduced and to restore it, he will take more risk, although the private risk taken after adjustment to the tax need not equal the pre-tax level. If the investor had retained the original asset combination, its total risk would have remained the same. But since the investor was shown to adjust his asset combination so as to increase his private risk above the unadjusted level to which it was lowered by the tax, total risk must have increased above the pre-tax level.

3. Under conditions of partial loss deduction, the yield is reduced by a greater percentage than risk. Both forces will be operating as in case 1, and the outcome will be uncertain. But there appears little doubt that the higher is the rate of loss offset, the higher will be the degree of risk taken after the tax.

The assumptions under which these conclusions have been reached are developed later on and are summarized in the final section.

A shift towards a more risky investment (or rather asset combination) may be accomplished by reducing the proportion of the investor's total assets held in cash, that is, by larger total investment, or through a change from less to more risky investments.

There is no question that increased risk taking in either or both forms is highly desirable (except during acute boom conditions) and that therefore a higher degree of loss deduction is of vital importance. The extent to which loss offset is possible in actual practice depends on the offset provisions in the tax law and upon the availability of other income in each instance.

There are limited provisions for loss offset in the tax law. Since a tax is imposed on net income, the law necessarily permits the offset of investment losses realized in a given period against income received in that period, subject, however, to the important limitation that, with minor exceptions, capital losses can be offset against capital gains only. The likelihood that sufficient other income will be available to the taxpayer is increased greatly if losses made in one period can be carried forward or backward against income made in other periods. The personal and corporation income tax law now provides for a limited carry-back and carry-forward (two years each) of business net operating losses and for a five-year carry-forward of long-term capital losses. Possible changes in the rate schedule introduce additional uncertainties into the investor's calculations.

The extent to which investors may utilize these provisions depends upon the availability of other income. Here the position of various taxpayers differs greatly. A large corporation or a large-scale financial investor may undertake a risky investment as a side line, and know that possible losses are covered by other income which is reasonably certain to be derived from the main line of business. It is not necessary, of course, that the losses should be realized in the form of capital losses; they may also take the form of a lower taxable income resulting from depreciation costs being charged against other income. Further, a large corporation is assured of the possibility of loss offset as long as the investment in question does not exceed the minimum net income (low as it may be relative to total invested capital) which the management is reasonably certain to derive during the period of carry-over. Thus, if a public utility or a life insurance company were to make a small investment (small relative to other income from operations or interest on gilt-edged bonds) in a very risky venture, it could be quite certain of a loss offset, and would thus have a great advantage over a small competitor who might consider the same venture. The discrimination is even more flagrant in the case of loss carry-back, which gives an 'old' corporation (that is, a corporation with past net income) the certainty of possible loss offset, thus placing it in a very advantageous position as compared with a new company. Inequities of this type will tend to increase economic concentration, and may lower the volume of new investment.

It is evident that the tax law should be adjusted to create the most favorable possible condition for loss offset for all types of investors. This raises numerous technical problems which are not considered in this paper. A careful analysis should be made of the length of the carry-over period required for this purpose, and, if necessary and feasible, unlimited carry-forward of losses should be permitted, supplemented by a limited carry-back. The possibilities of averaging income over a period of years should also be explored, and the present differential treatment of capital gains and losses, as well as the possibility of providing more flexible depreciation schedules, should be examined. These considerations by no means apply to the corporation tax only, but are equally if not more important with respect to the personal income tax.

A less orthodox alternative to an extended carry-over of losses might be considered, under which the Treasury would reimburse the taxpayer during the very period in which the net loss was made. Besides encouraging risk-taking, an arrangement of this kind might also contribute to cyclical stability by raising effective tax rates during prosperity and lowering them during depression. Even if some loss in revenue results, the condition for investment will be more favorable under a somewhat higher tax rate, together with more complete loss offset than under a lower tax rate accompanied by more imperfect offset conditions.

In the following five sections, the analysis is carried out in greater detail. In this next section the general rationale of investment behavior is described. In the following three sections the effects of taxation on risk-taking are examined under the assumptions of no loss offset, full loss offset and partial loss offset, respectively. Some limitations of the analysis are reviewed in the final section.

The Rationale of Investment Behavior

The essence of our problem is the change in the investor's behavior under the impact of the tax. Just as the usual theory of tax shifting is but an application of the principles of price theory to a particular change in data caused by the imposition of a tax, so the solution of the present problem consists in applying a theory of investment behavior to a similar change. Although the discussion of various investment problems is common in economic literature, no integrated theory of investment behavior applicable to the analysis of effects of taxation has come to our attention. While this is not the place to develop such a theory, it will be necessary to agree at the outset on those aspects of investment behavior which are directly related to our problem. For purposes of simplicity, our analysis is mainly concerned with the case of financial investment, some special characteristics of real investment being mentioned in the closing section. In addition, the following assumptions are made: (a) a *given* amount of investment funds is available to the investor; (b) investments are divisible into small units, that is, 'lumpiness' is excluded; (c) the investment market is perfectly atomistic, so that the investor can neglect the effect of his decisions on yields; (d) the investor's expectations, gross of the tax, are unaffected by the imposition of the tax and by resulting government expenditures.

To handle our problem, quantitative values for the yield and the degree of risk of an investment are needed; and in the absence of a better approach, they are obtained by means of a probability distribution which the investor will construct for each available investment opportunity.[2] Each possible yield, positive or negative,

2. For examples of the traditional probability approach, see Fisher (1906, ch. 16), and Pigou (1932, Appendix I). For a bibliography of more recent writings on risk theory, see Fellner (1943, p. 196).

The probability approach to risk theory implies that it is 'reasonable to set up the assumption of quantified probability estimates as an idealization of actual business practice' Hart (1940a, p. 52). Objections may be raised to this assumption, as in fact they may be raised against most any feature of the 'homo economicus'. For purposes of this paper, which does not discuss risk theory as such, the probability method is adopted, because no satisfactory alternative approach to the subject of risk theory has been developed. The theory of investment behavior, as developed by G. L. S. Shackle, divides expectations into those which would and would not cause 'surprise', and thus avoids having to attach numerical probabilities to all expected yields. It appears to us that the resulting indeterminacy makes it impossible to derive satisfactory tools for the comparison of relative advantages of different investments and therefore for the analysis of taxation effects (cf. Shackle, 1940, pp. 44–8, and 1942, pp. 77–94).

will include the recurrent income from the investment (such as interest or dividends), as well as the change in capital value which the investor expects to realize. Thus, no distinction is made here between capital gains and other income or capital losses and other losses. Each expected yield will be net of all monetary costs of investment. The dollar amounts are transformed into percentage yields on the amount invested by a process similar to that used by Keynes in defining the marginal efficiency of capital.[3] In constructing the probability distribution, the investor will consider all those circumstances which appear significant to him, such as the period of holding, possible developments during this period, and the conditions accompanying the sale. Thus, not only expectations regarding the specific investment and general market developments will be included, but also personal circumstances, such as a sudden need of cash because of a broken arm. Since income for tax purposes is always expressed in dollar amounts, our analysis is carried out in cash terms, cash being used as the numéraire.

From the probability distribution thus constructed, the investor will compute the mathematical expectation of the percentage yields, to be indicated by y.[4] It will prove helpful in the following discussion to separate y into its negative component r and its positive component g. Thus, if $q_1, q_2, \ldots, q_{k+1}, \ldots, q_n$ are the expected rates of return, such that $q_i < q_{i+1}$ and $q_k = 0$, and if the probability of the occurrence of q_i is p_i, so that

$$\sum_{i=1}^{n} p_i = 1,$$

we arrive at the following definitions:

3. That is, the investor will compute the rate of discount which equates the present value of the prospective returns with the amount invested. Cf. Keynes (1936, p. 135), and Fisher (1906, chs. 13 and 14).

4. The use of the mathematical expectation appears to us to be superior to that of the most probable value, employed by some other authors in similar problems. See, for instance, Fellner (1943, p. 198). If, for reasons of simplicity, the probability distribution is to be represented by one variable, the latter should reflect as much as possible the changes in any part of the probability distribution. The significance of this condition for an analysis of taxation effects will be seen presently.

$$r = -\sum_{i=1}^{k} q_i p_i \qquad \mathbf{1}^5$$

$$g = \sum_{i=k+1}^{n} q_i p_i \qquad \mathbf{2}$$

$$y = \sum_{i=1}^{n} q_i p_i = g - r \qquad \mathbf{3}$$

The magnitude of the actuarial value is not the only factor determining the investor's choice. Other characteristics must also be considered, though for purposes of this analysis their number must be limited.

Investment decisions are made in spite of uncertainty with respect to the relevant data and their implications. No investor is sure that his estimated probability distribution is entirely correct, but the degree of uncertainty will vary with different investors and different investments. It will be a factor in the investment decision. Yet it is extremely difficult to express the degree of uncertainty involved in workable terms.[6] For our purpose it is sufficient to say that the prevalence of uncertainty may induce the investor to require a somewhat higher return than would be required otherwise.

The very fact that the actuarial value is based on a probability distribution indicates that the investment involves some degree of

5. Since the values of all q's from the beginning to q_k are negative, r is positive.

6. The uncertainty factor has been emphasized in recent discussions of investment behavior, according to which the investor is, in fact, confronted not with a single probability distribution, but with a probability distribution of probability distributions. A. G. Hart has pointed out that the problem of uncertainty cannot be solved by boiling down the set of probability distributions into a single 'super' distribution, since the latter would conceal certain characteristics of the component distributions which are relevant for economic planning. This paper being a first step in the analysis of our subject, these complications, which will hardly affect the major results, are avoided here. Cf. Hart and Tintner (1942, pp. 110–18) and Hart (1940b). See also Makower and Marschak (1938, pp. 271 ff.), and Hicks (1935, pp. 1–19).

doubt as to whether or not the actual return will fall within specified limits. The investor will undoubtedly be interested in a number of limits, and in comparing two investments with different actuarial values may or may not wish to apply the same limits to each. Of all possible questions which the investor may ask, the most important one, it appears to us, is concerned with the probability of the actual yield being less than zero, that is, with the probability of a loss. This is the essence of *risk*.[7] Since the investor is not only interested in the probability of a negative return, but also in the chances of suffering losses of various magnitudes, the coefficient of risk should be defined more precisely as a function of losses and their probabilities. This can be done most simply by defining risk as the already familiar expression r, i.e. the summation of all possible losses multiplied by their respective probabilities as defined in **1**.[8]

7. The terminology employed here broadly agrees with that used in recent literature; cf., for instance, H. Makower and J. Marschak (1938, p. 271), and Hart and Tintner (1942, pp. 92, 110).

The term 'risk' has been given different connotations by various authors, but it has been generally described as a property of a known probability distribution. It has been expressed, for instance, as the probability of obtaining a smaller return than y (Pigou, 1932, p. 776), or as the coefficient of variation. The expression in the text appears to be most useful for our purposes, because among the factors underlying investment behavior and affected by a proportional tax we regard risk as defined in the text as by far the most important.

The term 'uncertainty' usually applies to anticipations where the probability distribution itself is not exactly known. This is in general agreement with Professor Knight's use of the term, although 'uncertainty' in his sense would appear to apply only where probability estimates are assumed not to be cardinal. See. H. Makower and J. Marschak (1938, p. 271), and A. G. Hart (1940, p. 111).

8. A further refinement of our definition of risk may be made. If the market pays a return on an entirely riskless investment, the investor when purchasing a given investment incurs not only the risk of losing a part of his present wealth, but also of losing the opportunity of obtaining a certain return from a riskless investment. If, therefore, the return on an entirely riskless investment is equal to l, expected losses should be measured, not from the zero point of the probability distribution, but from l. Thus, if in our original probability distribution of $q_1, q_2, \ldots, q^k, \ldots, q_m, \ldots, q_n$ there is a $q_m = l$, the adjusted degree of risk may be redefined as

$$r' = -\sum_{i=1}^{m}(q_i - l)\,p_i = -\sum_{i=1}^{k}q_ip_i + \left(-\sum_{i=k+1}^{m}q_ip_i + l\sum_{i=1}^{m}p_i\right) = r + \lambda.$$

By considering r, the most relevant aspect of the dispersion of the probability distribution is accounted for in our analysis. If an investor is to undertake an investment involving a possible loss of his wealth, a compensation will definitely be demanded. The case is less clear in regard to other aspects of the dispersion. If a choice is to be made between investments with different probability distributions, but which have the same yield and risk, it may well be that one investor would prefer the possibility of a large gain, although the probability of obtaining an even moderate return may be low, while another investor would prefer a greater probability of obtaining a moderate return, even though the possibility of substantial gain may be small. It is thus not clear that a greater dispersion, other things being equal, represents a disutility and commands a market return. This is not to say that the dispersion of the distribution will not be a factor in investment decisions. A more elaborate analysis would allow for additional variables defining the shape of the probability distribution, for example, in terms of the standard deviation, the probability of obtaining less or more than a given 'minimum yield', or the probability of suffering more or less than a given 'maximum loss'. For purposes of this analysis, however, it is assumed that the investor will consider changes in y and r only.[9]

From the preceding discussion we thus emerge with two tools of analysis: r – the degree of risk, and y – the yield of the investment, which is regarded as a compensation for risk taking. Aside from the already considered question whether a compensation is needed for the uncertainty and dispersion of the probability distribution, the definition of y as the compensation for risk taking may meet with two objections. First, it may be argued that y should also contain a compensation for the necessary 'effort' of making an investment. Second, the reader will wonder what has happened to the compensation for parting with liquidity.

In an economy like that of the United States, the difference between r and r' is likely to be of minor importance, since l may be expected to be quite small or zero. Therefore, this correction may be omitted for most of the argument and will be mentioned only where it may be particularly significant.

9. This limitation would probably not be acceptable for the analysis of a progressive tax, for which the entire shape of the probability distribution would be important.

As stated previously, y is defined as net of all monetary costs of investment, so that the only element that is disregarded is the personal 'effort' of making the investment. But this effort is subject to enormous economies of large scale, which are also available to smaller investors through the services of investment trusts. It appears to be of no great importance. In those few cases, however, where the element of personal effort may affect the results, it will be taken into consideration.[10]

The problem of liquidity remains to be considered. As expounded by Keynes, cash is held because of the speculative, precautionary and income (and business) motives (Keynes, 1936, chs. 13 and 15). The speculative motive refers to possible losses due to changes in interest rate, and thus represents a component of our concept of risk. The same holds true for the precautionary motive, which is concerned with the possibility of a loss due to the unavailability of cash at some future date. The analysis of the income motive results in a similar conclusion: the reason why an investor does not invest all his funds up to his last dollar is the knowledge that he will need some cash for current expenditures at an early date, so that the investment of the last portion of his funds would almost certainly result in a net loss, since investment expenses would be large relative to gross yield and a rush sale would probably be necessary. Thus, the three elements of the liquidity preference represent nothing but the fear of loss, and are therefore accounted for in our probability distribution and in the values of y and r.[11]

10. Thus, if it can be assumed that the net investment effort requires a minimum compensation, to be indicated by e, which is a constant percentage rate on the amount invested, then the adjusted compensation for risk-taking may be redefined as $y' = y - e$.

11. This view of the supply price for investment funds has certain implications for the theory of interest. If the return for waiting is zero (which, of course, depends upon institutional and other factors) and if Keynes' liquidity preference represents merely special types of risk the question must be asked why the return for these elements of risk (namely, marketability and changes in the interest rate) should be separated from other risk factors and identified as *the* rate of interest. This does not mean that for certain purposes a distinction between various types of risk might not be useful, but the more inclusive is the definition of interest – that is, the more complete the different types of risk the return for which is included – the clearer becomes the need for discarding the idea of *the* rate of interest and for talking about the returns available on different investments. We hope to develop this idea at a future date.

So far, the discussion has referred to single investments. Actually the investor is concerned with obtaining the most desirable use of all his assets, consisting of various investments and cash. It should be noted that a distinction is made here between an *investment combination*, which refers to that part of the investor's wealth which is not held in cash form, and an *asset combination*, which includes both investments and cash. It will be convenient to assume, at first, that the investor intends to invest all his funds, and then to introduce varying holdings of cash. To the extent that the probability distributions of various possible investments are independent of one another, their combination will reduce the degree of risk in accordance with the usual probability theory. But actually the probability distributions of most investments are somewhat interdependent, primarily due to their common dependence on general business conditions. A careful selection of investments may thus be more important than the choice of a large number of different investments.

Let the ordinate and abscissa of the points A and B in Figure 1 indicate the degree of risk and the yield of two different asset combinations consisting *entirely* of the investments A and B respecttively. Thus no cash is held at all. If the two investments are combined, the magnitudes of the r and y of each combination will depend upon the r and y of the components, the ratio at which they are combined, and their degree of independence. If they are completely interdependent, the magnitudes of y and r of the combinations will equal the weighted averages of the components and will hence be located on a straight line AB. If, as is more likely to be the case, they are more or less independent, the r of each combination will be more or less below the weighted average of the r of the components. This reflects the principle that diversification reduces the dispersion of a probability distribution. Therefore the rs and ys will fall on a curve such as ACB.

Besides investments, the investor's asset combination will also include a proportion of cash. Cash differs from investments by having a zero risk and zero yield. Cash holdings are riskless, since they cannot give rise to losses. This is the case because opportunity costs, that is, income not received because investment opportunities were missed, do not enter our analysis. Losses or gains in the real value of cash, due to price changes, are excluded likewise, because the entire analysis is in terms of cash. An expected appreciation or depreciation of investments due to general price changes is already accounted for in the estimating of probable gains and losses. Therefore in Figure 1 an asset combination consisting of cash only is located at the origin.

Beginning with an asset combination consisting of investments only, such as represented by a point C, the investor can move his combination towards the origin by increasing the proportion of his assets held in cash. The dotted curve CO described by this movement will be called the *cash-investment curve*. As the pro-

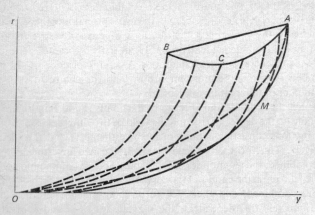

Figure 1   The optimum asset curve

portion of cash increases, the risk and the yield of the whole asset combination decline, since cash has zero risk and yield. The point C will move towards O, not along a straight line, but rather along a curve of the type CO, since r falls faster than y. The reason is that as the proportion of cash in the asset combination increases, it becomes less likely that a forced sale under unfavorable conditions will be necessary. Therefore the risk of the *investment* combination will decline, while its yield may even rise.[12]

12. It is quite possible that, as the investor moves down along the cash-investment curve, the yield of the whole asset combination may increase at first, since he will escape the probable loss that would result from the investment of the last portion of his funds. In order to analyse what happens on

The cash-investment curve, as drawn in Figure 1, does not indicate the proportion of cash in the asset combination corresponding to any given point on the curve. To measure the cash ratio, a third dimension would be needed. This is an important limitation of our analysis, since it makes it impossible to allocate changes in cash holdings and changes in the riskiness of investments held.

In order to find the best available asset combination, the investor will draw all possible cash-investment curves between each point indicating an investment combination and the origin, as shown by the dotted curves in Figure 1. It is evident that for each level of risk there will be a large (infinite) number of asset combinations with varying proportions of the investments A, B and cash. Of these, however, only the one with the highest yield is relevant.[13] The locus of these points of maximum yield, AMO, is *the* curve which describes the investor's evaluation of the market situation and which is the principal tool for our analysis. We shall call it the *optimum-asset curve*.[14]

In order to determine the investor's choice of the best position on the optimum-asset curve, a preference map between y and r can be constructed. Again y is measured along the abscissa and r along the ordinate. The essence of the map is a comparison between the investor's advantage of obtaining income and the disadvantage of jeopardizing his wealth. In our analysis both income and losses, measured in terms of y and r, are expressed as percentage rates on a given dollar amount of wealth. Therefore, any

the upper part of the curve, it would be necessary to allow for the possibility of borrowing, which may become profitable as the investor moves up along the curve. We prefer to disregard borrowing, so as not to complicate the general discussion.

13. It follows from subsequent analysis that the imposition of a tax will not change the yield rating of various asset combinations with the same degree of risk.

14. The optimum-asset curve can be expected to be smooth and continuous, because we have assumed an infinite divisibility of all assets. The investor can, therefore, combine the three assets, namely, the investment A, B and cash, in an infinite number of proportions which, most likely, will eliminate kinks. The case will be even stronger if more than two investments are considered.

changes in wealth will result in a change in the indifference map.[15] But since the amount of wealth is assumed to be constant, changes in percentage returns are equivalent to corresponding changes in income.

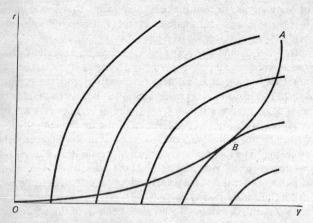

Figure 2   The equilibrium position

The indifference map presented in Figure 2 and in the other figures is constructed on the basis of the following conditions: it is assumed, first, that for any individual the marginal utility of income declines with increasing income, and second, that the marginal disutility of risk-taking rises with increasing risk. We also assume the marginal utility of income to be independent of risk and vice versa. Our analysis being limited to the immediate effects of a tax on investment, without regard for secondary effects such as changes in wealth, this assumption appears reasonable.

Since the slope of each indifference curve, or *the marginal rate of risk-taking*, equals the ratio of the marginal utility of income to the marginal disutility of risk, the slopes of the indifference curves must be positive: an increase in y along any indifference curve

15. The indifference map could also have been expressed in dollar amounts. Then the pattern would have been independent of changes in wealth, which would have been reflected in a shift of the optimum-asset curve. For the purposes of the present analysis, the approach chosen seemed more convenient.

must be accompanied by an increase in r and vice versa. The application of the two assumptions, stated above, to the preference map gives the indifference curves the following three properties:

1. The slope of any one indifference curve must be decreasing upward and to the right. This is the result of *either* one or both assumptions.

2. The slopes of the indifference curves must decline with increasing values of y for any given value of r – the result of the first assumption.

3. The slopes of the indifference curves must decline with increasing values of r for any given value of y – the result of the second assumption.

Property 1, used throughout our argument, is more certain than properties 2 and 3, since it holds true even if either one of the assumptions is omitted. Property 3 is not needed for our purposes.[16] Finally, property 2, which rests on the first assumption only, is used throughout our discussion, but sceptics who do not believe in it will find comfort in the footnotes below.[17]

The equilibrium position of the investor can now be easily found by establishing the point of tangency of the optimum-asset curve, ABO, with one of the indifference curves, as shown by point B on Figure 2.

Taxation without Loss Offset

We turn now to the effects of a tax on investment. By imposing a tax without loss offset, the Treasury shares in the investor's gains, while leaving his losses unchanged. We consider first the effects of

16. The second assumption and property (3) are included here for the sake of completeness only. They would enter into the analysis of related problems, such as the effects of insurance against loss on risk-taking.

17. If the marginal utility of income is assumed to be constant, the slopes of the indifference curves will be constant with increasing values of y for any given value of r. In other words, the curves will be horizontally parallel. If income utility is thus assumed constant, the second assumption (increasing disutility of risk-taking) must be applied, since the tax will produce no effects on risk-taking whatsoever, if both income utility and risk disutility are held constant. See also footnotes 22 (p. 396), 27 (p. 401) and 34 (p. 409).

For a more thorough discussion of the properties of indifference curves, see Schultz (1938, pp. 18–22), and Hicks (1939, ch. 1).

the tax on the magnitudes of y and r, and then the investor's reaction to this change.

Let the rate of the tax be indicated by t, $(0 < t < 1)$, and let y_t, r_t and g_t indicate the magnitudes of these variables after the tax. From **1** and **2** it is evident that

$$g_t = g(1-t) \qquad \qquad \textbf{4}$$

and

$$r_t = r, \qquad \qquad \textbf{5}$$

since by assumption, no losses can be deducted.[18]

Therefore,

$$y_t = g(1-t) - r = y(1-t) - rt \qquad \qquad \textbf{6}$$

from **6** we find that

$$y_t < y(1-t). \qquad \qquad \textbf{7}$$

Thus the rate of yield is reduced by a greater percentage than the rate of the tax. This, of course, should be expected, because all gains are reduced by the rate of the tax, while all losses are left unchanged. When $t \geqslant \dfrac{y}{g}$ we obtain $y_t \leqslant 0$. In other words, if the tax is sufficiently high, the rate of yield becomes zero or negative.

It is often stated that the yield of more risky investments is hit particularly hard by a tax. It is not clear whether this statement should be interpreted in the absolute or relative sense. To the extent that more risky investments have a higher yield, they will obviously suffer a greater absolute reduction. Similarly, out of any two investments with the same degree of risk, the one with a higher yield – that is, the more attractive one – will be hit harder in the absolute sense. It appears to us, however, that the relative reduction is the more significant of the two, and there the argument is far from evident.

Let a indicate the fraction by which y is reduced by the tax so that

$$a = \frac{y - y_t}{y}. \qquad \qquad \textbf{8}$$

18. If instead of r we use r', as defined in footnote 8 (p. 384), the tax will reduce the adjusted degree of risk somewhat. Since the tax reduced the yield of a perfectly safe investment as of all other investments, λ becomes $\lambda(1-t)$ and $r'_t = r + \lambda(1-t)$, which is smaller than $r' = r + \lambda$. But since λ is likely to be small, the reduction in risk will not be substantial.

Substituting the values of y and y_t from **3** and **6**, we obtain[19]

$$a = \left(1 + \frac{r}{y}\right)t. \qquad\qquad 9$$

Thus, a is not a function of risk, but of r/y. This expression may be called the degree of tax sensitivity, and will be indicated by s.

Figure 3 shows that s can be interpreted geometrically as being the slope of the line connecting any point representing a given asset combination with the origin. It also demonstrates that the degree of risk and the degree of tax sensitivity are different concepts, and that there is no apparent reason in general why a higher degree of risk should be accompanied by a higher degree of tax sensitivity. Thus, while the degrees of risk of the points p_1, p_2 and p_3 are $r_1 > r_2 > r_3$, their degrees of tax sensitivity are $s_3 > s_1 > s_2$. It must be noted, however, that if a comparison is

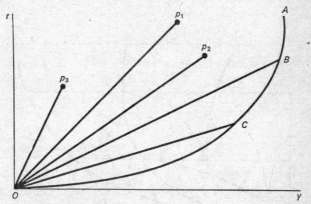

Figure 3   Tax sensitivity

made among points located on the same optimum-asset curve, $ABCO$, a point with a higher degree of risk (B) will also be more tax sensitive than a point with a lower degree of risk (C).[20]

19. $a = \dfrac{y - y^t}{y} = \dfrac{y - y(1-t) + r^t}{y} = \left(1 + \dfrac{r}{y}\right)t.$

20. The problem becomes more complex in the case of progressive taxation. To the extent that probability distributions with a higher degree of risk are also characterized by a longer right tail, they will probably be more tax sensitive than less risky distributions.

As the yield is cut by the tax, the investor may wish to change the asset combination chosen by him prior to the imposition of the tax. The adjustment will depend upon both the reduction in yields and the investor's preferences. It will be the result of the income and substitution effects. On the one hand, the tax will reduce the compensation per unit of risk y/r because y is reduced while r is left unchanged. The investor will therefore tend to take less risk. On the other hand, a reduction in y means that his total income is reduced, which will induce him to take more risk. The substitution and income effects will thus work in opposite directions, and the outcome will depend upon the circumstances of each case. The situation is somewhat similar to that in the labor market, where a fall in wage rates may or may not result in a decreased supply of labor. General opinion and empirical evidence would indicate, however, that a shift towards less risk appears more likely.

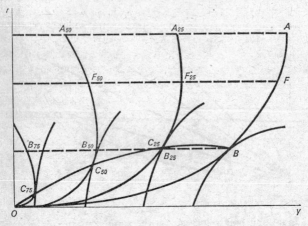

Figure 4   No loss offset

A geometrical analysis of the problem may permit some more definite conclusions. Let ABO (Figure 4) indicate the position of the optimum asset curve prior to the imposition of the tax, and let B be the equilibrium point. When a tax is imposed, each point of the asset curve suffers a reduction in y, in accordance with its degree of tax sensitiveness. It will move to the left along a horizontal line, since the degree of risk remains unchanged by the tax. Thus, any point F moves to F_{25}, F_{50}, etc., and so does the whole asset curve, ABO, which now becomes $A_{25}B_{25}O$, $A_{50}B_{50}O$, and so on, the subscripts indicating the rate of the tax. Because the tax sensitiveness of any point on the asset curve rises with risk, the upper part of the curve bends leftward as the tax rate increases, so that, as shown in Figure 4, its upper part becomes negative, if the tax is sufficiently heavy.

The investor who before the tax was located at the equilibrium point B, will, after a 25 per cent tax, find himself at B_{25}. This point is not an equilibrium position. He will therefore move up along the asset curve $A_{25}B_{25}O$ to the new equilibrium position C_{25}, located at the point of tangency of $A_{25}B_{25}O$ with an indifference curve, where his risk will exceed that taken before the tax. In the case of a 50 per cent tax, the corresponding adjustment would have been a downward move from B_{50} to C_{50}. It should be noted that the price of risk-taking y/r falls (increases) as the investor moves up (down) the optimum asset curve, which produces a secondary substitution effect and acts as a check to his movement.

Whenever an investor shifts to a more risky asset combination, he may do so by taking more risky investments or holding less cash or, most likely, by applying both methods at the same time.

As the optimum asset curve moves to the left, the new equilibrium positions describe the curve $BC_{25}C_{50}C_{75}O$, which will be called the *tax-asset curve* (Figure 4). It first rises and then gradually falls towards the origin. Its shape, proceeding this time from left to right, can be explained in the following manner. If the return on risk taking is close to zero – that is, if market prospects are extremely poor – the investor will take little risk, if any. As the market improves, he will take more risk. Finally, as his income increases, due to improved market conditions, he may once more become less willing to take risk. The result is determined by the interaction between the substitution and income effects.[21]

21. The faster the slopes of the indifference curves fall as the rate of yield increases along any given horizontal line, that is, the more the investor's marginal rate of risk-taking is (inversely) affected by the size of his income, the sooner will the tax-asset curve begin to fall. Since an increasing tax rate makes the investor move from right to left, an investor who 'tires' quickly of taking risk as his income increases, is more apt to shift to more risky investments as a result of the tax than is another investor whose willingness to take

It follows that if an investor (with a given amount of wealth) is optimistic about the market outlook, so that the optimum asset curve is further down and to the right, the effect of a tax on risk taking is more favorable or less detrimental than in the case of a darker market outlook. If the tax is very heavy, the investor may prefer to hold his entire assets in cash.

The subjective nature of the problem should be emphasized. The indifference curves, by their very definition, are only expressions of the investor's preferences, and the optimum asset curve represents his personal evaluation of the market situation. Since the same market situation may appear more favorable to one investor than to another, it is quite possible that a given tax may induce the more optimistic investor to take more risk, while driving his more pessimistic colleague out of the market. But the general conclusion is likely to hold that a relatively low tax imposed under depressed economic conditions, when expectations are bad, may have more harmful effects on investments than a much higher tax imposed under more favorable conditions.[22]

The argument is frequently presented that income taxes discourage risk taking, because (i) the yield for risky investments is particularly sensitive to taxation, and (ii) because more tax sensitive investments are avoided by the investor.[23] The first part of the argument has already been dealt with above (p. 392). In regard to the second part, it must be emphasized that tax sensitiveness is by no means the only factor which determines the investor's reaction to the tax. As has been shown, his choice depends both on the original position of the optimum asset curve, and on its movement, as well as on the slopes of the indifference curves. Unless special assumptions are made in respect to these factors, the choice need

---

risk is less affected by the size of his income. In the extreme case, the investor who insists on a given income, irrespective of the risk involved, will be taking higher and higher risk as the rate of the tax increases.

22. As promised above, the argument is reconsidered on the assumption that the marginal utility of income remains constant with an increasing y, so that the indifference curves are horizontally parallel. In that case, there is no income effect. The tax asset curve moves downward throughout, and the investor takes less risk.

23. See, for instance, Moulton (1940, p. 296), and for the version of the argument presented in the following paragraph, Black (1939, p. 222).

not be in favor of the less tax sensitive investment. As a matter of fact, the concept of tax sensitiveness is not a very essential part of the argument, and the whole problem could well be analysed without it.

Another version of the argument runs as follows. Prior to imposition of a tax, the investor is indifferent between a more risky investment, bearing, say, 10 per cent, and a less risky investment, bearing, say, 3 per cent, the difference of 7 per cent being just sufficient to compensate the investor for the additional risk of the second investment. If now a 50 per cent tax is imposed and both yields are cut by one-half (in fact, they are likely to be reduced by different percentages), the difference is reduced to 3·5 per cent, which is not sufficient to compensate for the difference in risk. Hence the conclusion that the investor will take the less risky investment. Evidently the argument implies that the investor will be indifferent between any two investments (or asset combinations) as long as the difference between their rates of yield remains constant, irrespective of the level of the yields themselves. This means that the indifference curves are assumed to be horizontally parallel, or in other words that the marginal utility of income is constant. For a discussion of this special case, the reader is referred to footnotes 17 (p. 391) and 22 (p. 396) above.

Taxation with Full Loss Offset

We shall now assume a complete offset of losses. This implies that the investor is assured of a sufficient amount of income derived from other sources (than the asset combination), and that adequate provisions for loss offset are made in the law. If he suffers a loss from his asset combination, he can then reduce his other taxable income by the magnitude of the loss. Thus, his total tax liability is decreased by an amount equal to the loss multiplied by the tax rate, so that this part of the loss is recovered. In other words, full loss offset means that whenever the investor suffers a loss, the Treasury reimburses him for a fraction of the loss equal to the tax rate. The Treasury thus becomes a partner who shares equally in both losses and gains.

Under these conditions, not only are the expected gains in the probability distribution cut by a percentage equal to the tax rate, but all losses are reduced likewise. We therefore have from **1, 2** and **3**

$$r_t = r(1-t) \qquad\qquad\qquad \textbf{10}$$
$$g_t = g(1-t) \qquad\qquad\qquad \textbf{11}$$
$$y_t = g_t - r_t = y(1-t) \qquad\qquad \textbf{12}$$

Thus, both the degree of risk and the yield are reduced by a percentage exactly equal to the rate of the tax. The question of tax sensitiveness does not arise here at all, because all asset combinations (or investments) suffer the same percentage reduction.[24] These results are in sharp contrast with those of the preceding case, where no loss offset was possible, so that we may expect the investor's reaction to be markedly different.

Before proceeding further, we must make a distinction between *total yield* and *private yield* and between *total risk* and *private risk*. The imposition of the tax reduces the yield and the degree of risk which are left to the investor, or his *private* yield and *private* risk, in the manner already described; but the *total* yield and the *total* risk of the given asset combination are entirely unaffected by the tax. The fractions of yield and risk which the tax takes away from the investor are simply transferred to the

24. This statement must be modified, if the minimum compensation for effort defined in footnote 10, p. 386, is taken into consideration. Then we have $y'_t = y_t - e$ and the percentage reduction of the adjusted yield is:

$$a' = \frac{y' - y'_t}{y'} = \frac{y - e - y(1-t) + e}{y'} = t\left(1 + \frac{e}{y'}\right).$$

It follows, therefore, that the yield is reduced by a greater percentage than the rate of the tax. If $t \geq \dfrac{y'}{y}$, we get $y'_t \leq 0$, so that the adjusted yield can become zero or negative, if the tax is sufficiently high. But since e is small, $\dfrac{y'}{y}$ is very close to 1, and therefore, to achieve this result, the tax rate must be very high.

The adjusted degree of tax sensitiveness now becomes $s' = \dfrac{e}{y'}$. Since e is a constant, s' depends on y' only and varies inversely with it. To the extent that a higher y' is accompanied by a higher r (or r'), more risky asset combinations are less tax sensitive. Again, since e is small, this difference in tax sensitiveness is hardly important.

Treasury.[25] The symbols y_t and r_t refer to private yield and degree of risk, respectively. Total yield and degree of risk, being unchanged by the tax, are still denoted by y and r. Since our main problem is the effect of the tax on total *risk* taking, not much use will be made of the difference between y and y_t; but the distinction between r and r_t will be extremely important. This distinction was not needed in the preceding case, where it was assumed that no loss offset was possible. Since in that case the Treasury did not share in risk, private risk and total risk were necessarily equal. From the point of view of the economy as a whole, it is, of course, total risk that is important, not private risk.

Faced with a reduction in private yield and private risk, the investor will try to readjust his asset combination. His reaction can again be studied in terms of the income and substitution effect. This time, however, the tax produces no initial substitution effect, because the price of risk taking (y/r) is unchanged, the yield and the degree of risk being reduced in the same proportion. The income effect will make the investor shift to an asset combination with higher risk. This increase in private risk taken (though not necessarily to or above the private risk taken before the tax) also implies an increase in total risk, since from **10**

$$r = r_t \times \frac{1}{(1-t)}.$$

Thus we reach the important and somewhat unexpected conclusion that the imposition of the tax will increase the total risk taken.

A geometric demonstration will help to clarify this result. Let ABO in Figure 5 be the position of the optimum asset curve before the tax, and let B be the optimum point. Since the imposition of the tax reduces y and r equally by the percentage of the tax rate, any point F on ABO moves towards the origin along a straight line FO, covering a fraction of the distance from F to O equal to the

25. The statement that the total degree of risk is unaffected by the tax is perhaps misleading, because it implies that the public and private risk are interchangeable. Quite possibly the concept of total risk is illegitimate, because it represents a combination of heterogeneous items. *Public* risk taking presents a most interesting problem, which certainly deserves further investigation. It remains true, however, that changes in 'total risk' – which for any given investment equals private risk before the tax – reflect the changes in the magnitude and direction of capital flows.

tax rate, so that if the new position of F is F_t we have $\dfrac{FF_t}{FO} = t$.
Similarly, the entire curve ABO moves to a new position, A_tB_tO, and the investor, who prior to the tax was at the equilibrium point B, now finds himself at B_t.

Finding himself at B_t, the investor discovers that, while holding the identical asset combination, his net return (after tax) has fallen by a fraction equal to the rate of the tax, and so has his private risk. He will then find that he can improve his position by moving from B_t to C_t, the point of tangency of the optimum asset curve, in its new position, with an indifference curve. Since, as shown before, the imposition of the tax will produce an income effect only, the point C_t must be above B_t. This statement can be readily proven geometrically.[26]

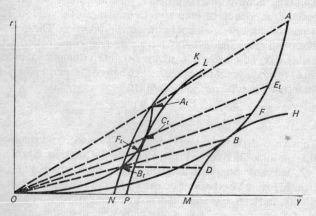

Figure 5   Full loss offset and constant tax

26. The *first* proposition is that the slope of KB_tN at B_t must be greater than the slope of HBM at B. This follows from the fact that (a) at the point B the slopes of ABO and HBM are equal and therefore are both smaller than the slope of HBM at D, since, by assumption, the slope along any given indifference curve falls with increasing y and r, and that (b) the slope of KB_tN at B_t must be equal or greater than the slope of HBM at D. A *second* proposition is that the slope of A_tB_tO at B_t will be equal to the slope of ABO at B: the slope of ABO at any point (y, r) is dr/dy. Similarly, the slope of A_tB_tO at a corresponding point (y_t, r_t) is dr/dy_t. But since $y_t = y(1-t)$

From the fact that private risk taken after adjustment to the tax exceeds private risk taken prior to this adjustment (although not necessarily private risk taken prior to the tax), it follows *that total risk taken after the tax will exceed total risk taken before the tax.* To find the total risk point, E_t, corresponding to the private risk point C_t, we can either apply the formulae $r = \dfrac{1}{1-t}\left(\text{and } y = y_t \dfrac{1}{1-t}\right)$, or draw the line C_tO and extend it to its intersection with ABO, which gives the position of E_t. The total risk (and yield) of any optimum asset combination being unaffected by the tax, it is still represented by its original position on the optimum asset curve. Since C_t is above B_t, E_t must be above B.[27]

The relationship between the level of total risk and the rate of tax remains to be considered. As the tax rate increases, the optimum asset curve ABO moves towards the origin, taking the positions $A_{25}B_{25}O$, $A_{50}B_{50}O$, etc., as shown on Figure 6, the subscripts indicating the corresponding tax rates. The new equilibrium positions located at its tangency points with the indifference curves describe the already familiar tax asset curve, $BC_{25}C_{50}C_{15}D$. This time, however, this curve indicates only the private degree of risk (and yield) taken by the investor under given tax rates, and will be referred to as the private tax-asset curve.

---

and $r_t = r(1-t)$, we have $dy_t = dy(1-t)$, $dr_t = dr(1-t)$ and hence $dr_t/dy_t = dr/dy$.

From these two propositions it follows that at B_t the slope of A_tB_tO must be smaller than the slope of KB_tN. Therefore, B_t cannot be the new point of equilibrium, at which the slopes of A_tB_tO and the indifference curve must be equal. Since the slope of A_tB_tO increases while moving upward and to the right, while that of any indifference curves decreases, the new equilibrium point C must be to the right and above B_t.

27. Continuing the story of footnote 22 (p. 396), we must review the argument on the assumption of a constant marginal utility of income. As explained in footnote 17 (p. 391), an increasing marginal disutility of risk-taking must then be assumed. The conclusion reached in the text that the imposition of the tax will increase the level of total risk taken still holds, because the price of risk-taking is unchanged, while the marginal disutility of risk is reduced by the reduction in private risk. It should be noted that the geometric proof given in the preceding note does not depend on the assumption that the slopes of the indifference curves fall along a given horizontal line.

In Figure 6 the private tax-asset curve first rises with an increasing tax rate from B to somewhat beyond C_{25}, and then falls towards the origin, this movement again depending upon the investor's evaluation of market conditions prior to the tax, and the shapes of the indifference curves.[28] Since the equal percentage

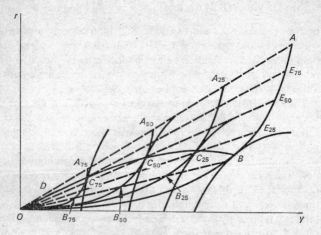

Figure 6   Full loss offset and variable tax

reduction of y and r leaves the ratio y/r unchanged, it may appear surprising that the private tax-asset curve should fall at all; that is, that under certain conditions the investor should fail to recover the degree of private risk taken before the tax. When a given, say 50 per cent, tax is imposed, the investor will find his original equilibrium point B moved to B_{50}, and again readjust his position in the direction of increased private risk by moving up along the new optimum asset curve $A_{50}B_{50}O$. If the latter were a straight line passing through the origin, he would be able to return to the

28. In Figure 6 the tax-asset curve is not continued beyond D, because as the tax continues to increase, there are no points of tangency between the subsequent positions of the optimum asset curve and the indifference curves below the line ADO. In order to make use of the tangency points above ADO, borrowing must be introduced, which is excluded in this paper. In the absence of borrowing, the tax-asset curve will proceed along the straight line DO.

original point B, thus taking just as much risk as he did prior to the tax; but as the slope of $A_{50}B_{50}O$ increases with increasing risk, the investor finds that the ratio y/r diminishes as he goes up along $A_{50}B_{50}O$; this secondary substitution effect will finally stop his upward movement. In the general case, it cannot be said whether any given tax will cause the investor to stop short of or exceed the *private* risk taken prior to the imposition of the tax. But as in the preceding case, a comparatively favorable market and lower tax rate will be conducive to a higher level of private risk.

From the point of view of the economy, the question whether the pre-tax level of private risk is recovered is relatively unimportant. What matters is the degree of total risk taken jointly by the investor and the Government. By extending the lines OC_{25}, OC_{50}, OC_{75}^{1}, etc. to their intersection with ABO, we find the corresponding points E_{25}, E_{50}, E_{75}, etc., indicating the degrees of total risk which will correspond to the investor's adjustment to various tax rates. We have already proved that all these points must fall above the pre-tax equilibrium B; it can be shown by a similar proof that the degree of *total* risk taken will be the higher the higher the tax rate. This, of course, is not an argument for a tax rate approaching 100 per cent. The simplifying assumptions upon which the conclusion rests must be kept in mind. In addition, the results for the economy would obviously be chaotic, if the Government were to invite everybody to invest his funds in whatever project he chooses with a 'no loss' (and 'no gain') guarantee.[29]

The General Case: Taxation with Variable Loss Offset

The discussion presented in the two previous sections will be recognized as the two extreme cases of the same problem. This can now be treated in its more general form by assuming a variable tax rate and variable degrees of loss offset.[30] Since the two extreme

29. If e, defined in footnote 10 (p. 386), which will become more important at very high levels of taxation, is taken into consideration, the conclusions reached in this section will have to be somewhat modified. The case becomes more like that of partial loss deduction, discussed in Section V.

30. A more detailed analysis of partial loss offset would include these considerations: (1) since the immediate offset of losses may not be possible, a loss of interest may result; (2) the extent to which loss offset will be possible may be uncertain, and thus in turn raise probability problems.

cases have been developed in detail, only the more important aspects of the general case are considered here.

Let the fraction of the loss that can be offset be indicated by z $(0 \leqslant z \geqslant 1)$. Then all expected gains are reduced by a percentage equal to t, while the losses are reduced by tz only. From **1**, **2** and **3** we have

$$r_t = r(1 - tz) \qquad\qquad \textbf{13}$$
$$g_t = g(1 - t) \qquad\qquad \textbf{14}$$
$$y_t = g(1 - t) - r(1 - tz) = y(1 - t) - rt(1 - z). \qquad \textbf{15}$$

The changes in the r and y of any given asset combination, under the impact of various rates of tax with varying degrees of loss offset, may again be determined algebraically from **13** and **15** or geometrically in the following manner:

Let M in Figure 7 represent the position of an asset combination

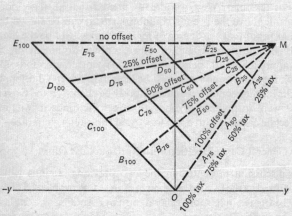

Figure 7 Variable offset and tax

prior to the imposition of the tax. If no loss offset is possible, the imposition of the tax will move the point along the horizontal line ME_{100}, and if full loss offset is provided, the point will move towards the origin along the line MO. Its new position A_{50} after, say, a 50 per cent tax and full loss offset, will be such that $MA_{50}/MO = 0.50$. If the tax rate is kept constant at 50 per cent, but the percentage of loss offset is allowed to vary, y_t and r_t will move along the line $A_{50}E_{50}$ which is given by the expression $r_t + y_t = g_t$, where g_t, being independent of z, is a constant. If the loss offset is, say, 75 per cent, the corresponding point on $A_{50}E_{50}$ is B_{50}, such that

$$\frac{B_{50}E_{50}}{A_{50}E_{50}} = 0 \cdot 75.[31]$$

Turning to the case of a *varying tax rate* with a constant loss offset of, say, 50 per cent, the locus of M is indicated by the straight line MC_{100} or – for varying rates of loss offset – by the family of lines MB_{100}, MC_{100}, and so forth, the slope in each case depending upon the degree of loss offset and the original position of M. Algebraically these lines [32] may be expressed as

$$r = y \frac{z}{\dfrac{y_1}{r_1} + (1-z)} + \frac{(1-z)(y_1 + r_1)}{\dfrac{y_1}{r_1} + (1-z)}, \qquad \mathbf{16}$$

where y_1 and r_1 indicate the coordinates of the point M prior to the tax.

The movement of M in Figure 7 is restricted to the area falling between ME_{100}, MO and OE_{100}, because it relates only to tax rates and loss offsets varying from 0 to 100. By assuming the Treasury to share in losses by over 100 per cent (that is, to guarantee a minimum positive return) or to impose negative taxes (that is, to grant subsidies) – and by allowing for even odder possibilities of negative loss deductions and more than 100 per cent tax rates – the point M may reach any point on the chart.

Using the described algebraic or geometric procedure, we can now turn to the movements of the optimum asset curve and the effects of the tax upon risk taking. In order to avoid the construc-

31. If r is the ordinate of the point M, it follows, by applying a standard procedure from analytic geometry, that the length of the line A_{50},E_{50}, is $rt\sqrt{2}$ and that of B_{50},E_{50}, is $rtz\sqrt{2}$. Their ratio is therefore z, as stated in the text.

32. We have here the standard problem of finding an equation of a line passing through two given points, the coordinates of which are (y_1, r_1) and (y_t, r_t) respectively. It should be noted that the expression **16** is independent of t, so that all points obtained from M by applying a constant loss offset and a varying tax will be on the same straight line.

tion of three dimensional diagrams, it will be necessary to treat separately the case of a variable tax rate with a given loss offset and that of a variable loss offset with a given tax rate.

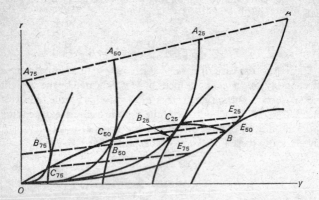

Figure 8   50 per cent offset and variable tax

Variable tax rate with a given loss offset. Let ABO in Figure 8 be the optimum asset curve, and let B be the equilibrium point prior to the tax. Under the assumption of a constant, say 50 per cent, loss offset and a variable tax rate, ABO moves to the left and towards the origin, taking the positions $A_{25}B_{25}O$, $A_{50}B_{50}O$, etc., the subscripts indicating the rate of the tax. The points of tangency of those curves with the indifference curves at C_{25}, C_{50}, etc. describe the familiar private tax-asset curve $BC_{25}C_{50}C_{75}O$.

In order to find the degrees of total risk corresponding to the new equilibrium points C_{25}, C_{50}, etc., we can either draw the lines $C_{25}E_{25}$, $C_{50}E_{50}$, etc. as given in **16**, where y_1 and r_1 are now the coordinates of the C points, or simply make use of the expression

$$r = r_t \frac{1}{(1 - tz)} \qquad\qquad \mathbf{17}$$

derived from **13**. It is important to note that the 'multiplier' $\dfrac{1}{1 - tz}$ increases with an increasing tax rate. Therefore, if the same level of private risk is produced by the imposition of two different tax

406

rates, the point corresponding to the higher rate will give a higher degree of total risk.[33] As the tax increases, the total risk rises, because the multiplier increases, and at the beginning also because the multiplicand (private risk) increases. After private risk begins to fall, total risk will continue to rise for a while, but eventually the diminution of private risk will overcome the increase in the multiplier, and therefore total risk will fall. With a given indifference map, market picture (i.e. position of the optimum asset line prior to the tax), and any positive degree of loss offset, there will thus be an *optimum tax rate* which produces the highest total risk. It also holds that this optimum tax rate will be higher than the rate which produces the highest private risk. In Figure 8 a tax of about 20 per cent will cause the investor to take the highest private risk, but the maximum total risk is not reached until the tax rate becomes about 25 per cent.

Variable loss offset with a given tax rate. Let *ABO* (Figure 9) be the optimum asset curve and *B* the equilibrium point before the tax.

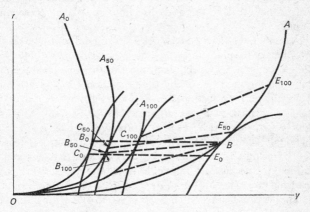

Figure 9 Variable offset and 50 per tax cent

33. The same conclusion can be reached by observing from **16** that the lines $C_t E_t$ are positively inclined, and that their slopes are the greater the smaller is the ratio $\dfrac{y_1}{r_1}$.

Three rates of loss offset will be considered: 100 per cent, 50 per cent and zero. As a result of a given, say 50 per cent, tax, ABO will move to new positions $A_{100}B_{100}O$, $A_{50}B_{50}O$, and A_0B_0O, the subscripts indicating the percentage of loss offset. Again, these positions can be determined either algebraically or geometrically by the methods already described.

The investor will find that his original equilibrium point, B, has moved to new locations, B_{100}, B_{50} or B_0, and will try to readjust his asset combination by moving along the new optimum asset curves to C_{100}, C_{50} or C_0, determined by their tangency with the indifference curves. From section IV we know that in the case of full loss offset the movement from B_{100} to C_{100} must be upwards; but in the other two cases the movement may be in either direction.

In general, no definite statement can be made as to whether the level of *private* risk taken by the investor goes up or down with decreasing percentage of loss offset. A lower rate of loss offset, very similar to an increased rate of tax, reduces the ratio y/r, and thus sets into motion the income and substitution effects already discussed in the section 'Taxation without Loss Offset' (p. 391). Again they work in opposite directions and the outcome is uncertain.

As before, the effect on *total* risk is most important. The relative positions of the points E_{100}, E_{50} and E_0, indicating the total risk of the asset combinations chosen by the investor, may again be determined according to **16** or by the expression **17**, $r = r_t/(1-tz)$. It was proved in the section 'Taxation with Full Loss Offset' (p. 397) that E_{100} must be above B, since, on the assumption of full loss offset, total risk taken is increased. While E_{50} and E_0 may fall either above or below B, there are strong reasons for believing that E_0 will be below E_{50}, and that E_{50} will be below E_{100}, because the multiplier $1/(1-tz)$ increases with an increasing rate of loss offset. In Figure 9, where $t = 50$ per cent, this multiplier rises from 1, with no loss offset, to 4/3, with a 50 per cent offset, and to 2, when full offset is assumed. If E_0 is to fall above E_{100}, the ordinate of private risk of C_0 must be more than twice as large as that of C_{100}. An investor for whom this was true would be characterized by an unusually strong income effect, forcing him to increase his risk taking sharply, notwithstanding a decline y/r. In general, it can be safely said that for any given tax rate the total risk of the investor's asset combination will be the greater, the higher the rate of loss offset.[34]

From the arguments presented above the following conclusions can be drawn: (1) with a given rate of loss offset, there will be an optimum tax rate at which total risk will be at its maximum; (2) with a given tax rate, total risk will, with minor exceptions, be the greater, the higher the rate of loss offset. From these two statements it also follows (3) that the optimum tax rate will be the higher, the higher is the rate of offset.

Qualifications

In the preceding analysis the problem has been considered in a simplified form. A review of the major limitations is now in order.

1. Our analysis has been based upon the probability approach to risk theory. Lacking better alternatives, this approach was introduced in order to obtain numerical values for y and r. It appears that, under the impact of a tax, these values behave in a manner quite compatible with common-sense considerations. If definitions of risk and yield were obtained on the basis of some different approach, their behavior under the impact of a tax would probably be very similar. If it is denied that numerical values *can* be obtained, no method for a precise analysis of the problem appears to be available.

2. We have assumed that the investor's behavior is concerned with changes in y and r, only because these variable appear to us the most most important. Undoubtedly there are other characteristics of the probability distribution in which the investor may be interested, such as the probability of obtaining less than a given minimum rate of return, the probability of suffering more than a given loss, the probability of obtaining very large gains, and so forth. Like r and y, each of these variables will also change as the result of a tax, but not necessarily in the same way. If the investor

34. As a final chapter of the story begun in footnote 21 (p. 395), it is again assumed that the marginal utility of income is constant while the marginal disutility of risk is rising. In this case, since a higher percentage of loss offset (with a given tax) produces a greater reduction in r and a smaller cut in y/r, it clearly follows that the degree of total risk taken will be the higher, the greater is the percentage of loss offset. This is the same conclusion as that reached in the text, except that it can now be stated without exceptions.

includes these additional variables, the outcome may in some cases differ from that described in the text.

3. Throughout our discussion the investor's wealth was assumed to be constant. Now, it is likely that as the result of the tax the investor's wealth will change, which in turn may change his indifference pattern. That is, his general attitude towards risk taking may become more or less favorable. This secondary adjustment has not been taken into account, since the analysis is limited to the immediate effects of the tax on the investor's decisions. The effect of taxation on wealth is in itself a complex problem, particularly because the effects of alternative taxes and/or expenditures must be taken into consideration.

4. Our analysis omits a consideration of the 'investment market'. It examines the intended reactions of any one investor to the imposition of a tax, and disregards the fact that all investors may want to shift towards more or less risk, thereby lowering or raising the price of risk taking. Moreover, the analysis assumes that the individual investor disregards the effects of his moves upon the investment market, an assumption which is clearly unrealistic with respect to important groups of investment decision, and which we hope to reconsider at a later date.

5. The probability approach as used here is more nearly applicable to the case of the financial investor than to 'real' investment decisions. The manager of a corporation about to decide which of his plants he should expand, and what equipment he should purchase, is confronted with fewer and more unique investment alternatives than is the financial investor, and is thus unable to achieve an equal degree of diversification. Certain considerations which might be of little importance for the financial investor, such as those related to maintaining competitive advantages, might be very significant for him. On the whole, however, it is likely that the rationale of real investment decisions would move along similar lines, and that the general conclusions here arrived at would also apply to the case of real investment.

6. The effects of a proportional tax only have been considered. If the case of a progressive tax is examined, additional complications arise. The entire shape of the probability distribution, and its right tail in particular, become of great importance, so that it is very doubtful whether it remains sufficient to describe the

distribution in terms of *y* and *r*. Given a progressive rate schedule, tax savings due to loss offset are likely to be made at different (mostly lower, but possibly higher) rates than those which would have been imposed on the gains. These considerations would modify some of the conclusions reached here, but the case for loss deduction would become even stronger. In an analysis of progressive rates, the related problem of discrimination against fluctuating incomes, and its elimination through averaging, becomes of particular importance.

References

BLACK, D. (1939), *The Incidence of Income Taxes*, Cass.

BOWMAN, M. J., and BACH, G. L. (1943), *Economic Analysis and Public Policy*, Prentice-Hall.

BUTTERS, J. K., and LINTER, J. (1944), *Effect of Federal Taxes on Growing Enterprises*, Study no. 1, Lockheed Aircraft Corporation, Harvard Business School, Division of Research.

FELLNER, W. (1943), 'Monetary policies and hoarding in periods of stagnation', *Journal of Political Economy*, vol. 51.

FISHER, I. (1906), *The Nature of Capital and Income*, Macmillan.

HART, A. G. (1940a), 'Uncertainty and inducements to invest', *Review of Economic Studies*, vol. 8.

HART, A. G. (1940b), 'Anticipation, uncertainty and dynamic planning', *Studies in Business Administration*, vol. 11, no. 1.

HART, A. G., and TINTNER, G. (1942), in H. E. Yntema (ed.), *Studies in Mathematical Economics and Econometrics*, University of Chicago Press.

HICKS, J. R. (1935), 'A suggestion for simplifying the theory of money', *Economica*, new series, vol. 2.

HICKS, J. R. (1939), *Value and Capital*, Oxford University Press, 2nd edn.

KEYNES, J. M. (1936), *The General Theory of Employment, Interest and Money*, Macmillan.

LERNER, A. P. (1943), 'Functional finance and the federal debt', *Social Research*, vol. 10, pp. 45–6.

MAKOWER, H., and MARSCHAK, J. (1938), 'Assets, prices and monetary theory', *Economica*, new series, vol. 5.

MOULTON, H. G. (1940), *Capital Expansion, Employment and Economic Stability*, Brookings Institution.

PIGOU, A. C. (1932), *The Economics of Welfare*, Macmillan.

SCHULTZ, H. (1938), *The Theory of Measurement of Demand*, University of Chicago Press.

SHACKLE, G. L. S. (1940), 'The nature of the inducement to invest', *Review of Economic Studies*, vol. 8, pp. 44–8.

SHACKLE, G. L. S. (1942), 'A theory of investment-decisions', *Oxford Economic Papers*, no. 6, pp. 77–94.

SIMONS, H. C. (1938), *Personal Income Taxation*, Chicago University Press.

TWENTIETH-CENTURY FUND (1937), *Facing the Tax Problem*, New York.

18 D. K. Stout

The Tax on Value Added

D. K. Stout, 'Value added taxation, exporting and growth', *British Tax Review*, September-October, 1963, pp. 321–35.

The Form of the Value Added Tax

The tax I am considering is a multiple stage tax imposed at a flat rate upon the annual sales proceeds of a company less all its purchases from other U.K. businesses (i.e. excluding direct imports). Purchases include services and all fixed capital and inventories purchased from other U.K. companies. Thus value added is understated for a growing or mechanizing company and overstated for one that is declining or letting its capital assets run down. Value added is further reduced by the deduction of the full values of export receipts during the year.

The tax is envisaged as being imposed at a rate which would provide the same real yield to the Revenue as the purchase tax and company profits tax which it is replacing. Thus on 1960 data, if the tax replaced the whole of company income tax and purchase tax, and fell upon company sector gross domestic product at factor cost, deducting replacement investment and exports and adding back imports, the rate of tax would be about 10 per cent. Exactly what the equal real yield rate would be would depend upon the extent to which the tax was shifted forward by price increases, and the extent to which it was avoided by net investment and export increases.

The discriminatory effects of the tax follow from the nature of the expenses and activities that are excluded in calculating its base.

The deduction of the whole of export receipts, and not merely export value added treats the exporter as if the whole of the tax that has fallen upon other U.K. companies from whom he himself bought has been passed on to him.[1] To the extent that this has not

1. Fully passing on entails raising price by $1/(1-t)$, not merely by $(1+t)$, where t is the value added tax rate. See p. 414.

happened, the deduction of export turnover goes further than would the substitution of purchase tax for profits tax with relief for exports. It does not merely not tax exports – it subsidizes them.[2] This is among the effects to be demonstrated.

The definition of value added net of all fixed capital purchases instead of net of depreciation is, of course, illogical but deliberate. It aims at correcting the biases against faster scrapping and mechanization discussed earlier. The general incentives to investment provided by capital allowances against profit disappear as profit tax disappears. The deduction of capital expenditures from the value added tax base provides the equivalent of a same year write-off, whether or not profits have been earned in that year; and the tax relief is more marked when the capital is substituted for direct labour (thus reducing value added) than when it is simply additional productive capacity, calling for complementary labour (and additional value added) to operate it.

It is necessary, of course, to treat all direct imports as value added (so that all imports are taxed once at the value added tax rate) to preclude the substitution of imported materials for home produced substitutes.

I see no reason why the provision of distribution and other services by the company sector should not be included in value added. On the other side of the account, the purchase of, for example, professional services from an individual not being a company would be an allowable deduction, notwithstanding that the provider of the service had paid no value added tax. For he would be subject to tax upon his income, though the tax on that income would tend to exceed the tax on his value added.

The periodic assessment of the differences between sales and purchases – identifiable flows over a period of time – should not present serious problems of administration and collection. There seems no need to imitate the French practice of invoicing the tax on each item individually, collecting the tax for the Revenue on all sales and reclaiming the tax as invoiced on all purchases, par-

2. It might still be asked why we should want to allocate resources inefficiently by subsidising exports. One answer is that since other countries do it, we may be allocating inefficiently if we do *not* follow suit. Another is that we are more interested in faster growth than in static 'optimum' allocation; and so long as we operate with a fixed exchange rate, balance of payments difficulties remain a chronic obstacle to faster growth.

ticularly if, unlike the French, the same rate of tax is applied in every industry. The French method seems calculated to lead to much more automatic forward shifting of the tax, and, as we shall see, the discriminatory effects of the tax proposal are much weakened by full forward shifting.

In the examples that follow, the discrimination introduced by a value added tax switch is considered for three paradigm cases of shifting. If

t = the rate of value added tax

s = the proportion of this tax rate passed on in the price of the product,

then the price of the product rises to $(1 + st)$ times the original price. The three cases considered are where

$s = \dfrac{1}{1-t}$, and price rises to $\dfrac{1}{1-t}$ of the old price;

$s = 1\quad$, ,, ,, ,, ,, $(1+t)$,, ,, ,, ,, ;

$s = 0\quad$, and prices do not change.

In practice, I should expect s to lie not far above zero in fast-growing industries and industries where there are substantial differences between the profit margins of competing firms; and not far from $s = 1$ in domestic sales in other industries. On average, the rise in prices might be close to $0.5t$, and the after tax profits results from an equal start position are shown in the full table (Table 5) for this degree of shifting also.

The case of $s = 1/(1-t)$ represents the extreme case of full shifting. If we imagine a firm, the price of whose product was p under the old tax régime, and which buys nothing at all from other firms, then if it takes no account of the compensating increase in its disposable profits with the removal of the profits tax, but insists upon trying to maintain its gross profits intact, it must try to sell the old output at a new price of $p + tp + t(tp) +, \ldots,$ or $\dfrac{p}{1-t},($ or $p_2 = p(1 + st)$ where $s = \dfrac{1}{1-t})$ since tax will be assessed on its *new* value added, inflated to the extent that it passes on the tax, and not on its old.

Discrimination Between Low Cost and High Cost Firms

In the examples that follow, two firms are compared, which start on an equal footing so far as profits are concerned (except in this first example), and that sell their output in the domestic market at the same price so that the initial value of the sales of each firm is 1000. Wherever a difference between their cost structures is assumed, it is always a difference of 100. The distribution between wage costs and outside purchases for the two taken together is chosen so that the yield from a 10 per cent value added tax imposed on both firms will equal, in real terms, the old yield from a 50 per cent profits tax. Disposable profits before the tax switch are thus fifty for each company (except in this first example where they are seventy-five and twenty- five) and profits tax revenue is 100. In all cases where it is supposed that part or all of value added tax is passed forward, value added tax revenue will correspondingly exceed 100.

In the numerical examples, the first two columns show the position of the two companies A and B before the switch to value added tax. The second pair show the position after a tax switch and assuming no price increases result; the other two pairs show the results if prices everywhere rise by the tax rate times the old price, and, finally if full shifting involving rises of $\frac{1}{1-t}$ occurs. It is assumed that the internal wage costs of the firm share in any general price rise. What happens to profits if wages do not change is shown in the final row of each table. In the tables, output is held constant before and after the tax switch. For simplicity, interest rates are assumed to be zero, so that relative profit margins indicate relative profitability. (The algebra and arithmetic is complicated a little if the equal start position is taken to be one where rates of return on capital are equal, but the conclusions are not essentially different.)

With everything except wages equal for A and B in this example, the tax has exactly the same effect upon the relative profitability of the two companies as would the substitution of an equal real yield tax at the same rates upon profits and payroll. Profits become larger in real terms for the low cost firm by half the difference between the taxes the two firms previously paid, and correspondingly lower for the high cost firm, whose profits, in this example are eliminated. There seems no reason for B, whose tax burden is reduced, to raise the price much, if at all, in these circumstances, particularly if it knows its costs are low by comparison with those

Table 1

Different Total Costs and Starting Profits

	Beforehand		s = 0		s = 1		s = $\frac{1}{1-t}$	
	A	B	A	B	A	B	A	B
Value of export sales	0	0	0	0	0	0	0	0
Value of home sales	1000	1000	1000	1000	1100	1100	1111·1	1111·1
Wages	450	350	450	350	495	385	500	388·9
Depreciation	500	500	500	500	550	550	555·6	555·6
Costs	950	850	950	850	1045	935	1055·6	944·4
Investment spending	500	500	500	500	550	550	555·6	555·6
Value added			500	500	550	550	555·6	555·6
Value added tax			50	50	55	55	55·6	55·6
Cost including tax			1000	900	1100	990	1111·1	1000
Disposable profits	25	75	0	100	0	110	0	111·1
Tax yield	100		100		110		111·1	
Profits if wages do not change			0	100	45	145	50	150

of its rival. Life would be very difficult for Firm A if it raised its price unilaterally. It is in industries where productivity differences are marked – whether because of lower total costs as shown above, or because of higher ratios of capital to labour as shown later – that I should expect the shifting of the tax forward to become damped towards s = 0, and the whole family of discriminatory effects to be correspondingly emphasized.

Discrimination Between Exporters and Home Producers

The example below isolates the discrimination in favour of exporting. The costs of the two firms are the same. Both before and after

Table 2

Different Ratios of Exports to Total Sales

	Beforehand		$s = 0$		$s = 1$		$s = \dfrac{1}{1-t}$	
	A	B	A	B	A	B	A	B
V (ex.)	0	500	0	500	0	500	0	500
V (home)	1000	500	1000	500	1100	550	1111·1	555·6
W	650	650	650	650	715	715	722·2	722·2
D = I	250	250	250	250	275	275	277·8	277·8
Costs	900	900	900	900	990	990	1000	1000
V − A			750	250	825	275	833·3	277·8
V − A − T			75	25	82·5	27·5	83·3	27·8
C + T			975	925	1072·5	1017·5	1083·3	1027·8
Disp. profits	50	50	25	75	27·5	32·5	27·8	27·8
Tax yield	100		100		110		111·1	
Profits if W unchanged			25	75	92·5	97·5	100	100

the tax change, A is selling entirely in the home market, at a price after the change that is marked up to the extent that the tax is shifted. Firm B sells half its output abroad at a constant price. Again the 10 per cent value added tax has the same real yield as the initial 50 per cent profits tax.

If the tax is *fully* passed on, then whether or not wages also rise, the benefit to the exporter is no different from that with export relief from purchase tax. If profits were equal before, they are equal after. If wages do not rise commensurately, all profits are to that extent higher. Conversely, if they do, then since the lower return over costs on exports is shared between home and overseas producers, instead of falling upon labour, profits are lower.

If the tax is not fully passed on, then whether or not wages rise, the profits of the firm that devotes the larger part of its sales to exports become higher than those of the other firm. The less the tax is passed on the greater the discrimination, until, in the example, when prices stay the same, Firm B is making three times the profit of Firm A.

The explanation of this is quite straightforward. The relief of export turnover from the value added tax base treats exporters as though they had had passed on to them in the investment goods (or components or, for that matter, any other purchases from outside, which are all treated by the value added tax in the same way as investment is) which they buy to produce exports with, the whole of value added tax at all previous stages. Thus, it assumes that the price of all these outside purchases will have risen to $1/(1-t)$ times the old price, and then relieves exporters of *this* tax, notionally prepaid in the price of their purchases, as well as of any tax on their own export value added. Thus, in the right hand column above, where tax is indeed fully shifted, B recoups tax prepaid in the price of its export capacity, and is able to make the same profit on its exports at their old price as on home sales at their new price. The tax treatment does not require any allocation of particular purchases to particular sales, but, conceptually, it can be looked at in this way:

Firm B	*No shifting*	*s = 1*	*Full shifting*
(a) tax prepaid in price of purchases	0	25	27·8
(b) tax paid on home value added	37·5	41·25	41·7
(c) relief on account of purchases entering exports	12·5	13·75	13·9
(d) tax prepaid in price of these purchases [½(a)]	0	12·5	13·9
(e) *export net subsidy* [(c) – (d)]	*12·5*	*1·25*	*0*
(f) tax bill [(b) – (c)]	25	27·5	27·8

The different tax treatment of home and export turnover will tend to lead to the setting of a lower price in the export market and, provided foreign demand is elastic, to an increase in export revenue.

Consider first how a given total output of, say, 300 would be distributed between home and export markets, before and after the tax change, by a profit maximizer who knew his demand functions in the two markets:

Suppose Demand at home = $344 - 2P_h$ (where P_h is home price)
Demand abroad = $396 - 3P_e$ (where P_e is export price)
Total output is fixed at 300.

Profits would be maximized, before the tax change, at a home price of 100 and an overseas price of 80. Home demand would be 144 and export demand 156.

If a 20 per cent value added tax is now introduced, and half the tax is shifted forward, the new profit maximizing position becomes:

| Home demand 132 | Home price 106 |
| Foreign demand 168 | Foreign price 76, |

a not inconsiderable shift into exports.[3]

More realistically, we may introduce a cost function and allow total output to vary. Consider a simple linear cost function of the form:

$$C = A + (b + c)Q \quad \text{with values } C = 16,000 + (12 + 16)Q$$

which are consistent with the above before-tax profit maximizing position at an output of 300. In this cost function, the b coefficient relates to variable costs incurred inside the firm, while the co-efficient refers to bought-in costs (depreciation, materials, components, etc.). Internal unit variable costs are being supposed not to rise with any forward shifting of the tax. The results are now these, under various shifting assumptions (see Appendix 2):

$(t = 0.2)$	before tax	$s = 0$	$s = 0.5$	$s = \dfrac{1}{(1-t)}$
Home demand	144	117	111·5	107
Export demand	156	160·8	158·9	156
Home price	100	113·5	116·2	118·5
Export price	80	78·4	79·0	80

Discrimination between More and Less Mechanized Firms

If wages do not rise when a switch is made from a profits tax to an equal real yield value added tax, then the extent of the discrimination in favour of the firm with a high ratio of replacement cost depreciation expenses to direct wage costs depends upon the extent to which the new tax is not shifted forward. If it is fully shifted, then the tax relief on these expenses exactly cancels out the differential tax paid by the mechanized firm in the price of its capital replacements. If depreciation expenses rise by less than $\dfrac{1}{(1-t)}$ times the old depreciation, the mechanized firm has the advantage of its lower value added.

3. See Appendix 1 for derivation of formulae.

However, if wages also rise when the tax is shifted, the old total level of real profits is earned by the two firms taken together, but is redistributed between them in proportion to their depreciation expenditures.

Table 3

Differing Ratios of Labour to Capital

	Beforehand		$s = 0$		$s = 1$		$s = \dfrac{1}{1-t}$	
	A	B	A	B	A	B	A	B
V (home)	1000	1000	1000	1000	1100	1100	1111·1	1111·1
Wages	450	350	450	350	495	385	500	388·9
Dep'n = I	450	550	450	550	495	605	500	611·1
Cost	900	900	900	900	990	990	1000	1000
VA			550	450	605	495	611·1	500
VAT			55	45	60·5	49·5	61·1	50
C+T			955	945	1050·5	1039·5	1061·1	1050
Disp. profits	50	50	45	55	49·5	60·5	50	61·1
Tax yield	100		100		110		111·1	
Profits if W unchanged			45	55	94·5	95·5	100	100

If, perhaps more relevantly, the ratio of disposable profits to depreciation is taken to be equal to begin with (so that wages are initially 460 and 340) then the ratio of profits to wages after the tax switch is 7·8 per cent for A and 11·8 per cent for B whatever the degree of shifting.

The effect described here applies equally to any differences between the proportion of work carried out inside the firm to that 'bought in.' That is to say 'Wages' can be taken to include work done by the firm in making its own components, and the 'Depreciation' row broadened to include components bought-in from specialist firms. If depreciation and normal wage expenses were then taken to be the same for the two firms in the previous table, the table would be showing the benefits, after tax, from buying-in from specialist suppliers rather than making for oneself.

D. K. Stout

Discrimination Between the Rapidly Growing or Rapidly Mechanizing or Modernizing Firms and Stagnating Firms

This effect follows in a straightforward fashion from the deduction of actual capital outlays, rather than depreciation costs, from sales receipts in the computation of value added for tax purposes. This capital allowance changes the relative profitability of fast and slow growers in much the same way that initial allowances do at present. There are two points of difference: since the base of the value added tax is broader and the rate lower, the benefit is to that extent less than in the case of an equivalent capital allowance against company income tax; on the other hand, the whole of the purchase, no matter how long-lived the item, is written off against value added in the year of payment.

Table 4

Different Investment Outlays

	Beforehand		$s = 0$		$s = 1$		$s = \dfrac{1}{1-t}$	
	A	B	A	B	A	B	A	B
V (home)	1000	1000	1000	1000	1100	1100	1111·1	1111·1
Wages	450	450	450	450	495	495	500	500
Dep'n	450	450	450	450	495	495	500	500
Cost	900	900	900	900	990	990	1000	1000
Investment	450	550	450	550	495	605	500	611·1
V−A			550	450	605	495	611·1	500
V−A−T			55	45	60·5	49·5	61·1	50
C+T			955	945	1050·5	1039·5	1061·1	1050
Disp. profits	50	50	45	55	49·5	60·5	50	61·1
Tax yield	100		100		110		111·1	
Profit if W unchanged			45	55	94·5	105·5	100	111·1

Conclusion

The foregoing profits results from the replacement of a 50 per cent profits tax by a value added tax (at 10 per cent) with the same real

The Economic Effects of Taxes

yield are summarized in Table 5, together with some results for combinations of inter-firm differences, and for a degree of shifting intermediate between s = 0 and s = 1.

If price-setters ignore profits tax relief and all shift the tax *fully* by raising prices all long the line to $p_2 = p_1/(1-t)$, *and if at the same time wages did not change*, then the benefit to exports would disappear, except in the sense that relief from purchase tax benefits exports; the benefit from a high degree of mechanization would disappear; the benefit from buying-in from specialist suppliers would disappear; the relative difference in profit margins would remain unchanged; and one would be left with a benefit from a high rate of investment only. However, the column on the far right is an absurdity: for, unless wages also rose to the same extent that prices rose, the goods would be unsaleable at their new price level. If tax is and can be shifted, then wages must rise. The *fourth* column then

Table 5

Summary of Profits Results from the Tax Substitution[4]

		Wages also rise				Wages do not rise			
s =		0	0·5	1	1/(1−t)	0	0·5	1	1/(1−t)
Exports	A	25	26·25	27·5	27·8	25	58·75	92·5	100
	B	75	53·75	32·5	27·8	75	86·25	97·5	100
Cap./ Lab. (Buying-in)	A	45	47·25	49·5	50	45	69·75	94·5	100
	B	55	57·75	60·5	61·1	55	75·25	95·5	100
Net invest.	A	45	47·25	49·5	50	45	69·75	94·5	100
	B	55	57·75	60·5	61·1	55	80	105·5	111·1
All 3	A	15	15·75	16·5	16·7	15	53·25	91·5	100
	B	85	64·25	43·5	38·9	85	96·75	108·5	111·1
Wages/ Profits	A	0	0	0	0	0	22·5	45	50
	B	100	105	110	111·1	100	122·5	145	150
All 4	A	−35	−36·75	−38·9	−38·9	−35	3·25	41·5	50
	B	135	116·75	98·5	94·4	135	146·75	158·5	161·1

4. See Appendix 3 for the formulae from which these results derive.

shows that the only benefit lost through full shifting is the subsidy to exports: the discrimination in favor of mechanization, buying-in, rapid investment growth and profitability all persist unaffected by the degree of shifting, when wages rise in step with price rises.

This does not alter the fact that a once-and-for-all increase in all prices and wages would be unfortunate, if it were to follow from the tax substitution. However, the fact that the disposable profits of Firm B are doubled (in the 10th row) if it does not raise its price at all makes me doubtful whether, to put it at its highest, the inflation that would follow from the complete sweeping away of all company income tax and its replacement by value added tax at the rate of 10 per cent would amount to more than a 3 or 4 per cent increase in the general level of prices and wages: and once the price adjustment to the new tax system had occurred, that would be that.

If the tax change were introduced gradually, and if businessmen were given plenty of simple illustrations, in advance, of what it would mean for their disposable profits if they did not raise prices, but sought to export, save labour, modernize and mechanize, then no noticeable price increases whatsoever need follow. In general, it is the firms that are already low cost, and that are anyway behaving in the ways described, that can lead on price.

Appendix 1

When output is given, and is to be distributed between the home and overseas markets in such a way as to maximize profits:

Let D = demand

P = price

Q = the given total output

R = Revenue

Subscripts h and e refer to the home and export markets

C = cost of purchases from outside the firm per unit of final product

t = value+added tax rate

s = proportion of the tax shifted forward by suppliers.

Assuming linear demand functions:

$$D_h = 1 - mP_h \text{ and } D_e = g - hP_e$$
$$R_h = P_h(1 - mP_h) \text{ and } R_e = P_e(g - hP_e)$$

$$\frac{\delta R_h}{\delta D_h} = P_h + (1 - mP_h)\frac{\delta P_h}{\delta D_h};$$

$$\frac{\delta P_h}{\delta D_h} = -\frac{1}{m}.$$

therefore $\dfrac{\delta R_h}{\delta D_h} = 2P_h - \dfrac{1}{m}$,

and $\dfrac{\delta R_e}{\delta D_e} = 2P_e - \dfrac{g}{h}$.

To maximize profits,

$$2P_h - \frac{1}{m} = 2P_e - \frac{g}{h}, \text{ subject to}$$

$$1 - mP_h + g - hP_e = Q. \text{ From this,}$$

$$P_h = \frac{hl + gm + 2lm - 2mQ}{2m(h+m)} \text{ and } P_e = \frac{hl + gm + 2gh - 2hQ}{2h(h+m)}.$$

Hence, $D_h = \dfrac{hl - gm + 2mQ}{2(h+m)}$ and $D_e = \dfrac{gm - hl + 2hQ}{2(h+m)}$.

After tax:

$$R_h = (l - mP_h)P_h - t(l - mP_h)(P_h - [1+st]C)$$

$$R_e = (g - hP_e)P_e - t(g - hP_e)(P_e - [1+st]C) + \\ + t(g - hP_e)P_e$$

$$= \frac{1}{h}(Q - 1 + mP_h)(1 + g - mP_h - Q) + Ct(1+st) \times \\ \times (Q - 1 + mP_h).$$

$$\frac{\delta R_h}{\delta D_h} = P_h + (1 - mP_h)\frac{\delta P_h}{\delta D_h} - tP_h - t(l - mP_h)\frac{\delta P_h}{\delta D_h} + t(1+st)C$$

$$= 2P_h(1-t) - \frac{l(1-t)}{m} + tC(1+st).$$

$$\frac{\delta R_e}{\delta D_e} = P_e + (g - hP_e)\frac{\delta P_e}{\delta D_e} - tP_e - t(g - hP_e)\frac{\delta P_e}{\delta D_e} + \\ + tP_e + t(g - hP_e)\frac{\delta P_e}{\delta D_e}$$

$$= 2P_e - \frac{g}{h} + tC(1+st).$$

To maximize profits, let $\dfrac{\delta R_h}{\delta D_h} = \dfrac{\delta R_e}{\delta D_e}$:

$$\frac{2(1+g-mP_h-Q)-g}{h}+tC(1+st) = 2P_h(1-t)-\frac{1(1-t)}{m}+ +tC(1+st),$$

Hence, $P_h = \dfrac{hl(1-t)+2lm+gm-2mQ}{2hm(1-t)+2m^2}$

$\quad\ \ D_h = \dfrac{hl(1-t)-gm+2mQ}{2h(1-t)+2m}$

$\quad\ \ P_e = \dfrac{hl(1-t)+2gh(1-t)+gm-2hQ(1-t)}{2hm+2h^2(1-t)}$

$\quad\ \ D_e = \dfrac{gm-hl(1-t)+2hQ(1-t)}{2h(1-t)+2m}.$

Appendix 2

When total output Q is free to vary,

Let C = total cost. Assume a simple linear cost function with constant marginal costs,

$$C = (B+C)+(b+c)Q,$$

where b is the unit variable cost of production incurred inside the firm, and B and C are internal overheads and overhead purchases from other firms.

Before tax:

$$b+c = 2P_h-\frac{1}{m} = 2P_e-\frac{g}{h};$$

$\quad P_h = \dfrac{m(b+c)+1}{2m}$

$\quad P_e = \dfrac{h(b+c)+g}{2h}$

$\quad D_h = \dfrac{1-m(b+c)}{2}$

$\quad D_e = \dfrac{g-h(b+c)}{2}.$

The Economic Effects of Taxes

After tax, if internal (wage) costs do not rise,

$$C = B+G(1+st)+bQ+c(1+st)Q$$

$$R_e = \frac{Q_e(g-Q_e)}{h}+tc(1+st)Q+tG(1+st)$$

$$\frac{\delta C}{\delta Q_e} = b+c(1+st)$$

$$\frac{\delta R_e}{\delta Q_e} = \frac{g}{h}-\frac{2Q_e}{h}+tc(1+st). \text{ To maximize profits,}$$

$$\frac{\delta C}{\delta Q_e} = \frac{\delta R_e}{\delta Q_e}, \text{ and hence}$$

$$Q_e = \frac{g-hb-hc(1+st)(1-t)}{2}$$

$$P_e = \frac{g}{2h}+\frac{b+c(1+st)(1-t)}{2}$$

(if $s = \frac{1}{1-t}$, then $Q_e = \frac{g-h(b+c)}{2}$ and the tax makes no difference.)

At home:

$$R_h = Q_h\left\{\frac{(1-Q_h)(1-t)}{m}-c(1+st)\right\}$$

$$\frac{\delta R_h}{\delta Q_h} = \frac{(1-t)(1-2Q_h)}{m}-c(1+st) = b+c(1+st) = \frac{\delta C_h}{\delta Q_h};$$

and $\quad Q_h = \frac{1}{2}-\frac{mb+2mc(1+st)}{2(1-t)}$

$$P_h = \frac{1}{2m}+\frac{b+2c(1+st)}{2(1-t)}.$$

In the diagram above, AR_h', MR_h', AR_e' and MR_e' are average and marginal revenue curves in the home and export markets after the tax switch. AR_h and AR_e, the average revenue curves before tax, remain the *demand* curves after tax. The vertical distance between AR_e' and AR_e is equal to the value added tax rate times AR. The vertical distance between AR_h and AR_h' is equal to the value added tax rate times $(AR_h-c(1+st))$. After tax is imposed, home price rises from P_h to P'_h and sales fall from Q_h to Q'_h; export price falls from P_e to P'_e and sales rise from Q_e to Q'_e. The subsidy per unit of exports is ST.

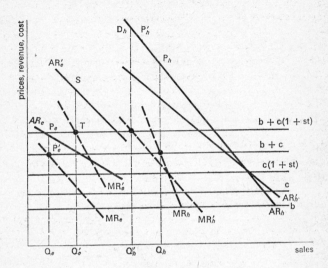

Figure 1

Appendix 3

To derive the equal real yield tax formula, and the equations for profit after tax, and the profit difference between companies A and B (i) when wages do not also shift; (ii) when they do:

V = initial sales value for one firm (same for each firm)
subscripts refer to firms A and B
dashed symbols show value for A minus value for B
where there is no subscript, the symbol stands for the sum of the values for A and B (except in the case of V)
h_A is initial proportion of home sales to total sales value
W_A = wages: the value of all work done within the firm
G_A = the surplus of investment expenditure over depreciation
α_A = profits after tax
r = rate of profit tax; t and s as already defined

427

R_A = total outside purchases (Investment + bought-in parts + materials, etc.)

C_A = total costs:

(i) When wages change,

$$\alpha_A = h_A(1+st)V - (1+st)C_A - t(1+st)(h_A V - R_A) + (1-h_A)V;$$

Hence, $\alpha' = h'stV + (1+st)(tR' - h'tV - C')$.

(ii) If wages do not change, $\alpha_A = h_A(1+st)V - (1+st) \times (C_A - W_A) - W_A - t(1+st)(h_A V - R_A) + (1-h_A)V;$

Hence, $\alpha' = h'stV + (1+st)(tR' - h'tV - R' + G') - W'$.

The rate of value-added tax with equal real yield to profits tax r:

$$r(2V - C)(1+st) = thV(1+st) - tR(1+st).$$

So

$$t^2s(R-hV) + t(sr[2V-C]+R-hV) + r(2V-C) = 0.$$

And

$$t = \frac{\sqrt{(hV-R-sr[2V-C])^2 + 4sr(2V-C)(hV-R)} + sr(2V-C) + R - hv}{2s(hV-R)}$$

Thus, when $s = \dfrac{t}{(1-t)}$, $t = \dfrac{r(2V-C)}{hV-R}$.

19 M. Krzyzaniak and R. A. Musgrave

The Shifting of the Corporation Income Tax

M. Krzyzaniak and R. A. Musgrave, *The Shifting of the Corporation Income Tax*, Johns Hopkins Press, 1964, pp. 1–21.

Introduction

The shifting and incidence of the corporation income tax have been theorized about at great length.[1] This discussion has been inconclusive, but a brief review of the main arguments will help in interpreting our empirical analysis.

To review the theoretical argument, we shall assume that the corporation tax is substituted for another tax of equal yield, thus permitting us to focus on differential incidence and to disregard the public-expenditure problem. Also, we shall assume that the tax substitution is in the context of a full-employment economy, thus permitting us to disregard effects on the level of employment, and to focus on the distribution, growth and allocation aspects of the problem.

Short-run adjustments

In the traditional approach, a distinction has been drawn between the short-run and the long-run effects of the tax. To avoid misunderstanding, it should be made clear just how these terms are to be used. Two sets of distinctions must be kept apart.

One distinction, theoretical in nature, is between effects which come about rapidly, and effects which are slow in working themselves out. The rapid type is referred to as 'short-run' effects, and the period is set sufficiently short (one or two years) so as to exclude

1. The following items are but a sample of the long literature on this topic: Edgeworth (1925, p. 97); also see Cournot (1938, p. 68); Wicksell (1896, pp. 11–20); Seligman (1925, pp. 59–84); Dalton (1936, pp. 81–5); Goode (1951a, pp. 47–54). Also see the Colwyn Report (1927); Robertson (1927); Coates (1927, pp. 65–113).

changes in capacity. The vehicle by which the 'short-run' effects come about must thus be through changes in prices received or wages (or other cost payments) paid, with capacity constant. The slow type is referred to as 'long-run' effects, and may come about only over a period sufficiently long to permit changes in capital stock, with corresponding adjustments in prices and costs.

Another distinction, observational in nature, is between results which show up if taxation effects are measured over a short period, as against results which show up only if a long period is examined. Long-run effects, as just defined, cannot show up in the first case; but short-run effects, as here defined, may prevail and be observed even if a long period is examined. The 'short-run' effect as here defined may thus have important consequences for the longer run; and if 'long-run' effects are absent or unimportant, the 'short-run' type of effects (which do not involve changes in capital stock) may indeed dominate even the observed long-run consequences of the tax.

Since the model here developed observes effects coming about within a year, and since fixed capital adjustments are hardly possible within that period, our results correspond to the theoretical concept of short-run effects.

Regarding the short-run effect, economists from Cournot on have argued that a profits tax will not affect optimum output under conditions of profit maximization, be it for monopoly or perfect competition. Consequently, prices and the gross (i.e., before tax) rate of return on capital must remain unchanged. This dictum was qualified later by recognition that taxable profits may contain variable cost elements, that changes in tax rates may act as a signal in oligopoly pricing, that the monopolist may use restraint in maximizing profits over the short run, aiming at a 'fair' net (after tax) rate of return, that the profits tax may play a role in wage demands in collective bargaining, etc. All these elements may cause some degree of adjustment in prices or wages and may affect the gross rate of return. Short-run shifting may result from market imperfections, without contradiction with conventional price theory.

The businessman, however, has been skeptical regarding the entire approach of marginal cost pricing. His position has been that taxes are treated as a cost when determining prices, be it as part of a 'full-cost-pricing' rule, by application of a conventional mark-up rate defined net of tax, or by pricing to meet a net of tax target rate of return. According to these formulae, a change in tax rate leads to an adjustment in price. The profits tax becomes a *quasi* sales tax. The fact that such a price policy is not consistent with the usual concepts of profit maximization does not disprove its existence. In all, it appears that the economist, speaking from his theoretical insight alone, cannot rule out the possibility of short-run shifting. Surprising or not, we shall find that our statistical results are compatible with the businessman's views.

Long-run adjustments

While the traditional view holds that the short-run effect of the tax is to reduce profits and the rate of return, this reduction is then expected to depress capital formation in the long run. Thereby the burden may be spread from owners of capital to other groups. This raises two problems: First, there is the question whether and how the level of capital formation is reduced; and second, there is the question of how such reduction in the rate of capital formation as results will affect factor shares and the rate of return on capital.

Theoretical reasoning regarding the effects of a profits tax on the level of private capital formation is most difficult. It can be no more conclusive than is the underlying theory of investment behavior. Unfortunately, the state of this theory is quite unsatisfactory. Different hypotheses give different answers. If the investment function is taken to be of the accelerator type, then the tax effect can operate only through changing the level of total expenditures. In the full employment context investment can not be affected by the tax. If the investment function is of the propensity-to-invest type, taxation effects may operate via the resulting reduction in the internal supply of funds. These effects will be restrictive, but the resulting reduction in investment cannot exceed the tax yield. Using a profitability type of investment function, the tax effects may operate via effects on the rate of return. In this case, much depends on the nature of the tax, especially on the loss treatment, and it is by no means certain that investment will be curtailed (see Domar and Musgrave, 1944, pp. 387–422; and Tobin, 1958, pp. 65–87). However, if it is, the magnitude of the reduction in investment may exceed tax yield. Such effects as result are likely to require more than a year and may extend over several decades. Again, many outcomes are possible and the problem cannot be solved by theorizing alone.

Assume now that the tax does reduce the rate of capital formation. The resulting effects on factor incomes then depend on the form of the production function for a growing economy. If it is in the nature of a constant return to scale-type Cobb–Douglas function, factor shares will remain unchanged. At the same time, the rates of return to capital and labor will change, depending on the parameters of the system. Looked at in absolute terms, capital and wage incomes in future years will be below the level which would have been obtained under higher investment. What these results indicate with regard to 'shifting' or 'incidence' of the tax, depends one one's definition of these terms. For instance, if incidence is defined in terms of resulting changes in the *distribution* of income after tax, the tax may be said to stay put, since the profit share after tax has declined; but if incidence is defined in terms of changes in *absolute* income, labor bears part of the burden. The results become more complicated if we assume a non-Cobb–Douglas type of production function, in which case factor shares before tax may change as well.

Complications

The preceding discussion assumed that the corporation tax is a truly general tax on profits. This must now be corrected since (1) the tax applies in the corporate sector only, and (2) different treatment is given to earnings on equity and debt capital. Also, (3) there is the problem of separating tax effects from government expenditure effects.

1. Since the tax applies to the corporate sector only, it may induce a movement of capital from this sector to the unincorporated sector. Particular corporations may be disincorporated, or there may be a reallocation of capital toward industries which are characterized by unincorporated firms, i.e., capital may flow from manufacturing to real estate. The latter adjustment may be expected to occur over a longer period. As a result of such capital movement, the gross rate of return in the corporate sector may rise

while that in the other sector falls.[3] In such a case, an isolated view of changes in the gross rate of return in the corporate sector may suggest shifting. At the same time, there may have been no shifting in the more significant sense of passing the burden from the total (corporate plus unincorporated) capital share to the labor share or to the consumer. Even though capital flows readily in response to differential returns, the total capital supply may be inelastic, and changes in the total capital share which result from reallocation

3. This aspect is emphasized by Harberger (1962, pp. 215–40, and 1959, pp. 231–51).

Without entering into an evaluation of Harberger's model, it may be useful at the outset to relate our analysis to his, even though this anticipates some of the later discussion:

i. Harberger's analysis is deductive, drawing conclusions regarding the consequence of the corporation tax from assumptions regarding market structure, production functions, etc. The analysis of this study takes an empirical approach, without *a priori* assumptions about market structure.

ii. Harberger allows for a time sufficiently long for all necessary adjustments, including adjustments in capital (be it inter-industry movement or total), to occur. Our analysis attempts to measure the consequences of a tax rate change which come about within a short period, i.e. a few years. Therefore, the effects of changes in capital stock in the corporate sector enter to a very limited degree only.

iii. Harberger's assumptions of competitive market structure, and, if we read it correctly, even his interpretation of the monopoly case (in terms of mark-up rather than factors such as restrained monopoly or oligopoly pricing) are hard to reconcile with our statistical results, or vice versa. If there is a quick and persistent recoupment of the tax prior to capital adjustments, the need for reduction of capital in the corporate sector and for equalization with other sectors (which is the essence of Harberger's analysis) is diminished.

iv. An excess burden problem, though in somewhat different form, may arise whether price changes through the Harberger mechanism or through revision of administered prices, as implied by our results.

v. Harberger de-emphasizes the possibility that total capital formation is depressed by the fall in the net rate of return (all sectors) which results in his system. But suppose such a result would follow. Then the implications for total capital formation and growth differ greatly, depending on whether an observed price rise in the corporate sector reflects (a) the rate of return being by 'administered' price and/or wage changes, in which case the net rate of returns is not reduced to begin with and no adverse effects on capital formation result; or (b) the net rate of return being equalized with the noncorporate sector through inter-sector capital flows, in which case total capital formation is retarded. This point seems to be missed in a recent statement by the Committee for Economic Development (1962, p. 22).

may be relatively minor. At the same time, by inducing capital movement to other industries, the tax may reduce the efficiency of resource allocation and give rise to an excess burden, such as is usually discussed in connexion with partial excise taxes. Such a burden may result even though the total gross-profit share remains unchanged.

In appraising the importance of capital movement to the unincorporated sector, it should be noted that what matters is not the absolute level of corporation tax alone, but the difference between the total rates which the tax system as a whole imposes on the investor in the corporate and in the unincorporated sectors. This involves individual income tax rates, capital gains treatment, and other aspects of the tax system as well.

2. Since the tax permits deduction of interest on debt capital but does not allow deduction of imputed interest on equity capital, it may induce substitution of debt for equity finance. This may result in an increase in the gross rate of return on equity, so as to leave the net rate unchanged. At the same time, there may be no change in the gross rate of return on total capital, i.e., the ratio of profits plus debt. As far as effects on the distribution of total income between capital and wage income are concerned, there has been no shifting. At the same time the position of investors in equity will have suffered relative to that of investors in debt. The net rate of return per unit of risk taking enjoyed by equity holders will decline relative to that enjoyed by bond holders (see Modigliani and Miller, 1958); and the ratio of profits after tax to interest payments will fall. Moreover, a further type of excess burden may arise.

The importance of these complications in the concrete setting of the U.S. corporation tax depends on how readily the unincorporated form of enterprise may be substituted for the corporate form, how readily capital may move to the unincorporated sector, and how readily debt finance may be substituted for equity finance. It may well be that these choices are determined largely by non-tax factors,[4] so that these two types of structural adjustments are relatively unimportant. Nevertheless, they must be kept in mind, especially when interpreting the behavior of various indicators of shifting.

3. In analysing various taxation effects – be it the broader problem

4. With regard to choice of financing instruments, this view is arrived at by Miller (1961).

of incidence or the narrower issue of resulting changes in the rate of return – the question always remains how such effects can be separated from the effects of other elements of budget policy (see Musgrave, 1959, ch. 10). In theoretical reasoning, one may consider the results of changing a particular tax rate while holding public expenditures and other taxes constant. This concept of 'absolute' effect serves the purpose of focusing on the specific tax change. But placed in a general equilibrium context, it is awkward because it implies aggregate-demands effects and resulting changes in price level or employment. This difficulty may be avoided by considering simultaneous changes in the tax rate and in public expenditures. This concept of 'budget' effect in turn has the disadvantage of mixing tax and expenditure effects, which is not the most interesting problem. A final possibility is to hold expenditures constant and to examine the effects of tax substitution. This approach of 'differential' effect may be the most satisfactory formulation of the problem, from a theoretical point of view.

The empirical results of our theoretical model do not fall neatly into any of these concepts. To begin with, it would be hardly possible to construct a model measuring 'differential' effects. The best we can do is to aim at 'absolute' effects, but even this proves difficult. It happens that changes in the corporate tax rate were highly correlated with public expenditure changes, making it difficult to isolate the two effects, and leaving us with a result which may come closer to that of budget effects than that of absolute corporation tax effects. To a lesser degree, this problem arises also with regard to changes in other taxes.

A Preliminary View

There have been a number of attempts in recent years to draw empirical conclusions on incidence, based on the observation of various time series, pertaining to profits, rates of return, and shares in national income.[5] These changes are then imputed to tax effects

5. For a discussion of recent work along these lines see Ratchford and Han (1957, pp. 310–24).

Also, see Adelman (1957, p. 152); Beck (1950, pp. 248, 253–6); Cary Brown (1954, pp. 240–41); Clendenin (1956, p. 396); Goode (1951b, p. 197); Lerner and Hendriksen (1956, pp. 199, 202); Lintner (1955, p. 235); Miller and Shelton (1955, p. 256); Musgrave, Carrol, Cook and Frane (1951, pp. 14–16); Shoup (1951, p. 187); Weston (1949, pp. 307, 309, 312, 315).

and taken as an indication of shifting. In interpreting the observed changes in these indicators, it must be kept in mind that there are many influences at work other than the tax factor, and that without isolating the latter, only a crude impression can be gained. The purpose of this study is precisely to undertake an attempt at such isolation, but by way of introduction, a brief look at the general picture will be useful. Even here, it is important to define how shifting is to be measured.

The concepts of 'shifting' and 'incidence' are not easily defined and mean different things to different people. For the immediate purposes of this chapter, we need only to say that 'shifting' of the corporation tax relates to the recovery of the burden which the tax imposes on the taxpayer, the 'burden' being the difference in his position as it is with the tax and as it would have been without the tax. The difference may be measured in terms of various 'indicators,' such as absolute profits, rates of return, or share in national income. The degree to which the potential burden (i.e., the burden which would result in the absence of any adjustment on the taypayer's part) is avoided or recovered, indicates the 'degree of shifting.'[6]

Indicators of shifting

We assume for the time being that the effect of the tax factor on the various 'indicators' has been isolated and consider what their movement tells us about shifting.

Types of indicators. Various possible indicators, most of which have been used in recent discussions, may be arranged as shown in Table 1 (p. 436).

A first way of looking at the problem is in terms of absolute profits according to indicators 1–4. For obvious reasons this is less instructive than observation of changes in rates of return or factor shares. The insight to be gained with regard to shifting from the historical pattern of financial data, such as given in this chapter, altogether depends on the validity of assuming that non-tax influences were absent on balance. This assumption is clearly absurd in the case of absolute profits, if only for the reason that the capital stock grows over time. It is less so regarding ratios such as rate of return or factor share which are at least partially self-correcting.

6. For further conceptual discussion, see ch. 5 and Appendix C [not included here].

Table 1

Indicators of Shifting

| Sector | Tax-induced change in | Expressed as | | | | |
| | | Absolute amounts | Rates of return on capital of | | Shares in value added of | |
			Corporations	All business	Corporations	All business
Corporations only	Profits only	1	5	—	9	11
	All capital earnings	2	6	—	10	12
All business	Profits only	3	—	7	—	13
	All capital earnings	4	—	8	—	14

The rate of return indicator is of major interest because it may be presumed that investment activity depends on the rate of return, with its consequences for the level of capital formation, capital allocation, and growth.[7] This is formulated most broadly in indicator 8 by relating all capital earnings (profits plus interest paid) to all capital. If the tax effect is to reduce the net rate of return, then investment as a whole has become less profitable. A quite narrow view of this relationship is given in indicator 5 by relating corporate profits to corporate equity. The effect of the tax on this rate of return clearly does not tell the whole story. By inducing debt finance or capital flow into unincorporated business, the profitability of investment may be restricted somewhere else. These effects are partially accounted for by indicators 6 or 7.

The share indicator is of interest primarily because it relates to the distributional effects of the tax.[8] The most comprehensive picture is given by indicator 14, which relates total capital earnings

7. Those who hold that investment depends on internal funds may prefer to examine effects on the ratio of profits plus depreciation to capital.

8. The definition of distributional consequences in terms of changes in factor shares deals with changes from the earnings side of relative income positions only. To gain a complete picture, tax effects on relative prices and resulting changes from the income uses side would have to be considered as well. See Musgrave (1959, ch. 10).

to total value added by business. If the tax reduces the share of capital, and if the capital share is distributed less equally by size groups than the labor share, then the tax tends to reduce income inequality. No such definite conclusion can be drawn if a narrower view of the share is taken, as in indicator 9. Indicators 10 to 13 again allow for varying degrees of comprehensiveness of the picture.

If one considers a period so short that capital is held constant, the absolute profit and rate of return indicators are in full agreement. If there are no non-tax factors affecting value added, there will also be a general agreement with the movement of share indicators. In the longer run, the absolute profit indicators are useless, while rate of return and share indicators may differ widely. Moreover, quite different time periods may be involved in the working out of effects on total capital formation, value added, inter-sector movements, and changes in type of finance.

It should be noted that these indicators do not tell us by what *mechanism* the shifting process comes about. To study the mechanism of shifting in the short run, changes in prices ('forward' shifting), in wages ('backward' shifting), and perhaps in profit margins are relevant, as well as inter-sector movements of capital and changes in financial structure. To examine the process of shifting in the long run, changes in investment and effects on productivity are relevant. In interpreting our approach to the problem, these factors underlying the mechanism of shifting had to be kept in mind; but for the time being, our concern is merely with the indicators as end results.

Zero and 100 per cent shifting. We now define what constitutes zero and 100 per cent shifting under the various indicators,

Table 2

Conditions of Zero and 100 Per Cent Shifting

Indicator	Zero shifting	100% shifting
Absolute profit (gross terms)	$\pi_g = \pi'$	$\pi_n = (1 - Z)\pi_g = \pi'$
Rate of return (gross terms)	$Y_g = Y'$	$Y_n = (1 - Z)Y_g = Y'$
Net share	$F_n = (1 - Z)F'$	$F_n = F'$
Gross share	$F_g = F'$	$(1 - Z)F_g = F'$

where π is profits, Y is the rate of return, F is the profit share, and Z is the tax rate. Throughout this study, the term '*gross* return' will be used to indicate return before deducting tax, and '*net* return' will be used to indicate return after deducting tax. Subscript g indicates gross and subscript n indicates net such that $\pi_n = (1 - Z)\pi_g$ by definition. Priming means value in absence of tax. The problem of how to define the degrees of shifting other than 0 to 100 per cent is more complicated and will be considered later.[9]

The definitions for the absolute profit and rate-of-return indicators are self explanatory. They are here stated in gross terms, but may be translated without change in meaning into net terms.[10]

The case of the share indicator is more difficult. An easy solution to the problem would be to take the absolute profit or rate-of-return definitions and translate them into share terms.[11] This, however, would be of no value because it would merely be a reformulation of the earlier concepts. The problem is to find definitions for the share indicator which are meaningful in terms of share analysis. Looking at the matter in this way, it appears that for the share case there is a substantive difference between the net and gross formulation.

9. See ch. 5 and Appendix C [not included here].
10. We then have

Indicator	Zero Shifting	100% Shifting
Absolute profit (net terms)	$\pi_n = (1 - Z)\pi'$	$\pi_n = \pi'$
Rate of return (net terms)	$Y_n = (1 - Z)Y'$	$Y_n = Y'$

11. Using the absolute profit indicator and assuming a system where profits (π) and wages (W) are the only two shares, we have

		100% Shifting	
Indicator	Zero Shifting	Forward	Backward
Net share	$F_n = \dfrac{\pi' - T}{\pi' - T + W'}$	$F_n = F'$	$F_n = \dfrac{\pi'}{\pi' + W' - T}$
Gross share	$F_g = F'$	$F_g = \dfrac{\pi' + T}{\pi' + T + W'}$	$F_g = F' + \dfrac{T}{\pi' + W'}$

where the net profit share is $F_n = \dfrac{\pi_n}{\pi_n + W}$ and the gross profit share $F_g = \dfrac{\pi_g}{\pi_g + W}$. It will be noted that this formulation gives different gross measures for 100 per cent shifting, depending on the direction of shifting. This direction must be known, therefore, to interpret the observed change in shares.

439

One purpose of the share approach to shifting is to examine distributional implications. The relevant issue here seems to be the change in the distribution of income after tax or the change in the net profit share F_n. Assuming an economy with two factor shares, profits π and wages W, and a profits tax only, we have $F_n = \dfrac{\pi_n}{\pi_n + W}$. This readily suggests that 100 per cent shifting be defined as a situation where $F_n = F'$. In other words, the share of profits in value added available for private use remains unchanged. Similarly one may define zero shifting as a situation where the share of profits in value added available for private use is reduced by the rate of tax, this is to say $F_n = (1-Z)F'$.

Another purpose of the share approach is to consider what has happened to factor shares in the context of national income and factor-price analysis. What is relevant here is the change in the gross share F_g, where $F_g = \dfrac{\pi_g}{\pi_g + W}$. Now we have a ready definition of zero shifting as $F_g = F'$, a situation where the profit share (including tax) in total value added remains constant. Correspondingly, we define 100 per cent shifting as $(1-Z)F_g = F'$, a situation where the share of profits (including tax) in total value added rises by the tax share in total value added.

While both these share indicators are independent of the 'direction' of shifting, the movement of profits and of the rate of return for any given degree of shifting depend on its direction. Such is the case because a given behavior of the profit share may be the net result of many different pairs of wage and profit changes.[12]

12. This is shown in the following table which gives the required value of π_n, net profit after tax, for the various indicators. T is the tax liability equal to $Z\pi_g$.

In reading Table 3, note that zero shifting in the share sense does not exclude wage or price adjustments leading to changes in absolute profits and to shifting in terms of the absolute profit indicator. Indeed, we find that net profits must decline if there is to be zero shifting in the share sense. The extent of the required decline depends on the direction of the shifting. For all but one case (zero shifting according to the gross-share indicator, with forward adjustment), the required decline in net profits exceeds that for zero shifting under the absolute profit indicator. Also it may be noted that the required π_n is larger with forward than with backward adjustment, and that given the direction of adjustment, the required π_n for the gross-share measure is larger than for the net-share measure.

The evidence

We now turn to the historical evidence provided by the various indicators. Over the last decades, tax rates have risen sharply, and it is interesting to consider what have been concurrent changes in factor shares and rates of return on capital. These changes, as noted before, are the result of many forces, including (but by no means only) tax influences. Since the latter are not isolated, only crude conclusions on tax influences can be drawn. This gives additional reason to prefer the general indicators, especially indicators 8 and 14 of Table 1, where non-tax influences on inter-sectional and interfinancial movements will not distort the picture.

Absolute level of profits. Simple observation of the absolute level of corporation gross profits, corresponding to indicator 1 of Table 1, is altogether misleading. The *ceteris paribus* assumption in this case is entirely untenable, the absolute level of profits having been affected by powerful non-tax factors, such as the increase in capital stock due to growth.

Nevertheless, the absolute profit picture may be considered briefly. Gross profits rose from $10 billion in the late twenties to over $40 billion in the fifties. Corporation tax rates rose from 10 to 52 per cent, liabilities rose from over $1 billion to over $20 billion,

---

Table 3
Conditions of Zero and 100 Per Cent Shifting Under Share Indicators Stated in Terms of Net Profits

| Indicator | Required value of net profits π_n for | |
	Zero per cent shifting	100 per cent shifting
1. Net share		
(a) adjustment backward $(W = W' - T)$	$\left(1 - \dfrac{2T}{W'}\right) \pi' - T$	$\left(1 - \dfrac{T}{W'}\right) \pi'$
(b) adjustment forward $(W = W')$	$\left(1 - \dfrac{T}{W'}\right) \pi' - T$	π'
2. Gross share		
(a) adjustment backward $(W = W' - T)$	$\left(1 - \dfrac{T}{W'}\right) \pi' - T$	π'
(b) adjustment forward $(W = W')$	$\pi' - T$	$\left(1 + \dfrac{T}{W'}\right) \pi'$

---

and profits after tax rose from \$8 billion to \$25 billion. For 100 per cent shifting, and given the *ceteris paribus* assumption, gross profits should have increased from \$10 billion to \$29 billion.[13] The observed increase having been to \$40 billion, shifting would have been much above 100 per cent. Defining the degree of shifting as the ratio of actual increase in gross profits (corrected for initial tax rate) to the increase needed for full recovery of the additional burden due to the rise in tax rate, one would arrive at shifting of 157 per cent.[14] All this has no meaning, however, since other influences were clearly present.

Profit share. Changes in gross shares are shown in Table 4, corresponding to indicators 9 to 14 of Table 1. While the more general indicators 11 to 14 would again be preferable on conceptual grounds, the data for the non-incorporated sector are much less reliable than those for the incorporated sector. On these grounds, indicators 9 and 10 are to be preferred. Indicator 10 includes interest income on debt capital, measured here as interest paid by the corporate sector to the outside. It thus has the advantage that tax effects on the financial structure are neutralized; but it has the disadvantage that non-tax effects on interest income from debt capital are included.

We begin with indicator 9. The most meaningful comparison, perhaps, is that between 1922–9 and 1948–57, as both represent periods of high employment. Over this period the corporation tax rate rose from about 10 to 52 per cent. The gross share or corporation profits as a per cent of corporate value added rose from

13. The condition for 100 per cent shifting was defined previously (Table 2) as $\pi_g - \pi' = Z\pi_g$. Since we are now dealing with an increase in tax rates, we must compare the equilibrium with 100 per cent shifting at the new tax rate Z_1 with that at the old tax rate Z_0.

$$\text{Thus } \pi_{g,1} - \pi' = Z_1\pi_{g,1}$$
$$\text{and } \pi_{g,0} - \pi' = Z_0\pi_{g,0}$$

Deducting the second from the first equation, we obtain

$$\pi_{g,1} - \pi_{g,0} = \pi_{g,1}Z_1 - \pi_{g,0}Z_0$$

as the condition for 100 per cent shifting of the incremental tax rate.

14. The formula for 100 per cent shifting in the preceding note suggests that the degree of shifting S be defined as

$$S = \frac{\pi_{g,1} - \pi_{g,0}}{\pi_{g,1}Z_1 - \pi_{g,0}Z_0} = \frac{\pi_{g,1} - \pi_{g,0}}{T_1 - T_0} \quad \text{if } T = Z\pi_g.$$

See p. 37 [not included here], where this formula is used for $Z_0 = 0$.

19·2 to 22·6 per cent. Full shifting would have required an increase to 27 per cent. The data needed for estimating the implicit degree

Table 4
Factor Shares (Gross) in Income Originating in Corporate and Total Business Sections

No.	Indicator	1922–9[b]	1929[c]	1930–9[c]	1936–9[c]	1940–9[c]	1948–57[c]
	As per cent of corporate value added:						
9	Corporate profits before tax	19·2	21·8	9·8	14·8	23·8	22·6
10	Corporate profits before tax plus interest paid by corporations to non-corporate sector	23·0	25·4	15·4	19·2	24·7	22·8
	As per cent of total value added by business:[a]						
11	Corporate profits before tax	—	14·3	6·3	9·6	15·5	15·7
12	Corporate profits before tax plus interest	—	16·6	9·9	12·4	16·1	15·8
13	Corporate profits before tax and income of unincorporated business	—	35·5	27·0	31·1	37·3	33·2
14	Corporate profits before tax, income of unincorporated business and total interest paid	—	38·8	32·0	34·7	38·2	33·6

[a] Unincorporated business does not include operations of mutuals, co-operatives, trade associations, and non-profit organizations.
[b] Source: Osborne and Epstein (1956, pp. 8–20).
[c] Source: U.S. Department of Commerce (1958, Table 1–12, pp. 134–5).

of shifting are hardly available, but a rough calculation suggests 44 per cent.[15]

15. In line with the gross share definition in Table 2 the formula for the degree of shifting (gross share) is

$$S_g = \frac{F_{g,1} - F_{g,0}}{\dfrac{T_1}{\pi_{g,1} + W_1} - \dfrac{T_0}{\pi_{g,0} + W_0}} .$$

For full shifting $S_g = 1$.

In arriving at the ratios 27 and 44 per cent, we estimated first the ratio of tax to corporate value added for 1922–9. The values for π_g and T are obtained

Indicator 10, which includes interest income, shows approximately zero shifting for the period. This is the particular result which is featured in Adelman's study (see Adelman, 1957). The result of lower shifting with inclusion of interest income is in line with the hypothesis that the increase in tax has induced substitution of debt for equity finance. But again, the *ceteris paribus* assumption does not hold. The interest share in fact declined rather than rose, due largely to a decline in interest rates. There was only a minor substitution of debt for equity finance; and such substitution as occurred appears to have been due to non-tax factors (see Miller, 1961). Though indicator 10 may be conceptually better, the evidence of indicator 9 seems preferable because we know that certain additional *ceteris paribus* assumptions implicit in indicator 10 do not hold.

The share picture, pertaining to indicators 11 to 14 does not permit comparison with the twenties and, as noted before, the data for the unincorporated sector are less satisfactory. However, the general picture seems to be fairly similar to that for the corporate sector, thus not supporting the hypothesis of a strong tax-induced shift between sectors.[16]

So far, reference has been to gross shares only. The net picture, though more interesting, is more difficult to come by. Corporate profits after tax as a per cent of corporate value added net of tax are estimated at 16·0 per cent for 1922–9 and at 12·7 per cent for 1948–57.[17] A heroic estimate suggests that this implies shifting of 42 per cent,[18] which is only slightly below that for the gross share picture.

---

from *Statistics of Income* for the years 1922–9. They are then scaled from 1929 back so as to agree in 1929 with figures from *U.S. Income and Output* (U.S. Department of Commerce, 1958). Using the gross shares as given by Osborne and Epstein (1956), we arrive at the non-profit income. The data for 1948–57 are given in *U.S. Income and Output* (U.S. Department of Commerce, 1958).

16. This is in line with our conclusions for the differential-rate approach.

17. The additional information needed is net-profits, which for the 1922–9 period were obtained by deducting adjusted tax liability from adjusted gross profits as derived in footnote 15 for gross shares.

18. In line with the net-share of definition of Table 2, the formula for the degree of shifting (see. p. 438) is now

$$S_n = 1 + \frac{F_{n,1} - F_{n,0}}{Z_1 F_{n,0} - Z_0 F_{n,1}}.$$

Rates of return. Changes in the rate of return are shown in Table 5. These correspond to indicators 5 and 6 of Table 1.

The table is given in terms of net rates of return, because (given the *ceteris paribus* assumption) *any* increase in the net rate suggests shifting in excess of 100 per cent, a result which holds for most cases. The results are shown for a 'total capital base' (ratio of profits plus interest paid to equity plus interest bearing debt) and for an 'equity base' (ratio of profits to net worth).

The case of all manufacturing corporations, total capital base, is shown in line 2 of Table 5. The increase in the net rate or return was 11 per cent when comparing the late twenties with the mid-fifties, and 36 per cent when the base is the late thirties. In both cases shifting exceeded 100 per cent. This is in line with the results obtained by Lerner and Hendriksen (1956). In order to determine

Table 5

Net Rates of Return after Tax[a] All Corporations and All Manufacturing

No.	Description	Average (Per cent)			Percentage change from	
		1927–9	1936–9	1955–7	1927–9 to 1955–7	1936–9 to 1955–7
1.	Statutory tax rate	11 to 13·5	15 to 19	52·0	40·0	35·0
2.	All manufacturing, total capital base					
	Rate of return after tax	7·6	6·3	8·5	11·2	35·6
	Turnover	109·0	118·5	195·0	78·8	64·5
	Margin	6·9	5·2	4·3	−37·8	−16·3
3.	All manufacturing, equity base					
	Rate of return after tax	8·0	6·3	9·4	18·2	50·6
	Turnover	134·7	113·0	240·8	78·8	113·2
	Margin	5·9	4·6	3·9	−33·8	−14·7
4.	All manufacturing, equity base, adjusted for price change (inventory valuation profits excluded)					

445

Table 5 (cont.)

Rate of return after tax	n.c.[a]	6·5	6·3	n.c.[a]	−2·1
Turnover	n.c.[a]	141·4	225·1	n.c.[a]	59·1
Margin	n.c.[a]	4·7	2·8	n.c.[a]	−40·2

5. All manufacturing, equity base, adjusted for price change (inventory valuation profits included)

Rate of return after tax	7·8	6·7	7·3	−6·5	9·0
Turnover	135·4	141·4	225·1	66·3	59·1
Margin	5·8	4·6	3·2	−43·9	−30·1

6. All corporations, equity base

Rate of return after tax	7·0	4·0	7·5	20·5	87·5
Turnover	85·7	69·8	176·6	106·0	152·8
Margin	8·2	5·6	4·8	−41·8	−15·2

[a] Inventory valuation adjustment series not available.

degrees of shifting, it is more convenient to proceed from changes in the gross rates of return,[19] shown for certain key cases in Table 6. The degrees of shifting on the total capital base are 107 and 134 per cent for the two periods respectively.

As before, the results cannot be taken at face value because non-tax factors did not remain constant. However, it is of interest to see how the change in the date of return was reflected in changes in margins and in the rate of turnover. The net rate of return is the product of net margin and turnover, so that

$$Y_n = \frac{S}{K} \frac{\pi_n}{S}$$

where Y_n is net rate of return, π_n is net profit, S is sales and K is capital. S/K is turnover and the ratio $\frac{\pi_n}{S}$ is net margin. Comparing 1927–9 with 1955–7, we find that the 11 per cent rise in Y_n was accompanied by a 79 per cent rise in turnover and a decline in net margins by 38 per cent. Suppose now that the *ceteris paribus* assumption holds. What does the rise in turnover and drop in net margin tell us about the process of shifting? If, on the one hand,

19. Unlike for the share indicator, the gross or net approach now gives the same degree of shifting, but computation is simpler in gross terms.

the shifting had been accomplished through price rise, given inelastic private demand for the total corporate product and increased government outlays, it would have increased sales, thus raising turnover. Since Y_n did not rise appreciably, this would have lowered margins. Thus, the observed rise in turnover and decline in margins are compatible. If, on the other hand, the tax was not recouped by price rise, the decline in the margin could have been balanced by an increase in turnover due to retardation in capital formation. Thus, the evidence is compatible with various types of adjustments. Moreover, the picture is far from conclusive, since many other factors operating on margins and turnover did not remain constant.

The general picture does not change greatly if we consider equity finance only. As shown in line 3 of Table 5, the increase in the rate of return is greater, as is the degree of shifting shown in Table 6. The degrees of shifting for the two periods are now 124 and 136 per cent respectively. The difference in the behavior of the rate of return on equity and total capital reflects a slight rise in the debt to equity ratio (with debt yield being lower than equity yield), as well as a rise in equity yield relative to debt yield.

The reader may wonder whether the 'true' rise in the rate of return is not overstated by failure to allow for inflation and by inclusion of inventory valuation profits, thereby giving a misleading impression of high shifting. To test this hypothesis, the data were adjusted to correct for inflation,[20] as shown in lines 4 and 5 of Table 5. The increase in the net rates of return is dampened, with shifting falling slightly short of 100 per cent for the period 1927–9 to 1955–7 and slightly exceeding 100 per cent for the period 1936–9 to 1955–7. The corresponding degrees of shifting as shown in Table 6 are 98 and 114 per cent. While allowance for inflation dampened the results somewhat, it does not change the picture of heavy shifting.[21]

Turning now from manufacturing to all corporations (equity base), we find (line 6 of Table 5) that the rise in the rate of return from the twenties to the fifties was similar to that for manufacturing only. However, for the later period the increase for all corporations

20. For methods of adjustment, see p. 76 [not included here].
21. For a discussion of the significance of the inflation adjustment for shifting see p. 56 [not included here].

Table 6

Degrees of Shifting: All Manufacturing[a]

No.	Description	Average gross rate of return as percentage			Shifting[b]	
		1927–9	1936–9	1955–7	1955–7 to 1927–9	1955–7 to 1936–9
1.	Equity base	8·7	7·9	18·9	1·239	1·362
2.	Total capital base	8·1	7·5	16·1	1·070	1·344
3.	Equity base, adjusted for price change (inventory valuation profits excluded)	—	7·9	15·2	—	0·985
4.	Equity base, adjusted for price change (inventory valuation profits included)	8·6	8·2	16·2	0·999	1·138
5.	Equity base, companies with assets under $50 M	—	7·8	16·9	—	1·243
6.	Equity base, companies with assets over $50 M	—	8·1	20·2	—	1·406
7.	15 largest manufacturing companies (price leaders)	—	10·9	27·5	—	1·468
8.	15 largest manufacturing companies (price followers)	—	11·5	25·5	—	1·402
9.	26 steel companies	—	9·0	26·9	—	1·568
10.	12 textile companies	—	9·6	10·3	—	0·2136
11.	Average rate of statutory tax	10·0	17·0	52·0	—	—

[a] The formula is: $S_{01} = \dfrac{Y_{g,1} - Y_{g,0}}{Y_{g,1}Z_1 - Y_{g,0}Z_0} = \dfrac{Y_{g,1} - Y_{g,0}}{L_1 - L_0}$ where L is tax liability divided by capital.

[b] Effective rates used to estimate shifting.

was much greater, suggesting shifting (given the *ceteris paribus* assumption) of nearly 200 per cent.

Changes in the rate of various subgroups (chosen to permit comparison with our later analysis) are shown in Table 7. The

Table 7

Net Rates of Return after Tax;[a] Subgroups of All Manufacturing

No.	Description	Average		Percentage change from 1936–9 to 1955–7
		1936–9	1955–7	
	All manufacturing, equity base			
1.	Companies with assets up to $50 M	6·3	8·1	+28·1
2.	Companies with assets over $50 M	6·8	10·3	+51·6
	Industry groups, total capital base			
3.	Pulp and paper	5·0	9·1	+82·2
4.	Rubber and products	5·6	9·2	+64·0
5.	Leather, hide, and products	3·7	6·5	+77·5
6.	Food and kindred products	5·9	7·2	+23·1
7.	Stone, clay, and glass	6·6	10·8	+64·3
	Industry samples, equity base			
8.	26 steel companies	7·1	13·6	+90·8
9.	12 textile companies	7·6	5·1	−33·1
10.	15 largest manufacturing companies (price leaders)	9·1	14·4	+58·4
11.	15 largest manufacturing companies (price followers)	9·4	13·4	+42·9

[a] For sources, see ch. 3, Section B [not included here].

comparison by asset-size groups indicates shifting in excess of 100 per cent for both groups, but a somewhat higher degree of shifting for the larger group. As shown in Table 6, the degrees of shifting are 124 per cent for the smaller and 141 per cent for the larger group. This would seem to be in line with the hypothesis that shifting is facilitated by strength of market position. Individual industry groups on the total capital base all show shifting in excess of 100 per cent, but with wide variation. The samples of individual firms in the steel industry, computed on the equity base, show shifting well in excess of 100 per cent, while those in textiles fall far short of full shifting. Our sample for the fifteen largest companies tending to be price leaders shows high shifting, in line with the picture for all companies with assets over $50 million. Again these results cannot be taken at face value, as they are altogether subject to the assumption that non-tax influences were absent.

Conclusion

If the various indicators are interpreted on the extreme assumption that non-tax influences were totally absent, we find shifting under the profit and rate-of-return approaches to be 100 per cent for all-manufacturing and most of its subgroups. At the same time, shifting in all-manufacturing under the share approach is below 50 per cent. Discarding the absolute profits indicator as meaningless, how could one reconcile the results (in the context of the *ceteris paribus* assumption) for the rate of return and the share approaches?

Since the comparisons cover a span from 20 to 30 years, both 'short' (quick) and 'long-run' (slow) types of adjustments may have occurred. For instance, the tax might have reduced the net rate of return in the short run, shifting being initially less than 100 per cent. This retarded capital formation, thereby holding down the profit share but allowing the rate of return to rise. This interpretation is more or less in line (not entirely, since the gross capital share rose somewhat) with a Cobb–Douglas type of production function with perfectly competitive markets and an elastic capital supply. As will be seen later, this explanation is not supported by our short-run analysis. An alternative interpretation, supported by this analysis, is that the rate of return was pushed up in response to the tax by short-run types of adjustments, thus involving short-run shifting, and that this had no effect on factor inputs, but that the nature of the production function was such that the gross capital share would have declined in absence of tax. Other explanations involving changes in various factor inputs may also apply.

Altogether different explanations may be developed if the

ceteris paribus assumption is dropped. Non-tax factors such as changes in market structure might have occurred. If we add the hypothesis that rising union strength tended to depress the gross rate of return, reconciliation of the results becomes even harder and strengthens the presumption that substantial shifting of the short-run type occurred. The alternative hypothesis of structural changes favoring capital helps the explanation and reduces the need for postulating high short-run shifting. But these other changes would have had to be very large to sustain the assumption of zero short-run shifting.

It appears that there are many ways of interpreting the results for particular indicators, and of reconciling them with each other. General observation of the data leaves the impression that there probably has been substantial shifting, even in the short run, but no definite conclusion is possible. We shall return to these findings after presenting our econometric results for short-run shifting.

References

ADELMAN, M. A. (1957), 'The corporate income tax in the long run', *Journal of Political Economy*, vol. 65.

BECK, M. (1950), 'Ability to shift the corporate income tax: seven industrial groups', *National Tax Journal*, vol. 3.

CARY BROWN, E. (1954), 'The corporate income tax in the short run', *National Tax Journal*, vol. 7.

CLENDENIN, J. C. (1956), 'Effect of corporate income tax on corporate earnings', *Taxes*, vol. 34.

COATES, W. H. (1927), 'Incidence of the income tax', *Appendices to the Report of the Commission on National Debt and Taxation*, H.M.S.O.

COLWYN REPORT (1927), *Report of the Commission on National Debt and Taxation*, Hansard 2700, H.M.S.O.

COMMITTEE FOR ECONOMIC DEVELOPMENT (1962), *Reducing Tax Rates for Production and Economic Growth*, December.

COURNOT, A. (1938), *Researches into the Mathematical Principles of the Theory of Wealth*, I. Fisher (ed.), Macmillan. (First published 1838.)

DALTON, H. (1936), *Principles of Public Finance*, Routledge, 9th edn.

DOMAR, E. D., and MUSGRAVE, R. A. (1944), 'Proportional income taxation and risk taking', *Quarterly Journal of Economics*, vol. 58.

EDGEWORTH, F. Y. (1925), *Papers Relating to Political Economy*, vol. 2, Macmillan.

GOODE, R. (1951a), *Corporation Income Tax*, Wiley.

GOODE, R. (1951b), 'Some considerations on the incidence of the corporation income tax', *Journal of Finance*, vol. 6.

HARBERGER, A. C. (1959), 'The corporation income tax: an empirical appraisal', *Tax Revision Compendium*, vol. 1, Committee on Ways and Means.

HARBERGER, A. C. (1962), 'The incidence of the corporation tax', *Journal of Political Economy*, vol. 70, no. 3.

LERNER, E. M., and HENDRIKSEN, E. S. (1956), 'Federal taxes on corporate income and the rate of return on investment in manufacturing, 1927 to 1952', *National Tax Journal*, vol. 8.

LINTNER, J. (1955), 'Effects of a shifted corporate income tax on real investment', *National Tax Journal*, vol. 8.

MILLER, M. H. (1961), 'The corporation income tax and corporate financial policies', *Research Paper*, prepared for the Commission on Money and Credit.

MILLER, M. H., and SHELTON, J. P. (1955), 'Effects of a shifted corporate income tax on capital structure', *National Tax Journal*, vol. 8.

MODIGLIANI, F., and MILLER, M. H. (1958), 'The cost of capital, corporation finance and the theory of investment', *American Economic Review*, vol. 48.

MUSGRAVE, R. A. (1959), *The Theory of Public Finance*, McGraw-Hill.

MUSGRAVE, R. A., CARROL, J. J., COOK, L. D., and FRANE, L. (1951), 'Distribution of tax payments by income groups: a case study for 1948', *National Tax Journal*, vol. 4.

OSBORNE, H. D., and EPSTEIN, J. B. (1956), 'Corporate profits since World War I', *Survey of Current Business*, U.S. Department of Commerce, January.

RATCHFORD, B. U., and HAN, P. B. (1957), 'The burden of the corporate income tax', *National Tax Journal*, vol. 10, no. 4.

ROBERTSON, D. H. (1927), 'The Colwyn committee, the income tax and the price level', *Economic Journal*, vol. 37, no. 142, pp. 566–81. Reprinted in R. A. Musgrave and C. Shoup (eds.), *Readings in the Economics of Taxation*, American Economic Association, 1958, Irwin, pp. 297–311.

SELIGMAN, E. R. (1925), *Studies in Public Finance*, Macmillan.

SHOUP, C. S. (1951), 'Some considerations of the incidence of the corporation income tax', *Journal of Finance*, vol. 6.

TOBIN, J. E. (1958), 'Liquidity preference as behaviour towards risk', *Review of Economic Studies*, ser. 2, vol. 25.

U.S. DEPARTMENT OF COMMERCE (1958), 'National income and gross national product by legal form of organization, 1929–57', *U.S. Income and Output*, A Supplement to the Survey of Current Business, January.

WESTON, J. F. (1949), 'Incidence and effects of the corporate income tax', *National Tax Journal*, vol. 2.

WICKSELL, K. (1896), *Finanztheoretische Untersuchungen des Steuerwesen Schwedens*, Jena, Germany.

Further Reading

W. J. BLUM and H. KALVEN, Jr, *The Uneasy Case for Progressive Taxation*, University of Chicago Press, 1953.

J. M. BUCHANAN and G. TULLOCK, *The Calculus of Consent*, University of Michigan Press, 1962.

J. M. BUCHANAN (ed.), *Public Finances: Needs, Sources and Utilisation*, for N.B.E.R., 1965.

J. M. BUCHANAN, *Public Finance and Democratic Process*, University of North Carolina Press, 1967.

J. M. BUCHANAN, *The Demand and Supply of Public Goods*, Rand McNally, 1968.

Canadian Royal Commission on Taxation Report, Government Printer, Ottawa, 1966.

G. COLM, *Essays in Public Finance and Fiscal Policy*, Oxford University Press, 1955.

A. DOWNS, *An Economic Theory of Democracy*, Harper & Row, 1957.

J. DUE, *Sales Taxation*, Routledge & Kegan Paul, 1957.

O. ECKSTEIN, *Public Finance*, Prentice-Hall, 1964.

F. Y. EDGEWORTH, *Papers Relating to Political Economy*, vol. 2, 1925.

J. M. FERGUSON, *Public Debt and Future Generations*, University of North Carolina Press, 1964.

R. GOODE, *The Individual Income Tax*, Brookings Institution, 1964.

H. M. GROVES, *Federal Tax Treatment of the Family*, Brookings Institution, 1963.

B. P. HERBER, *Modern Public Finance*, Irwin, 1967.

H. M. HOCHMAN and J. D. RODGERS, 'Pareto-Optimal redistribution', *American Economic Review*, vol. 59, 1969, pp. 542-57.

L. JOHANSEN, *Public Economics*, North Holland, 1965.

N. KALDOR, *An Expenditure Tax*, Allen & Unwin, 1955.

N. KALDOR, *Indian Tax Reform*, Ministry of Finance, India, 1956.

M. KRZYZANIAK and R. A. MUSGRAVE, *The Shifting of the Corporation Income Tax*, Johns Hopkins, 1964.

A. DE VITI DE MARCO, *First Principles of Public Finance*, first English edn, 1936.

J. MARGOLIS and H. GUITTON (eds.), *Public Economics*, Macmillan, 1969.

JOHN STUART MILL, *Principles of Political Economy* (1848), Ashley edn, 1909.

R. A. MUSGRAVE, *Theory of Public Finance*, 1959. The standard textbook on the subject.

R. A. MUSGRAVE and A. T. PEACOCK (eds.), *Classics in the Theory of Public Finance*, International Economic Association, 1962. This volume includes Wicksell's 'A new principle of just taxation'.

Further Reading

R. A. MUSGRAVE and C. S. SHOUP (eds.), *Readings in the Economics of Taxation*, American Economic Association, 1959.

A. C. PIGOU, *The Economics of Welfare* (1920), pt 2, Macmillan, 4th edn, 1928.

A. C. PIGOU, *Public Finance* (1928), 2nd edn, 1929; 3rd edn, 1947, Macmillan. The 2nd edn contains in pt 3 a valuable discussion of the place of loans in public finance.

A. R. PREST, *Public Finance*, 3rd edn, 1967.

Report of the Committee on Turnover Taxation (Richardson), Cmnd 8830, 1953.

DAVID RICARDO, *The Principles of Political Economy and Taxation* (1817), chs. 8–18, Sraffa edn, 1952.

E. R. ROLPH, *The Theory of Fiscal Economics*, University of California Press, 1954.

E. R. ROLPH and G. F. BREAK, *Public Finance*, 1961.

Royal Commission of the Taxation of Profits and Incomes, 1st Report Cmnd 8761, 1953; 2nd Report Cmnd 9105, 1954; Final Report Cmnd 9474, 1955, H.M.S.O.

W. J. SCHULTZE and C. LOWELL HARRISS, *American Public Finance*, Prentice-Hall, 1965.

SHOUP MISSION, *Report on Japanese Taxation*, Tokyo, 1949.

C. SHOUP, *Public Finance*, Columbia University Press, 1969.

HENRY SIMONS, *Personal Income Taxation*, Chicago University Press, 1938.

ADAM SMITH, *The Wealth of Nations* (1776), Book 5, Everyman edn, 1956.

W. VICKREY, *Agenda for Progressive Taxation*, Ronald Press, 1947.

A. WILLIAMS, *Public Finance and Budgetary Policy*, Allen & Unwin, 1961.

Acknowledgements

Readings in this volume are acknowledged from the following sources:

Reading 1	University of Chicago Press
Reading 2	University of Chicago Press
Reading 4	The Macmillan Company and George Allen & Unwin Ltd
Reading 5	*Manchester School of Economic and Social Studies* and W. Vickrey
Reading 6	*Public Finance*
Reading 8	The Macmillan Company of Canada Ltd and Macmillan & Co. Ltd
Reading 9 (a, b, d, c)	*Review of Economics and Statistics*
Reading 10	Princeton University Press
Reading 11	University of Chicago Press and J. M. Buchanan
Reading 12	W. W. Norton & Company Inc.
Reading 13 (a)	American Economic Association and W. G. Bowen, R. G. Davis and D. H. Kopf
Reading 13 (b, c)	*Review of Economics and Statistics*
Reading 14	*Economic Journal* and C. S. Shoup
Reading 15	Richard D. Irwin, Inc. and J. M. Buchanan
Reading 16	*Public Finance*
Reading 17	Harvard University Press
Reading 18	*British Tax Review*
Reading 19	Johns Hopkins Press

Author Index

Author Index

459

Index

462

Subject Index

Subject Index

465

Index

Index